MODERN CAMBRIDGE ECONOMICS

MONEY, INTEREST AND CAPITAL

MODERN CAMBRIDGE ECONOMICS

General Editors: Phyllis Deane   Geoffrey Harcourt
Jan Kregel   Stephen Marglin

Phyllis Deane
The Evolution of Economic Ideas

Joan Robinson
Aspects of Development and Underdevelopment

A.K. Bagchi
The Political Economy of Underdevelopment

Éprime Eshag
Fiscal and Monetary Policies and Problems in Developing Countries

Michael Ellman
Socialist Planning (2nd Edition)

MONEY, INTEREST AND CAPITAL

A study in the foundations of monetary theory

Colin Rogers

Department of Economics
University of Adelaide

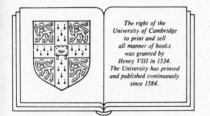

The right of the
University of Cambridge
to print and sell
all manner of books
was granted by
Henry VIII in 1534.
The University has printed
and published continuously
since 1584.

CAMBRIDGE UNIVERSITY PRESS

CAMBRIDGE

NEW YORK   NEW ROCHELLE   MELBOURNE   SYDNEY

Published by the Press Syndicate of the University of Cambridge
The Pitt Building, Trumpington Street, Cambridge CB2 1RP
32 East 57th Street, New York, NY 10022, USA
10 Stamford Road, Oakleigh, Melbourne 3166, Australia

© Cambridge University Press 1989

First published 1989

Printed in Great Britain at the University Press, Cambridge

British Library cataloguing in publication data
Rogers, Colin
Money interest and capital: a study in
the foundations of monetary theory.–
(Modern Cambridge economics).
1. Monetary system. Theories
I. Title
332.4'01

Library of Congress cataloguing in publication data
Rogers, Colin, 1948–
Money, interest, and capital.
(Modern Cambridge economics)
Bibliography.
Includes index.
1. Money.   2. Interest.   3. Capital.   I. Title.
II. Series.
HG221.R683   1989   332.4   88–20364

ISBN 0 521 35138 3 hard covers
ISBN 0 521 35956 2 paperback

AL

To my father, Arthur Victor Rogers

CONTENTS

ILLUSTRATIONS

TABLES

SERIES PREFACE

The Modern Cambridge Economics series, of which this book is one, is designed in the same spirit as and with similar objectives to the series of Cambridge Economic Handbooks launched by Maynard Keynes soon after the First World War. Keynes's series, as he explained in his introduction, was intended, 'to convey to the ordinary reader and to the uninitiated student some conception of the general principles of thought which economists now apply to economic problems'. He went on to describe its authors as, generally speaking, 'orthodox members of the Cambridge School of Economics' drawing most of their ideas and prejudices from 'the two economists who have chiefly influenced Cambridge thought for the past fifty years, Dr Marshall and Professor Pigou' and as being 'more anxious to avoid obscure forms of expression than difficult ideas'.

This series of short monographs is also aimed at the intelligent undergraduate and interested general reader, but it differs from Keynes' series in three main ways: first in that it focuses on aspects of economics which have attracted the particular interest of economists in the post Second World War era; second in that its authors, though still sharing a Cambridge tradition of ideas, would regard themselves as deriving their main inspiration from Keynes himself and his immediate successors, rather than from the neoclassical generation of the Cambridge school; and third in that it envisages a wider audience than readers in mature capitalist economies, for it is equally aimed at students in developing countries whose problems and whose interactions with the rest of the world have helped shape the economic issues which have dominated economic thinking in recent decades.

Finally, it should be said that the editors and authors of this Modern Cambridge Economics series represent a wider spectrum of economic doctrine than the Cambridge School of Economics to which Keynes referred in the 1920s. However, the object of the series is not to propagate particular doctrines. It is to stimulate students to escape from conventional theoretical ruts and to think for themselves on live and controversial issues.

PHYLLIS DEANE
GEOFFREY HARCOURT
JAN KREGEL
STEPHEN MARGLIN

PREFACE

Post-war monetary theory has been dominated by the neoclassical synthesis, the attempt to reconcile the general equilibrium theories of Wicksell and Walras with the analysis of the *General Theory*. It is now widely recognised that this endeavour has led to a dilemma for monetary theory. The best-developed models of the economy have no role for money so monetary theorists are forced to proceed without sound theoretical foundations.

This study proposes a solution to the dilemma by adopting a Marshallian perspective of the flaws in Wicksell's capital theory to reassess the monetary analysis of the *General Theory*. Seen in historical context the analysis begins with a reassessment of Wicksell's attempt to extend the relevance of the quantity theory of money to an economy with a well-developed banking system. This endeavour was taken up by Keynes in the *Treatise on Money* and ultimately led, in the *General Theory*, to the abandonment of the quantity theory and Say's Law. Analytically, the monetary analysis of the *General Theory* appears as a generalization of Wicksell's monetary and capital theory to a monetary system in which the real forces of productivity and thrift cannot determine the rate of interest. A capitalist economy is such a system.

In a capitalist economy producing heterogeneous capital goods which are financed by the banking system the rate of interest emerges as a key independent variable which can determine long-period equilibrium. In such a system the principle of effective demand then replaces Say's Law as the relevant analysis of output and employment and the concept of monetary equilibrium replaces the quantity theory. The concept of monetary equilibrium falls within the tradition of what Schumpeter (1954) called Monetary Analysis as monetary forces are integrated with real forces in the determination of long-period equilibrium positions. The neutrality of money is abandoned and the quantity theory appears as a special case of monetary equilibrium in the sense that the quantity equation holds at all long-period monetary equilibria but the quantity theory is no longer of any analytical significance.

On the basis of these properties the analysis suggested in this study provides the theoretical foundations for a unified Keynesian analysis of output and employment. In particular the notion of monetary equilibrium provides a sound theoretical foundation for Post Keynesian monetary theory and strengthens the general Keynesian perspective by identifying the necessary conditions for the existence of a long-period unemployment *equilibrium* to which the usual Keynesian stories of perverse dynamic adjustment can readily be appended. In other words, this study is an attempt to support the view that the capitalist system is not self-adjusting, by clarifying the theoretical basis on which it rests.

In forming my ideas on these issues I have over the years received encouragement, advice and criticism from a number of people. In this regard I would like to thank Greg Brown, Tony Seeber, Philip Mohr, Chris Torr, Ludwig Lachmann, Karl Mittermaier, Victoria Chick, Marc Lavoie, Basil Moore, Kevin Hoover, Geoff Harcourt, Jan Kregel and Peter Groenewegen. It goes without saying that none is responsible for any remaining errors or inaccuracies in the work, for which I accept full responsibility.

I am also most grateful to many people who at various stages assisted with the typing of the manuscript. In particular Mrs van Rensburg at the University of South Africa, and Debbie Beckman and Kerri Braini at the University of Adelaide. In addition Anne Grossman had the thankless task of removing most, if not all, of my lapses from acceptable grammar.

OVERVIEW

REAL ANALYSIS AND MONETARY ANALYSIS: AN INTRODUCTION

THE CURRENT DILEMMA IN MONETARY THEORY

In his study on money and inflation, Frank Hahn (1982b: 1) points to one horn of a dilemma facing neoclassical monetary theorists when he reminds us that: 'The most serious challenge that the existence of money poses to the theorist is this: the best developed model of the economy cannot find room for it.' But, if the best developed neoclassical model of the economy has no role for money, then Keynesian and monetarist analysis is hung on the other horn of the dilemma: based as it is on the neoclassical synthesis, it is proceeding without sound foundations in neoclassical theory. The neoclassical monetary theorist must, it seems, choose between monetary theory and sound theoretical foundations – a dilemma for the theorist.

Now, although Hahn's own position is narrowly based on a neo-Walrasian perspective, the dilemma to which he points applies to all neoclassical monetary theory, whether it be the Keynesian or monetarist version of the neoclassical synthesis or the Friedmanian quantity theory tradition. The objective of this study is therefore twofold: firstly, to show that the dilemma raised by Hahn applies to all the varieties of neoclassical monetary theory; and, secondly, to propose a solution to the dilemma by establishing where the foundations of monetary theory should be laid so as to avoid the quicksands of neoclassical theory. To this end the study which follows is divided into two parts. The first is essentially critical and is concerned with illustrating the dilemma facing all versions of neoclassical monetary theory. The second is constructive and offers an analytical framework in which the foundations of monetary theory can be laid.

For this endeavour it proves useful to employ a somewhat unfamiliar taxonomy of monetary theories which requires some clarification.

In this respect a fundamental distinction is drawn between *Real* and *Monetary Analysis* where these terms are used in the sense defined by Schumpeter (1954: 276). In terms of Schumpeter's definitions all neoclassical monetary theories are classified as Real Analysis because real and not monetary forces determine long-period equilibrium positions. As Kohn (1986: 1192) has recently pointed out, Real Analysis proceeds on the assumption that all the essential features of the economy can be understood in real terms. Consumers trade real factor services for real goods; firms convert real inputs into outputs and capital markets allocate real resources between consumption and investment. Money is nothing more than a veil to be drawn aside to reveal these real forces at work. Monetary Analysis on the other hand, proceeds on quite the opposite assumption. Money is not a veil but an integral part of the capitalist process. The face cannot be analysed independently from the veil. Hence Monetary Analysis attempts to integrate real and monetary forces in the determination of long-period equilibrium and it is in this tradition that the foundations of monetary theory are to be found. At this fundamental level the failure of all the varieties of neoclassical monetary theory can be traced to the fact that they fall within the tradition of Real Analysis.

A further classification of importance which is associated with the distinction between Real and Monetary Analysis is that between credit and commodity money. Commodity money was historically the dominant form of money as most monetary systems were based on precious metals. However, with the evolution of the banking system, credit has become the predominant form of money. Precisely when this dominance became sufficiently pronounced to be analytically significant is difficult to pinpoint but both Thornton (1802) and Wicksell (1898a,b) paid particular attention to credit. Modern monetary theories, of course, acknowledge the existence of credit. Nevertheless, all these monetary theories are based on analytical principles which tacitly assume that credit has, or can be made to behave as though it has, the same properties as commodity money. As Hicks (1967a: 159) notes with reference to Ricardo and his contemporaries, the idea is to get credit (secondary money) to behave like commodity money (primary money). Schumpeter (1954: 717) makes essentially the same point by describing these theories as money theories of credit rather than credit theories of money. The former lies within the tradition of Real Analysis and the latter within Monetary Analysis. With the evolution of the banking and financial system, Real Analysis is no longer an appropriate framework for the analysis of capitalist economies employing bank money.

REAL ANALYSIS: CRITIQUE

Monetary theories in the tradition of Real Analysis can be further categorised by examining their theoretical structure, method of analysis and associated methodology. Examining neoclassical monetary theories in terms of these characteristics proves invaluable in providing an accurate taxonomy of the diverse range of monetary theories that exist in the Keynesian, monetarist and quantity theory traditions. To illustrate the power of this taxonomy, consider first, the distinction in theoretical structure between neo-Walrasian and Wicksellian theory. Both are neoclassical general equilibrium theories but both have distinct properties and hence distinct monetary theories. Specifically, it is shown in chapter 2 that the Wicksellian model employs a concept of capital which is open to the Cambridge critique. As Scott Moss (1980: 78) has observed, 'a number of issues lie hidden beneath the capital theory battlefield like unexploded mines'. One of these mines explodes under Wicksellian monetary theory.

It is often overlooked that Wicksell's capital theory provided the basis for his analysis of the natural rate of interest. But once this is realised it is apparent, on reflection, that the Wicksellian notion of the natural rate of interest is open to the Cambridge critique. This suggests in turn that, as the natural rate of interest is the fulcrum of the loanable funds theory, the latter is also a casuality of the Cambridge critique. This point is missed by Leijonhufvud (1981) and Kohn (1981b, 1986) who call for a return to the loanable funds tradition.

The neo-Walrasian model, on the other hand, does not employ the Wicksellian notion of capital and is thus not open to the Cambridge critique. However, it is shown in chapter 3 that although neo-Walrasian models avoid the Cambridge critique they suffer from an equally fatal defect in the sense that money is always an inessential addition to the analysis. For example, the most sophisticated model of the economy, to which Hahn refers in the opening quotation, is the Arrow–Debreu model – a model in the neo-Walrasian tradition. But the difficulty extends beyond the Arrow–Debreu model because *all* the neo-Walrasian models – including the temporary equilibrium versions – cannot find a role for money as they are models of *perfect* barter. The problem lies at the heart of the neo-Walrasian system which rests on a notion of equilibrium that requires the pre-reconciliation of choices – even in the case of fix-price or so-called non-tâtonnement models. The limitations of this notion of equilibrium have not as yet been generally recognised because it is one of the seductive properties of the neo-Walrasian system that inessential additions may be made in many directions, e.g. to incorporate production, intertemporal analysis or money, but these extensions, although they appear to make the analysis more 'realistic' or relevant, only amount to inessential elaborations to a model of perfect barter. From the point of view of monetary theory, this ultimately leads to the fundamental dilemma which has also been well posed by Ostroy (1973: 608) when he asks, 'How to make money appear without making the standard theory disappear?' To date this question remains unanswered, the dilemma unresolved, as the incorporation of money in an essential (as opposed to inessential) way has not been achieved by neo-Walrasian theorists.

Seen from this perspective, it is clear that both the major general equilibrium streams within neoclassical monetary theory, the Wicksellian and the neo-Walrasian, fall within the tradition of Real Analysis and that both are subject to fatal defects. The extent of the dilemma facing neoclassical monetary theorists is therefore apparent once it is realised that the foundations of both Wicksellian and neo-Walrasian monetary theory have collapsed. The need for replacing these foundations becomes even more pressing when we consider the Keynesian and monetarist models inspired by the neoclassical synthesis.

Examining the theoretical structures of the neoclassical synthesis in chapter 4 reveals that both neo-Walrasian and Wicksellian models are currently in use. For example, both Wicksellian and neo-Walrasian versions of the IS–LM model are common in the literature. Such is the neoclassical synthesis. The theoretical foundations are often thought to be neo-Walrasian but, in the more policy-oriented debates, it is the Wicksellian theme which predominates. It should therefore not come as a surprise, in chapter 5, to find that an examination of the theoretical structures used by the Keynesians and monetarists reveals a similar picture. For example, Hahn (1980b) assesses the theoretical foundations of monetarism from a neo-Walrasian perspective while both Tobin (1969) (a Keynesian) and Brunner–Meltzer (1976) (monetarists) employ a common Wicksellian structure to assess issues of policy. In the latter case it is little wonder that many commentators have concluded that only empirical and not theoretical issues divide modern monetary theorists.[1] However, although it may have some truth content, such a conclusion is seriously misleading because it fails to recognise the fundamental issue raised by the

---

1. Friedman (1976) holds this view but perhaps for different reasons.

current dilemma in neoclassical monetary theory – the lack of any sound theoretical foundations. Theoretical issues are therefore still very much on the agenda.

Looking at Keynesian and monetarist analysis from the perspective of method and methodology also proves illuminating. In particular, the Keynesians appeared at one point to have abandoned the traditional method of economic theory: namely the use of long-period equilibrium to isolate the persistent forces at work in the economy. In terms of traditional terminology, persistent forces are analysed with reference to some notion of long-period equilibrium while short-period positions are classified as transitory. All monetary theorists in the tradition of Real Analysis have, at least since Hume, recognised that money is neutral only in the long period. It has always been conceded that money may very well be non-neutral in the short period. For the Keynesians (or Keynes for that matter) to claim that the demonstration of a short-period unemployment equilibrium is the essence of Keynes's contribution then makes no sense from the perspective of the history of thought.[2] In any event the Keynesians now appear to have accepted the traditional method of economic analysis, and examine the long-period implications of their Wicksellian-type models (Tobin and Buiter, 1976). The traditional method of economic analysis thus remains very much in use.

Friedman in particular, has always employed the traditional method (Eatwell, 1983c), but questions of methodology loom larger when we consider his quantity theory analysis in chapter 6. Although at face value it is clear enough that Friedman's quantity theory falls within the tradition of Real Analysis (he accepts that in the long period real forces determine equilibrium and money is neutral) he cannot be classified with monetarists such as Brunner and Meltzer because he does not employ their general equilibrium framework. A study of Friedman's work reveals instead, that, although it is embellished with references to Wicksellian or neo-Walrasian concepts, and various methodological red herrings, he remains essentially an inductivist, i.e. he attempts to derive theories by observing the 'facts'. The inductivist element in Friedman's approach would therefore seem to be paramount. In particular, it explains why he has never been able to produce a complete theoretical framework, being content, instead, to settle for the view that the quantity theory philosophy is indicative of a 'general approach' in the Marshallian tradi-

---

2. Keynesians should not be misled by Keynes's statement that in the long-run we are all dead. This statement is not associated with the *General Theory* but was made in the *Tract on Monetary Reform* (1923: 80) when Keynes was criticizing certain naive interpretations of the quantity theory.

tion. Keynesians, and monetarists, using the Wicksellian structure
thus suffer from frustration when debating with Friedman because all
his references to Wicksellian or neo-Walrasian concepts are quite
irrelevant to his own position[3] – an empiricist vision of the quantity
theory. At the level of theory it seems that, if anything, Friedman
(1985) has abandoned attempts to restate the quantity theory as a
theory of the demand for money, in favour of a return to the traditional quantity theory and its stress on an exogenous money stock. There
may have been a change in tactics from advocating 100 per cent
reserve banking (Friedman, 1953c), to monetary base control
(Friedman, 1985), but the strategy of rendering the money stock
exogenous remains as the *sine qua non* for monetary stability.

These illustrations provide an overview of the issues and the power
of the taxonomy in establishing that the current dilemma in monetary
theory extends to all versions of neoclassical monetary theory in the
tradition of Real Analysis. At the same time, however, they suggest
how this dilemma can be avoided, i.e. by turning to Monetary
Analysis for the foundations of monetary theory.

MONETARY ANALYSIS: FOUNDATIONS

In terms of Schumpeter's definition, Monetary Analysis is based on
the premise that both real *and* monetary forces determine long-period
equilibrium positions. With reference to the traditional method of
economic theory this means that monetary phenomena are included
in the analysis of persistent forces. In the tradition of Monetary
Analysis money is no longer neutral. Exponents of this tradition are,
however, in the minority when we come to examine the history of
monetary thought. Nevertheless, the undue concentration on Real
Analysis by monetary theorists would seem to be a fundamental error.

The basis for this error appears to lie in a failure of modern
monetary theorists to take account of changes in the structure of the
economy. Early monetary theories in the tradition of Real Analysis
may well have been applicable to the predominantly agricultural,
commodity money, economies that then existed. Specifically, in any
economy of self-employed farmers and artisans using commodity
money, concepts such as Say's Law, the quantity theory of money,
and notions such as real saving and investment may indeed make

3. To a serious theorist, however, they appear as incoherent. As a theorist one cannot
   be a neo-Walrasian, Wicksellian and Marshallian simultaneously without suffering
   a nervous breakdown or becoming a confirmed cynic.

sense. The question facing modern monetary theorists, however, and one to which they have paid far too little attention, is whether these properties still apply to capitalist bank money systems. Keynes and Marx were both of the opinion that this was not the case and that a capitalist economy based on the division of labour and a sophisticated financial sector using credit was not subject to Say's Law or the quantity theory of money. Keynes, in particular, argued that in a capitalist system, supply need not create its own demand – there was many a slip twixt the cup and the lip – and that the principle of effective demand should replace Say's Law in such an economy. Consequently, the abandonment of an analysis based on Say's Law appears as a necessary condition for the development of Monetary Analysis. A key step in this analysis is the recognition that the money rate of interest in a bank money economy is not subject to analysis in terms of either classical or neoclassical theoretical principles. The behaviour of the rate of interest can then play a crucial role in breaking Say's Law.

It is on this basis that the second component of this study proceeds with a re-evaluation of Keynes's attempt at Monetary Analysis as a possible foundation for monetary theory. It should be stressed, however, that the analysis which follows is not intended as an exercise in Keynesian exegesis. It may have some implications for such an exercise but that is not the main objective. The major objective is to provide a coherent analytical foundation for monetary theory in the tradition of Monetary Analysis. In terms of modern terminology this implies a contribution to Post Keynesian monetary theory in the tradition of such writers as Davidson, Kregel, Kaldor, Chick, Moore and Minsky. With this in mind, chapter 7 examines some important properties of Monetary Analysis and introduces some further unfamiliar interpretations of apparently familiar ideas. This need arises mainly because most readers will only be acquainted with the neoclassical approach which has dominated monetary theory since the 1940s.

The first step in this endeavour is to come to terms with the implications of the distinction between credit and commodity money. Although most monetary theorists are aware of this distinction the analytical implications do not appear to have been fully appreciated. Instead, the tradition of Real Analysis is implicitly based on the view that credit poses no particular problems so long as it can be made to behave as if it were commodity money. Monetary theories developed on the basis of commodity money can then be safely applied to bank money economies. Or so it was – and still is – thought.

The fundamental property of credit is that the analytical principles of neither classical nor neoclassical theory can be applied to determine its natural price, i.e. the natural rate of interest. From the perspective of classical theory, credit is not a commodity and therefore it is not subject to the laws of production. Consequently, classical analytical principles cannot be applied to determine the natural rate of interest as would be the case with the natural price of commodity money. Similarly, neoclassical theoretical principles, in the guise of the Wicksellian model, also cannot be applied to define the natural rate of interest except as a purely logical exercise in a one-commodity world. On the other hand, neo-Walrasian analysis is trapped in the money-less world of perfect barter. Thus, as far as both versions of neoclassical general equilibrium analysis are concerned, it is also the case that the money rate of interest cannot be given a coherent explanation. Hence we reach the general conclusion that *economic theory cannot be applied to explain the natural rate of interest*. Rigorously speaking, the money rate of interest must then be treated as an exogenous variable in a bank money economy.

The fundamental theoretical implication of this conclusion is that it opens up a role for the principle of effective demand. The principle of effective demand emerges as an essential feature of a bank money system because in such a system the rate of interest can set a limit to the profitable expansion of output in the long-period before full employment is reached. In other words the principle of effective demand explains the existence of a long-period equilibrium with unemployment. A key element in the demonstration of this possibility is the concept of monetary equilibrium. The term was apparently introduced by Myrdal (1939) to describe Wicksell's condition of equality between market and natural rates of interest. The term is, however, sufficiently general to apply to all analyses of the relationships between the rates of return on financial and non-financial assets. Within Real Analysis the term monetary equilibrium makes little sense however, because long-period equilibrium is defined only in terms of real forces – monetary equilibrium would then be a transitory phenomenon of little interest. In Monetary Analysis, the term monetary equilibrium is apposite as monetary forces can determine long-period equilibrium positions. It should be noted, however, that the concept of monetary equilibrium employed here differs fundamentally from that suggested by Gale who excludes banks and any notion of credit (Gale, 1982: 6, 1983: 15).

In developing the foundations of Monetary Analysis we therefore use the term monetary equilibrium to describe the relationship between the rate of interest and the marginal efficiencies of all assets. A shorthand definition of monetary equilibrium is the equality between the rate of interest and the marginal efficiency of capital. But the relationship between these two variables proceeds on quite a different basis from the relationship between the money and natural rates of interest in the Wicksellian general equilibrium tradition of Real Analysis. Wicksell's long-period equilibrium is readily shown to be a special case of monetary equilibrium.

Before presenting a formal demonstration of these results some important issues concerning method and methodology are considered in chapter 8. Most importantly, the Marshallian partial equilibrium method emerges as a useful tool. In this respect it is important to realise that the Marshallian partial equilibrium *method* is not restricted to microeconomic analysis. On this score we have an unexpected ally in Friedman who argues that Marshallian analysis is not restricted to microeconomics (Hoover, 1984b: 64). On reflection this seems reasonable, as it is apparent that the neoclassical general equilibrium analysis developed by Walras was intended as what we would now call a microeconomics analysis of the millions of markets in the economy. Only later was it applied by the neo-Walrasians to macroeconomic questions, e.g. by Lange and Patinkin. The Marshallian partial equilibrium *method* was, in fact, applied by Keynes to macroeconomic aggregates in the *Treatise on Money* and it is on this basis that it must be compared with the general equilibrium *method*. General equilibrium is thus not synonymous with macroeconomics. The term macroeconomic equilibrium is therefore suggested so as not to prejudice the issue; macroeconomic equilibrium can then be examined using either the partial or the general equilibrium *methods*. In view of the difficulties with neoclassical general equilibrium theory it is perhaps time that we reconsidered the partial equilibrium method.

The partial equilibrium method has, in fact, some attractive features. For example, it is associated with a sequential notion of causality in which certain institutionally determined exogenous variables are treated as 'causes'. By comparison, the general equilibrium method can, at best, deal only with contemporaneous causality. It is therefore unable to deal with disputes between Keynesians and monetarists on the direction of the causal relationship between money and income. Only by applying the partial equilibrium method in an attempt to reach agreement on which are the important exogenously determined variables would it be possible to make headway with this dispute. In addition, the partial equilibrium method is based on the belief that it is possible to analyse economic problems on a one-at-a-time basis before allowing for their interaction. Interestingly, it seems that Friedman also attempts to apply this method (Hoover, 1984b: 65), although this application is constrained by his empiricist bias and peculiar Chicago view of neoclassical theory. Nevertheless, the partial equilibrium method is designed to provide the theorist with an 'organised and orderly method of thinking out particular problems' in the real economy (Keynes, 1936: 247). As the general equilibrium method of simultaneous solution has proved itself to be only partially successful in the analysis of imaginary economies, and totally unsuccessful in analysing the real economy, this is perhaps a sufficient basis for adopting the partial equilibrium method. These concepts then provide a basis for the change in perspective necessary to develop an analytically coherent monetary theory in the tradition of Monetary Analysis which integrates real and monetary forces.

Having accepted that the money rate of interest must be treated as an exogenous variable in a bank money economy, Marshallian analytical principles are then applied, in chapter 9, to define the concept of monetary equilibrium. The concept of monetary equilibrium links the rate of interest (a monetary phenomenon), via the marginal efficiency of capital, to investment, output and employment (real phenomena), in a manner which is not open to the Cambridge critique of neoclassical capital theory. Furthermore, the concept of monetary equilibrium applies the classical notion of long-period equilibrium as a state of rest in which the rates of return on all forms of converting present into future wealth are equalised. This, it seems, is the notion which lies behind the general theory of asset-holding in the enigmatic chapter 17 of the *General Theory*.

Employing Marshallian techniques, and with some assistance from Kaldor, Kregel and Conard, it is then a relatively straightforward exercise to provide a formal analysis of the relationship between the rate of interest and the marginal efficiencies of all durable assets in terms of their demand and long-period or normal supply prices. It is then also apparent that the long-term money rate of interest, as an exogenous variable, can determine monetary equilibrium in the sense that it sets the rate of return to which all other marginal efficiencies must adjust in long-period equilibrium. The equality between the rate of interest and the marginal efficiency of capital occurs via adjustment in the demand prices of capital goods relative to their normal or long-period supply prices and determines whether capital goods can be produced at a profit. The rate of interest therefore plays an important role in the production of capital goods, i.e. it influences the rate of investment. In other words, the money rate of interest may rule the roost and this has implications for output and employment in long-period equilibrium.

Chapter 10 then applies the concept of monetary equilibrium and the principle of effective demand to re-examine three well-known macroeconomic models. These are (1) the Fundamental Equations of the *Treatise on Money*, (2) the aggregate demand and supply model of the Post Keynesians, and (3) the IS–LM model of the mainstream Keynesians. All of these models are re-interpreted from the perspective of Monetary Analysis.

In this regard it is shown that the Fundamental Equations of the *Treatise* suggest the existence of multiple equilibria but that the analysis is incomplete, lacking, as it does, any notion of the principle of effective demand. This suggests that only with the abandonment of the natural rate of interest and the quantity theory of money does Keynes move beyond the Real Analysis of the *Treatise* to the Monetary Analysis of the *General Theory*.

In the *General Theory* Keynes presented the principle of effective demand as a refutation of Say's Law that 'supply creates its own demand'. In terms of Say's Law there would appear to be no limit to the *profitable* expansion of output until full employment imposes a resource constraint. Supply – the production of commodities – would generate the demand to sell the output at a profit. By contrast, the principle of effective demand asserts that there may well be a limit to the profitable expansion of output before full employment (Chick, 1983: 71).

The concept of monetary equilibrium explains why this is so. With the rate of interest treated as an exogenous variable which establishes monetary equilibrium, the rate of investment then determines what Keynes called the point of effective demand. There is, moreover, no mechanism whereby the money rate of interest, as an exogenous variable, can automatically adjust to just that level which generates a rate of investment and a point of effective demand that produces full employment. The money rate of interest as determined by monetary policy can determine a point of effective demand which establishes an equilibrium at almost any level of output and employment. What is more, the economy is then in long-period equilibrium, in the classical sense of a state of rest, as entrepreneurs have no incentive to expand production and employment. That is, at the level of output determined by the point of effective demand, the rates of return on converting all forms of present into future wealth are equalized, i.e. entrepreneurs are earning normal profits. The point of effective demand therefore provides a limit to the profitable expansion of output and Say's Law is broken.

This, in outline, is the monetary theory of the principle of effective demand proposed in this study. It offers a formal analysis of the ideas proposed by Kregel (1983) and provides the basis for the foundations of Monetary Analysis. In this sense it provides, also, a synthesis of much of Post Keynesian monetary theory.

The analysis has several unique features. Firstly, the concept of monetary equilibrium proposed here provides an analysis of the principle of effective demand which differs from that suggested by most Post Keynesians and the so-called neo-Ricardians. The Post Keynesians define the principle of effective demand in terms of expected proceeds (Asimakopulos, 1984), and stress the necessity of a marginal propensity to consume of less than one for the refutation of Say's Law (Chick, 1983: 72). In somewhat similar fashion the neo-Ricardians define the principle of effective demand in terms of the proposition that saving and investment are brought into equality by variations in the level of income (Milgate, 1983: 78). By comparison, the definition of the principle of effective demand employed here applies the concept of monetary equilibrium to define the point of effective demand as an equilibrium in the classical sense of a uniform rate of return on all assets. Thus the analysis is conducted initially within the confines of a static equilibrium model in which both short- and long-period expectations are realized (Kregel, 1976). The principle of effective demand is therefore defined without reference to the discrepancy between *ex ante* and *ex post* saving and investment or the use of the notion of expected proceeds.

Secondly, as the existence of multiple monetary equilibria is the norm rather than the exception, it is readily demonstrated that the quantity equation holds at all monetary equilibria. The quantity theory then fails because it is seen to presuppose the existence of monetary equilibrium at full employment. This is another way of showing that the principle of effective demand refutes the quantity theory of money. The concept of monetary equilibrium proposed here also integrates real and monetary forces in the definition of the principle of effective demand. The notion of the neutrality of money is then abandoned and replaced by an analytically sound definition of the point of effective demand which may determine a long-period equilibrium with unemployment. Furthermore, this analysis may be applied directly to the Weintraub–Davidson model of aggregate demand and supply. Flexible wages and prices can then lead to greater employment only if they can induce a more favourable monetary equilibrium, i.e. only if flexible wages and prices can influence the money rate of interest, the marginal propensity to consume and/or the marginal efficiency of capital, so as to produce a new monetary equilibrium and point of effective demand with increased employment.

Thirdly, the concept of monetary equilibrium proposed here implies the rehabilitation of liquidity preference theory and allows for a re-interpretation of the IS–LM model from the perspective of Monetary Analysis. As neither classical nor neoclassical analytical principles can be applied to determine the money rate of interest it must be treated as an exogenous variable. Treating the money rate of interest as an exogenous variable restores the conventional rate of interest in liquidity preference theory to a role analogous to that of the natural rate in Wicksell's theory. The conventional rate of interest then provides the centre of gravitation in a purely monetary analysis of the rate of interest, and the loanable funds theory emerges as a special case of liquidity preference theory. This interpretation of liquidity preference theory also provides an analysis of the interest rate that is compatible with the Kaldor (1982)–Moore (1986) theory of endogenous bank money.

Finally, following the properties of the concept of monetary equilibrium to their logical conclusion ultimately leads us to Shackle's vision of Keynesian kaleidics. The route to Keynesian kaleidics can be traced by considering Kregel's (1976) classification of models used by Keynes and the Post Keynesians. In terms of Kregel's distinction between static, stationary and shifting equilibrium, the formal analysis presented in this study refers only to the static model. That is to say, monetary equilibrium is defined only for a given rate of interest and we consider a static equilibrium solution. This facilitates the demonstration of the properties of monetary equilibrium without the complication introduced by expectational errors. In terms of Joan Robinson's notion of an historical model, we are concerned with the development of the formal relationships in the model before attempting to apply it to any actual situation.

The analysis is, however, readily extended into the realms of stationary and shifting equilibria. But once this is done we come face to face with Shackle's notion of Keynesian kaleidics. To see this, note that the formal definition of monetary equilibrium and hence the point of effective demand, rests on the notion of the conventional or normal rate of interest as an exogenous variable. What this means is that long-period equilibrium positions in the static equilibrium model are not defined in terms of objective real forces as is the case with the concept of equilibrium employed by monetary theories in the tradition of Real Analysis. The conventional rate of interest, which determines monetary equilibrium in a bank money economy, simply has no objective theoretical basis in either classical or neoclassical theory. This in turn suggests that the existence and stability of the static equilibrium solution rests on the existence and stability of the conventional rate of interest. Referring again to Kregel's classification, a given state of long-period expectations is defined with reference to a given conventional rate of interest, i.e. the belief that the existing conventional rate will persist. If this convention is abandoned and no attempt is made to re-establish stability in the mistaken belief that interest rates should be allowed to fluctuate under the influence of 'objective' market forces, the world of shifting equilibrium results. This outcome is possible because expectations become elastic (in the Hicksian sense) once the convention of stability is broken. Deviations from a conventional rate that is perceived by participants in the capital, money or foreign exchange markets to have been abandoned are then not self-correcting. Unless a new conventional rate can be established with its attendant centrifugal forces, in the guise of inelastic expectations, we encounter the supposedly nihilistic result stressed by George Shackle (1967: 247, emphasis added):

The interest rate in a money economy. This was the enigma that led Keynes to the *nihilism* of his final position . . . The interest rate depends on the expectations of its own future. It is expectational, subjective, psychic, indeterminate. And so is the rest of the economic system. The stability of the system, while it lasts, rests upon a convention: the tacit general agreement to *suppose* it stable. This stability, once doubted, is destroyed, and cascading disorder must intervene before the landslide grounds in a new fortuitous position. Such is the last phase of Keynesian economics. But Keynes had shown governments how to prolong the suspension of doubt.

Here Shackle is drawing out the implications of the model of shifting equilibrium in which existing conventions have been broken. Once the conventions have been broken, and no new conventions established, it is no longer possible to define the static case of monetary equilibrium. It is in this sense that long-period equilibrium in a static model of a bank money economy is a species of conjectural equilibrium.

This conclusion has interesting implications for monetary policy particularly when that policy has been influenced by monetarism. All monetary theorists are in search of policies that will promote stability in the financial markets and the economy as a whole. The monetarists seek to achieve such monetary stability by fixing the money stock and allowing interest rates to find their own market determined levels. The analysis of monetary equilibrium presented here suggests that monetarist-inspired policy will have consequences for stability which are the polar opposite of those expected by the monetarists. Far from creating the conditions for stability, attempts to fix the quantity of money or adjust interest rates to so-called market-related levels will succeed only in breaking the existing conventions in financial markets. The basis of stability will then be lost and the economy cut free, as it were, from its moorings as expectations become elastic.

Consequently, from the perspective of Monetary Analysis, the irony of the monetarist free market philosophy is that instead of promoting stability – the suspension of doubt – the attempt to achieve so-called market-determined interest rates runs the risk of destroying the basis of stability on which financial markets rest for their efficient operation. Stability requires inelastic expectations and, in a world of bank money, that stability must be imposed as an integral part of monetary and macroeconomic policy; it does not arise spontaneously. An essential component of monetary policy in a bank money system is the establishment of credible conventions in terms of which the centrifugal forces of inelastic expectations can ensure the necessary stability of the system. Adopting a policy explicitly aimed at destroying the previous conventions on which stability rested, e.g. by encouraging the increased variability of interest rates, may lead only to increased instability and not to an optimal allocation of resources as suggested by neoclassical general equilibrium theory. If anything, it seems that the lesson to be learnt from the monetarist episode is that stability cannot be achieved in a bank money economy, as the monetarists suggest, by attempting to make it behave as if it were a commodity money system.

I

REAL ANALYSIS: CRITIQUE

2

WICKSELLIAN MONETARY THEORY

INTRODUCTION

At one time, prior to the *General Theory*, Wicksell's monetary theory represented the most sophisticated attempt to complement the static formalism of the quantity theory. Wicksell's ideas, in particular the distinction between the natural and market rates of interest, were adopted by many economists, including both Keynes – in the *Treatise* – and Dennis Robertson (1934). Post-war developments in monetary theory have, however, all but obscured the Wicksell connection, to use Leijonhufvud's (1981) phrase. Despite a number of papers by Harrington (1971), Laidler (1972), Bailey (1976), Honohan (1981) and Kohn (1981b), and Leijonhufvud's best efforts, the significance of the Wicksell connection for post-war monetary theory remains obscure – buried as it is beneath Keynesian, neo-Walrasian and monetarist revolutions and counter-revolutions.

Nevertheless, as Leijonhufvud (1981: 131) correctly perceives, the theory of the real (or natural) rate of interest lies at the centre of some of the confusion and inconclusive quarrels in monetary theory.[1] The

---

1. At this point it is appropriate to warn the reader about possible ambiguity surrounding the concept of a real rate of interest. Wicksell often appears to use the term as a synonym for the natural rate. That is, the real or natural rate is the variable which equates *real* saving and investment and is distinguished from the money or market rate of interest. By contrast, in neo-Walrasian theory all own rates of interest are real rates in the sense that money is an *inessential addition* to the model (see the discussion in chapter 3). The issue is further complicated by the fact that Fisher's *definition* of the real rate is not connected to either of these theoretical concepts. Leijonhufvud (1981: 155 n37) draws attention to this latter distinction which is also discussed by Robertson (1966: 70–71) who enquires

 . . . briefly what the relation is between the doctrine that fluctuation is to be explained in terms of a gap between the *natural* rate of interest and the *actual* rate, and the doctrine [Fisher's] that it is to be explained in terms of a gap between the

theory of the natural or real rate of interest is crucial as it forms the hub around which all else rotates in Wicksellian monetary theory. From the Wicksellian perspective the debate between the loanable funds and liquidity preference theories is a case in point. Rejection of the loanable funds theory in favour of the liquidity preference theory entails abandoning the natural rate of interest. As Leijonhufvud (1981: 135) notes, 'The denial of the LF (loanable funds) mechanism makes a nonsense of the very notion of a "natural rate" of interest. The Wicksellian theme is lost.' Conversely the natural rate of interest lies at the heart of a Wicksellian statement of the loanable funds theory and both stand or fall together.

The importance of this observation becomes apparent once it is realised that the natural rate of interest links Wicksell's capital theory with his monetary theory. This would suggest that developments in post-war capital theory have implications for Wicksell's monetary theory that need to be carefully assessed. In this regard it will be argued here that although Leijonhufvud (1981: 131) claims to get to the bottom of the Wicksell connection – and of the Two Cambridges controversy in particular – he in fact fails completely to appreciate the significance of that debate for Wicksellian monetary theory. In particular he fails to notice that the capital debate has, for all useful purposes, exposed the impossibility of defining the natural rate of interest. As a consequence of the capital debate it is now possible to see that neither the existence nor the stability of a Wicksellian long-period equilibrium – in terms of which the natural rate is derived – can be established outside of a one-commodity world. A failure on either of these criteria then leaves the natural rate of interest without

real rate of interest (nominal rate less the rate of inflation) and the nominal *money* rate. The answer is, of course, to be sought in the fact that the so-called 'real' rate is not really a rate of interest at all, but a hypothetical change which takes into account changes in the real value of the money principal borrowed.

Fisher's *definition* of the real rate of interest is thus not equivalent to Wicksell's notion of the natural rate. On this point see the comments by Schumpeter (1954: 1118–3). Interestingly, Kohn (1981b: 862, expression (4)) appears to overlook this distinction when discussing Robertson's loanable funds analysis because he employs Fisher's *definition* of the real rate. On the question of the general equilibrium pedigree of Fisher's analysis there is evidence to support the view that, ultimately, it represented an attempt to incorporate elements of Wicksellian or 'Austrian' capital theory into a Walrasian framework. For example, Pasinetti (1969: esp. 508 n5) notes that Fisher introduced the notion of 'rate of return' so as to admit a role for the productivity of capital, in addition to time preference, in the determination of interest. On the other hand, Fisher (1930: 42) suggests the use of a Walrasian approach and is so interpreted by Dougherty (1980) and Tobin (1985: 32–4) who suggest that the Arrow–Debreu model offers a formal restatement of Fisher's theory of interest. But on either interpretation Fisher's analysis is subject to the criticisms raised in this and the following chapter.

any analytical foundation and, somewhat ironically, the market rate of interest is left hanging by its own bootstraps. With the benefit of hindsight this charge by Hicks (1939: 164) against the liquidity preference theory is seen to rebound with greater force against the loanable funds theory.

The significance of the Wicksell connection for modern monetary theory is thus not that we should embrace the loanable funds theory – as Leijonhufvud (1981) would have us do – but that the capital debate has effectively undermined the Wicksellian statement of the loanable funds theory by eliminating the analytical foundations of the natural rate of interest. This conclusion has some destructive implications for the elements of the Wicksell connection still extant in modern monetary theory. Such elements can be traced in some text book presentations of the IS–LM model, the Keynes versus 'classics' debate and in the monetary framework of Tobin (a Keynesian) and Brunner and Meltzer (monetarists). All of these structures fall with the collapse in the Wicksellian real interest rate mechanism and this theme will be taken up in subsequent chapters. For the moment the objective is to outline the implications of the capital debate for Wicksellian monetary theory. The first step is to present the reader with a synopsis of Wicksell's monetary theory.

WICKSELL'S MONETARY THEORY

Wicksell's monetary theory must be understood as an attempt to extend the application of the quantity theory of money to an economy which has moved beyond the use of metallic money to the use of credit and loans (Patinkin, 1965: 587–8). As Wicksell (1898b: 73–5, emphasis in original) argues:

If, then, we test the assumptions on which the quantity theory rests, we easily find that this doctrine would be quite true, assuming a state of affairs where everybody buys and sells for cash and with money of their *own*, that is to say, neither commodity credits nor money loans exist . . .

. . . under these conditions the quantity theory is perfectly true and correct; but it need hardly be pointed out how little they conform to reality, at any rate with present day developments in the monetary system . . . in reality, at least in the business world proper, all purchases are made against credit for a longer or shorter period, and every businessman, however solvent, repeatedly has occasion to seek monetary credit for his business.

In such a credit money system the quantity of metallic money no longer bears a simple quantitative relationship to the price level.

Instead Wicksell (1898b: 77–8, emphasis in original) argues that it is the rate of interest which plays a key role in determining the level of commodity prices:

Logically speaking it does not seem possible to give any other answer to our question than the following: assuming a pure credit economy, the exchange value of money and the level of commodity prices must depend on the price at which 'money' (i.e. in this case credit) itself can be obtained, in other words on *the rate of interest on money*. A low rate of interest must lead to rising prices, a high rate to falling prices. And this is in full agreement with the basic principles of the quantity theory, because a surplus of material money would manifest itself, among other ways, in a lower interest on money.

Wicksell goes on to illustrate this point by considering the impact of changes in the rate of interest on the prices of assets with differing holding periods. In the case of a three-month trade bill, for example, a 1 per cent change in the interest rate would cause, at most, a $\frac{1}{4}$ per cent change in its price. But if capital is committed for an infinite period, as is the case with a building for example, the price effect is much more marked in terms of the familiar relationship:

$$i = \frac{r}{R}$$

where i = the annual rate of interest, r = the annual rental on the building, and R = the capital value or demand price of the building. If the interest rate falls by 1 per cent then the capital value of the building might increase by as much as $33\frac{1}{3}$ per cent. If a similar building could still be erected at the cost of the initial capital value then building becomes a profitable activity and, assuming the full employment of resources (which Wicksell (1901, II: 195) usually took to be an empirical fact or a useful first approximation), competition in the building industry would result in a rise in wages and prices.[2] This rise in prices would only cease once the rate of interest had returned to its original level – as it would do, according to Wicksell (1898b: 79–80), when the rising price level had eliminated the surplus money that had initially caused the decline in the interest rate:

This interesting circumstance has already been pointed out by Ricardo from the point of view of the quantity theory: an increase in the amount of money must at first lower the rate of interest at the same time as raising the prices of commodities, but whereas the increase in prices would be permanent, the decrease in the rate of interest would only be temporary, because as soon as

2. This relationship between the prices of assets and the market rate of interest is quite general and independent of the analysis of the natural rate of interest. It will resurface when we examine Keynes's monetary theory in chapter 9.

prices had adapted themselves to the increase in the amount of money, the surplus of money would no longer exist, and, therefore, neither would the reason for keeping the rate of interest down.

In this argument Wicksell is apparently referring to a real balance effect which operates in the case of an exogenous money stock. On the other hand, in the case of a pure credit economy, no such effect is operative and the price level is indeterminate.[3] In a mixed system of metallic money and credit the existence of an exogenous metallic money element was therefore treated as a stabilising influence on the price level in accordance with the properties of the quantity theory of money. Nevertheless, Wicksell argues that in a credit money system, it is not only changes in the quantity of money which cause changes in the price level, as postulated by the quantity theorists. Movements in the natural rate of interest could cause movements in the price level even with a fixed stock of metallic money. In terms of the previous example taken from the building industry, if new houses with a capital value of R can only command lower rents of $r'(< r)$ then if the banks still maintain an interest rate of i, housing construction will no longer be profitable. As Wicksell (1898b: 81) notes, 'In order to be able to grant any building loans, banks would have to reduce their interest to $i'[= r']$ per cent and at this rate of interest home-building would only just be profitable . . .'

Alternatively, if banks maintain the interest rate at i then wages and prices in the building industry will fall as workers and builders attempt to find employment. Wicksell argues, therefore, that it is not sufficient to look only at movements in the money rate of interest to determine the effect on commodity prices. It is movements in the money rate relative to the natural rate that are important. In the above examples a fall in the money rate to meet the natural rate did not cause any price changes while a stationary money rate resulted in a fall in prices because it lay above the then lower natural rate. The relationship between the money and natural rates of interest Wicksell (1898b: 82, emphasis in original) then presented in terms of the following general principle:

3. At times there seems to be some ambiguity in Wicksell's treatment of the money supply. In the 'pure credit' model the money supply appears to be perfectly elastic. On the other hand, as an extension of the quantity theory tradition, Wicksell's analysis also incorporates a real balance effect and the existence of bank reserves. In fact Patinkin (1965, note E) argues that it is the loss of reserves by the banks that ultimately forces them to raise the market rate to the natural rate. From the perspective of modern monetary theory this distinction appears to involve the debate on the endogeneity or exogeneity of the money supply and we will take it up in later chapters.

At any moment in time in any income situation there is always a certain rate of interest, at which the exchange value of money and the general level of commodity prices have no tendency to change. This can be called *the normal rate of interest*; its level is determined by the current natural rate of interest, the real return on capital in production, and must rise or fall with this. If the rate of interest on money deviates *downwards*, be it ever so little, from this normal level, prices will, as long as the deviation lasts, rise continuously; if it deviates upwards, they will fall indefinitely in the same way.

The relationship between the money and natural rates of interest is then employed by Wicksell (1901, II: 182) to explain Tooke's evidence that the money interest rate and the price level tended to rise or fall together. This latter phenomenon was later labelled by Keynes as the Gibson paradox and was explained by Wicksell along the following lines.

The natural rate of interest is constantly subject to fluctuations caused by changes in technology, labour supply and rising or falling wages (Wicksell, 1898b: 82). A rise in the natural rate of interest would, however, initially go undetected by the banks with the result that the money rate would lag behind the natural rate. With the money rate below the natural rate, for example, the demand for resources would, with full employment assumed, lead to a rising price level. The rising price level would in turn reduce the surplus money that had arisen because of the discrepancy between money and natural rates of interest, and the banks would be forced by changed circumstances to increase their money rate of interest. Hence rising prices and rising interest rates could be accounted for in terms of Wicksell's analysis and, what is more, be accounted for in a fashion which he considered to be quite compatible with the quantity theory of money, provided that the quantity theory was suitably adapted to allow for the existence of a banking system and credit money.

It should, therefore, be clear at this stage that Wicksell sought to extend the applicability of the quantity theory of money to an economy with credit money. The concept of the natural rate of interest then played a key role in that attempt. For, without the natural rate it is not possible to tell whether interest rates are too high or too low. The impact of the market rate of interest on the price level is obscured and the resolution of the Gibson paradox breaks down. In addition it is apparent that the quantity theory is still retained – despite the reference to a pure credit economy. This much is evident from the role played by the real balance effect in adjusting the money rate of interest to the natural rate. In a pure credit money economy this mechanism would be absent. This is an issue to which we will return in later chapters.

Finally, it is necessary to highlight the fact that Wicksell's monetary theory falls within the tradition of Real Analysis in the sense that money or credit has no influence on the natural rate of interest. Wicksell (1898b: 84, emphasis added) makes this point quite explicitly:

It is now possible to observe quite clearly, be it only under certain simplifying conditions, the phenomena of capital and interest on capital, as they would appear if liquid capital . . . was in reality *lent in kind without the intervention of money*. In the former case, i.e. if capital was lent in kind, there would undoubtedly develop, through the supply of and demand for the available capital a certain rate of interest on the lending market, which would be the natural rate of interest on capital in the strictest sense.

The natural rate of interest is thus defined independently of the existence of money or credit and deviations between the market or money rate and the natural rate, however caused, are resolved by adjustment of the money rate to the natural rate which acts as the centre of gravitation for the system. It is for these reasons that we should reject Kohn's (1986) recent classification of Wicksell within the tradition of Monetary Analysis.

THE THEORETICAL FOUNDATIONS OF THE NATURAL RATE OF INTEREST: A MARGINAL PRODUCTIVITY THEORY

As we have seen, the natural rate of interest plays a central role in Wicksell's monetary theory. Without a coherent theory of the natural rate of interest the Wicksellian statement of the loanable funds theory collapses and the extension of the quantity theory tradition to a credit money economy breaks down. The theoretical properties of the natural rate of interest therefore require careful attention from monetary theorists. To this end it is necessary to examine Wicksell's theory of capital as developed from the work of Jevons and Böhm-Bawerk – particularly the latter.

Wicksell (1901, I: 144–5) begins his discussion of the concept of capital by distinguishing between *real capital* in all its forms – building, machinery, implements and tools, raw materials and all the resources that have to be saved to support labour during the process of production – and *capital as a sum of exchange value*, a certain amount of the medium of exchange. He notes that the term capital has been employed to refer to either financial or real capital. Further, although the other factors of production, such as land and labour, could also be measured either in technical units or as a sum of exchange value, the treatment of capital in the analysis of production was not symmetrical with that of labour and land.

In simple terms the reason for this asymmetry arises from the relationship between capital and interest. To begin with, it is apparent that in order to determine the rate of interest – the return on capital – capital must be measured as a sum of exchange value. Capital must be measured in the same units as output – as exchange *value* and not in technical units. As Wicksell (1901, I: 149, emphasis in original) argues:

If capital also were to be measured in technical units [like land or labour] . . . productive capital would have to be distributed into as many categories as there are kinds of tools, machinery, and materials, etc. and a unified treatment of the role of capital in production would be impossible. Even then we should only know the *yield* of the various objects at a particular moment, but nothing at all about the value of the goods themselves, which it is necessary to know in order to calculate the rate of interest, which, in equilibrium is the same in all capital.

Apart from pointing out the technical necessity of defining capital in value terms, Wicksell also suggests that it is necessary for theoretical reasons; namely, that in equlibrium the rate of interest must be the same on all capital. This condition is, of course, the classical condition of long-period equilibrium defined in terms of a uniform rate of return on all assets. It is the notion of equilibrium employed by Wicksell to define the natural rate of interest. To define such an equilibrium, however, capital must be treated as a mobile homogeneous entity so that it may move between sectors to equalize the rate of interest/ profit.[4] Capital defined as value capital (financial capital) can fulfil this role but capital defined in technical or quantity terms cannot. Wicksell (1893: 167, emphasis in original) noted this fact in his review of Walras's general equilibrium system:

Walras calls 'capital' and treats as 'capital' *only* durable goods . . . A necessary consequence of this is the peculiar fact that these equations of production and exchange can *give no information at all about the level of the rate of interest*. If

4. The change in the concept of profit between classical and neoclassical theory has caused much confusion over the years. In classical theory, profits are the dual of the surplus – Walsh and Gram (1980) – while in Wicksellian theory the natural rate of interest is equated with the marginal productivity of capital or the marginal productivity of 'waiting' (Wicksell 1901, I: 177). But once capital was inserted into the neoclassical production function in the analysis of income distribution, the marginal productivity of capital or 'waiting' was automatically equated with the rate of profit – the share of capital in output. However, some authors, e.g. Howard (1983: 111) note that the Wicksellian theory is a theory of interest only. On the question of identifying profits with interest see the discussion in Conard (1963: 12) and Schumpeter (1954: 720).

only durable goods are regarded as capital, then a certain *rent* is fixed for each group of these by the above mentioned equations but *not* the *capital value* of the goods itself, nor, consequently, the rate of interest either.

What Wicksell is saying here is that if capital is measured in technical terms – on a par with land and labour, say – then it is not possible to define the natural rate of interest. It is not possible because there is no sense in which capital – defined as an array of machines, – can be imagined to re-arrange itself between sectors so as to produce a uniform rate of interest/profit. Financial capital can behave in this fashion – in the long period – but not real capital. It is on this issue that Walrasian and Wicksellian general equilibrium theories part company and we will return to this point in the following chapter. For the moment we continue with the examination of Wicksell's attempt to reconcile the apparent contradictory properties of homogeneous financial capital with heterogeneous real capital.

To make some progress along this route while avoiding the difficulties into which Walras and his followers have been led, and which need not concern us here, Wicksell (1901, I: 149) turns to the observation that all capital goods can be interpreted as composed of saved-up labour and land: 'All capital goods, however different they may appear, can always be ultimately resolved into labour and land.' Capital may thus be regarded as a single homogeneous mass of saved up labour and land. The current wage and rental on land can then be employed to determine the *value* of capital. But what is more, the marginal productivity of saved-up labour and land is greater than that of current labour and land. This discrepancy arises from the scarcity of saved-up labour and land relative to current labour and land and accounts for the existence of interest. As Wicksell (1901, I: 154, emphasis in original) puts it: '*Capital is saved-up labour and saved-up land. Interest is the difference between the marginal productivity of saved-up labour and land and current labour and land.*' These ideas are then formalised by Wicksell (1901, I: 156–206) in terms of a series of models beginning with the simple case of investment over a single year and progressing to more complex cases. In the simple model, accumulated capital consists of A labour-years and B acre-years. If l represents wages per labourer and r rent per acre, then the value of capital is given by $Al + Br$. The rate of interest, i.e. the *natural* rate of interest, is then determined by examining the marginal productivities of current and saved-up labour and land in 'a particular business' which employs a workers, b acres of land and a_1 and b_1 units of saved-up labour and land respectively. The production function of this enterprise is given by $F(a,b,a_1,b_1)$ and the marginal productivities of the inputs, the partial derivatives with respect to each variable, i.e.

$F_a = l, \dot{F}_b = r$ and $F_{a_1} = l', F_{b_1} = r'$, are employed to determine the natural rate of interest. The natural rate of interest is then defined in terms of the discrepancy between l' and l or r' and r, e.g.:

$$\frac{l' - l}{l} = i$$

Also, long-period equilibrium requires that 'interest, at any rate within the limits of the single year's investment here contemplated, must, according to our definition, be the same in all enterprises and all kinds of employment', and especially that 'the marginal productivity . . . of saved-up land must stand in the same relation to that of current land as does saved-up labour to current labour' (Wicksell, 1901, I: 155). Therefore, in long-period equilibrium,

$$\frac{l' - l}{l} = \frac{r' - r}{r} = i$$

indicating that a uniform rate of interest is earned on both forms of capital, i.e. saved-up land and labour.

Wicksell continues with the analysis of more complex cases until he presents what he calls theory of exchange value in its final form. But even then the production functions still contain only current and saved-up labour and land. It seems that Wicksell (1901, I: 203) is ambivalent about the attempt to introduce capital as a value magnitude into the production function directly. Later neoclassical economists have been less cautious, with the consequences revealed by the capital theory debates.

THE CAPITAL DEBATE BRIEFLY REVISITED

The definition of the natural rate of interest in terms of the marginal productivities of capital, i.e. saved-up land and labour, inevitably leads us to examine the relationship between Wicksell's treatment of capital and the issues raised by the capital debate. This issue is fundamental to Wicksellian monetary theory because if the Cambridge critique applies to Wicksellian capital theory then the derivation of the natural rate of interest will break down. To see that this is, in fact, the case and that the natural rate of interest cannot be defined outside of a one-commodity model it is necessary to consider some of the conceptual issues raised by the capital debate.

Joan Robinson initiated what was to become known as the capital debate or the Two Cambridges controversy when she complained about ambiguity surrounding the treatment of capital in the neoclassical production function. The neoclassical production function, as every student knows, is written in the form $Q = f(K,L)$ where $Q = $ the rate of output of commodities, $L = $ the quantity of labour and $K = $ the quantity of capital. But when it comes to measuring these quantities Joan Robinson (1953–4: 81, quoted by Harcourt 1972: 16) observed that the discussion was rather cryptic:

He [the student] is instructed to assume all workers alike, and to measure L in man-hours of labour; he is told something about the index-number problem involved in choosing a unit of output; and then he is hurried on to the next question, in the hope that he will forget to ask in what units K is measured. Before ever he does ask, he becomes a professor, and so sloppy habits of thought are handed down from one generation to the next.

As we have seen, Wicksell was well aware of the difficulties that might lie in wait for the treatment of capital on a par with land and labour in the production function.[5] The fundamental problem which Joan Robinson pointed to was that the neoclassical production function implied circular reasoning. If capital was to be treated as a homogeneous *value* magnitude in the production function then it could not be treated as an exogenous variable and one of the determinants of the rate of interest. To determine the value of capital it would be necessary to know the rate of interest; but the value of capital was needed to determine the rate of interest! The difficulty here is that the value of capital cannot be treated as an exogenous variable in the production function or a Wicksellian general equilibrium model because capital as a value magnitude is a function of prices which are endogenous variables. As Petri (1978: 252) notes, Wicksell was aware of this danger. While discussing his theory of exchange value in its final form, Wicksell (1901, I: 202) observed that, 'it would clearly be meaningless – if not altogether inconceivable – to maintain that the amount of capital is already fixed *before* equilibrium between production and consumption has been achieved. Whether expressed in terms of one or the other, a change in the relative value of the two commodities would give rise to a change in the value of capital.' But what is more, this difficulty arises *even if capital is treated as saved-up labour and land*: 'But even if we conceive capital generically,

---

5. As Wicksell (1901, I: 149, emphasis in original) noted:

Whereas labour and land are measured each in terms of its own *technical* unit (e.g. working days or months, acres per annum), capital, on the other hand, as we have already shown, is reckoned, in common parlance, as a sum of *exchange value* – whether in money or as an average of products. In other words each particular capital-good is measured by a unit extraneous to itself. However good the practical reasons for this may be, it is a theoretical anomaly which disturbs the correspondence which would otherwise exist between all the factors of production.

See also Howard (1983: 108).

as being a certain quantity of labour and land accumulated in different years, a change in the value of commodities would also alter the conditions of production and thus necessitate a larger or smaller change in the composition of capital.' Despite these observations Wicksell (1901, I: 204–5) went on to impose the condition that, in equilibrium, the sum total of capital has a particular exchange value. This condition he imposed to close the model but as we will see below that leaves Wicksellian capital theory open to the charge of circular reasoning – the charge brought by Joan Robinson in the opening salvo of the Two Cambridges controversy.

In response to this charge, some neoclassical economists, notably Samuelson (1962), attempted to show that under certain conditions heterogeneous capital goods could be aggregated into a homogeneous entity called 'capital'. This model could then be used to formalise the properties of neoclassical (Wicksellian) interest theory. However, as both Pasinetti (1969) and Garegnani (1970) showed, the conditions necessary to equate Fisher's (1930: 155) rate of return to the marginal product of capital or to generate Samuelson's surrogate production function were analytically equivalent to assuming a one-commodity world. In such a world the neoclassical principles do, at least, apply[6]. But as we shall see, there are serious objections on methodological grounds to the use of such models.

The up-shot of all this is that it is now generally conceded that the capital debate has exposed the logical anomalies in Wicksellian capital theory – what many neoclassical economists call the aggregative version of neoclassical theory to distinguish it from the neo-Walrasian version. But from the perspective of monetary theory this means that it is also generally agreed (if not realized) that it is *not possible to define the natural rate of interest outside of a one-commodity model*. This conclusion is analytically equivalent to Kregel's (1971: 95) conclusion that 'when the underlying marginal analysis is thoroughly studied, it can be shown that a rate of profits [interest] does not exist in the neoclassical [Wicksellian] models.'

Other issues raised in the capital debate, such as reverse capital deepening and reswitching, add to the difficulties associated with attempts to define the natural rate of interest. Reverse capital deepening refers to the case where there is a positive relationship between the value of capital and the rate of interest. Reswitching refers to the possibility that the same value of capital may be associated with two or more rates of interest. Between them these two possibilities rule out

6. The problem of circular reasoning which arises with the attempt to measure capital as a quantity of *exchange value* does not arise in a one-commodity world. As output and capital are the same commodity, say corn, relative price changes cannot influence the 'value' (= quantity) of capital.

the generation of a monotonically declining relationship between the rate of interest and the value of capital. The demand for capital may then appear as in Figure 2.1 (where demand for 'capital' means the value of capital associated with the technical choices induced by a given rate of interest (Petri, 1978: 252)). This means that even if the existence of a long-period equilibrium solution to the Wicksellian model could be established, i.e. even if the natural rate of interest could be defined, the stability of that equilibrium would in general be problematic.

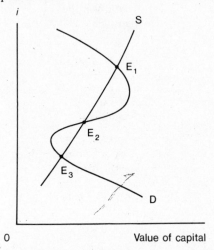

Fig. 2.1 Demand and supply in the capital market

For example, equilibrium E_2 in Figure 2.1 is unstable and cannot act as a centre of gravitation for the system in the determination of long-period equilibrium. What is more, it cannot be taken for granted that an unstable equilibrium would be bounded on either side by stable equilibria as is the case in Figure 2.1. Like that of existence, the question of stability of Wicksellian general equilibrium is also problematic. On the basis of the failure in terms of these two criteria it seems that neoclassical general equilibrium theorists would have little use for the Wicksellian model. In this regard the reaction of neoclassical economists to the implications of the capital debate reveals at least two types of response.[7]

7. A possible third response may be identified and includes those neoclassical economists who continue to accept the neoclassical production function 'on faith'. An example of this view is found in Blaug (1980: 207) who argues that there is nothing irrational about ignoring logical anomalies in a theory until they are shown to be empirically important. However, in view of the work by Fisher (1971) and Shaikh (1980) it is difficult to understand how empirical evidence can resolve the issue in this case. Empirical evidence cannot be applied to solve a *logical* problem.

Firstly, there are those who acknowledge the limitations of the Wicksellian model or what they call the aggregative neoclassical production function and seek instead to develop neoclassical general equilibrium theory within the context of neo-Walrasian analysis. This step successfully avoids the problems thrown up by Wicksellian capital theory but, as we will see in chapter 3, neo-Walrasian monetary theory encounters a new set of insoluble puzzles. Examples of theorists who have followed the neo-Walrasian route are Dougherty and Frank Hahn. Dougherty (1980: 17) considers that the aggregate version of neoclassical theory has been given the *coup de grâce* and offers a Walrasian interpretation of Fisher, while Hahn (1972: 8) remarks:

It is extremely unfortunate, and to some extent the fault of its practitioners, that neoclassical theory has come to be identified with this aggregative version. On purely theoretical grounds there is nothing to be said in its favour. The view that nonetheless it 'may work in practice' sounds a little bogus and in any case the onus of proof is on those who maintain this.

What Hahn and Dougherty identify as the aggregate version of neoclassical theory is, of course, the Wicksellian version under discussion in this chapter. Neo-Walrasian monetary theorists therefore seek to avoid the implications of the capital debate by dropping Wicksell's treatment of capital in favour of that used by Walras. The implications of that step will be examined in chapter 3.

Secondly, there are those neoclassical economists who rely on a methodological defence for the continued use of the Wicksellian version of neoclassical general equilibrium theory or, if used in isolation, the 'aggregate' neoclassical production function. These theorists acknowledge that the marginal productivity theory must be restricted to models in which a single commodity is produced by itself and labour. It is nevertheless claimed that this analysis serves as a useful 'parable' reflecting the fundamentals of neoclassical interest theory.[8] But as Harris (1973) has noted, this claim is without foundation. The assumptions used to generate the neoclassical 'parables' are clearly highly restrictive and yet necessary. The assumptions are highly

8. Harcourt (1976: 42) lists the 'parables' as follows:

    (i)   a negative association between the rate of profit (interest) and 'capital' per man;

    (ii)   a negative relationship between profits and the 'capital':output ratio;

    (iii)   a negative association between the rate of profit (interest) on sustainable steady-state levels of consumption per head;

    (iv)   the marginal productivity theory of distribution.

See also Pasinetti (1969: 516–19) or Garegnani (1983) who provide some illustrations of the derivation of the neoclassical 'parables' in a corn model.

restrictive in the sense that if subject even to slight variation beyond the one-commodity case the logical difficulties exposed by the capital debate re-emerge. What heuristic function they perform (apart from the negative results) is thus far from obvious. Harris (1973: 110) therefore concludes that 'no theory based upon such foundations can lay claim to validity or generality or even to any significance as a "parable" or illustration of what exists in reality.' Thus as a methodological defence the 'parables' story is particularly weak.

Yet, despite the apparent weakness of the neoclassical position, there is a general perception that the Cambridge critique – although valid when applied to the 'aggregate' production function – has no serious implications for neoclassical general equilibrium theory. This view appears to be based on the belief that the neo-Walrasian approach to general equilibrium theory provides a sound theoretical foundation for neoclassical economics which is not open to the Cambridge critique. As far as the Cambridge critique is concerned this view is sound. Those who wish to attack neo-Walrasian theory must seek other grounds. Nevertheless, from the perspective of monetary theory the Wicksell connection still plays an important if not dominant role as Leijonhufvud (1981) has noted. The implications of the capital debate are therefore fundamental to understanding these issues in monetary theory and a more formal discussion is presented in the following section.

A FORMAL CRITIQUE OF THE WICKSELLIAN CONCEPT OF THE NATURAL RATE OF INTEREST

The collapse of the Wicksellian real interest rate mechanism – and with it the Wicksellian statement of the loanable funds theory – can now be demonstrated more formally. Following Petri (1978) it can be shown that the attempt to treat capital as a homogeneous value magnitude can only succeed in a one-commodity model. In a multi-commodity model where output is produced using labour and an array of heterogeneous capital goods, the determination of long-period equilibrium, in terms of which the natural rate of interest is defined, requires that capital be treated as a homogeneous value magnitude. But in that case the value of capital cannot be treated as an exogenous variable in terms of which the prices of capital goods and the natural rate are to be defined. The attempt to define the natural rate of interest in such a model collapses in the face of the charge of circular reasoning.

The model presented by Petri (1978) represents an economy with one consumption good, c, which is produced by labour, l, and land, b, with the aid of two types of circulating capital goods, m and n. The capital goods are produced by land and labour to capture Wicksell's treatment of capital as saved-up labour and land. There is only one type of land and one type of labour with production inputs applied at the beginning of the production period and outputs emerging at the end.

The equations describing this model are listed in Table 2.1. The production functions are represented by equations (2.1), (2.6) and (2.10) and are all linearly homogeneous with l_c, l_m, l_n, and b_c, b_m, b_n, the amounts of labour and land, respectively, used in the production of c, m and n. In equilibrium the wage rate, w, and rental rate, r, which are paid at the end of the production period, must equal the value of the marginal products of the inputs. The consumption good is taken as *numéraire* so the values of the marginal products in the production of consumption goods are given by their physical marginal products. In the production of capital goods the real wage and rental rates are calculated in terms of the prices of the capital goods, p_m and p_n. These results are presented in equations (2.2)–(2.5), (2.7), (2.8), (2.11) and

Table 2.1. *A Wicksellian general equilibrium model.*

$c = f(l_c, b_c, m, n)$	(2.1)		$n = h(l_n, b_n)$		(2.10)
$\dfrac{\partial f}{\partial l_c} = w$	(2.2)		$\dfrac{\partial h}{\partial l_n} = \dfrac{w}{p_n}$		(2.11)
$\dfrac{\partial f}{\partial b_c} = r$	(2.3)		$\dfrac{\partial h}{\partial b_n} = \dfrac{r}{p_n}$		(2.12)
$\dfrac{\partial f}{\partial m} = v_m$	(2.4)		$p_n n = w l_n + r b_n$		(2.13)
$\dfrac{\partial f}{\partial n} = v_n$	(2.5)		$l_c + l_m + l_m = L$		(2.14)
$m = g(l_m, b_m)$	(2.6)		$b_c + b_m + b_n = B$		(2.15)
$\dfrac{\partial g}{\partial l_m} = \dfrac{w}{p_m}$	(2.7)		$\dfrac{(v_m - p_m)}{p_m} = \dfrac{(v_n - p_n)}{p_n}$		(2.16)
$\dfrac{\partial g}{\partial b_m} = \dfrac{r}{p_m}$	(2.8)		$i = \dfrac{(v_m - p_m)}{p_m}$		(2.17)
$p_m m = w l_m + r b_m$	(2.9)		$p_n m + p_n n = \bar{K}$		(2.18)

(2.12). Equations (2.9) and (2.13) show that the value of the capital goods produced must equal the costs of production as a result of the linear homogeneity of the production functions. Equations (2.14) and (2.15) specify the full employment of labour and land, which reflects the assumption of sufficient substitutability between these two factors whose supply is considered to be independent of prices. Equation (2.16) establishes that, in equilibrium, the rentals of the capital goods, v_m and v_n, must guarantee the same rate of return over the supply prices of the two types of capital goods. This rate of return is the natural rate of interest, i, which, because it is assumed that capital goods only last one period, gives the simple form of equation (2.17). The market or money rate of interest does not enter the model because it plays no role in determining the natural rate, which is the variable under scrutiny here.

At this point it is necessary to pause and point out that so far the model consists of only 15 independent equations with 16 unknowns.[9] To close the model, we therefore require at least an additional equation. The Wicksellian solution is to add an equation which specifies that the demand for capital equals the supply of capital.[10] Equation (2.18) specifies this condition in that the demand for capital, $p_m m + p_n n$, is equal to the total *value* of capital, $\bar{K}$, with which the economy is endowed. Note that in equation (2.18) the capital endowment, $\bar{K}$, is fixed and that it is measured in *value* terms.[11] This

9. The unknowns are: c, l_c, b_c, m, l_m, b_m, n, l_n, b_n, w, r, v_n, v_m, p_m, p_n, i. Note that equation (2.9) is not independent. Since the production function in equation (2.6) is linearly homogeneous $m = (\partial g/\partial l_m) \, l_m + (\partial g/\partial b_m) \, b_m$. Multiplying both sides by p_m and substituting w for $p_m(\partial g/\partial l_m)$ and r for $p_m(\partial g/\partial b_m)$ produces (2.9). The same is true for equation (2.13).

10. There are alternative ways of closing the system. The Walrasian solution is to fix m and n as part of a given quantity of capital in the sense that the endowment of each capital good is taken as given. But this means that the model cannot, in general, determine a long-period equilibrium solution. To see this, note that if the endowment of capital goods forms part of the given data, equations (2.1) and (2.18) are replaced by

$$c = \mathrm{f}(l_c, b_c, \bar{m}, \bar{n})) \ (2.1') \text{ and } K = p_m \bar{m} + p_n \bar{n} \qquad (2.18')$$

And, assuming stationarity for simplicity (Petri, 1978: 252), two more equations $m = \bar{m}$ and $n = \bar{n}$ are added. The value of capital is no longer given but the model is now overdetermined having gained two more equations but only one endogenous variable. This is a typical result when attempting to give a Walrasian model a long-period equilibrium solution and is discussed in greater detail in the following chapter. Attempts by Walras and later neo-Walrasians to get around this difficulty have failed. On this question, see Petri (1978: 253) or Tosato (1969) and the discussion of Hahn's model in chapter 3.

11. Note also that, 'To give a marginal product equal to the *rate of interest*, "capital" must be conceived as a magnitude homogeneous with the product and must therefore be measured as the *value* of the means of production and not in physical units as is the case with labour and land (Garegnani, 1970: 422, emphasis in original). See also Howard (1983: 107).

feature is crucial to the attempt to derive a long-period equilibrium defined in terms of a uniform rate of return. By closing the model in terms of equation (2.18), a measure of the endowment of capital is given but its composition is free to vary so that rates of return may be equalized (equation (2.16)), in the determination of the natural rate of interest (equation (2.17)). This, of course, mimics the result obtained by Wicksell in his definition of the natural rate in terms of the marginal productivities of saved-up labour and land. It differs from that result in that the marginal productivity of capital, for m and n in this case, rather than the marginal productivity of land-capital or labour-capital (i.e., saved-up land and labour) now plays a direct role in defining the natural rate of interest. As we noted, Wicksell (1901, I: 204) was ambivalent on this issue and attempted instead to value capital in terms of its constituent labour- and land-capital components. Later neoclassical theorists have not been so cautious and explicitly introduce 'capital' as an argument in the production function. Capital must then be specified as either a real quantity or a value magnitude. But in the latter case the exercise will only be successful if the capital endowment can be defined independently of the values of any endogenous variables.

In terms of the above model, however, equation (2.18) indicates that $\bar{K}$ cannot be defined independently of p_n and p_m. It is on this basis that Joan Robinson made her famous charge of circular reasoning against the neoclassical production function.[12] To take as given the value of capital, $\bar{K}$, which is itself a function of the endogenous variables p_m and p_n, to determine the natural rate of interest, via equations (2.16) and (2.17), is to argue in a circle. More technically the Wicksellian model attempts to treat a variable as both exogenous *and* endogenous simultaneously! As Petri (1978: 252) then concludes: 'If the circularity of this procedure is admitted equation [(2.18)] must be dropped and one cannot even begin to discuss the existence or stability of solutions; the whole theory crumbles.' Treating the endowment of capital as a *value* magnitude therefore leads to the conclusion that the analysis is indeterminate and the existence of a long-period equilibrium solution simply cannot be demonstrated.[13] Add to this the problems of capital reversal and reswitching and it is apparent that

12. As Garegnani notes, '. . . is not possible to determine the equilibrium if one does not know the amount of capital and it is not possible to determine the amount of capital if one has not already determined the equilibrium' (quoted by Petri, 1978: 252n).
13. In this respect it is necessary to reject Dougherty's (1980: 14) argument that Joan Robinson's claim of circular reasoning is not well founded. The claim has nothing to do with the simultaneity of the system of equations, as Dougherty seems to think, but with the distinction between exogenous and endogenous variables. Dougherty

this Wicksellian version of neoclassical general equilibrium theory collapses.

SAVING, INVESTMENT AND LOANABLE FUNDS IN A WICKSELLIAN MODEL

Before leaving the Wicksellian scheme it is useful to re-examine the concept of the natural rate of interest from the perspective of the relationship between saving and investment. As all students are introduced to 'classical' interest rate theory in terms of a demand and supply analysis in which 'the' rate of interest equates something called *real saving* and investment (Makinen, 1977: ch. 1), this perspective may prove helpful in revealing the properties of Wicksellian monetary theory.

The relationship between saving, investment and market versus natural rates of interest is explained by Wicksell (1901, II: 193, emphasis in original) in the following terms: 'The rate of interest at which *the demand for loan capital and the supply of savings exactly agree*, and which more or less corresponds to the expected yield on newly created capital will then be the normal or natural real rate.' Recall, also, that in Wicksell's analysis the natural rate is defined on the assumption that it represents the state of affairs that would result if capital was lent *in kind*, without the intervention of money. Furthermore, in terms of the distinction between the marginal productivities of saved-up and current labour and land it appears that *saving is investment by definition* because capital is saved-up labour and land. And, in this sense, it could be said that the forces of productivity and thrift determine the natural rate of interest. The relationship between saving and investment in this scheme is also virtually identical to that of a simple one-commodity model, e.g. the corn model. In such a model, saving consists of corn not consumed. The corn which is saved is, of course, the seed corn which is used to plant next season's crop. Hence saving is embodied in next season's capital and is investment. Chick (1983: 184) explains the historical relevance of this analysis:

Classical theory had its beginnings in the setting of an agricultural economy, where the archetypal form of saving was the seed-corn: production not consumed, a real resource. (Being real [and highly divisible], there is no

argues that the simultaneity of the system makes it impossible to say 'what determines what' because equilibrium is determined simultaneously. But that observation applies to the *endogenous* variables and not to the attempt to treat a variable as both endogenous and exogenous. Dougherty's observation misses the point. See also Harcourt (1972: 21).

problem of aggregation.) Income, the harvest, *is* predetermined. When corn is held back from consumption it is saving, when sown, investment. The saving is done (slightly) prior to the investment in the nature of things and is only done for the purpose of investment.

Within the confines of a simple corn model it is therefore legitimate to talk in terms of real saving and investment and it is even possible to apply neoclassical marginal analysis to determine a natural rate of interest/profit (Garegnani, 1983). However, once we move beyond the confines of the corn model the relationship between the forces of productivity and thrift is no longer so close. In particular, when capital consists of machines which are produced – not saved directly (but which may be imagined to embody saved-up labour and land) – and saving consists of money income not spent, how are the forces of productivity and thrift related? The answer given by Wicksell and other 'classical' economists such as Dennis Robertson, is that the demand and supply of loanable funds (money/credit) continues to reflect the real forces of productivity and thrift. For example, Robertson (1966: 203) summarizes the 'classical' theory in the following terms:

The convenient sense of the word 'classical' . . . stands for an analysis conducted on the assumption that the monetary system operates in such wise as to interpret and not to distort the influence of 'real' forces. Put loosely, I take the theory to be that on these assumptions the rate of interest depends on the demand for and supply of investible funds, behind the former standing the forces of productivity, behind the latter those of thrift.

It is quite clear from this description that Robertson envisages that the demand and supply of loanable funds – money and financial flows – simply reflects the underlying real forces of productivity and thrift. On occasions Robertson (1966: 160, 162) actually refers to the marginal productivity of loanable funds as a principal determinant of the rate of interest. The financial flows, of course, influence the market or money rate of interest relative to the natural rate, which somehow embodies the real forces of productivity and thrift.

An illustration of the analysis can be found in Robertson's (1934, [1966: 64–74]) paper on 'Industrial Fluctuations and the Natural Rate of Interest'. The main features of the analysis can be illustrated with reference to Figure 2.2 which is a simplified version of Robertson's diagram. Equilibrium exists initially with the market rate i_0, equal to the natural rate r_0. Owing to some technological advance the demand for loanable funds, DD′ shifts outwards to D_1D_1' establishing what Robertson calls a new *quasi-natural* rate at r_1. If the banks maintain the market rate of interest of i_0, however, the initial rate of lending exceeds the rate of available saving by the amount of newly created bank money, MM_1. From here on Robertson examines the stability of the quasi-natural rate, r_1, in the face of rising wages as the money or actual rate of interest pursues the natural rate. The details of that discussion are not of direct concern to us here. Rather, the more fundamental questions concern the nature and interpretation of the demand and supply schedules in Figure 2.2.

It is clear from the previous quotation from Robertson that the real forces of productivity and thrift lie behind the DD′ and SS′ schedules respectively. A complete exposition of the loanable funds theory therefore requires that we introduce the forces of productivity and thrift that stand behind the demand and supply schedules of loanable funds. The relevant analysis is illustrated by Makinen (1977: 20) in terms of Figure 2.3. In this scheme bonds have been introduced as the form in which savings are held and investment is financed, i.e. the demand for loanable funds generates a supply of bonds, $S_B(I)$. Figure 2.3(a) represents the real forces of productivity and thrift that lie behind the demand, D_{LF}, and supply, S_{LF}, of loanable funds. As Makinen (1977: 19) puts it, the money *value* of desired saving is supplied to the financial markets as loanable funds, while corresponding to the real *value* of desired investment in Figure 2.3(a) is the demand for loanable funds in Figure 2.3(b). But in view of the

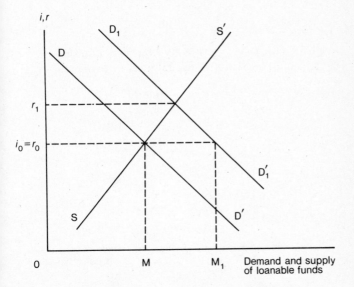

Fig. 2.2 Robertson's analysis of loanable funds theory

analysis presented so far, that immediately raises the question: what is real saving? And, in view of the capital debate, what are we to make of the definition of the natural rate of interest? Can the existence of the natural rate simply be assumed? Finally the monotonically declining relationship between the natural rate of interest and the *real value* of capital in Figure 2.3(a) raises the question of stability.

In attempting to answer these questions it soon becomes apparent that the notion of real saving is not sustainable in a world in which capital goods are produced. In such an economy saving is a monetary phenomenon and, unlike the corn model, does not occur in kind. (That Wicksell nevertheless sought to define the natural rate as the rate which would emerge if capital were lent in kind was a point made in previous discussion.) So although we may imagine a supply of money savings generating the upward sloping supply of loanable funds in Figure 2.3(b), there is no way in which we can relate that function to the real savings function in Figure 2.3(a). Recall from the discussion in footnote 1 that in Wicksell's analysis real saving does *not* refer to nominal saving deflated by the price level. This Fisherian concept of real saving is not relevant to Wicksell's definition of the natural rate. At best, the savings function in Figure 2.3(a) refers to the single commodity world of the corn model. In an economy in which capital goods are produced the supply curve of the capital goods sector is the relevant supply curve. But that relates the *price* of capital goods to the flow of output of capital goods; it cannot then be employed to define the natural rate of interest along the lines attempted in Figure 2.3(a).

On the demand side, it has already been demonstrated that to define the natural rate of interest, capital must be treated as a value

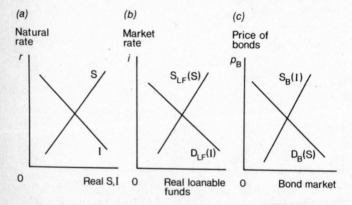

Fig. 2.3 The markets for loanable funds

magnitude but that this can only be achieved in a one-commodity model where the *value* and the *quantity* of capital are coincident. Also, it is only under these conditions that a monotonically declining demand function for the *real value* of capital can be derived as illustrated in Figure 2.3(a). The more general result is that illustrated in Figure 2.1.

In view of these observations it must be concluded that the analysis of the natural rate of interest illustrated in Figure 2.3(a) cannot be sustained if it is to be applied to an economy producing an array of heterogeneous capital goods. Consequently, all that remains of the loanable funds theory is the market rate of interest in Figure 2.3(b) (and the prices of bonds in Figure 2.3(c)). But in that case the loanable funds market has been cut free from the traditional analysis of the forces of productivity and thrift. This is a conclusion which was anathema to 'classical' economists in the tradition of Robertson or Hicks as is evidenced by their description of such a state in terms of the bootstraps analogy or, in Robertson's (1966: 174) case, of a grin without a cat! Neverthless, this is one of the inescapable conclusions of the capital debate; the natural rate of interest cannot be defined outside of a one-commodity model and that means that the money rate of interest is cut free from the forces of productivity and thrift.

CONCLUDING REMARKS

In this chapter we have examined Leijonhufvud's Wicksell connection from the perspective of the capital debate to demonstrate that the Wicksellian natural or real interest rate has no sound theoretical foundations. Within a multi-commodity model, neither the existence nor the stability of the long-period equilibrium solution can be established. Consequently, within the context of the Wicksellian loanable funds theory, the natural rate of interest is a concept which must be abandoned and the market rate of interest is left hanging by its own bootstraps.

Nevertheless, the use of the natural rate of interest to capture the link between the real and monetary sectors is suggestive of a fundamental idea that is worth retaining. It will be argued in later chapters that this can be done by employing Keynes's notion of the marginal efficiency of capital. The latter concept applies Marshallian principles to incorporate the influence of the market or money rate of interest on the demand prices of capital goods relative to their long-period supply prices. The concept of the marginal efficiency of capital is thus applicable to a world in which capital goods are produced, not saved. When

Wicksell's concept of the natural rate is replaced by Keynes's marginal efficiency of capital the relationship between the real and monetary sectors highlighted by Wicksell (and earlier by Thornton, 1802) can be placed on a secure theoretical footing which avoids the pitfalls exposed by the capital debate. In this regard although it cannot be claimed that Keynes was aware of the ramifications of the capital debate as they are understood today, it does seem that he was aware of the dangers inherent in Wicksell's approach. When discussing alternative theories of the rate of interest Keynes (1973b: 212–13) makes the following observations:

If the rate of interest is not determined by saving and investment in the same way in which price is determined by supply and demand, how is it determined? One naturally began by supposing that the rate of interest must be determined in some sense by productivity – that it was, perhaps, simply the monetary equivalent of the marginal efficiency of capital, the latter being independently fixed by physical and technical considerations in conjunction with the expected demand. It was only when this line of approach led repeatedly to what seemed to be circular reasoning, that I hit on what I now think to be the true explanation.

He then goes on to refer to liquidity preference theory and concludes that although it may not carry us very far it does, at least, provide a firm and intelligible basis on which to proceed. We will take up this theme in chapters 9 and 10.

3

NEO-WALRASIAN MONETARY THEORY

Having acknowledged the difficulties associated with Wicksellian capital theory, most neoclassical theorists have opted for the neo-Walrasian approach to general equilibrium theory. From the perspective of monetary theory the difficulties associated with the Wicksellian real interest rate mechanism are thereby avoided. Instead of taking the *value* of capital as given, neo-Walrasian general equilibrium models treat the endowment of capital, and its distribution, as a given array of *quantities*, e.g. as an array of machines. The immediate implication of this step is that interest rates are not related in any way to the notion of a natural rate but are derived on the basis of an intertemporal specification of the model. To this end neo-Walrasian models employ the concept of time-dated commodities to derive own rates of interest for each commodity. In general the uniformity of rates which characterized Wicksellian long-period equilibrium is lost and, if imposed, renders the model over-determined unless one or more of the initial endowments are treated as endogenous. Moreover, although this latter step is logically and mathematically feasible, it does not appear to have any economic rationale. In particular, neo-Walrasian analysis has no theory of competition that may be used to explain the existence of uniform rates of interest on all commodities.

Neo-Walrasian and Wicksellian interest rate theories thus have quite distinct analytical foundations and interpretations. The same is true of the quantity theory. Within the context of neo-Walrasian theory, the quantity equation imposes what is now referred to as the transaction or finance constraint. It is not a demand and supply relationship as in the Cambridge interpretation of the quantity theory but is instead a technical relation which specifies the rate at which

45

trades can occur with the aid of a monetary medium.[1] Further investigation of this issue then reveals the fundamental flaw in neo-Walrasian monetary theory – the inessential nature of 'money'; that is, the quantity equation or the finance constraint imposes a medium of exchange function on one of the commodities in what is otherwise a model of *perfect barter*. The point is simply that neo-Walrasian models do not need money. Such models Hahn (1973b:231, emphasis added) describes as inessential monetary economies and defines as follows: 'The main content of the monetary theory of an inessential economy is implicit in its construction: *there is nothing we can say about the equilibrium of an economy with "money" that one cannot say about the equilibrium of a non-monetary economy.*' Introducing a transaction constraint or a real balance effect cannot change this fact.

The inessential nature of neo-Walrasian monetary theory can be traced initially to the use of a concept of equilibrium based on tâtonnement and recontract in which all exchanges and production decisions are pre-reconciled *before* trade commences. Traders know the rates of exchange between all commodities so all the problems associated with ordinary barter are avoided. The model is one of perfect barter. It is therefore difficult to justify a role for money as a medium of exchange. It is not even clear that a unit of account is required in such a world. Neo-Walrasian models do, however, have the seductive property that 'money' may always be added without altering any of the perfect barter results. It is this latter property which has misled many neo-Walrasian theorists to concentrate on superficial issues such as the supposedly invalid 'classical' dichotomy (Patinkin, 1965) or the finance constraint (Clower, 1967; Kohn, 1981a), in an attempt to integrate real and monetary forces within a neo-Walrasian framework. But these attempts overlook the fundamental point that neo-Walrasian monetary and interest rate theory remains *real* theory because 'money' is always an inessential addition to a model of perfect barter. As Hahn (1973b:233) noted over a decade ago, the finance or transaction constraint is an inessential addition to a neo-Walrasian model.

This conclusion is not overturned when we examine the more recent overlapping generations models, or models which drop the auctioneer and introduce an Edgeworthian analysis of the exchange process. A role for 'money' is found in most overlapping generations

---

1. Valavanis (1955) and Hickman (1950) made this point during the so-called Patinkin controversy but its significance was not appreciated at the time. The Patinkin controversy is, in fact, an important illustration of the sterility of neo-Walrasian monetary theory and is discussed in full in the next chapter.

models because, as the only durable asset, it acts as a store of value. But, as Gale (1983:15) describes it, 'The "money" appearing in these models is of the "as if" variety, a confetti asset rather than a full-blown medium of exchange.' McCallum (1983b:195) makes essentially the same point when he concludes that the Sargent and Wallace (1983) model presents a 'flawed picture of a commodity-money economy, the problems arising because the model's "gold" does not serve as a medium of exchange'. In that case we must acknowledge Yeager's (1968) observation that if we cannot introduce the medium of exchange function we are not dealing with money at all. An additional problem in these models is that any interest-bearing asset would dominate 'money' in its role as a store of value.

Attempts to extend the neo-Walrasian tradition by focussing on the Edgeworth recontract process also ran into the dilemma of neo-Walrasian monetary theory so aptly posed by Ostroy (1973:603): 'How to introduce money without making the standard theory disappear?' Adding 'money' in an inessential fashion is one response to the dilemma but it leaves the theorist without any analytical framework to tackle the issues posed by the existence of credit and the banking system, e.g. Gale (1982:6, 1983:15). By comparison with Wicksell this appears as a retrogressive step. But more importantly it seeks to avoid the dilemma of neo-Walrasian monetary theory by ignoring it! This response is surely inappropriate. As Shubik (1985:127–8) explains, the implications of the dilemma must be faced: 'Attempts to merely extend general equilibrium theory without recognizing fundamentally different rules of the game concerning government, central banks, legal enforcement, power to collect taxes, etc., are doomed to failure … Money and credit are system properties. They cannot be defined independently of the structure of exchange and production in which they operate.' Here Shubik is suggesting that the dilemma of general equilibrium theory (neo-Walrasian) can only be resolved by abandoning the standard formalism. In this respect he is echoing Clower's (1975:12) conclusion that neo-Walrasian theory is 'categorical rather than non-categorial – closed to extension in certain crucial directions'. Clower suggests that this property is responsible for the present perplexity in macroeconomic theory and goes on to ask: 'if neo-Walrasian theory is bankrupt – as, for practical purposes it most surely is – where do we go from here?'

A constructive answer to this question will have to wait until part two of this study. For the moment the objective is to highlight the bankruptcy of neo-Walrasian monetary theory and to consider some failed attempts to avoid the dilemma posed by Ostroy and Hahn.

VARIETIES OF INTERTEMPORAL EQUILIBRIUM

The inessential nature of 'money' in neo-Walrasian theory is clearly revealed in its most sophisticated model – the Arrow–Debreu model. In the Arrow–Debreu specification a complete set of futures markets exists for all time-dated commodities, and problems associated with expectations and uncertainty are avoided by also defining commodities as contingent on the state of nature. Moreover, the state of nature is a 'complete specification of everything that might affect the usefulness or availability of commodities to anyone, such states being defined in such a way that exactly one must occur' (Allingham, 1983:7). The objective of defining commodities in this way is that it enables the future to be collapsed into the present! (Allingham, 1983:7; Hahn, 1982b:132; Gale, 1982:198). All decisions are thus coordinated or pre-reconciled at an instant in time in the first period when equilibrium is established, and the trading that results, as this infinitely long time slice unfolds, then occurs in accordance with these predetermined decisions. In such a world money obviously has no role to play. As Hahn (1982b:1) put it: 'A world in which all contingent future contracts are possible neither needs nor wants intrinsically worthless money.'

Nevertheless, having reached the conclusion that the best developed neo-Walrasian model of the economy has no role for money, all is not considered lost. Neo-Walrasian theorists seek instead to find a role for money in less comprehensively specified intertemporal models. To begin with it is generally agreed that the assumption of a complete array of contingent futures markets must be dropped. Such models are referred to as neo-Walrasian Temporary Equilibrium (TE) models and it is within this framework that attempts have been made to develop a 'useful' neo-Walrasian monetary theory (see, e.g. Grandmont, 1974; 1977:535; Gale, 1982:ch.5; Hahn, 1982b:3–4; Cowan, 1983). Nevertheless serious problems remain.

The initial difficulty encountered by these TE models arises from the need to model expectations. If a complete array of contingent futures markets does not exist then current plans will be influenced by expectations of future prices and states of nature. The recognition of this possibility does, however, pose some difficult, and as yet unresolved, problems for TE theorists. As Hahn (1980a:132–3, emphasis in original) has acknowledged:

Once these [futures] markets are incomplete, rather terrible things happen to the theory. The economy will now have trading at every date – we are dealing with a sequence economy [a TE model]. Agents' actions at any date will now depend on their beliefs concerning *future* events ... and the prices which will rule *given those events*. But we have no theory of expectations comparable to our theory of household or firm choice; that is to say, we certainly have no axiomatic foundations for such a theory and scarcely have we a psychologically plausible account ... Put at its mildest, the sequence economy has presented problems of market expectations which are not yet resolved.

The difficulties associated with the treatment of expectations should not, however, be interpreted as a minor technical problem. Rather they are in one sense fundamental to attempts to introduce money into neo-Walrasian models. Relaxing the assumption of a complete array of contingent futures markets was seen as a way of justifying a role for money precisely because it appeared to allow for expectations and uncertainty – elements excluded from the Arrow–Debreu model. But if the problems associated with expectations are unresolved, by implication, attempts to justify a role for money along these lines are in similar difficulties. Despite these reservations let us proceed to examine how expectations have been treated in TE models.

Expectations have been tackled in one of two ways — neither of which is considered to be satisfactory (Hahn, 1980a). Firstly, expectation formation may be taken as entirely exogenous to the model and changes in expectations left unexplained.[2] Most theorists now consider such a treatment as entirely *ad hoc* (Gale, 1982:59), and hence unsatisfactory, although it was the method employed prior to the craze for Rational Expectations. Secondly, under the Rational Expectations hypothesis each agent is assumed to predict correctly, on average, the equilibrium prices associated with the future states of nature. Agents in the model use the structure of the model to make these predictions: and, as Hahn (1982b:4) and others have reminded us, this implies that agents have knowledge of the future structure of the model which is beyond reach. But more important from the point of view of monetary theory is the realization that the Rational Expectations hypothesis reduces the TE structure to what Hahn (1973b) calls an inessential sequence economy, that is to say, a sequence economy which produces results isomorphic to the Arrow–Debreu model – a moneyless world! Introducing the Rational Expectations hypothesis into neo-Walrasian TE models thus defeats attempts to find a rationale for the role of money on the grounds of the existence of expectations and uncertainty.

Hahn (1973b:230–33) points out that for a neo-Walrasian TE

2. It is commonly assumed that expectations are unit elastic in these exercises.

model to produce results isomorphic to the Arrow–Debreu model it is necessary that:

(i)   there is no sequential learning;
(ii)   the prices at all dates are known to all agents;
(iii)   transaction costs are zero.

Imposing the Rational Expectations hypothesis has the effect of removing the need for sequential learning (first criterion); it provides stochastic knowledge of all prices at all dates such that price expectations are on average correct as each agent knows the model that generates these prices, i.e. he employs the 'relevant' economic theory (Muth, 1961)(second criterion); and finally the tâtonnement assumption of neo-Walrasian theory ensures that transaction costs are zero (third criterion). Employing the Rational Expectations hypothesis in neo-Walrasian TE models thus brings us face to face with the non-monetary properties of these models. These non-monetary properties of neo-Walrasian theory are, of course, inherent in the structure of the theory itself, irrespective of any treatment of expectations which may be imposed on that structure. The Rational Expectations hypothesis merely serves to highlight that fact. Consequently in what follows we concentrate on the theoretical structure of neo-Walrasian monetary and interest rate theory.

THE FOUNDATIONS OF NEO-WALRASIAN MONETARY THEORY

In view of the above observations, the following illustrations of the non-monetary nature of neo-Walrasian monetary and interest rate theory will proceed on the basis of some form of TE model. No particular attention will be paid to the treatment of expectations, however, and it may be assumed, for the sake of simplicity, that agents only live one period and are replaced by their identical offspring who inherit any durable commodities that may remain at the beginning of the next period (Gale, 1982:16). That gets rid of the problem of expectations, but does not solve it.

When it comes to selecting a particular neo-Walrasian TE model the intertemporal specification is clearly important for the analysis of interest rates but less so for examining the role of the finance constraint. Consequently, to illustrate the properties and non-monetary nature of neo-Walrasian interest rate theory, a model presented by Hahn (1982a) in his critique of the neo-Ricardians will be used. For our purposes this model provides a useful illustration of the non-monetary properties of neo-Walrasian interest rate theory which makes for easy comparison with the Petri model discussed in chapter

2. The statement of the finance constraint presented by Grandmont and Younes (1972) is then used to provide a concrete illustration of the inessential addition of 'money' to a neo-Walrasian model. The Grandmont and Younes version of the finance constraint is also particularly useful because it is general enough to capture a wide variety of interpretations of the concept that exist in the literature. In particular it is easily related to the treatment of the quantity theory in the neo-Walrasian models employed in the Patinkin controversy – which is to be discussed in the next chapter.

Neo-Walrasian theory of interest rates

The model presented by Hahn (1982a) provides an elementary ill-ustration of the use of time-dated commodities in an intertemporal setting. And although the model is far from comprehensive, it contains sufficient detail to illustrate the properties of neo-Walrasian interest rate theory. It is in any event easily generalized.

For the sake of simplicity (Hahn, 1982a:362), the model consists of only two time periods, t and $t + 1$, say, with initial endowments of period t wheat, $\bar{W}_t$, barley, $\bar{B}_t$, and one unit of labour, L. The intertemporal feature of the model is derived by noting that wheat and barley available in period $t + 1$ are not the same goods as period t wheat or barley. Seen from period t the model has five prices:

$$P_W^t, P_B^t, P_W^{t+1}, P_B^{t+1}, w$$

where w is the wage of one unit of period t labour which gets paid in period $t + 1$. The price vector is normalized by:

$$P_W^t + P_B^t + P_W^{t+1} + P_B^{t+1} + w = 1 \qquad (3.1)$$

The model is assumed to refer to a production process in which the endowments of wheat, barley and labour can be employed to produce $t + 1$ wheat or barley. Writing

$$Q = (P_W^t, P_B^t, P_W^{t+1}, P_B^{t+1}, w)$$

as a five vector, the unit 'profit' function for the production of wheat or barley must have the form:

$$\pi_i(Q) = 0, i = W_{t+1}, B_{t+1} \qquad (3.2)$$

where π_i refers to what Hahn (1982a:360) calls the 'pure profit' per unit. That is to say, pure profits must be set to zero because if $\pi_i < 0$ the ith commodity will not be produced while if $\pi_i > 0$ competitive producers would attempt to produce an unbounded amount, which contradicts the assumption of finite endowments. Now there are difficulties of interpretation associated with this analysis which will be taken up below, so for the moment we simply note that as a consequence of (3.2) the prices of commodities equal their costs of production:

$$P_j^{t+1} = \Sigma a_{ij} P_i^t + a_{0j} w, \qquad i, j = \text{W, B}$$

where the a_{ij}'s represent the most 'profitable' input coefficients from those available; it is not necessary to assume fixed input coefficients.

The model is completed by introducing the excess demand functions for wheat, barley and labour:

$$X_i^t = X_i^t(Q, \bar{W}_t, \bar{B}_t), \qquad i = \text{W, B, L}$$

As is usual in neo-Walrasian models, these excess demand functions satisfy Walras's Law:

$$P_W^t X_W^t + P_B^t X_B^t + w X_L^t \equiv 0$$

which means that we only require two of them to determine the equilibrium solution. Dropping the labour equation gives:

$$X_i^t(Q, \bar{W}_t, \bar{B}_t) = 0, \qquad i = \text{W, B} \qquad (3.3)$$

The model comprising (3.1), (3.2) and (3.3) then contains five equations in five unknowns, and, subject to the usual restrictions on preferences, the existence of an equilibrium can be established (Hahn, 1982a).

The intertemporal equilibrium solution to the model then implies that own rates of interest can be calculated on both wheat and barley. These rates of interest are defined as follows:

$$r_i = \frac{P_i^t - P_i^{t+1}}{P_i^{t+1}}, \qquad i = \text{W, B}$$

and it is important to note the following characteristics of these rates. Firstly, own rates of interest are defined for all commodities once the prices of the time-dated commodities are known, so clearly no additional analytical insights are obtained by deriving the implied interest rates (Walsh and Gram, 1980:234–6,407–8 and Howard, 1979:52). Furthermore, own rates may be negative for some commodities. This may appear a little odd but it does not mean that any gains can be made by shifting resources to commodities with positive own rates – for an illustration see Howard (1983:86–9). Secondly, and more importantly, the own rates of interest on wheat and barley do not satisfy the condition $r_W = r_B$ in equilibrium – except by chance. In other words, the equilibrium generated by the above example of an intertemporal neo-Walrasian TE model does not generate the equality of interest rates illustrated by equations (2.16) and (2.17) in Petri's statement of the Wicksellian system. This inequality of own rates is almost a defining characteristic of neo-Walrasian interest rate theory and simply reflects the alternative treatment of capital in neo-Walrasian models.[3]

However, it is possible to impose the Wicksellian-type condition $r_W = r_B$ by finding a particular set of endowments of wheat and barley that generates just that set of intertemporal prices to yield the condition $r_W = r_B$. More technically, this means that the model is overdetermined if the condition $r_W = r_B$ is imposed (recall footnote 10 in chapter 2) but that a solution can be obtained if one of the endowments, $\bar{W}_t$ or $\bar{B}_t$, is treated as an endogenous variable. Because the marginal conditions of utility and 'profit' maximization apply to the functions of the model, e.g. the excess demand functions in (3.3), most neo-Walrasian theorists follow Hahn (1982a) and conclude that the Wicksellian-type solution of equal own rates of interest is simply a special case of the more general neo-Walrasian analysis. Nevertheless, this interpretation is based on a fundamental conceptual error as a result of which it is not at all clear what economic rationale can be given to this algebraic manipulation.

To demonstrate these properties and the associated conceptual error, consider the following manipulations of the model. As it stands the equilibrium solution to Hahn's model does not produce $r_W = r_B$ unless the relative prices of wheat and barley are the same in both periods, i.e.

$$\frac{P_W^t}{P_B^t} = \frac{P_W^{t+1}}{P_B^{t+1}},$$

and it is unlikely that any arbitrarily given endowment would produce that result. To see this, define

$$R_i = \frac{P_i^t}{P_i^{t+1}}, \quad i = \text{W, B}$$

so that $r_i = R_i - 1, i = \text{W, B}$, and note that, despite the differences in own rates of interest, no gain can be made by holding wheat rather than producing barley. Converting period t wheat into period $t + 1$

3. It will be recalled that Wicksell (1893:167, emphasis in original) considered this to be a fatal flaw in Walras's analysis. He noted that:

Walras calls 'capital' and treats as 'capital' *only* durable goods, but not raw materials and half-finished products and not the means of subsistence of the workers ... In this interpretation the true role of capital in production is completely overlooked. A necessary consequence of this is the peculiar fact that these equations of production and exchange can *give no information at all about the level of the rate of interest*. If only durable goods are regarded as capital, then a certain *rent* is fixed for each group of these by the above-mentioned equations but *not* the *capital value* of the good itself, nor, consequently, the *rate* of interest either.

wheat is equivalent to converting period t wheat into period t barley, converting the period t barley into period $t + 1$ barley at the rate R_B, and then converting the period $t + 1$ barley into period $t + 1$ wheat. Simple algebra shows the two routes to produce an equivalent rate of return,[4] i.e.

$$R_W = \left(\frac{P_W^t}{P_B^t}\right) R_B \left(\frac{P_B^{t+1}}{P_W^{t+1}}\right)$$

Imposing the condition $r_W = r_B$, or $R_W = R_B$, then, obviously implies the equality of relative prices in both periods: but it also renders the model overdetermined! This result emerges if we impose the definition of $R_i = R$ and rewrite equation (3.1) as:

$$RP_W^{t+1} + RP_B^{t+1} + P_W^{t+1} + P_B^{t+1} + w = 1 \qquad (3.1')$$

The model now consists of five equations in four unknowns and is thus overdetermined (Hahn, 1982a:365). Nevertheless, an analytical solution can be found if one of the exogenous variables, $\bar{W}_t$ or $\bar{B}_t$, is treated as an additional unknown.

The relevant analytical point can be explained with reference to Figure 3.1 which illustrates possible (but arbitrarily drawn) market-clearing loci for the intertemporal wheat and barley markets. The abscissa measures the endowment of wheat, for example, which may be treated as an endogenous variable if the Wicksell-type condition of equal rates of interest is imposed. The ordinate measures the two rates of interest on wheat and barley and illustrates the case that for wheat endowments greater than W_t' the wheat rate of interest is negative. The labour market has been dropped by applying Walras's Law.

Looking at these properties of neo-Walrasian interest rate theory, a number of serious difficulties of interpretation must be faced. To begin with, there is the neo-Walrasian contribution to the confusion between profits and interest that characterizes neoclassical theory. In this case confusion arises because neo-Walrasian models have abandoned the classical analysis of production as a surplus-generating process. Instead neo-Walrasian theory is concerned with the efficient allocation of *given* resources, and production is modelled, like exchange, as an application of this criterion (Walsh and Gram, 1980).

This point can, perhaps, best be made with reference to the familiar Marshallian concepts of normal and excess profits. The latter is in fact the remnant of the classical concept of surplus which is

4. By definition, $\frac{P_W^t}{P_W^{t+1}} = \left(\frac{P_W^t}{P_B^t}\right)\left(\frac{P_B^t}{P_B^{t+1}}\right)\left(\frac{P_B^{t+1}}{P_W^{t+1}}\right)$. This result, although often described

as a terminal state (Howard, 1983:89) should not be confused with the Marshallian normal profit condition, for reasons which are spelt out in the text.

eliminated by the marginal productivity theory of distribution in Wicksellian general equilibrium models.[5] Nevertheless, in Marshallian analysis excess profits (or losses) may exist in the short period but the mobility of capital ensures that only normal, and hence uniform, profits are earned in the long period. The existence of quasi-rents or excess profits therefore provides the signal or dynamic for the attainment of a long-period equilibrium solution. Wicksell (1898a) employed a similar concept in his analysis of the cumulative process which was, after all, a disequilibrium state relative to the long-period equality of market and natural rates of interest. By comparison, in the neo-Walrasian model illustrated in Figure 3.1 we find that 'firms' *always* earn zero 'pure profits' – both when $r_W \neq r_B$ and when $r_W = r_B$! In neo-Walrasian theory, interest rate equality therefore is not a necessary characteristic of equilibrium and there is no mechanism of competition whereby the wheat endowment can converge on W_t^0 in the long period. What role then do normal and excess profits play in this story? In Wicksellian or Marshallian theory a discrepancy between rates of interest or the existence of excess profits is a symptom of short-period disequilibrium relative to long-period equilibrium where the natural rate of interest is equated with normal profits. In neo-Walrasian theory, however, this mechanism is missing. In fact, it

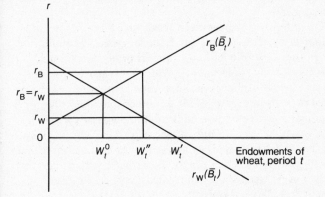

Fig. 3.1 Hypothetical market-clearing loci in intertemporal wheat and barley markets.

5. During Wicksell's (disequilibrium) cumulative process excess profits/losses accrue which may induce entrepreneurs to attempt to change their scale of operations (Wicksell, 1898a:ch.9). Similar ideas are found in Keynes's use of the Fundamental Equations in the *Treatise*, which embody standard Marshallian ideas. In this sense excess profits appear as disequilibrium phenomena which do not play a role in the neoclassical (equilibrium) theory of distribution.

is now apparent that the concepts of normal and excess profits cannot be applied in this way to neo-Walrasian models. To see why, consider the following points.

In his discussion of Walras's production model Morishima (1977:48) highlights what he considers to be the rather paradoxical conclusion that Walras's Law does not hold in Walras's production model! This result is not surprising, however, because Walras's Law, which states that the value of excess demands must always sum to zero for any price vector, is a concept introduced by Lange (1942). In Walras's production model we find instead that it is only the value of the excess demands *plus* the aggregate excess profit which identically sums to zero (Morishima, 1977:49). Hence Walras's Law *à la* Lange does not hold in Walras's production model. Walras was, after all, attempting to apply the traditional method of long-period equilibrium analysis in terms of which excess profits only exist in the short period (Petri, 1978). To impose Walras's Law the neo-Walrasians then adopt one of two approaches to get rid of the excess profits. They either:

(i) impose the condition of zero excess profits as Hahn did in the above model, or

(ii) assume that excess profits exist but are distributed to households in proportion to their ownership of capital goods, for instance.

On the first point it is important to recall that this approach does not mean that Walras's Law only holds for long-period equilibrium where excess profits are zero and only normal profits are earned.[6] As we saw above, interest rates in neo-Walrasian theory cannot be interpreted as normal profits even when rates of interest are equal, such as when $r_W = r_B$ in Figure 3.1. It is not possible to interpret the result $r_W \neq r_B$ as a short-period equilibrium and $r_W = r_B$ as a long-period equilibrium in the traditional sense of these terms. In the model these two conditions represent *mutually exclusive* equilibria that are not dynamically related by the existence of excess profits in terms of the distinction between short- and long-period equilibrium. The neo-Walrasian model is not open to this traditional interpretation. (Alternative notions of long-period equilibrium have been employed in the neo-Walrasian literature and will be discussed in the appendix to this chapter.) Furthermore, having defined away the notion of

6. Walras attempted to interpret his model along these lines but ran into difficulties. See Petri (1978) for a discussion of this issue. The main difficulty is that Walras's treatment of capital rules out the determination of a long-period equilibrium defined in terms of a uniform rate of profit/interest. Recall the earlier illustration of the point in Hahn's model.

excess profits, the associated notion of normal profits is also lost. Thus, despite the fact that Hahn (1982a:356n1) defines profits as 'the rate of interest used to discount future receipts', these 'profits' cannot be interpreted as normal profits in the sense that the term is used in classical or Marshallian economics.

As far as the second point is concerned it seems, at first sight, not unreasonable to include profit income in the budget constraints of households. Certainly, profits earned in one period could be paid out the next or if not paid out could imply some form of wealth effect which should be taken into account. However, the treatment of excess profits in neo-Walrasian models cannot be justified on these grounds because the excess profit in the budget constraints of households must equal that of the firms *in the same period* if Walras's Law is to hold. In effect this means that so-called excess profits form part of the endowment which determines the level of demand, which in turn is supposed to generate these profits. In other words it appears that excess profits are both spent and earned simultaneously! This anomaly is a symptom of the fact that the concept of excess profits is simply not compatible with the neo-Walrasian specification of the production process as a variation on the theme of the efficient allocation of given resources. As Walsh and Gram (1980:243n3, emphasis in original) explained:

This, of course, was the position of Walras (zero profits). Ironically, even in certain modern versions of post-Walrasian theory, in which net receipts *are* allowed to be positive in equilibrium, the resulting 'profits' must somehow be assigned to the *consuming* agents. This is done by means of additional parameters that fix the share that each consumer has in the net receipts of each producing agent (subject to the condition that such shares add up to 100 per cent for each producer). Sometimes the shares are interpreted as dividends from common stock or as the proceeds from a partnership ... On this interpretation, however, the question arises as to how the shares are to be assigned. If they reflect differences in entrepreneurial skill with which enterprises are managed then it would be more in keeping with the theme of the allocation of given resources to identify such special skills as inputs to be allocated, like any other factor service. If the shares are implicit returns to physical assets, such as machinery, then, again, the ownership of such factors should be specified and the rental rate for, say, machine-services should appear as a factor price in the analysis. In short, in an allocation model, all incomes must *ultimately* be imputed to the value of some factor of production – calling any such income 'profit' is just a misleading use of language.

What Walsh and Gram are saying is that the Marshallian concept of excess profits is simply not defined in neo-Walrasian theory and extending the model to deal with production amounts only to another inessential extension of the analysis (Rogers, 1983).

The above investigation of the problems of interpretation involved in neo-Walrasian interest rate theory thus reveals another case of the inability of neoclassical theory to distinguish between profit and interest. In Wicksellian general equilibrium models the natural rate of interest is equated with the normal rate of profit and derived from the marginal productivity of capital. The notion of a rate of interest not related to the productivity of capital, which is used to discount the excess profits to determine the value of an item of capital, is not a concept that has any meaningful analytical interpretation within Wicksellian theory. In neo-Walrasian general equilibrium theory, on the other hand, only own rates of interest are defined, and are done so in such a way that they are unrelated to the Marshallian concepts of normal and excess profit. Nevertheless, both versions of neoclassical theory can be found with explicit reference made to profits, with the result that considerable confusion remains. But, as Bauer (1939) pointed out long ago:

the value of a capital asset would depend on the expected quasi-rents and the rate of interest at which these will be discounted, and the value will rise either if quasi-rents rise, or if the rate of interest falls; thus variations in these have exactly opposite results [on investment] which surely would not be the case if they belonged to the same genus. ·

Neo-Walrasian theory is particularly open to confusion on this score, lacking as it does any notion of excess profit. Moreover, apart from these difficulties of interpretation with neo-Walrasian interest rate theory – which reflect in the main the treatment of production as an allocation and not a surplus-generating process – it is also apparent that the theory is entirely non-monetary. This latter property is most clearly revealed by an examination of the role of the finance constraint.

Money and the finance constraint

Not surprisingly, the role of money in neo-Walrasian models has come under extensive attack in the post-war period, most notably from Patinkin (1965) and Clower (1965). The criticism by Patinkin and Clower is, however, misconceived as they both miss the significance of the central issue exposed by Hahn – the inessential nature of 'money' in neo-Walrasian models. Instead, both Patinkin's real balance effect and Clower's finance constraint are examples of analysis which reflect the failure to note the inessential nature of 'money' in neo-Walrasian models. That is to say, they illustrate that 'money' can be added to a neo-Walrasian model but that such a step is unnecessary because none of the perfect barter results are thereby altered. The point can most readily be made using a generalization of Clower's notion of the finance constraint presented by Grandmont and Younes. Patinkin's critique of the invalid 'classical' dichotomy and his interpretation of the quantity theory in a neo-Walrasian setting is then seen to be an error because the quantity equation emerges as a particular application of the finance constraint.

Patinkin's case will be discussed in full in the following chapter. Here we concentrate on showing that the finance constraint is an inessential addition to a neo-Walrasian model. The generalization of the finance constraint presented by Grandmont and Younes (1972) is employed in a neo-Walrasian TE model with the following characteristics. (Patinkin employs much the same structure.)

The analysis is conducted in a simple exchange model where 'money' is the only durable commodity and store of value. Time is divided into a number of discrete periods and market equilibrium is established at the beginning of each period – on Hicksian 'Mondays'. All markets operate via the tâtonnement process and all commodities other than 'money' are perishable, i.e. they cannot be carried over from one period to the next. The fact that 'money' is durable establishes its role as a store of value. The quantity of 'money' is fixed and all consumption goods have positive prices. Each 'Monday' agents receive a bundle of real income in kind – the 'manna drop' – which acts as their initial endowment. Once equilibrium is established, via the tâtonnement process, plans are irrevocable for the remainder of the week.

To ensure that 'money' had a medium of exchange function, Clower (1967) argued that in a monetary economy 'money' bought goods and goods bought 'money' but goods did not buy goods. The latter condition he considered to be a property of a barter model. To formalize this idea he suggested that in addition to the usual budget constraint agents should face a finance constraint. In terms of the above TE framework Grandmont and Younes (1972) present these ideas in the following form. Each agent's endowment of real income is denoted by ω and the initial 'money' holding by $m(t-1)$. In terms of the usual utility-maximizing exercise, agents determine their consumption for the current period, $q(t)$, and the 'money' balances, $m(t)$, that will be carried over to the next period. Taking a representative agent, and the price vector $p(t)$, the agent must choose a combination of $q(t)$ and $m(t)$ subject to both a budget and a transaction or finance constraint. The transaction constraint imposes the condition that 'money' must be used to make all exchanges in terms of Clower's aphorism.

The budget constraint has the form:

$$p(t)q(t) + m(t) = p(t)\omega + m(t - 1) \qquad (3.4)$$

and simply states that the value of consumption, $p(t)q(t)$, plus the 'money' balances to be held over, $m(t)$, cannot exceed the value of income endowment, $p(t)w$, plus the initial 'money' balances. In addition the equilibrium consumption plan must also satisfy the finance constraint:

$$q(t) \text{ is feasible} \qquad (3.5)$$
$$\langle = \rangle \, p(q - \omega)^+ \leqslant m(t - 1) + \sum_n k_n p_n (q - \omega)_n^-$$

where $(q - \omega)^+$ and $(q - \omega)^-$ are agents' net purchases and sales, respectively, from their income endowment, and the k's are parameters satisfying $0 \leqslant k_n \leqslant 1$ for all commodities.[7] The latter parameters are important because they provide the generalization of Clower's statement of the finance constraint. For example, if $k_n = 0$, $\forall n$, then 'money' received from current sales cannot be used to make current purchases – as in Clower's (1967) original statement of the finance constraint. If we impose the condition that $m(t) = m(t - 1)$, as Archibald and Lipsey (1958) do for the case of full equilibrium, then the value of purchases, $p(q - \omega)^+$, is constrained to equal the value of sales, $p(q - \omega)^-$, and $k_n = 1$. The implications of these observations will be taken up in the following chapter. At this point we need to concentrate on the central issue. Is the finance constraint in (3.5) a necessary addition to the model? On investigation it appears that the answer is no.

To see why, consider first that it is generally acknowledged that the TE solution determined via a tâtonnement process is analytically distinct from the actual trading which takes place later. In other words there is an analytical distinction between the tâtonnement algorithm and the use of 'money' as a medium of exchange in the trading process. Kohn (1979:9) describes the relationship as follows: 'Money has no role to play in the mechanism of the tâtonnement algorithm ... The special role of "money" is not found in the dynamics of the tâtonnement algorithm but in the trading process ... the actual exchange of commodities; not the happenings of Monday, but in the activities of the rest of the week.' But if the equilibrium

---

7. For example, if $k_n = 0$, $\forall\, n$, then 'money' received from current sales cannot be used to make current purchases, while if $k_n = 1$ the entire 'money' proceeds are available for such purposes. Obviously if $0 < k_n < 1$ only part of these proceeds are available.

solution is determined by the tâtonnement algorithm, why is 'money' needed to make the exchanges? Surely the tâtonnement has costlessly pre-reconciled *all* plans and rates of exchange between *all* commodities? Consequently the problems usually associated with barter, e.g. the double coincidence of wants, do not arise in neo-Walrasian models – a well-known (but nevertheless often overlooked) fact. The exponents of the finance constraint certainly appear to have overlooked this point. For example, Clower (1969:16) states that Patinkin's model is logically indistinguishable from the traditional theory of barter. But that is surely not correct. Patinkin's model is a model of *perfect barter* in which all the problems of the traditional analysis of barter do not arise. More recent exponents of the finance constraint make a similar mistake when they justify the role of 'money' on the basis of frictions in the trading process. For example, Grandmont (1977:554) argues that the constraint (3.5) 'is supposed to reflect the fact that "money" is used as an intermediary in every exchange, *and the difficulty of buyers and sellers to get together during the market period*'. Patinkin (1965) similarly attempted to justify the assumption of a positive accounting price for 'money' on the basis of uncertainty over the timing of receipts and payments. But although these frictions may be added to make the exchange process appear more realistic, they are nonetheless inessential additions to a neo-Walrasian model.[8] They have no theoretical basis in neo-Walrasian theory. As Hahn (1965:130–31) pointed out: 'explanations which turn on ... inconvenience of indirect transactions are not easy to accommodate in a model such as Patinkin's [a neo-Walrasian model]. These are all imperfections which find no place in the model.' Hahn's comments apply to neo-Walrasian theory in general, and although the finance constraint may make sense in another context, introducing it into a neo-Walrasian model does not change the properties of the model imparted by the tâtonnement assumption. The point is simply that 'the inessential economy does not need money and one must give reasons for grafting on to it monetary constraints. These reasons have not been given' (Hahn, 1973b:233). More than a decade later convincing reasons are still wanting.

8. Grandmont and Younes (1972:357) make a similar mistake when they claim that only when $k_n = 1$ in (3.5) does the medium of exchange function become redundant and the exchange process frictionless. But the finance constraint is an arbitrary or inessential elaboration of a model in which the medium of exchange function is always redundant – as can be seen from the fact that k_n is an arbitrary parameter imposed on the model by the theorist. It has no basis in neo-Walrasian theory.

Existence and stability of equilibrium

The previous discussion leads to the conclusion that 'money' is an inessential addition to a neo-Walrasian temporary equilibrium model. That is, there is nothing we can say about the equilibrium in these models that cannot be said about the equilibrium of the equivalent non-monetary perfect barter model. In that case there may seem to be little point in examining the formal analysis of the existence and stability of such an equilibrium. Nevertheless it is instructive to pursue the issue because it provides additional support for the above conclusion.

Hahn (1965) was the first to pay attention to the question of the existence of an equilibrium in a monetary economy when he pointed out that a Patinkin-type (neo-Walrasian) model always contained a 'non-monetary' solution. That is, the model has an equilibrium in which no one uses 'money' because it has a zero accounting price. Now setting the accounting price of 'money' equal to zero means that it has no value in exchange and, as Howitt (1973:488) points out, would not be demanded by anyone free of 'money' illusion. Of course not; in a world of perfect barter, who would need money? This aspect of Hahn's examination of the existence properties therefore again reveals the inessential nature of 'money' in neo-Walrasian theory. As early as 1965 Hahn had thus reached the conclusion that Patinkin had 'failed to provide a model which can serve as an adequate foundation of monetary theory' (Hahn,1965:131). Yet a similar conclusion applies to the more recent attempts at the proof of existence in temporary equilibrium 'monetary' models. Moreover as we shall see, Howitt's (1974) analysis of stability is conducted in terms of the same model. The issue is *not* resolved by adding the finance constraint.

In his survey article, Grandmont (1977) points out that a positive accounting price for 'money' is ensured by the assumption that traders expect the future accounting price to be positive. Thus, even if the current accounting price was zero, traders would have a demand for 'money' balances because of its expected future positive value. As Cowen (1983:9) remarks, this is like attributing the existence of the Cheshire Cat to its smile rather than vice versa. Clearly, to explain money's present value on the basis of its expected future value, without explaining the latter, amounts to no more than *assuming* that 'money' has a positive accounting price, *an assumption which must ultimately be made if 'money' is to be used as a medium of exchange in a model in which no such function is required.* The difficulties with the proof of existence in neo-Walrasian models first exposed by Hahn therefore continue as properties of the temporary equilibrium models. These difficulties reflect the fact that 'money' is an inessential addition to neo-Walrasian models and as such its medium of exchange function is not necessary for the determination of an equilibrium solution. The existence proofs currently in use are therefore valid only for non-monetary models and there is no reason to believe that their results can be transferred to monetary models. As Hahn (1965:134) was at pains to point out, in a model that includes debt, i.e. credit money, the possibility of bankruptcies introduces discontinuities which would render the existence of an equilibrium problematic, if not impossible. Consequently neo-Walrasian models are still best characterized as models to which 'money' is an inessential addition. For models or theories in which money does matter, the question of existence remains unresolved and therefore the issue of stability is not even raised.[9]

That this issue is still on the agenda, is evidenced by McCallum's (1983a:36) recent survey of overlapping-generations models in which he concludes that in the basic model 'the same bundles are attainable (with a given capital stock) in equilibria in which "money" is valuable and valueless'. But this is no more than a restatement of Hahn's (1965,1973b) assessment of neo-Walrasian monetary theory. It simply reflects the fact that 'money' as a medium of exchange is always an inessential addition to the basic neo-Walrasian model of perfect barter.

CLOWER'S GENERAL PROCESS ANALYSIS

As a means of illustrating the dilemma facing neo-Walrasian monetary theorists, it is interesting to reconsider Clower's position in more detail. It will be recalled that Clower (1967) initially introduced the finance constraint in an attempt to provide a role for money in what he perceived to be Patinkin's (1965) barter analysis. However, as Ostroy (1973:597) observed, this step generated the paradoxical conclusion that the introduction of money had led to a loss in efficiency. Monetary exchange appeared from this perspective to be more restrictive than barter exchange! More recently Clower (in Walker,1984:267) acknowledges that this result is contrary to common sense and enquires as to the possible cause. The simple

---

9. The stability analysis of non-monetary models is in sufficient difficulty without considering the added complications introduced by money. See Hahn (1980a) and Fisher (1976).

answer, of course, is that if the model is initially one of perfect barter, then incorporating any additional constraints, e.g. the finance constraint, will inevitably involve a loss of efficiency. There is therefore no paradox because this is precisely the result that we would expect from tampering with the perfect barter world of the neo-Walrasian tâtonnement process where traders are provided with the real rates of exchange for all commodities. It is difficult to imagine a more efficient system. In such a world there is simply no necessary role for money as a medium of exchange.

As a result of this perceived anomaly with Clower's initial attempt to introduce a role for money via the finance constraint, Ostroy (1973) and Howitt (1974) independently proposed analyses of what they call the 'microfoundations of monetary exchange'. Clower now perceives these developments as providing the theoretical framework for what he calls a general process analysis (Walker, 1984:part IV). On closer inspection, however, Clower adopts an ambivalent stance when it comes to a confrontation with the dilemma of neo-Walrasian monetary theory. For example, at one point he describes his analysis as an attempt to establish necessary conditions for monetary exchange in an otherwise strictly Arrow–Debreu economy (Walker, 1984:239). On another occasion he suggests that general process analysis includes general competitive analysis as a limiting case (Walker, 1984:249). These observations tend to suggest that despite acknowledging that neo-Walrasian theory is categorical (and theoretically bankrupt science fiction!), Clower has not yet come to terms with the fundamental dilemma of neo-Walrasian monetary theory, viz. 'How to make money appear without making the standard theory disappear?' The ambivalence inherent in Clower's position is thrown into sharper focus when we compare the Howitt (1974) analysis to that of Ostroy (1973) and Ostroy and Starr (1974).

In a recent paper on the genesis and control of inflation Clower indicates that Howitt (1974) employs a simple but nevertheless formal model of general process analysis (Walker, 1984:245). An inspection of this model reveals, however, that it retains a strictly neo-Walrasian structure. In particular, both Walras's Law and the homogeneity postulate continue to apply and Howitt (1974:141) explicitly remarks on the similarity between his model and the neo-Walrasian system. But more significantly, Howitt (1974:135, 140) notes both that the long-period equilibrium solution to his model is identical to that of Patinkin and that, except for his addition of the finance constraint, his formal model of the transactor's decision process is the same as that proposed by Archibald and Lipsey (1958). But as the Patinkin and Archibald–Lipsey models are neo-Walrasian structures, how are these theoretically bankrupt models to provide the microeconomic foundations for Clower's general process analysis?

The neo-Walrasian pedigree of Howitt's model becomes even more apparent when it is realized that he is incorrect to claim that Archibald and Lipsey do not include a finance constraint. As we show in greater detail in the following chapter, the quantity equation employed by Archibald and Lipsey is formally equivalent to the finance constraint introduced by Clower and later employed by Howitt. At this stage the equivalence can be demonstrated informally in terms of Clower's interpretation of the finance constraint as the imposition of the condition that only money buys goods (or goods buy money) but goods do not buy goods. That is, money must at least perform its function as a medium of exchange. But augmenting the neo-Walrasian system of equations with the quantity equation along the lines suggested by Patinkin or Archibald and Lipsey is equivalent to imposing this medium of exchange function on an otherwise perfect barter system. After all, the equation of exchange includes a term indicating the *velocity* at which the 'money' stock is to circulate so as to achieve the equilibrium trades. Once this is recognized, it is a relatively simple matter to show that the Archibald and Lipsey (1958) analysis of the quantity equation is formally equivalent to the imposition of Clower's finance constraint. Therefore, Howitt's (1974: 140) analysis does not, as he claims, provide a rationale for the role of money in the exchange process. In fact, Howitt's model is simply an example of how 'money' can be added in an inessential way to a neo-Walrasian model.[10]

On an earlier occasion Clower (1975:13) indicated that the work by Ostroy (1973) and Ostroy and Starr (1974) offered the basis for the first steps in breaking out of the sterility of the neo-Walrasian framework. And at times Ostroy (1973:608–9) appears to suggest that to resolve the dilemma of standard (neo-Walrasian) theory it is necessary to abandon that framework. However it is not clear that this step is actually taken; for although Ostroy and Starr resolve Clower's paradox by demonstrating the efficiency of monetary exchange over *ordinary* barter it is not entirely clear where their analysis leads. The fact that it deals with the logistics of exchange as a 'do-it-yourself' affair has led some observers to interpret it as a variety of the Edgeworthian contracting process. For example, Weintraub (1979:153) classifies the Ostroy and Starr analysis as Edgeworth disequilibrium

10. Kohn's (1981a) defence of the finance constraint will be discussed in more detail in chapter 4. Here we merely note that he does not address the question of the inessential nature of 'money' in neo-Walrasian general equilibrium theory.

theory even though it consists of a 'curious amalgam of neo-Walrasian analysis (equilibrium prices must come from a market, or meta-model conceptual experiment) and disequilibrium trading dynamics'. But following Weintraub's line of reasoning may ultimately lead us to the type of analysis presented by Gale (1982, 1983) in which 'money' appears in the form of an 'as if' confetti-type asset. This is surely not the world that Clower is looking for.

An inspection of the analysis that Clower cites as the theoretical foundation for general process analysis thus leads us to the conclusion that either:

(i)   it is based on standard neo-Walrasian theory, or
(ii)   the intention is to abandon standard neo-Walrasian theory but as yet no formal analytical foundations exist.

The analysis of monetary exchange presented by Howitt supports the first interpretation. For although it may provide an analysis of a so-called non-tâtonnement adjustment mechanism similar to that of Hahn and Negishi (1962) or Arrow and Hahn (1971:324–46) Howitt's analysis is not *general* in the sense claimed by Clower because it amounts to no more than an inessential elaboration of the neo-Walrasian model. Thus, despite his apparent rejection of neo-Walrasian theory (Walker, 1984:266–7; Eichberger, 1986), it appears that Clower on occasion fails to reconcile his theoretical intentions with the formal analytical properties of his models.[11] His verbal expression reveals an intention to abandon the neo-Walrasian system but as yet there exists no suitable alternative framework in terms of which these intentions can be realised. If that is the case then he implicitly adopts a methodological position similar to that of Frank Hahn (1982b).

CONCLUDING REMARKS

In this chapter, the properties of neo-Walrasian monetary and interest rate theory have been examined with two objectives in mind. Firstly, to show that the concepts employed, although classified as neoclassical, differ in important respects from the Wicksellian version of neoclassical theory. And secondly, to highlight the inessential role of 'money' in neo-Walrasian theory. The dilemma facing neo-Walrasian theorists is implicit in the recognition that the most sophis-

11. A similar conclusion applies to Clower's application of the dual decision hypothesis which, contrary to Clower's intentions, was readily incorporated into neo-Walrasian theory (Rogers,1985; Eichberger,1986).

ticated version of the theory – the Arrow–Debreu model – has no role for money. In a perfectly synchronized world money simply has no function. To avoid this conclusion, temporary equilibrium models are used to deal with a sequence of markets which do not exhibit the comprehensive synchronization or pre-reconciliation of choices that renders money redundant in the Arrow–Debreu model. Nevertheless, attempts to find a rôle for money in less comprehensively specified neo-Walrasian models have also come to naught.

Faced with their self-imposed (if implicit) constraint that neo-Walrasian theory is not to be given up (we have seen that, ultimately, even Clower appears to accept this constraint), theorists working in this field have been unable to provide the foundations of monetary theory. 'Money' may be incorporated into a neo-Walrasian model but it will always amount to no more than an inessential extension of the model. This is the seductive property of neo-Walrasian theory that is responsible for its popularity but it also accounts for its ultimate sterility. A symptom of this sterility is provided by the fact that from a neo-Walrasian perspective monetary exchange appears less efficient than barter. But this is only an apparent paradox which is readily solved when we recognize the perfect barter properties of neo-Walrasian models and resolve the dilemma of neo-Walrasian monetary theory by allowing that theory to disappear. Only then will it be possible to make headway with essential monetary theory.

Some neo-Walrasian theorists are aware of the dilemma and have acknowledged that many of the important issues at stake in monetary theory cannot be understood within a neo-Walrasian framework (Hahn, 1982b:ix). Nevertheless, reluctance to abandon one's investment in the techniques of neo-Walrasian modelling leaves the dilemma unresolved. As Coddington (1975) once observed when explaining the failure of dynamics within neo-Walrasian theory, it is not possible to use a model which specifies the conditions under which no change is called for, to explain why change is occurring. By the same token it is not possible to develop a monetary theory in a model in which money is not needed. This, it seems, is the fundamental contradiction of neo-Walrasian monetary theory.

Appendix 3

LONG-PERIOD EQUILIBRIUM IN
NEO-WALRASIAN THEORY

With the rise to prominence of the temporary equilibrium method in the neo-Walrasian literature, the claim has been made that neo-Walrasian theory as a whole is not compatible with the traditional method of economic analysis – the use of long-period equilibrium as the centre of gravitation towards which the persistent forces in the system are tending (e.g. Eatwell and Milgate, 1983). Although technically correct this claim is possibly open to misinterpretation because concepts of long-period equilibrium have always existed in neo-Walrasian theory. These concepts of long-period equilibrium are, however, quite different from the traditional definition of long-period equilibrium as a state in which a uniform rate of profit is earned. To illustrate the point we will consider the Archibald and Lipsey (1958) distinction between weekly and full equilibrium.

In their critique of Patinkin, Archibald and Lipsey pointed out that he had only presented the analysis of weekly or temporary equilibrium, and that the analysis needed to be extended to deal with full or long-period equilibrium. In particular, Archibald and Lipsey (1958:2) quoted Hicks's definition of a stationary economy which 'is in full equilibrium, not merely when demands equal supplies at the current prices, but when the same prices continue to rule at all dates'. As we will see in chapter 4, in Patinkin's analysis money holdings are changing from week to week which means that prices are also changing, so that the model is not in a full equilibrium as defined by Hicks. Two questions then naturally require answers. Firstly, will the weekly or temporary equilibria converge to full equilibrium and, secondly, if attained, what are the characteristics of full equilibrium? In answering these questions it proves useful to refer to a recent discussion of these issues by Gale (1982).

Following Gale's (1982:16) example, which is a formalization of one of the Archibald and Lipsey (1958:6–7) arguments, we consider a simple model consisting of two individuals with identical preferences. There are two goods, one a perishable consumption good and the other a durable money commodity like gold which performs the store of value function. Each individual lives for one period and then expires and is replaced by an identical offspring who inherits his share of the gold. Within each week each individual maximizes the utility of current consumption and the gold stock subject to his budget constraint. This constraint is determined by the inherited gold stock and the endowment of real income acquired at the beginning of the period.

The dynamics of this system's adjustment to full equilibrium can be illustrated in an Edgeworth box diagram (Figure 3A.1). The analysis is analogous to that presented by Archibald and Lipsey (1958:6) in terms of their Figure 4. The initial endowment point must be somewhere on the horizontal line XY in the box because the income endowment remains constant from period to period while the gold endowment varies as a result of the trading process in which gold also acts as the medium of exchange. Assuming we start at point A, the weekly equilibrium must lie somewhere on the contract curve to the northwest, say at point B. Point B therefore represents a weekly equilibrium. In the next period, the successors to this pair of consumers inherit their ancestors' gold stock and receive the same real income endowment. The endowment for this period must therefore lie directly below point B at point C. The tâtonnement process then repeats itself and it is clear that over successive periods the weekly equilibria will converge on point G which represents full or long-period equilibrium. There are, however, several – what can only be described as extremely peculiar – characteristics of this concept of full equilibrium that require comment.

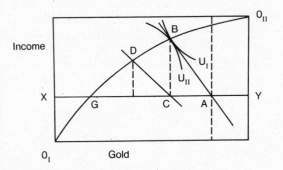

Fig. 3A.1 Adjustment to full equilibrium

To begin with, it transpires that if we follow the process of adjustment from weekly or temporary equilibria to the long-period equilibrium as sketched by Archibald and Lipsey (1958:6–7) or Gale (1982:16–17) then we end up in *a long-period equilibrium in which no trade occurs!* Interestingly, this autarky result is not unusual in neo-Walrasian theory (see, for example, the illustration in Hahn, 1982b:ch.1). Inspection of Figure 3A.1 reveals that at point G both consumers receive an income which, together with their inherited gold stocks, places them on the contract curve. There is therefore no need for consumers to engage in trade to maximize utility. Consequently, they will simply consume their entire income endowment leaving their gold stocks untouched, to be inherited by the next generation. The model is in a Pareto-optimal position and, assuming no exogenous shocks rock the boat, the system will continue *ad infinitum* in the same state, with the consumers living off the 'manna from heaven' and engaging in no trade. This is obviously an absurd notion of long-period equilibrium. But even worse, its attainment is only possible in terms of the highly restrictive assumptions used in the simple model presented above. As Gale (1982:18–19) points out, with an alternative generational structure (to allow for expectations) or the introduction of Patinkin's real balance effect, the attainment of long-period equilibrium is in doubt. For example, when the real balance effect is taken into account the horizontal dimension of the Edgeworth box in Figure 3A.1 becomes a function of prices and point C may lie to the right of point A. The simple argument to prove convergence therefore no longer works. Consequently, the very notion of a long-period equilibrium, as well as the possible convergence to such an equilibrium, is highly problematic even in this overly simplistic model. This suggests, as a general proposition, that the real balance effect leads only to complications for stability analysis in neo-Walrasian theory (Grandmont, 1983).

Some of these anomalies can, however, be avoided by introducing an alternative specification of long-period equilibrium also proposed by Archibald and Lipsey (1958:14), but only, it seems, at the expense of a change in the concepts of, and the relationship between, short- and long-period equilibrium.

Archibald and Lipsey (1958:14) suggest that to prevent money balances from changing each period it is necessary to impose the condition that the value of sales equals the value of purchases for each individual as a characteristic of long-period equilibrium. Money balances will then remain unchanged over consecutive periods. In terms of the Grandmont and Younes (1972) finance constraint, if $m(t)$

must equal $m(t - 1)$, then purchases must equal sales, i.e.

$$p(q - \omega)^+ = \sum_n k_n p_n (q - \omega)_n^- .$$

(Recall the previous argument that the finance constraint is formally equivalent to the use of the quantity equation in a neo-Walrasian model. This analysis provides a simple illustration of that claim.) With reference to the Edgeworth box diagram this condition can be illustrated as in Figure 3A.2. In this case both the gold and income endowments are *fixed* and determine the equilibrium at G' on the contract curve. As both endowments are now fixed for every period the same equilibrium and relative prices are determined each period unless a change in tastes occurs. Note also that trade occurs each period because A does not lie on the contract curve. This alternative notion of full or long-period equilibrium proposed by Archibald and Lipsey therefore avoids the conclusion that no trade occurs in long-period equilibrium but at the expense of redefining a short-period equilibrium, such as B in Figure 3A.1, as a long-period equilibrium! The question of convergence to this long-period equilibrium via a series of temporary equilibria is then no longer considered; the question of convergence simply no longer arises!

The above properties of long-period or full equilibrium in neo-Walrasian theory should be clearly distinguished from those of the classical concept employed by Marshall, Ricardo and Sraffa, for example. In terms of the classical concept of long-period equilibrium, the state of a uniform rate of profit is attained by the mobility of capital between different lines of production. Excess or abnormal profits/losses provide the signals in terms of which capital is reallocated. In neo-Walrasian theory, however, no such mechanism of

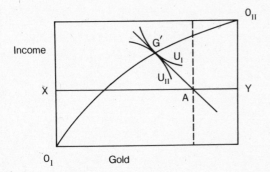

Fig. 3A.2 Reclassification of weekly equilibrium as full equilibrium

competition exists. Instead, some distribution of the possible endowments must be found by the theorist to generate the condition of constant relative prices over time. Hahn's imposition of uniform own rates of interest in an intertemporal setting is another example of this neo-Walrasian concept of long-period equilibrium, as will be recalled from the discussion in chapter 3. As Hahn demonstrates, in any neo-Walrasian intertemporal analysis a distribution of endowments can always be found which will generate constant relative prices, i.e. an example of full equilibrium can always be found. However, such an equilibrium should not be conceived of as a long-period equilibrium or centre of gravitation in the traditional sense. The neo-Walrasian full equilibrium solution is analytically identical to that of any arbitrary temporary equilibrium in the sense that it belongs to the same set of mutually exclusive temporary equilibria. Only in this limited sense is full equilibrium a special case of temporary equilibrium. There is no mechanism of competition to explain why full equilibrium should act as a centre of gravitation for a series of temporary equilibria.

4

THE NEOCLASSICAL SYNTHESIS REVISITED

INTRODUCTION

The previous chapters have examined the foundations of neoclassical monetary theory in terms of both its Wicksellian and neo-Walrasian versions. Despite the limitations exposed in this discussion it is these two versions of neoclassical theory which formed the basis of the neoclassical synthesis. The origins of this development can be traced to Hicks as references to both the Walrasian and the Wicksellian general equilibrium models can readily be detected in his early work. For example, in his famous paper entitled 'Mr Keynes and the Classics', Hicks (1937:158) remarks that:

When generalised in this way, Mr Keynes's theory begins to look very like Wicksell's; this is of course hardly surprising. There is indeed one special case where it fits Wicksell's construction absolutely. If there is 'full employment' ... if IS is horizontal, we do have a perfectly Wicksellian construction; the investment rate becomes Wicksell's *natural* rate, for in this case it may be thought of as determined by real causes; if there is a perfectly elastic monetary system, and the money rate is fixed below the natural rate, there is a cumulative inflation; cumulative deflation if fixed above.

The reference to a Wicksellian interpretation of the IS–LM model is repeated by Hicks (1950:139n2, 1957:62) and, as we will see, the interpretation need not be as narrow as he appears to suggest. In *Value and Capital*, however, Hicks (1939:57–61) changes direction and focuses his attention on the neo-Walrasian interpretation of IS–LM which was later taken up and perfected by Lange (1942) and Patinkin (1958,1965). It is within this Walrasian context that the debate over the loanable funds and liquidity preference theories is often encountered. (An illustration of the futility of the debate when conducted in this context is presented in the appendix to this chapter.) Hence it should not be overlooked that the most famous product of the neo-classical synthesis – the IS–LM model – is readily given both a Wicksellian and a neo-Walrasian interpretation.

The distinction is particularly important for identifying the theoretical issues at stake. For example, in discussions of the neoclassical synthesis attention is usually focused on the relationship between Keynes and the 'classics'. However both Keynes and the classics (proper) have been misrepresented in this debate in terms of either neo-Walrasian or Wicksellian theoretical structures. The objective of this chapter is, therefore, not to examine the relationship between Keynes and the 'classics' but rather to highlight the Wicksellian and neo-Walrasian elements in the debate. To this end no attempt is made to present an exhaustive catalogue of Wicksellian and neo-Walrasian elements. Instead two examples will be selected to illustrate the points made in chapters 2 and 3.

In this respect the Wicksell connection is seen to play a prominent role in the Keynes versus 'classics' debate of the textbooks. As traditionally presented, this debate consists of a comparison between two Wicksell-type neoclassical models, one labelled Keynesian and the other 'classical'. Not surprisingly, the Keynesian interpretation of the theory has been forced to rely on the existence of traps or rigidities to demonstrate the possibility of an unemployment equilibrium. But having adopted the Wicksellian rules of the game, it is now generally recognized that these arguments are theoretically trivial and amount to no more than short-period disturbances which will be overcome in the long period. As a result Keynesian theory has been undermined in the eyes of some observers. What these observers have overlooked, however, is the fact that both this so-called Keynesian analysis and the 'classical' model to which it is compared are Wicksellian in structure. As it is the latter structure which collapses as a result of the capital debate, both the pseudo-Keynesian and 'classical' models fall with it. This issue will not be taken any further in this chapter as the discussion here serves only to provide an illustration of the Wicksell connection which will reappear in Tobin's brand of Keynesianism and Brunner–Meltzer monetarism. The latter debate between Keynesians and monetarists is then seen to echo the earlier Keynes versus 'classics' debate.

The example of the neo-Walrasian element in the neoclassical synthesis will be examined in somewhat more detail as it provides the opportunity to correct some errors. The example selected is taken from the Patinkin controversy on the invalid 'classical dichotomy' and it is argued that Patinkin's claims against the invalid 'classical dichotomy' are in error. It will be shown that introducing the quantity equation into a neo-Walrasian model imposes a finance or transactions constraint of the type suggested by Clower (1967). The general form of this constraint was presented by Grandmont and Younes (1972) but both Hickman (1950) and Valavanis (1955) had earlier attempted to show that this was the correct interpretation of the quantity equation in a neo-Walrasian setting. Unfortunately the significance of the point was not appreciated at the time. With the benefit of hindsight the significance of this conclusion is that it reveals the quantity equation as an inessential addition to a neo-Walrasian model. It is then apparent that the issue at stake in the Patinkin controversy is the inessential nature of 'money' in neo-Walrasian monetary theory and not the so-called 'classical dichotomy'. Patinkin's attempt to integrate real and monetary theory via the real balance effect is therefore not only unnecessary but fails to address the central issue. As was the case with the Wicksell connection these issues are of interest for more recent developments in monetary theory, not the least of which is Friedman's (1974) claim that all theorists employ the quantity theory augmented by the Walrasian system of equations for long-period analysis.

THE KEYNESIAN REVOLUTION AND THE WICKSELL CONNECTION

The Keynesian revolution was celebrated in the early post-war years by the famous (infamous?) 'Keynes versus classics' debate which purported to show how Keynesian macroeconomics differed from the 'classics'. The debate was conducted in terms of two models, one labelled Keynesian and the other 'classical'. Inspection of these two models reveals, however, that they are both variations of neoclassical theory; in particular the Wicksellian version.[1] This much emerges after an inspection of the specification of the 'classical' system found in most textbooks.

The 'classical' model

The following set of equations represents a typical example of the 'classical' system.[2]

1. For a discussion of classical macroeconomics see Cochrane (1970,ch.3) or Walsh and Gram (1980).
2. See, for example, Ackley (1961, part II: 157, 1978, part II) Makinen (1977, part I: 27) or Pierce and Shaw (1974:ch.6).

The 'classical' model

$$y = y(N) \quad \text{(production function)} \tag{4.1}$$

$$\frac{dy}{dN} = \frac{W}{P} \quad \text{(demand for labour)} \tag{4.2}$$

$$N = N\left(\frac{W}{P}\right) \text{(supply of labour)} \tag{4.3}$$

$$MV = Py \quad \text{(quantity theory)} \tag{4.4}$$

$$S = S(r) \quad \text{(saving function)} \tag{4.5}$$

$$I = I(r) \quad \text{(investment function)} \tag{4.6}$$

$$S = I \quad \text{(equilibrium in capital market)} \tag{4.7}$$

Now, although it may not be immediately obvious,[3] the above model represents a naive version of a Wicksellian model of the type presented by Petri (1978) and discussed in chapter 2. The Wicksellian features do emerge, however, when we enquire into the interpretation of equations (4.5) to (4.7) which generate equilibrium in the *capital* market.

From our previous discussion of Robertson's treatment of the loanable funds theory, it will be recalled that the analysis of expressions (4.5) to (4.7) involves the interaction between the natural and market rates of interest. This relationship can be re-examined in terms of Makinen's (1977:20) explanation of expressions (4.5) to (4.7). Behind the analysis of these expressions lies the idea of three markets: a market for *real* capital, a money or loanable funds market, and a bond or equities market.[4] These markets are illustrated in Figure 4.1. (Recall the discussion in chapter 2.) The demand for capital (real investment) is a decreasing function of the natural rate of interest while real saving is an increasing function. The other curves in the money and equities markets are the mirror images of the S and

---

3. Particularly as no capital appears in the production function, expression (4.1). It is nevertheless implicitly there (Ackley,1961:93). Whether it is a fixed *value* or a fixed *quantity* is, however, a question that these writers never considered explicitly. It seems that all they had in mind was Keynes's definition of the short period in terms of a given capital stock.

4. Leijonhufvud (1981:155) considers that the terms market rate and natural rate are different names for two values *of the same variable*. The market rate is then treated as the actually observed value while the natural rate is the hypothetical rate that would exist if the system were in equilibrium. He then concentrates all his attention on Figure 4.1(b), the loanable funds market, without apparently realizing that he has in the process abandoned Wicksell's derivation of the natural rate of interest. His oversight here seems to be a reflection of his failure to appreciate the implications of the capital debate.

I curves. If either of the S or I curves shifts, the corresponding curves in the other markets also shift (Makinen, 1977:20). For example, the demand for real investment (capital) is reflected in the money market as the demand for money and in the equities market as the supply of equities. Similarly, real saving is reflected as the supply of money and the demand for equities. In terms of this analysis, the supply and demand schedules for real saving and investment are clearly the dominant factors, with the money and equities markets operating as a veil. However, as we noted previously, the notion of *real saving* is problematic outside of the simple corn model. In the corn model real saving represents the corn not consumed. By contrast, in a world in which capital goods are *produced* (rather than saved as is the case with seed-corn) the market for real capital is no longer directly related to the money or equities markets in the simple fashion illustrated in Figure 4.1. In particular, the notion of real saving loses its corn model interpretation and at best can be interpreted as the value of money saving deflated by some index of the price level. But as we noted in chapter 2, real saving in this Fisherian sense is not equivalent to the concept of real saving required to define Wicksell's natural rate of interest in terms of the marginal productivity of capital (where capital is saved-up labour and land). Consequently, in an economy where capital goods are produced, the savings function in Figure 4.1(a) cannot represent real saving but, at best, can be interpreted as the supply curve of the capital goods sector. This means that, in a world in which capital goods are produced, the demand and supply schedules for real capital are functions of the price of capital goods and not the natural rate of interest.

This confusion of the saving–investment mechanism is one aspect of 'classical' monetary theory to which Keynes took strong exception.

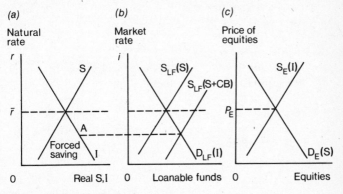

Fig. 4.1 Loanable funds theory

For example, when Marshall defined interest as 'the price paid for the use of capital in any market', Keynes (1936:186n1, emphasis in original) objected in the following terms:

It is to be noticed that Marshall uses the word 'capital' not 'money' and the word 'stock' not 'loans'; yet interest is a payment for borrowing *money*, and the 'demand for capital' in this context should mean 'demand for loans of money for the purpose of buying a stock of capital goods'. But the equality between the stock of capital goods offered and the stock demanded will be brought about by the *prices* of capital goods, not by the rate of interest. It is equality between the demand and supply of loans of money, i.e. debts, which is brought about by the rate of interest.

The closest we get to the concept of a natural rate of interest in a system in which capital goods are produced is the calculation of the *marginal efficiency of capital*. Keynes (1936:135) defines the marginal efficiency of capital as the rate of discount that would equate the demand price of a capital good, i.e. the present value of the series of annuities, given the returns expected from the capital asset during its lifetime, to its supply price (where the supply price is not the market price but the price that would just induce a manufacturer to produce an additional unit of the capital good in question). Here Keynes appears to be treating the market price as the spot price and the supply price as the flow supply price (Davidson, 1978:ch.4; Chick, 1983:118–30). By comparison, from the perspective of saving and investment, it will be recalled that Wicksell (1901,II:193, emphasis in original) defines the natural rate of interest in this way: 'The rate of interest at which *the demand for loan capital and the supply of savings* exactly agree, and which more or less corresponds to the expected yield on newly created capital, will then be the normal or natural real rate.' As Lindahl (1939:262) pointed out, Wicksell treated the natural rate as equating *ex ante* saving and investment and this definition is consistent with Robertson's description of 'classical' interest theory discussed in chapter 2.

In Keynes's analysis, by contrast, the marginal efficiency of capital is not the variable which equates the demand and supply of loan or real capital. Seen in terms of Marshallian comparative statics (Marshallian three-period analysis) the rate of interest is *always* equated with the marginal efficiency of capital as a result of changes in the demand prices of capital goods relative to their long-period supply prices. Hence, equality between the marginal efficiency of capital and the rate of interest is maintained as a result of changes in the demand prices of capital goods. The marginal efficiency of capital does not operate so as to equate the demand and supply of real capital as is the case with Wicksell's concept of the natural rate of interest. Furthermore, although this relationship between the money rate of interest and the prices of durable assets is, in fact, the same as that outlined by Wicksell and discussed in chapter 2, it does not entail the definition of the natural rate of interest in terms of the marginal productivity of capital. For these reasons (and others to be outlined in chapters 9 and 10) we can agree with Schumpeter (1954:1119n) that the marginal efficiency of capital is not equivalent to Wicksell's natural rate of interest as has been suggested by some writers, e.g. Lindahl (1939:261).

But in the neoclassical model sketched above, it is the natural rate of interest derived from the *marginal product of capital* that plays the dominant (albeit implicit) analytical role in expressions (4.5) to (4.7), and, as we now know from the capital debate, to relate the marginal product of capital to the natural rate of interest requires that capital be defined as *value* capital. As Howard (1983:107) explains:[5]

The procedure must allow the rate of [interest] to be an inverse function of the scarcity of capital and to bear a relation of equality to its marginal product. This last requirement means capital must be measured in values. Unless capital is defined to be value capital it would not be possible for its marginal product to be equal to the rate of interest ... In other words, the rate of (interest) is a pure number; it expresses a percentage per unit of time. If a marginal product is to be equal to it, it must be expressible as a pure number. The marginal value product of a unit of physical capital is the (infinitesimal) small addition to the value of net outputs over the (infinitesimal) small addition to the physical capital that is associated with it. It is therefore not a pure number except in special cases [e.g. in a one-commodity model]. To make it such we have to make a unit of capital a unit of value, i.e. to measure capital goods in terms of their values.

Treating the rate of interest as the equilibrating mechanism in the market for capital therefore brings us full circle to the problems discussed in terms of Petri's (1978) statement of Wicksell's model. This suggests that although the 'classical' model is rather sketchily presented in most textbooks it is nevertheless open to the Cambridge critique. In that case, only in terms of a simple one-commodity model will the stories it tells be valid in general.

5. This point has been known for some time. As Rosenstein-Rodan (1936:274n1) noted: 'Wicksell's natural rate of interest is defined under the assumption of one factor and one product. It becomes difficult to give it a precise meaning when there are many products, as Wicksell himself has realized. Lindahl ... and Myrdal ... have therefore rightly pointed out that the natural rate of interest must not be interpreted as a physical but as a value productivity.' But compare Schumpeter (1954:1119n).

In terms of such a story the system depicted in expressions (4.1) to (4.7) operated in the following way to generate full employment (Pierce and Shaw, 1974:176). The rate of interest operated to equate saving and investment and so establish Say's Law, i.e. to equate aggregate demand and aggregate supply. However, this was not considered to be sufficient to guarantee full employment. The latter required flexible wages in the labour market combined with the quantity theory of money. Any disturbance to the system that led to too high a real wage in the labour market would then be automatically corrected by a fall in both the *money* and the *real* wage. Competition in the labour market ensured a fall in money wage while the quantity theory ensured that the real wage also fell. This latter point is important, because if the wage and price level fell proportionally, the real wage would remain unchanged, maintaining the level of unemployment. In terms of expression (4.4), this result cannot occur if M and V do not change. For, if P is assumed to be falling at the same rate as W, resulting in a constant real wage, W/P, then y would be unchanged and the quantity equation violated. M, V and y would be unchanged but P is supposed to be lower. Hence it is concluded that as P falls so does W, but not in proportion, so that W/P falls and y increases, maintaining the quantity equation.

The quantity theory therefore plays an important role in the process of adjustment to full employment. It nevertheless leaves open the possibility that the process of adjustment could be long and drawn out as a result of a fall in velocity or a decrease in the money supply. A more sophisticated analysis of the adjustment process was, of course, offered by Wicksell (1898a:ch.9) in terms of his famous cumulative process. The process could be set in motion by the commercial banks increasing the money supply, as illustrated by $S_{LF}(S + CB)$ in Figure 4.1(b), and lowering the market rate of interest below the natural rate. The increased demand for resources (with the system operating at full employment) pushed up prices and the inflation continued until the two rates were brought back to equality,[6] either as a result of a real balance effect or as a result of a loss of reserves by the commercial banks (Patinkin,1972a). A deflationary process was the

6. Inflation was a symptom that the market and natural rates of interest were not equal and Wicksell's analysis therefore offers a solution to the Gibson Paradox. In terms of empirical work carried out by Tooke, and later Gibson, a positive correlation between price levels and the rate of interest was detected. In a situation where the market rate is below the natural rate, as a result of technical innovation say, the price level will be rising and the market rate will also begin to rise as the commercial banks lose free reserves (Makinen,1977:65–8). It is also interesting to note that Wicksell and Myrdal considered the money supply to be endogenous in an economy with a well developed banking sector (Moore,1986; Rousseas,1986).

reverse of the inflationary situation, with the market rate of interest above the natural rate.

The loanable funds theory then fits naturally into this framework by enabling the analysis of the money market, i.e. the loanable funds market in Figure 4.1(b), so that it *reflects* the properties of the market for real saving and investment (capital). Following Ackley (1961:158), the 'classical' model can then be examined in a disequilibrium state by replacing expressions (4.4) and (4.7) with

$$S + DH + \Delta M = I \qquad (4.8)$$

$$DH = MV - Py \qquad (4.9)$$

where DH = dishoarding and ΔM represents the change in the money supply. Expression (4.8), with the source of funds on the left-hand side, captures the idea behind the loanable funds theory. But as Ackley (1961:160) points out, the model is now indeterminate.[7] However, this is simply a reflection that the model has been placed in a *disequilibrium state* relative to its long-period equilibrium solution. From (4.8) we see that so long as either DH or ΔM is positive, real saving need not equal investment. In the case where the market rate is below the natural rate, *forced saving* is occurring as I is greater than S; as, for example, at point A in Figure 4.1(a).[8] The loanable funds theory therefore attempts to identify the sources of the disturbances to the market rate of interest in the money market. As Ackley (1961:160) notes, it is essentially a disequilibrium process analysis. This can be seen from the fact that if expression (4.7) holds then both $DH = 0$ *and* $\Delta M = 0$, and we are back to the simple quantity equation (4.4) in place of expression (4.9). Interestingly, Kohn (1981b, 1986) has recently refocused attention on this disequilibrium analysis by championing the cause of what he calls Robertson–Wicksell sequence analysis.

On this topic, Kohn (1986) argues that Keynes's break with the 'classics' is not one of substance but one of method. According to

---

7. Specifically, there are eight endogenous variables, y, N, W, P, r, s, i, DH and only seven equations.
8. The notion of *forced saving* was the subject of some controversy in the literature. In particular Ricardo rejected the idea (Schumpeter,1954:724), possibly because for the classical economists saving was *always* equal to investment while forced saving requires that investment should exceed saving. The latter possibility can occur in a *neoclassical* disequilibrium analysis (as at point A in Figure 4.1(a)) but not in a classical model. In addition, there seems to be some confusion as to how real saving can be forced to increase to point A if the natural rate remains fixed. If saving occurs in the form of money, how is it that real capital increases? It seems that these difficulties reflect the attempts to apply the corn model analysis to a model in which capital goods are *produced*, i.e. not saved as in the corn model. For a discussion of the concept of forced saving, see Wicksell (1901,I:135) and Hayek (1932).

Kohn the *General Theory* represents a revolution in method in the sense that Keynes abandoned the sequence analysis of the loanable funds theory employed by Robertson and other 'classical' monetary theorists, in favour of an equilibrium analysis. Now, as Shackle (1967:162) pointed out, it is certainly true that the *General Theory* is comparative statics while the *Treatise* is sequence analysis or dynamics. Nevertheless the *General Theory* represents more than a change in method. As we will see it represents a change in theory from Real to Monetary Analysis. In particular, Keynes abandons the natural rate of interest and the associated notion of a unique long-period equilibrium with full employment and replaces it with the marginal efficiency of capital and the possibility of multiple long-period equilibria. Kohn (1986:1197) misses this change in the theory and as a result he misapplies Schumpeter's taxonomy of monetary theories and classifies Wicksell's monetary theory within the tradition of Monetary Analysis!

For Kohn (1986:1197) money is a veil in long-period equilibrium and monetary factors are only of importance in understanding the movement of the economy towards that equilibrium. In other words Kohn attempts to reserve the principles of Monetary Analysis for the analysis of periods of transition between long-period equilibria and Real Analysis for statements about the long-period equilibrium. But as we know, these are the characteristics of Real Analysis and monetary theorists in this tradition have, at least since Hume, acknowledged that money is non-neutral in the short period (Patinkin, 1972a). The analysis of the *Treatise* falls within this tradition as it seeks to extend the static formalism of the quantity theory to examine the periods of transition in terms of the Fundamental Equations. (The Fisherian tradition also offers a comprehensive analysis of the period of transition between long-period equilibria (Makinen,1977:ch.3). It is therefore not surprising to find that the 'classical' model of the textbooks has always offered a comprehensive analysis of the short-period or disequilibrium (relative to the long-period) adjustment process in the tradition of Real Analysis. Kohn's interpretation is simply the latest in this venerable tradition and as we will see it has no significance for assessing the theoretical contribution of the *General Theory*. This conclusion can perhaps be reinforced by noting that Kohn's interpretation supports the widespread but erroneous view that the *General Theory* offers no significant theoretical contribution, as unemployment equilibrium is due to wage rigidity – the 'classical' explanation of unemployment! From this perspective it appears that the *General Theory* consists only of a collection of astute empirical observations, which is, of course, the conclusion that emerges when we assess the so-called Keynesian model of the textbooks.

The pseudo-Keynesian challenge to the 'classics'

It is well known that the Keynesian model, to which the 'classical' structure was compared, differed only in three respects: (i) the introduction of liquidity preference theory, (ii) saving as a function of income rather than the rate of interest, and (iii) rigid wages. The model therefore differs from the 'classical' system only in terms of expressions (4.12), (4.13) and (4.14). Although it seems that this type of comparison originated with Hicks (1937) and Modigliani (1944) it is readily apparent that these innovations do not offer an effective challenge to the theoretical structure of the 'classical' model. They are all minor modifications or changes in functional form without any change of substance. This was apparent from the start when Hicks (1937:152) suggested that (ii) was an insignificant addition and that (i) was the vital distinction. However, Hicks had assumed rigid wages and it was left to Modigliani (1944:76) to point out that this was the crucial assumption. But this is the 'classical' explanation of unemployment! We are therefore led to the conclusion that the comparison is posed in such a way that the Keynesian model offers no substantive theoretical contribution. To see this consider each of the differences in turn.

> *The pseudo-Keynesian model*

$$y = y(N) \tag{4.10}$$

$$\frac{dy}{dN} = \frac{W}{P} \tag{4.11}$$

$$W = W_0 \tag{4.12}$$

$$M = Py + L(i) \text{ or } MV(i) = Py \tag{4.13}$$

$$S = S(y) \tag{4.14}$$

$$I = I(i) \tag{4.15}$$

$$S = I \tag{4.16}$$

To begin with, the liquidity preference analysis, i.e. the speculative demand for money, is simply tacked onto the transactions demand of the quantity equation. But there is simply no way in which this approach is going to produce a monetary theory of the rate of interest to replace the real loanable funds theory of the 'classical' model. It is also obvious that to determine the rate of interest in terms of expression (4.13) the transactions demand must already be known. This leads to the well-known charge that the simple Keynesian model is indeterminate[9] and opens the door for the neoclassical synthesis of these two aspects of the analysis in terms of the IS and LM curves (Hicks, 1937:152–3). Nevertheless, the apparent indeterminacy of the simple Keynesian-cross analysis does raise a fundamental theoretical issue which we will take up in later chapters.

The inclusion of savings as a function of income also poses no problems for the 'classical' model.[10] It does, however, raise some interesting issues that appear to have been overlooked in the literature. It will be recalled that underlying the saving–investment analysis of the 'classical' model is the idea of *real* saving and investment. But, as we have seen, outside of a simple corn model the notion of real saving does not make a great deal of sense. These issues are, nevertheless, not faced by the Keynesian treatment of saving as a function of income. Instead, the neoclassical synthesis of 'classical' and Keynesian features of the model opens the door to the reinstatement of the concept of real saving in the derivation of the IS curve along Wicksellian lines. The IS curve is then readily interpreted as an equilibrium locus of quasi-natural rates of interest associated with different levels of income at which real saving equals investment. Similarly, the demand and supply of money – whether analysed on liquidity preference or loanable funds grounds – determines an equilibrium locus of market rates of interest.

Finally, it is now clear that the Keynesians got themselves into such a muddle on these issues that they even passed off the 'classical' explanation for unemployment as Keynesian! The rigid wage assumption explanation for unemployment is in fact the 'classical' explanation.[11] As Keynes (1936:257, emphasis added) remarked: 'For

9. See the discussion in Weintraub (1977:54). In his criticism of 'classical' interest rate theory, Keynes (1936:181) made a similar charge. He argued that 'classical' theory was indeterminate, as saving was a function of income. In terms of Figure 4.1a, this meant that a shift in the investment function would increase income and shift the savings function. Although it is not clear whether Keynes is referring to the natural or the market rate of interest the former seems the most likely (see Keynes,1936:180n1).

10. Ackley (1961:404) concludes: 'The only difference is that, now, a shift in either the production function or the supply of labour will alter the rate of interest, because, by altering y, they will change the level of saving relative to investment. But this is a minor difference of little importance for short-period economic policy, because the production function and labour supply change only slowly and steadily.'

11. As Chick (1983:132) points out, 'The idea that the *General Theory* is based on fixed wages is blatantly incorrect. This point is now generally acknowledged; see Fender (1981,ch.3) and Meltzer (1981). However, Kohn (1986) has recently resurrected a more sophisticated version of the rigidity argument.

the classical theory has been accustomed to rest the supposedly self-adjusting character of the economic system on the assumed fluidity of money wages; and *when there is rigidity, to lay on this rigidity the blame of maladjustment.*'

A general Wicksellian IS–LM model

The shared theoretical structure of the 'classical' and Keynesian models can be illustrated with reference to the following general Wicksellian specification of the IS–LM structure.[12]

$$S = S(r, y, P) \left. \begin{array}{l} \\ \\ \\ \end{array} \right\} \text{IS curve} \hspace{2cm} \left\{ \begin{array}{l} (4.14') \\ (4.15') \\ (4.16) \end{array} \right.$$

$$I = I(r, y, P)$$

$$S = I$$

$$m^{\mathrm{d}} = m^{\mathrm{d}} (i, y, P) \left. \begin{array}{l} \\ \\ \\ \end{array} \right\} \text{LM curve} \hspace{1.5cm} \left\{ \begin{array}{l} (4.17) \\ (4.18) \\ (4.19) \end{array} \right.$$

$$m^{\mathrm{s}} = m^{\mathrm{s}} (i, y, P)$$

$$m^{\mathrm{s}} = m^{\mathrm{d}}$$

$$r = i \hspace{2cm} \text{'Monetary' equilibrium} \hspace{2cm} (4.20)$$

This specification combined features from both the 'classical' and Keynesian models, with r = the quasi-natural rate of interest (to indicate that the natural rate is not unique), i = the money or market rate of interest, y = the level of nominal income and P = the general price level. Expression (4.18) is sufficiently general to allow for the extreme case of exogenous money while expression (4.20) is the Wicksellian condition for 'monetary' equilibrium.

The Wicksellian interpretation of the model follows by fixing income at the full employment level, y_{f}, and allowing for a variable price level. The IS and LM loci can then be derived for the full employment level of income, y_{f}, as illustrated in Figure 4.2. The IS curve consists of the combinations of quasi-natural rates of interest and the price level that equate the full employment level of real saving and investment. The LM curve consists of combinations of the market rate of interest and price level which equate the full employment demand and supply of money. Any attempt by the monetary authority or the banking system to set a market rate of interest i' below *the*

---

12. Similar specifications of the IS–LM model can be found in Mundell (1963) and Harrington (1971).

natural rate, $\bar{r}$, for example, can only be achieved by increasing the price level. Whether such a situation can be maintained then depends on what is assumed about the money supply process. Recall that Wicksell argued that deviations of the market rate from the natural rate would ultimately be reversed by a real balance effect or as the banking system lost reserves. Only if the money supply was perfectly elastic, as is the case in the pure credit economy, would the banks have no incentive to increase the market rate. The reverse occurs if the market rate rises above the natural rate, with a deflation of the price level resulting. Various possibilities can then be examined in terms of Figure 4.2 by postulating changes in either the natural rate – shift of the IS curve – or money rate – shift of the LM curve. Harrington (1971:283–6) provides some examples in terms of a slightly different interpretation of the Wicksellian version of the IS–LM model.

The Keynesian interpretation of what is essentially a Wicksellian construct is based on the assumption of a fixed price level. It is not clear whether it is the full employment price level, but for the sake of comparison it will be assumed here that this is the case. The IS and LM curves then represent equilibrium loci between quasi-natural and market rates of interest and levels of real income, y, given the price level P_f, as illustrated in Figure 4.3. In addition, Keynesian interpretations have, following Keynes but for different reasons, dropped the distinction between natural and market rates of interest and refer only to 'the' rate of interest, i. On the basis of this change in interpretation the Keynesians attempted to justify the existence of an

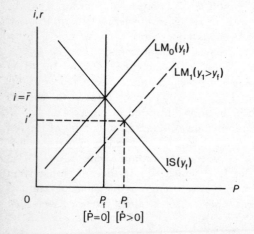

Fig. 4.2 A Wicksellian interpretation of IS–LM

unemployment equilibrium – at, for example, y_e in Figure 4.3. Now the obvious response to this Keynesian claim is that a flexible price level would restore full employment equilibrium, and both the Pigou effect (shifting IS curve) and Keynes effect (shifting LM curve) were offered as theoretical, not necessarily practical, solutions. Similarly, when the model is extended to include the labour market (in the complete Keynesian system) full employment equilibrium is reinforced unless money illusion or rigid wages assumptions are used. A recent example of this result is provided by Kohn (1981b:861) who concludes 'that the loanable funds theory supports the existence of an unemployment equilibrium if and only if the money wage is completely rigid'.

The whole point, of course, is that these Keynesian adjustments to the model amount to no more than *ad hoc* restrictions imposed to produce a Keynesian rabbit out of a neoclassical ('classical') hat. What is more, it is apparent that the Keynesian interpretation of the model is then concerned with the period of transition while the neoclassical or monetarist interpretation is concerned with long-period equilibrium. The debate between monetarists and Keynesians can then be portrayed as a dispute between two special cases of a more general Wicksellian model as is, in fact, suggested by Harrington (1971). This interpretation is now quite standard and is incorporated in the textbook distinction between Keynesian and neoclassical (quantity theory) versions of IS–LM, e.g. Levacic and Rebmann (1982). However, it is now recognized that this brand of spanner-in-the-works Keynesianism is an inappropriate framework for examin-

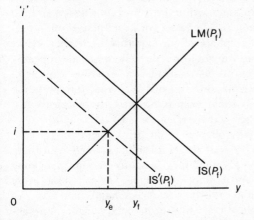

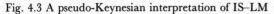

Fig. 4.3 A pseudo-Keynesian interpretation of IS–LM

ing the theoretical contribution of the *General Theory* (Eatwell and Milgate, 1983:ch.15). Nevertheless, the significance and implications of the Wicksell connection for this version of the IS–LM framework are not widely appreciated. In particular, Leijonhufvud (1981) and Kohn (1981b), who suggest a return to the loanable funds theory and the analytical framework of the *Treatise*, fail to realize that the Wicksell connection leaves both this brand of Keynesianism and the associated 'classical' model open to the Cambridge critique. In a sense this strengthens a broader Post Keynesian position by neutralizing the significance of Pigou or wealth effects. However, even if existence is taken for granted, the properties of Wicksellian capital theory still pose problems of stability which must be resolved if the Pigou effect is to work in principle. For only in a one-commodity world would the necessary functional forms exist to ensure stability (recall Figure 2.1). That is to say, even if existence is assumed, in a multi-commodity world the Pigou effect cannot be relied on *in theory*, let alone in practice, to restore full employment equilibrium. It seems that the pseudo-Keynesians would be well advised to abandon the Wicksell connection.

THE NEO-WALRASIAN REVOLUTION

In addition to the Wicksell connection, the neoclassical synthesis also incorporated its own neo-Walrasian revolution. This neo-Walrasian interpretation of 'classical' theory was initiated by Hicks (1939) and Lange (1942) but popularized by Patinkin's (1965) discussion of 'classical' and Keynesian issues within the context of a neo-Walrasian version of the IS–LM model. The latter construct played an important role in the post-war phase of the liquidity preference versus loanable funds debate but will not be discussed here (see the appendix to this chapter). The central task instead is to examine the role of money and the quantity equation in the neo-Walrasian interpretation of 'classical' theory. Note that, when using the term 'classical', it is plain that Patinkin (1965) was referring to neo-Walrasian theory.

In a celebrated debate, often referred to as 'the Patinkin controversy', Patinkin argued that 'classical', i.e. neo-Walrasian, monetary theory, involved a fundamental contradiction by dividing the analysis into a 'real' and a 'monetary' sector. The dichotomy arose from the property that in the real sector demands and supplies depended only on relative prices, while the monetary sector, represented by the quantity equation, determined the absolute price level.[13] An equiproportional change in all money prices would then apparently leave the real sector in equilibrium while, in terms of the quantity equation, the monetary sector revealed a disequilibrium state; hence the contradiction.

It can be shown, however, that this claim of a contradiction arises only because of the failure to examine correctly the real sector's relationship to the quantity equation. On this point it is interesting to note that Archibald and Lipsey (1958:1) and others argued that the 'classical dichotomy' was valid but that they were unable to make their claim stick because they either made some analytical errors and/or lacked the tools of an adequate 'disequilibrium' analysis. But with the benefit of hindsight, we can see that in the context of neo-Walrasian theory the quantity equation in fact imposes a finance or transaction constraint of the type suggested by Clower (1967). Examined from this perspective it is easily shown that Patinkin's demonstration of the 'classical dichotomy' involves a violation of these finance constraints. In other words, adding the quantity equation to the equations of the real sector, in a neo-Walrasian model, implies the medium-of-exchange function of money, which requires that goods can only be exchanged for money and not bartered directly. This imposes a finance constraint, in addition to a budget constraint, on all traders in the model. Once this is recognized[14] it is obvious that the money endowment, and its distribution in the case of a short-period (weekly) equilibrium solution, are implicit arguments in the demand and supply functions of the real sector and Patinkin's dichotomy disappears. To reveal this the analysis suggested here combines Clower's dual decision hypothesis with the finance constraint to show that Patinkin's dichotomy does not arise in neo-Walrasian theory. At

13. Gupta (1969) contends that the argument was directed against what is now known as a 'pure outside-money' model in which money consists of government issued fiat money. In a sense, this assessment is correct although it overlooks the real issue which is that money is treated as a commodity in monetary theories in the tradition of Real Analysis. By contrast, inside money is a concept which is compatible with a credit theory of money in the tradition of Monetary Analysis.

14. Valavanis (1955) and Hickman (1950) seem to have been the only participants in the debate who correctly perceived the relationship between the real and monetary sectors. They pointed out that the quantity theory acted as a technological restriction on the rate at which trade could occur with the help of a monetary medium. Although Archibald and Lipsey (1958:2) state that the quantity equation is based on the view that money is used solely as a medium of exchange, and also note the Valavanis–Hickman observation, they cannot make use of it because they substitute *equilibrium values* into the quantity equation when the model is in a disequilibrium state (Archibald and Lipsey,1958:16).

the same time it provides an illustration of Clower's recent explanation that the dual decision hypothesis and the finance constraint are alternative formulations of a single thought-experiment (Walker, 1984:264–5).

A corollary of the conclusion that the 'classical dichotomy' is a non-issue is that Patinkin's attempt to integrate the real and monetary sectors using the real balance effect is redundant. If anything, the real balance effect is already there and as we noted in the appendix to chapter 3, leads only to difficulties with stability analysis. The whole question of the 'classical dichotomy' is therefore best interpreted as a false trail which obscures the fundamental issue – the inessential nature of 'money' in neo-Walrasian monetary analysis.

To substantiate this argument, we first present the 'classical dichotomy' in general terms as developed by Patinkin so as to demonstrate its neo-Walrasian pedigree. We then illustrate the absence of any dichotomy by applying the finance constraint and the dual decision hypothesis to reveal the flaw in Patinkin's argument. It is readily shown that the quantity equation imposes a transaction constraint of the type suggested by Clower (1967) and generalized by Grandmont and Younes (1972).

Patinkin on the 'classical dichotomy': some corrections

Patinkin (1972b) begins his case against the 'classical dichotomy' by setting out the excess demand equations in a model with n commodities (with prices $p_1, p_2, \ldots, p_n$), and money, which are divided into a 'real subset',

$$
\left.
\begin{aligned}
X_1\left(\frac{p_2}{p_1}, \ldots, \frac{p_n}{p_1}\right) &= 0 \\
&\ \ \vdots \\
X_n\left(\frac{p_2}{p_1}, \ldots, \frac{p_n}{p_1}\right) &= 0
\end{aligned}
\right\}
\tag{4.21}
$$

where the $X_n(\ )$ are the excess demand equations[15] for commodities,

15. In a neo-Walrasian model excess demand refers to excess demand over and above the initial endowment. An excess supply (i.e. a negative excess demand) occurs when the amount demanded by an individual is less than his initial endowment (Patinkin, 1965:ch.1).

and a 'monetary subset' consisting of the quantity equation,

$$p_1\left[Q_1^* + \left(\frac{p_2}{p_1}\right)^* Q_2^* + \ldots + \left(\frac{p_n}{p_1}\right)^* Q_n^* \right] = \bar{M}V \qquad (4.22)$$

where the $(p_i/p_1)^*$ are the equilibrium relative prices that emerge in the solution of (4.21) and Q_i^* are the corresponding equilibrium quantities; $\bar{M}$ is the given stock of money and V is a stable (in this case, fixed) velocity of circulation. The relative prices are therefore determined in the 'real subset' of equations while the absolute or money prices are determined by the quantity equation or the 'monetary subset'.

Patinkin objected to this dichotomy on the grounds that the excess demand function for money derived from the 'real subset' was not compatible with the excess demand for money implied by the quantity equation. More technically, the excess demand function for money, say $\theta(\ )$, as derived from the 'real subset' is, by Walras's Law,[16] of the form

$$\theta(\ ) = -\sum_{i=1}^{n} p_i X_i \left(\frac{p_2}{p_1}, \ldots, \frac{p_n}{p_1}\right) \qquad (4.23)$$

which is homogeneous of degree 1 in the p_i and hence appears to be inconsistent with (4.22) which is homogeneous of degree 1 in p_i *and* $\bar{M}$.[17] Patinkin (1972b) argues that the economic meaning of this

16. Walras's Law states that the sum of the value of the excess demands for all commodities, including money, must be zero in all states of the model, equilibrium or disequilibrium (Lange, 1942). In terms of Patinkin's notation Walras's Law would then be written as

$$\sum_{i=1}^{n+1} p_i X_i(\ ) \equiv 0$$

where the $(n + 1)$th commodity is 'money'. Clearly the negative of

$$\sum_{i=1}^{n} p_i X_i(\ )$$

must then be the excess demand for money as represented in (4.23).

17. Writing (4.22) as

$$\sum_{i=1}^{n} p_i Q^* = \bar{M}V$$

the excess demand function for money appears to have the form

$$X_i = \sum_{i=1}^{n} p_i Q^* - \bar{M}V$$

With V fixed this excess demand for money is then homogeneous of degree 1 in p_i and $\bar{M}$. If all prices and $\bar{M}$ are increased in proportion, the excess demand for money will increase by an identical proportion.

criticism is that the 'real subset' (4.21) does not contain money balances and hence a change in those balances has no effect on the 'real subset'. Now this argument is simply incorrect and involves an oversight on Patinkin's part. It is well known, and Patinkin (1965:35) even points it out himself, that the excess demand functions in (4.21) have as implicit arguments the endowments of the n commodities *including money*! All of this is also stated explicitly by Archibald and Lipsey (1958:2) who assume an indifference system between real balances and consumption goods: see especially their Figure 1. It is from this system that the excess demand functions in (4.21) are derived as Patinkin (1965:ch.1) himself explains. If this were not so then Walras's Law need not hold and Patinkin would be unable to write expression (4.23). This can also be seen from the fact that if at least one of the individuals did not hold money, the medium-of-exchange function implied by the quantity equation would not make sense because no one would have any money with which to engage in trade! Hence, when the quantity equation is added to the model, 'money' ceases to be solely a unit of account (assuming the commodity designated as 'money' was fulfilling that role) and becomes also a medium of exchange. If 'money' is then not included as part of the endowment, the model simply ceases to make any economic sense. All this suggests that there is no Patinkinesque dichotomy in neo-Walrasian monetary theory and the one that Patinkin attacks is of his own manufacture. There is, of course, a dichotomy in the trivial sense that relative prices are determined in the 'real subset' and the absolute price level by the quantity equation. But this dichotomy does not lead to the contradictions that Patinkin finds.

This argument is most clearly illustrated using a model presented by Hickman (1950) to generate some numerical examples. The objective here will be to show that Patinkin's analysis of the dichotomy in terms of the disequilibrium implications of the above model is fundamentally flawed. Patinkin's objection to the dichotomy was ultimately concentrated on what he perceived to be its dynamic disequilibrium implications. For example, Gupta (1969:118–19) summarizes the conclusions of the debate as follows:

As Patinkin (1965:176–7) has stated in his demonstration against the validity of the 'classical dichotomy', and as was also emphasized by Baumol ... in a symposium on an earlier criticism of Patinkin by Archibald and Lipsey (1958), the invalidity or inconsistency of a dichotomized system does not necessarily lie in the non-existence of an equilibrium (solution) but in the necessity of having an integrated system (in which the real and monetary sectors have become interdependent) when one comes to specify the adjustment mechanism ensuring the stability of the said equilibrium (solution).

Kohn (1979:4) reaches the same conclusion: 'Patinkin's objection to the dichotomy lies in what he believes to be its dynamic (disequilibrium) implications.' But it is precisely in the so-called dynamic analysis that Patinkin's lack of disequilibrium tools leads to the oversight regarding the transaction constraint imposed by the quantity equation. In this regard the distinction between effective and notional functions is particularly helpful in revealing Patinkin's error which, at one point, amounts to employing equilibrium values in a disequilibrium situation. At the time of the debate, in the early fifties, the analysis of disequilibrium states was particularly sketchy, which no doubt partly explains this oversight. There is, however, no excuse now.

A simple model of weekly equilibrium: transactions structure

The arguments presented above can now be illustrated using a simple model which featured prominently in the debate. This model was developed by Hickman (1950) and consists of only two commodities and money. For the sake of simplicity we will also assume that there are only two traders. The equations of the model are as follows:

$$
\left.
\begin{array}{llll}
 & \textit{Demand} & \textit{Supply} & \textit{Excess demand} \\
\textit{Commodity I} & D_1 \equiv \dfrac{d_1 p_2}{p_1} & S_1 \equiv \dfrac{s_1 p_1}{p_2} & X_1 \equiv \dfrac{d_1 p_2}{p_1} - \dfrac{s_1 p_1}{p_2} = 0 \\[2mm]
\textit{Commodity II} & D_2 \equiv \dfrac{d_2 p_1}{p_2} & S_2 \equiv \dfrac{s_2 p_2}{p_1} & X_2 \equiv \dfrac{s_2 p_1}{p_2} - \dfrac{s_2 p_2}{p_1} = 0 \\[2mm]
\textit{Money} & D_3 \equiv p_1 S_1 + p_2 S_2 & S_3 \equiv p_1 D_1 + p_2 D_2 & X_3 \equiv p_1 X_1 - p_2 X_2 = 0
\end{array}
\right\} \quad (4.24)
$$

To these equations of the 'real subset' is added the quantity equation:

$$
p_1 D_1 + p_2 D_2 = \bar{M} V \tag{4.25}
$$

Now it is immediately obvious that money must appear as an implicit argument in the 'real subset' if the system is to satisfy Walras's Law as required by Patinkin. This can be seen by comparing Patinkin's use of Walras's Law, as in expression (4.23) above, with X_3 in (4.24). This also implies that money is used as a medium of exchange, as was argued by Valavanis (1955) and Hickman (1950) and embodied later by Clower (1967) in the maxim that money buys goods and goods buy money but goods do not buy goods, i.e. they are not bartered. It also implies that money must appear among the endowments of the functions in the 'real subset'. This we will see most clearly in the numerical example presented below.

To generate a solution the determinant of the matrix of coefficients of X_1 and X_2 must be set to zero which implies that $s_2 = d_1 (d_2/s_1)$.

Making this substitution and solving X_2 for $p_1/p_2 = \sqrt{d_1/s_1}$ ensures a consistent solution.[18] Using the numerical example presented in Archibald and Lipsey (1958) it is then possible to illustrate all the features of this model. Setting $d_1 = 4$ and $s_1 = 16$ generates $p_1/p_2 = 0.5$, from excess demand function X_1, and $D_1 = S_1 = 8$. Consistency requires $s_2/d_2 = d_1/s_1$, hence arbitrarily setting $d_2 = 4$ produces $s_2 = 1$. The numbers have been selected so as to avoid awkward fractions. Substituting these values into X_2 confirms that $p_1/p_2 = 0.5$ and $D_2 = S_2 = 2$. The relative prices and equilibrium quantities are thus determined in the 'real subset' without recourse to X_3, which of course does not mean that the model exhibits Patinkin's invalid dichotomy. To determine the absolute price level, values of $\bar{M}$ and V must be given for the quantity equation. If $V = 3$ and $\bar{M} = \$10$ we have $8p_1 + 2p_2 = 30$ and with $p_1/p_2 = 0.5$ this yields $p_1 = \$2.50$ and $p_2 = \$5$. So much for the solution.[19] What is now of interest is the economic interpretation that lies behind this solution, for it is here that the confusion arises.

Patinkin's analysis proceeds in terms of the temporary equilibrium theory outlined earlier (chapter 3). On the Monday of each week traders receive an endowment of real income to add to their money holdings from the previous period. (Again we see that the money holdings form part of the initial endowment at the beginning of the period.) The equilibrium solution is then determined via a tâtonnement process and only after this does trade, in the form of exchange

18.
$$\begin{vmatrix} d_1 & -s_1 \\ -s_2 & d_2 \end{vmatrix} = 0 \quad \therefore \quad d_1 d_2 - s_1 s_2 = 0$$
$$\therefore \quad s_2 = d_1(d_2/s_1)$$

Substituting into X_2 produces

$$d_2 p_1/p_2 - (d_1(d_2/s_1))p_2/p_1 = 0$$
$$d_2(p_1/p_2)^2 - d_1(d_2/s_1) = 0$$
$$(p_1/p_2)^2 = \left(\frac{d_1}{d_2}\right)(d_2/s_1) = d_1/s_1$$
$$p_1/p_2 = \sqrt{d_1/s_1}$$

19. Note also that both Walras's Law and the quantity equation are satisfied by the equilibrium values in the model. Walras's Law is the identity

$$\sum_{i=1}^{2} p_i S_i + p_3 S_3 \equiv \sum_{i=1}^{2} p_i D_i + p_3 D_3$$

which is obviously true when

$$D_i = S_i \text{ and } D_3 = S_3$$

Substituting the relevant values into the quantity equation (4.25) produces $(8 \times 2.5 + 2 \times 5.0) = 30$.

of goods for money, take place. Archibald and Lipsey (1958:2) describe the process in the following terms: 'The *tâtonnement*, in which equilibrium prices are found, is quite distinct from the actual trading which takes place afterwards.' (Recall the discussion in chapter 3.)

Now, although this distinction is valid and holds for all neo-Walrasian analysis, it does not imply that these two aspects of the model are incompatible or that they reflect a dichotomy between real and monetary sectors. The two aspects of the model must be compatible because if they were not it would imply that the tâtonnement process could generate a solution that was not feasible! The quantity equation therefore, in addition to determining the absolute price, describes the mechanics of the exchange process which occurs during the week in such a way that it is compatible with Monday's tâtonnement solution. In terms of more modern jargon the quantity equation implies a transaction constraint of the Grandmont–Younes (1972) form, i.e. the equilibrium solution is feasible if and only if, for each trader, the value of purchases using money is less than or equal to the value of sales plus initial money holdings.

To see this, consider a simple example of the transactions structure implicit in the equilibrium solution derived from the Hickman model. The structure is illustrated in Figure 4.4 and for the sake of simplicity it is assumed that there are only two traders. An inspection of Figure 4.4 now reveals that there is no meaningful sense in which this model can be dichotomized. In particular the money endowment of \$10 must be held by individual A, i.e. the supplier of good 2. If individual B held the \$10 on Monday then the equilibrium solution generated by the tâtonnement would not be feasible! Trade would come to a halt

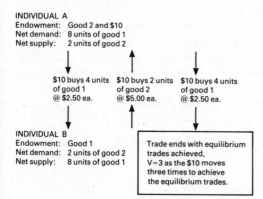

INDIVIDUAL A
Endowment: Good 2 and \$10
Net demand: 8 units of good 1
Net supply: 2 units of good 2

\$10 buys 4 units of good 1 @ \$2.50 ea. \$10 buys 2 units of good 2 @ \$5.00 ea. \$10 buys 4 units of good 1 @ \$2.50 ea.

INDIVIDUAL B
Endowment: Good 1
Net demand: 2 units of good 2
Net supply: 8 units of good 1

Trade ends with equilibrium trades achieved, V=3 as the \$10 moves three times to achieve the equilibrium trades.

Fig. 4.4 Endowments and transactions structure: weekly or temporary equilibrium

after individual B had acquired the two units of good 2 but individual A had acquired only four units of good 1, leaving an excess demand of four units! Individual B would have no further incentive to trade because he would have achieved his equilibrium position. The excess demand functions in (4.24) are therefore only defined on the implicit assumption that the given money stock is in the hands of individual A who is the supplier of commodity 2.

More formally, the quantity equation (4.25) implies the transaction constraint (3.5) holds for each trader:

$$q(t) \text{ is feasible } \langle = \rangle \quad p(q - \omega)^+ \leqslant m(t - 1) + \sum_n k_n p_n (q - \omega)_n^-$$

In the case of individual A, the relevant values are, $p(q - \omega)^+ = \$20$ (purchases); $m(t - 1) = \$10$ (initial money balances) and $\sum_n k_n p_n (q - \omega)_n^- = \$10$ (sales) as k and $n = 1$ in this simple example. The same constraint is satisfied for individual B so it is safe to conclude that the equilibrium trades, $q(t) = (8;2)$ are feasible. The quantity equation in a neo-Walrasian model should (as Valavanis (1955) argued) be interpreted as imposing a transaction constraint and not as a demand and supply relationship. But Patinkin failed to see that his critique of the 'classical dichotomy' involved a violation of these finance constraints. The point is most easily illustrated by examining Patinkin's argument about the disequilibrium adjustment of the above system.

Temporary disequilibrium and the transactions structure

Starting from the equilibrium solution, Patinkin introduces an equi-proportionate change in commodity prices. He then argues that:

(i)   because the commodity markets depend only on relative prices they remain in equilibrium. By Walras's Law the money market will also remain in equilibrium so there are no forces released to correct the price level, which is therefore indeterminate;

(ii)   from the quantity equation, with $\bar{M}$, V and Q_i assumed constant, there is an excess demand for money as

$$\sum_{i=1}^n p_i Q_i > \bar{M} V.$$

Hence forces will be released to correct the price level, which is therefore determinate (Patinkin, 1965:176).

Comparison of (i) and (ii) reveals then another aspect of the contradiction which Patinkin perceives as reflecting the invalid 'classical dichotomy'. Now it is easy to demonstrate that Patinkin's argument is incorrect in both parts (i) and (ii). It is incorrect in part (i) because, despite the 'homogeneity postulate' (that is, the property that commodity excess demand functions are homogeneous of degree zero in prices), an increase in the price level *will affect the commodity markets* as the finance constraints are violated. And it is incorrect in part (ii) because Patinkin substitutes equilibrium quantities into the quantity equation when the model is in a *disequilibrium state*.

What happens is this. When prices are doubled, with V held constant, the finance constraints implied by the quantity equation are violated and the equilibrium trades are no longer feasible! To see this, consider the transactions structure implied by the disequilibrium state with absolute prices doubled and $\bar{M}$ and V held constant (Figure 4.5). Inspection of this structure reveals that when the price level doubles, with $\bar{M}$ and V held constant, it is no longer possible to achieve the equilibrium trades. In other words, the equilibrium trades $q(t) = (8;2)$ are no longer feasible as the finance constraint for at least one trader is violated. In the case of trader A, for example, $p'(q - \omega)^+ = \$40$ which is greater than $m(t - 1) = \$10$ plus $\sum_n k_n p_n (q - \omega)_n^- = \$20$. In this case trader B's finance constraint is satisfied but if V is held constant he cannot achieve his equilibrium trades. If V is allowed to vary (to $V = 5$) trader B will achieve his equilibrium trades but will have no further incentive to trade. Trader A will therefore not be able to continue because trader B will be holding the $10. What this suggests is that, in general, a doubling of the price level will throw the commodity markets into disequilibrium, contrary to Patinkin's point (i).

As far as point (ii) is concerned, it is also apparent that when correctly interpreted the quantity equation does not reveal an excess

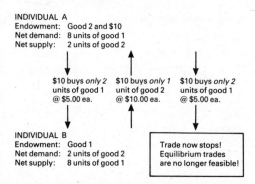

INDIVIDUAL A
Endowment: Good 2 and $10
Net demand: 8 units of good 1
Net supply: 2 units of good 2

$10 buys *only 2* units of good 1 @ $5.00 ea.

$10 buys *only 1* unit of good 2 @ $10.00 ea.

$10 buys *only 2* units of good 1 @ $5.00 ea.

INDIVIDUAL B
Endowment: Good 1
Net demand: 2 units of good 2
Net supply: 8 units of good 1

Trade now stops!
Equilibrium trades
are no longer feasible!

Fig. 4.5 Transactions structure: temporary disequilibrium

demand for money. In fact the quantity equation cannot be interpreted as a demand and supply relationship in neo-Walrasian theory.[20] To interpret Patinkin's model correctly in a temporary disequilibrium state it is necessary to introduce the distinction between *effective* and *notional* functions due to Clower (1965). (Recall that Clower treats the finance constraint and the dual decision hypothesis as alternative formalizations of the same thought-experiment.) From the transactions structure presented in Figure 4.5 it is clear that both traders are constrained by the fact that velocity is fixed.

Both, in fact, suffer from a constrained demand for commodities: four units in the case of individual A and one unit in the case of individual B. Hence, Walras's Law must now be written to include effective, as well as notional, functions.[21] In terms of the above model, Walras's Law then appears as

$$\sum_{i=1}^{2} p_i' (\hat{D}_i - S_i) + (D_3 - \hat{S}_3) \equiv 0 \qquad (4.26)$$

where the p_i' are the new prices and the $\hat{\ }$ over a variable represents the constrained or *effective* values. Substituting the relevant values into Walras's Law then produces $5(4 - 8) + 10(1 - 2) + (60 - 30) = 0$ which reveals an excess supply of commodities matched by an excess demand for 'money'.[22] Substituting the constrained trades

20. It was so interpreted in the Cambridge version of the quantity equation, which points to an important but overlooked distinction between the interpretation of the quantity theory in neo-Walrasian models and the Cambridge tradition. Tsiang (1966:344n21) is a notable exception here but Archibald and Lipsey (1958) treat the two interpretations as equivalent, which is a mistake that leads them to the conclusion, also incorrect, that Walras's Law does not apply to disequilibrium states in a neo-Walrasian model.

21. A full discussion of the relationship between effective demand functions and Walras's Law is presented in Rogers (1985) and Rhodes (1984). The concepts involved were not available to the participants in the Patinkin controversy.

22. In terms of the values used in the model we have,

$$\sum_{i=1}^{2} p_i' (\hat{D}_i - S_i) + (D_3 - \hat{S}_3) \equiv 0$$

where

$$p_1' = 5.0$$
$$p_2' = 10.0$$
$$p_3 = 1$$
$$\hat{D}_1 = 4 \text{ (constrained demand for good 1)}$$
$$S_1 = 8 \text{ (notional supply of good 1)}$$
$$\hat{D}_2 = 1 \text{ (constrained demand for good 2)}$$
$$S_2 = 2 \text{ (notional supply of good 2)}$$
$$D_3 = \sum_{i=1}^{2} p_i' S_i = 60$$
$$\hat{S}_3 = \sum_{i=1}^{2} p_i' \hat{D}_i = 30$$

into the quantity equation produces

$$\sum_{i=1}^{2} p_i' \hat{D}_i = \bar{M} V \tag{4.27}$$

and inserting the relevant values, $(5 \times 4) + (10 \times 1) = 30$, which satisfies the quantity equation and is not in conflict with the fact that an excess demand for 'money' exists in terms of Walras's Law (recall footnote 20 on the interpretation of the quantity equation in this model). Thus, from expression (4.26), we can see that when the price level doubles, a corrective movement on prices immediately emerges in both the real *and* 'money' markets. An excess supply of commodities and an excess demand for 'money' will cause prices to fall until the initial price level is restored, given that $\bar{M}$ and V do not change. It may, therefore, safely be concluded that neo-Walrasian monetary theory does not suffer from Patinkin's dichotomy. Although the tât-onnement algorithm is analytically distinct from the trading process, the quantity equation imposes a finance constraint on each trader that is consistent with the tâtonnement equilibrium.

With the benefit of hindsight, we can see that Patinkin's concern over the contradictions implied by the 'classical dichotomy' was not well founded. In fact, the contradictions that he derives are of his own making and arise as a result of a failure to interpret his neo-Walrasian model correctly. Correctly interpreted, Patinkin's neo-Walrasian model does not reveal any contradictions, and consequently concern over the 'classical dichotomy' is seen to be a false trail which misled both Clower (1967) and Archibald and Lipsey (1958) to conclusions about 'classical' neo-Walrasian monetary theory that reflect Patinkin's original errors. For example, Walras's Law applies in all states of the model, both equilibrium and disequilibrium, and is not in conflict with the 'classical dichotomy' as claimed by Archibald and Lipsey (1958). Also Clower's (1967) claim that Patinkin's model is a barter model, and that the distinction between barter and monetary systems rests on the postulate that money buys goods and goods buy money but goods do not buy goods, is seen to be seriously misleading. For, although Patinkin's model is a non-monetary model in the sense that 'money' is always an inessential addition, it does satisfy Clower's maxim, which seems to indicate that the latter cannot provide a suitable criterion for distinguishing between a monetary and a non-monetary system. Recall that it was shown in chapter 3 that the transaction constraint and hence the quantity equation is an inessential addition to a neo-Walrasian model so that although we have corrected a number of errors in the debate, the fundamental flaw in neo-Walrasian monetary theory remains.

CONCLUDING REMARKS

In any examination of the neoclassical synthesis, it is necessary to identify the Wicksellian and neo-Walrasian elements. Failure to do so will only add to the already considerable confusion which surrounds discussion of the neoclassical synthesis and the Keynesian revolution. In this regard each element has made its own peculiar contribution.

Attempts have been made to extract Keynesian results from what are essentially Wicksellian structures by imposing traps and rigidities, despite the fact that Keynes (1936:243) formally abandoned both Wicksell's concept of the natural rate of interest and the spanner-in-the-works explanations of unemployment. A similar story may be told for the neo-Walrasian contribution, and the sorry episode is well documented in the literature. Nevertheless, in neither case have the fundamental issues received sufficient attention. From the point of view of monetary theory, these are:

(i)   the capital debate has undermined the Wicksellian concept of a natural rate of interest; and

(ii)   'money' is an inessential addition to neo-Walrasian models.

It has been demonstrated that these two points are the fundamental issues at stake in the monetary theory of the neoclassical synthesis. If these two points are accepted then together they effectively demolish the twin foundations of neoclassical monetary theory. Unfortunately, these issues have not been generally perceived through the smoke of battle thrown up by the Keynesian revolution and the monetarist counter-revolution. Instead, attention has been diverted to secondary issues of the type illustrated in this chapter. As a result, history repeated itself when the same issues remained to confound the debate between Keynesians and the second generation of 'classicists' – the monetarists.

Appendix 4

THE NEO-WALRASIAN REVOLUTION

Another facet of the neoclassical synthesis that requires attention is the role played by neo-Walrasian analysis. The developments to be outlined here played no role in the construction of Tobin's Wicksellian brand of Keynesian analysis but they did offer an alternative interpretation of the loanable funds versus liquidity preference analysis and today the neo-Walrasian model provides the framework within which some theorists attempt to evaluate issues of macro-economic theory and policy. For example, McCaleb and Sellon (1980) interpret Patinkin's version of the IS–LM model as 'the standard version'. Nevertheless, both Wicksellian and neo-Walrasian versions of the IS–LM model are thoroughly entangled in the current literature and they need to be carefully identified in any discussion.

The neo-Walrasian interpretation of 'classical' theory was initiated by Hicks (1939) and Lange (1942) but was popularized by Patinkin's (1958,1965) discussion of 'classical' and Keynesian issues within a neo-Walrasian version of the IS–LM model. And, as Clower (1975:10) points out, no one imagined that neo-Walrasian general equilibrium theory could not be applied to deal with Keynesian issues:

That any even moderately 'general' economic model should be anything but *noncategorical*, therefore, would hardly occur naturally to any but a very perverse mind. That the elaborate neo-Walrasian model set out in Hicks's *Value and Capital* might fail to satisfy this condition would have seemed correspondingly incredible to any sensible person at the outset of the neo-Walrasian revolution.

The neo-Walrasian system can be portrayed in different but equivalent ways. Here we will follow Lange's (1942) exposition. The relevant properties of this analysis can be illustrated in terms of the derivation of Walras's Law. The model consists of n commodities one of which, say the nth commodity, acts as numeraire (the medium of exchange function can be imposed later). Let P_i be the price of the ith commodity which means that $P_n \equiv 1$. With $D_i(P_1, P_2, \ldots, P_{n-1})$ and $S_i(P_1, P_2, \ldots, P_{n-1})$ the demand and supply functions for the ith commodity, the equilibrium relative prices are determined by the $n - 1$ equations

$$D_i(P_1, P_2, \ldots, P_{n-1}) = S_i(P_1, P_2, \ldots, P_{n-1}), \quad (4A.1)$$
$$i = 1, 2, \ldots, n - 1.$$

Note that these functions are only defined for a given distribution of endowments – see, for example, Patinkin (1965:35) or Quirk and Saposnik (1968:153–5). Also each demand and supply function represents the net demand and supply over and above the endowment. For example, each budget constraint is written as

$$\sum_{i=1}^{n} P_i(X_{ij} - \bar{X}_{ij}) \equiv 0,$$

where $\bar{X}_{ij}$ is the endowment of the ith commodity held by trader j. If $X_{ij} > \bar{X}_{ij}$, we have a net demand, D_i, and if $X_{ij} < \bar{X}_{ij}$, a net supply, S_i. There are only $n - 1$ independent demand and supply functions because the demand and supply functions for money are derived from the components of:

$$\sum_{i=1}^{n-1} P_i D_i \equiv S_n \text{ and } \sum_{i=1}^{n-1} P_i S_i \equiv D_n \qquad (4A.2)$$

The total demand, in money value, for all n commodities is then:

$$\sum_{i=1}^{n} P_i D_i \equiv \sum_{i=1}^{n-1} P_i D_i + D_n \equiv S_n + D_n \qquad (4A.3)$$

and the total money value of the supply of commodities is:

$$\sum_{i=1}^{n} P_i S_i \equiv \sum_{i=1}^{n-1} P_i S_i + S_n \equiv D_n + S_n \qquad (4A.4)$$

We therefore obtain Walras's Law

$$\sum_{i=1}^{n} P_i D_i \equiv \sum_{i=1}^{n} P_i S_i \qquad (4A.5)$$

which states that the sums of the *value* of total demand and total supply are *identically equal*. Walras's Law is also often encountered in the form which reads: if, in a system of n markets, $n - 1$ of the markets are in equilibrium the nth market is also in equilibrium. But it should be apparent that this statement is simply a paraphrasing of (4A.5) for the general equilibrium state. Hence Walras's Law should not be interpreted to mean that the system is always in equilibrium but only that the sum of the value of excess demands is always zero for any state of the model, equilibrium or disequilibrium. For example, rearrangement of (4A.5) produces the more familiar statement of Walras's Law in terms of excess demands as:

$$\sum_{i=1}^{n} P_i(D_i - S_i) \equiv 0 \qquad (4A.6)$$

The properties of this analysis can be highlighted using a simple three-commodity example, i.e. $n = 3$ in the above discussion. If we now impose the further condition that the numeraire is also the medium of exchange, then:

$$\sum_{i=1}^{2} P_i D_i = S_3 \text{ and } \sum_{i=1}^{2} P_i S_i = D_3$$

The relationship between the prices P_1 and P_2 that maintain equilibrium in the two commodity markets can then be examined and related to the equilibrium locus of the medium of exchange (commodity 3) – the so-called 'money' market – in terms of Figure 4A.1. The prices of the two goods are plotted on the axes; the price of P_3 as numeraire is set equal to 1. Each point in the space then represents a relative price ratio (P_1/P_2) and the point marked GE is that price ratio for which demand equals supply for all three commodities. Assuming that the two goods are substitutes and that no complementarity is present (Hicks, 1939:68), the market-clearing loci for the commodities 1 and 2 will both run from the northeast quadrant to the southwest quadrant. For example, an increase in the price of com-

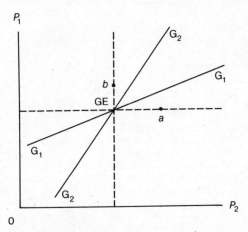

Fig. 4A.1 Market-clearing loci for commodities 1 and 2

modity 1 from P_1^e to P_1 will generate an excess supply as illustrated in Figure 4A.2. Equilibrium could be restored, however, by increasing the price of commodity 2 which would shift the demand curve to the right in the market for commodity 1 (Bilas,1967:261). Recall that the two commodities are assumed to be substitutes. Note also that Patinkin (1965) refers to the process whereby the demand and supply functions in each 'market' are derived as 'individual experiments' and the process of deriving the market-clearing loci as 'market experiments'. In the above example the supply curve is assumed to remain fixed. A higher price for commodity 1 must therefore be accompanied by a higher price for commodity 2 to maintain equilibrium in the market for commodity 1. The same argument applies for commodity 2 but the two loci do not coincide except at the GE point. In a three-commodity model it follows from Walras's Law that either of the markets for commodities 1 and 2 may be in equilibrium without the other being in equilibrium. All that Walras's Law requires is that the sum of the value of the excess demands be zero. Furthermore, it is reasonable to expect the price of a commodity to be more influential in its own market. The slope of G_1 will then be flatter than G_2 in Figure 4A.1 (Hicks,1939:69).

Examining points off the curves then enables us to establish the excess demand state of each market in terms of Walras's Law. For example, at point *a* the price of P_1 is too low to maintain equilibrium for commodity 1, given the price of P_2. An excess demand for commodity 1 therefore exists at all points below the G_1 locus and an excess supply at all points above it. Similarly at point *b* the price of P_2 is too low to maintain equilibrium for commodity 2, given the price of P_1.

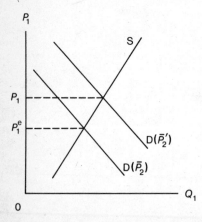

Fig. 4A.2 Market experiment to derive market-clearing loci

Consequently, excess demand exists at all points above G_2 and excess supply at all points below it. These possibilities are shown in Figure 4A.3. The position of the medium of exchange locus in this figure, can now be deduced from Walras's Law. To one side of the locus an excess supply of money will result and to the other side an excess demand for money. Hence by Walras's Law the money market locus cannot pass through either region II or region IV in Figure 4A.3. It must therefore pass through regions I and III and from Walras's Law we can deduce that points to the right represent an excess demand for money and points to the left, an excess supply of money. The slope is, of course, not crucial. All neo-Walrasian models subject to Walras's Law display this relationship between the market-clearing loci, and the neo-Walrasian version of the IS–LM model made use of this property in a futile attempt to distinguish between liquidity preference and loanable funds theories of the rate of interest.

More recently the same model has been employed by McCaleb and Sellon (1980) in an attempt to assess the significance of portfolio balance (wealth) and government financing constraints. They argue that if these constraints are imposed on what they call the standard version of the IS–LM model, i.e. the neo-Walrasian version, indeterminacy may result. Although technically correct this interpretation overlooks entirely the conceptual and analytical differences between Wicksellian–Keynesian and the neo-Walrasian versions of the IS–LM model. As we have already noted, there is no unique or standard

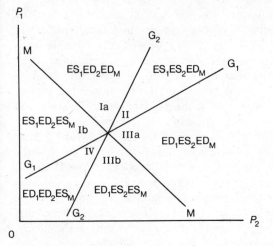

Fig. 4A.3 Classification of 'market' states in a three-commodity neo-Walrasian model

version of the IS–LM model, and, if anything, the Wicksellian–Keynesian version is more common in the literature. Attempting to impose features of the Wicksellian–Keynesian version on the neo-Walrasian version as McCaleb and Sellon suggest will inevitably lead to the sorts of problems that they encounter. But the fundamental question concerning the relevance of each of these theoretical structures is totally overlooked. It is simply taken for granted that the neo-Walrasian model is the 'standard version'. But as Clower (1975), Hahn (1981) and others have noted over the years, the neo-Walrasian model is totally unsuited to the assessment of macroeconomic or monetary policy issues. Some idea of the conceptual errors implied by any such attempt can be gained by re-examining the liquidity preference versus loanable funds debate.

Hicks and Patinkin on liquidity preference versus loanable funds

Hicks (1939:ch.12) and Patinkin (1958,1965:375) used the neo-Walrasian framework to evaluate the loanable funds and liquidity preference theories of the rate of interest. Although Coddington (1983:74–5) and Patinkin (1976:140) give qualified approval to the neo-Walrasian position, apparently on the grounds that Keynes failed to adopt the appropriate general equilibrium view of his theory(!), we will attempt to show that the neo-Walrasian interpretation of the debate is entirely misconceived and involves fundamental error.

The neo-Walrasian version of the IS–LM model presented by Patinkin (1958) involves the goods, money and bond markets as illustrated in Figure 4A.4. The dispute between the loanable funds and liquidity preference theories can be examined with reference to Figure 4A.4 by noting that the two theories apparently produce conflicting results in regions II and V. If we consider the general equilibrium solution W, however, there is no conflict. Hence it was concluded that as far as static equilibrium was concerned it did not matter which of LM or BF was dropped by applying Walras's Law (Johnson,1971:13). But out-of-equilibrium, in 'dynamic' analysis, the two theories supposedly give different predictions in regions II and V. For example, in region V the liquidity preference theory, from an excess supply of money, indicates that the interest rate should *fall*. The loanable funds theory, with an excess supply of bonds, indicates that the price of bonds should *fall* and hence the rate of interest should *rise*. The two theories thus apparently give conflicting conclusions on the movement of the rate of interest although the loanable funds explanation appears the more plausible.

A careful reassessment of the above argument now provides an interesting illustration of the fallacy of misplaced concreteness as it arises from the use of neo-Walrasian models. The first point to note about this specification of the IS–LM model is that, unlike the Wicksellian–Keynesian version, income is treated as a stock and not a flow! Income in the neo-Walrasian model refers to the initial endowments given to traders, i.e. the 'manna drop'. The implications of this property become apparent when we examine the concept of 'the' rate of interest employed in Figure 4A.4. As we saw in the discussion of neo-Walrasian interest rate theory in chapter 3, own rates of interest exist for all commodities in a general intertemporal specification of any neo-Walrasian model. In addition, it was shown with reference to Figure 3.1 that a distribution of endowments could be found which would equalize these own rates of interest. Seen in this light, Figure 4A.4 is just a more complex version of Figure 3.1. The analytical principles involved are identical. But in that case there is no conflict between loanable funds and liquidity preference theories on the grounds raised by Hicks or Patinkin.

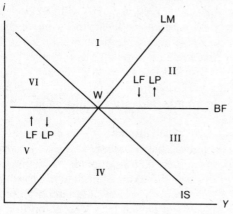

LF loanable funds
LP liquidity preference
I $ES_M; ED_B; ES_G$
II $ED_M; ED_B; ES_G$
III $ED_M; ES_B; ES_G$
IV $ED_M; ES_B; ED_G$
V $ES_M; ES_B; ED_G$
VI $ES_M; ED_B; ED_G$

Fig. 4A.4 Patinkin's neo-Walrasian version of IS–LM

To see why, consider Figure 4A.4 in terms of the properties of neo-Walrasian interest theory outlined in chapter 3. Firstly, the general equilibrium solution, W, should be interpreted as corresponding to that distribution of endowments of 'money', 'bonds' and 'income' which generates uniform own rates of interest on each of these commodities. In other words, W in Figure 4A.4 is a graphical illustration of Hahn's uniform rate of interest result illustrated in Figure 3.1 (with which, incidentally, he seeks to attack the neo-Ricardians by erroneously associating their use of long-period equilibrium with this notion of full equilibrium). For any other distribution of endowments, i.e. at any other point on the 'income' abscissa, own rates of interest will then differ for each of the three commodities as measured on the market-clearing loci – this is the general result in a neo-Walrasian model. At positions off the market-clearing loci, in disequilibrium states, markets are not clearing and time-dated prices are still, as it were, in motion. There is moreover no reason why the own rates of interest on each commodity should not all appear to move in different directions depending on the state of excess demand in each intertemporal 'market'. Such a result is in fact to be expected as we know from Walras's Law that excess demands will be matched by excess supplies so individual prices are likely to be moving in opposite directions. In a three-commodity intertemporal model such as this there is therefore no fixed relationship between the time-dated prices for commodity 1 and those for commodity 2, for example. This means that, in terms of neo-Walrasian interest rate theory, a rising 'bond' rate of interest is quite compatible with a falling 'money' rate in region V.

The difficulty arises, of course, when attempts are made to impose the observed real world relationship between money rates of interest and bond prices onto this type of neo-Walrasian model. The inverse relationship between bond prices and the rate of interest observed in the real world is simply not a property of any intertemporal neo-Walrasian model, so imposing it will obviously involve a contradiction. But the contradiction arises from misinterpreting the neo-Walrasian model and not from any conflict between liquidity preference and loanable funds theories.

Now, although Patinkin derives Figure 4A.4 in a somewhat different fashion and his model is not given a general intertemporal specification as the rate of interest is calculated for only one commodity – 'bonds' – the argument presented here applies *mutatis mutandis*. In particular the rate of interest is used by Patinkin as a kind of shift parameter when deriving market-clearing loci of the type illustrated in Figure 4A.4. Despite these differences on matters of detail,

Patinkin's discussion of the contradiction between loanable funds and liquidity preference theories involves the same confusion between the properties of the model and reality which are outlined above. Even with Patinkin's restrictive intertemporal specification of the model – in terms of a single rate of interest on 'bonds' – there is no reason why, *in the model*, an excess demand for the medium of exchange – 'money' – has any bearing on the interest rate on 'bonds'. On the latter issue the moneyless neo-Walrasian model has nothing to say for reasons which have been well documented above. Rather, the episode provides an illustration of the trivial distractions thrown up by neo-Walrasian monetary theory.

Other examples of the confusion generated by neo-Walrasian monetary theory have been documented by Tsiang (1966:329). He points out that Walras's Law is not applicable to 'an economy where money as the necessary medium of exchange and generally accepted means of payments is demanded for transactions purposes'. Today we know that this conclusion is sound, as the medium of exchange function of money is an inessential addition to a neo-Walrasian model. In addition, Tsiang (1966:331n4) concludes that the budget constraints in neo-Walrasian models are best interpreted as 'fair exchange constraints' (here he anticipates Clower's (1965) use of Say's Principle) and points to the errors that arise if the net acquisition of the medium of exchange under Walras's Law is associated with the demand for money as that term is understood in the Cambridge cash balance equation (Tsiang, 1966:334n8,334n21). Although we may not wish to agree with Tsiang's (1956,1966) arguments on the equivalence of liquidity preference and loanable funds theories (for reasons that will become clearer in chapters 9 and 10), the confusion to which he pointed continued to dog attempts to extract Keynesian conclusions from fix-price neo-Walrasian models, inadvertently initiated by Clower (1965) and promoted by, for example, Barro and Grossman (1976) and Malinvaud (1977). The false trails and sterility of this type of analysis have been documented by Rogers (1983,1985).

5

KEYNESIANS AND MONETARISTS

INTRODUCTION

Any discussion of Keynesians and monetarists must inevitably come to terms with the wide diversity of approaches that exist under these headings. To some extent this task has already been performed in terms of our distinction between neo-Walrasian and Wicksellian elements of the neoclassical synthesis. Employing this distinction, it appears that as far as the Keynesians are concerned the Wicksellian version forms the dominant theoretical foundation. In this chapter we will show that this is particularly true of James Tobin who is selected as the most sophisticated representative of the Keynesian position. By contrast the Post Keynesians, because they reject the neoclassical synthesis, are not open to the objections raised here. On the monetarist side we have already noted the need to distinguish between Friedman and monetarists such as Brunner and Meltzer. Friedman will be discussed in detail in chapter 6 so here we will be concerned with the Brunner–Meltzer brand of monetarism and the objective will be to show that they employ the same neoclassical–Wicksellian structure as Tobin. This leaves only the new 'classical' macroeconomics of monetarism mark II as a further monetarist alternative. The latter is relegated to a brief discussion at the end of this chapter on the grounds that it offers nothing new in terms of resolving the theoretical issues at stake. As Fusfeld (1980) puts it, Rational Expectations arrives too late to save neoclassical economics. Rational Expectations, as the defining characteristic of the approach, may be applied to virtually any type of model, neo-Walrasian, Wicksellian or whatever. It therefore offers no solutions to the theoretical issues discussed in chapters 2 and 3.

The chapter opens with a modern restatement of the Wicksellian version of the neoclassical synthesis by Sargent (1979). This model bridges the gap between the Keynesian and 'classical' models of chapter 4 and the Tobin and Brunner–Meltzer models of this chapter. It is then shown how the latter models employ a relationship between the return on equities and the marginal productivity of capital which mimics Wicksell's distinction between market and natural rates of interest. The Tobin and Brunner–Meltzer models therefore suffer from all the limitations discussed in chapter 2. Together with the conclusions of chapter 3 this leaves neoclassical monetary theory, as practised by many Keynesians and monetarists, without any coherent theoretical foundations and paves the way for Friedman's empiricist approach to the quantity theory.

A MODERN RESTATEMENT OF THE WICKSELL CONNECTION

The discussion of the 'Keynes versus classics' debate in chapter 4 indicated that there were no significant analytical differences between the two models. Both were, in fact, examples of a Wicksellian-type neoclassical model in which capital is defined as *value* capital. Nevertheless, the pseudo-distinction between 'classical' and Keynesian models still persists in the literature. For example, Sargent (1979:46–7) provides a recent illustration of the distinction between Keynesian and 'classical' models drawn on the basis of the wage rigidity assumption! The focus of attention in the recent literature has, however, shifted away from a Keynes or 'classics' classification to a distinction between Keynesian and neoclassical models on the basis of their different treatments of the capital market. However, on the basis of our previous experience, it would be wise to examine this terminology more closely.

Neoclassical or perfect-market models are now characterized as those models in which there is a perfect market for capital; either for real capital goods themselves or for the equity value of the capital goods, i.e. in the equities market. (There is obviously an important difference between assuming a perfect market for equities and a perfect market for real capital – both newly-produced and existing – and we will take up the issue below.) The defining characteristic of a perfect-market model is that the marginal product of capital is equated to the real cost of capital in equilibrium (Benavie,1977; Sargent, 1979:10). By contrast, the Keynesian model is characterized by the absence of such a perfect capital market and the consequent divergence between the marginal product of capital and the real cost of capital. Sargent (1979:11) rationalizes the existence of this discrepancy by assuming that firms are not allowed to trade in equities. The existence of this divergence provides a rationale for the derivation of an investment demand function in the Keynesian model that does not arise in the neoclassical model.

However, in view of the previous discussion of the relationship between the natural and market rates of interest, the divergence between these two rates is not novel. As we know, such a distinction lies behind the saving–investment analysis of the Wicksell-type model employed in the 'Keynes versus classics' debate. In addition the dispute over forced saving, i.e. whether fictitious capital (money) could create real capital is of long standing within neoclassical theory (Schumpeter,1954:724–5), so it is difficult to see how the divergence between the marginal product of capital (the natural rate) and the market rate of interest (or any other measure of the real cost of capital) can be described as Keynesian.

To remain consistent with the tradition of these ideas it therefore seems advisable to acknowledge that we are dealing here with the short-period (disequilibrium) and long-period solutions to a Wicksell-type neoclassical model. This much is apparent when we consider the conceptual difficulties exposed by Benavie (1977) when he proposes to add clay capital to the neoclassical model or putty capital to the Keynesian model so as to produce a more general model! This exercise appears to suffer from a number of conceptual oversights. To see this, recall that the neoclassical or long-period solution requires that real capital be treated as value capital (putty) as in the Wicksellian model discussed in chapter 2. The neo-Walrasian model of chapter 3, by contrast, treats capital as an array of machines (clay). As we noted in chapter 2, the concern with 'putty–clay' or 'jelly' by neoclassical theorists represented an attempt to reconcile the homogeneous nature of financial or value capital with the heterogeneous nature of real capital. But the capital debate revealed that it is not possible to produce a hybrid model which generates both the long-period solution of the Wicksellian model and (by comparison) the short-period solution of the neo-Walrasian model. The two theoretical structures are quite different and are, if anything, distinguished by their different treatments of capital, i.e. as putty *or* clay; they cannot be combined into a more general framework. The models presented by Benavie and Sargent should therefore be interpreted as dealing with short and long-period solutions to a Wicksellian general equilibrium model. Calling the short-period solution to such a model Keynesian and the long-period solution neoclassical is only going to prolong the confusion generated by the 'Keynes versus classics' debate.

Nevertheless, the relationship between the markets for real capital, money and equities, implied by the savings–investment analysis of the early models of the neoclassical synthesis, now received attention either under the guise of the Keynesian investment function or as part of the analysis of the transmission mechanism. The portfolio balance analysis popularized by Tobin, and now embraced by almost all monetary theorists, plays a key role and offers a modern restatement of Wicksell's analysis. To illustrate this argument we will now examine a modern restatement of the neoclassical synthesis due to Sargent (1979). The objective will be to highlight the Wicksellian-type neoclassical features of the analysis and to relate them to Tobin's portfolio theory so as to prepare the ground for an explicit examination of his analysis in the following section. As far as possible the notation of previous sections will be retained.

THE WICKSELL CONNECTION RESTATED: SARGENT

In contrast to earlier statements of the neoclassical synthesis, more recent versions take explicit account of the role of capital. The following is an illustration, from Sargent (1979:18,79), of the long-period equilibrium solution of such a model. The version of the model presented here includes only those features relevant to the discussion. The role of the government, for example, which is included by Sargent, is here omitted. Note also that the model is based on the assumption that only a single good is produced (Sargent,1979:6), so the neoclassical 'parables' do at least apply. The model consists of seven equations:

Sargent's Wicksellian model

$$y \quad = \quad y(K, N) \tag{5.1}$$

$$y_N \quad = \quad w/p \tag{5.2}$$

$$N \quad = \quad N(w/p) \tag{5.3}$$

$$y_K \quad = \quad (r + \delta) \tag{5.4}$$

$$M/p \quad = \quad m(r, y) \tag{5.5}$$

$$C \quad = \quad C(r, y) \tag{5.6}$$

$$y \quad = \quad C + I \tag{5.7}$$

The endogenous variables of this model are N, w/p, y, C, I, r and p while the exogenous variables are K, M and δ (depreciation). The interesting points to note are, firstly, that the marginal product of capital y_K is equal to the cost of capital (the rate of interest plus the rate of depreciation) but Sargent does not distinguish between natural and money rates of interest. The forces of thrift are captured in expression (5.6) and by implication the *natural* rate of interest is included in the money market, expression (5.5). Secondly, there is no investment demand function other than that implied by expression (5.4). The latter embodies the same analytical principles used to derive expression (5.2) which is usually referred to as the demand for labour function.[1] It is difficult to see, therefore, in what sense this model lacks a demand for capital (investment) function. (See Garegnani's (1978:346) discussion.) Finally, the equilibrium solution obviously implies that when $y_K = r + \delta$ saving equals investment (expression 5.7); that is, when the marginal product of capital equals the cost of capital.

The short-period solution to the model now requires that we allow $y_K \neq r + \delta$ and that we pay particular attention to the portfolio balance of households. When the possibility that $y_K \neq r + \delta$ exists, such an occurrence is usually rationalized on the basis that a perfect market does not exist in which firms could trade capital at each moment so as to maintain the equality $y_K = r + \delta$. Hence it is possible that $y_K > r + \delta$ and firms will then demand more capital. It is also implied that when $y_K < r + \delta$ firms will seek to run down their capital stock (Chick, 1973:91–102). In this respect it is often not clearly stated whether firms are dealing in equities or real capital.

The so-called Keynesian investment demand function then relates firms' demand for capital to the gap between the marginal product of capital and the cost of capital (Sargent, 1979:10). That is, we replace (5.4) with:

$$I = I\left[\frac{y_K - (r + \delta)}{r}\right] \tag{5.4'}$$

which can be written more compactly as:

$$I = I(q - 1) \tag{5.4'}$$

where

$$q = \left[\frac{y_K - (r + \delta)}{r}\right] + 1$$

1. The notation used is

$$y_N \equiv \frac{\partial y}{\partial N}$$

But as Davidson (1967,1983) has explained, there are good reasons why we should not consider these functions to be demand curves. Nevertheless they are so construed in neoclassical theory.

Notice that if $q = 1$, i.e. if $y_K = r + \delta$ then $I = 0$ and (5.4′) falls away to be replaced by (5.4). Further insight into the role of expression (5.4′) in the model is obtained if we examine the portfolio decisions lying behind expression (5.5). It is here that the relationship between the monetary and real sectors is analysed in terms of a portfolio balance decision. It is usually assumed that, in addition to money, two other assets may be held by households but not by firms. These are a savings bond issued by the government and equities issued by firms to finance investment (Sargent, 1979:11). Bonds earn a rate of interest, r, and if considered to be perfect substitutes for equities they must generate the same rate of return or they would not be held. The bond rate of interest is therefore the rate to be used in discounting the firms' net cash flow ('profits') to determine the value of firms' equities.

The 'profits' paid out in the form of dividends by the firms, at an instant in time, s, are given by:

$$p(s)y(s) - w(s)N(s) - \delta p(s)K(s)$$

The nominal value of firms' equities at instant t, denoted by $V(t)$, is then:

$$V(t) = \int_t^\infty [p(s)y(s) - w(s)N(s) - \delta p(s)K(s)]e^{-r(s-t)}\,ds$$

Ignoring the anticipated rate of inflation and assuming the firms and households expect the price and wage levels to follow the paths:

$$p(s) = p(t)e^{(s-t)}; \quad w(s) = w(t)e^{(s-t)}$$

and also assuming that the rate of real dividend will remain unchanged over time at the current rate, it follows that:

$$V(t) = [p(t)y(t) - w(t)N(t) - \delta p(t)K(t)] \int_t^\infty e^{-r(s-t)}\,ds$$

which reduces to:[2]

$$V(t) = \frac{p(t)y(t) - w(t)N(t) - \delta p(t)K(t)}{r}$$

The latter expression can then be rewritten as:[3]

$$\frac{p(t)[y(t) - (w(t)/p(t))N(t) - y_K(t)K(t)]}{r}$$

2.

$$\int_t^\infty e^{-r(s-t)}\,ds = -\frac{1}{r}e^{-r(s-t)} \Big|_t^\infty = \frac{1}{r}$$

3. The simplification is obtained by adding and subtracting the term $p(t)y_K(t)K(t)$ and noting that:

$$\frac{-(r + \delta)p(t)K(t)}{r} + p(t)K(t) = -\delta p(t)K(t)$$

$$+ \frac{[y_K(t) - (r + \delta)]p(t)K(t)}{r} + p(t)K(t)$$

Applying the marginal productivity theory of distribution reduces the first term in the expression to zero. We may note in passing that this illustrates that the marginal productivity theory of distribution is not an independent part of the analysis but an integral part of a unified neoclassical theory of output and distribution (Milgate, 1982:41–6). The expression then simplifies to:

$$V(t) = \left[\frac{y_K - (r + \delta)}{r} + 1 \right] p(t)K(t)$$

which in turn reduces to:

$$q = \frac{V(t)}{p(t)K(t)} \tag{5.4''}$$

and is simply a restatement of the argument which appears in the investment function (5.4′). It now states that investment, or the demand for capital, is related directly to the ratio of the value of equities to the replacement value of the capital stock. As Sargent (1979:13) points out, this is precisely how Tobin (1969:326) defines his Keynesian investment schedule. But before we turn to Tobin's analysis, additional features of the above model will repay attention.

The portfolio decisions of households are analysed in terms of a wealth constraint at each point in time and households allocate their wealth between money, bonds and equities. If the latter two assets are treated as perfect substitutes, the wealth constraint is written in the usual fashion as:

$$(V + B + M)/p = W$$

and the division between M and $B + V$ is described by the asset demand functions:

$$M^D/p = m(r, y, W)$$
$$(B^D + V^D)/p = b(r, y, W)$$

such that for each value of r, y and W, total wealth is allocated between M and $B + V$. Portfolio equilibrium requires that:

$$M^D/p = M/p$$
$$(B^D + V^D)/p = (B + V)/p$$

Thus, if the money market is in equilibrium, so is the bonds/equities market. Now this condition is described by Sargent (1979:14) as Walras's Law but it is clearly *not* equivalent to Walras's Law as defined in a neo-Walrasian model because the commodity market is excluded. On reflection this is not surprising as the theoretical foundations of the model sketched by Sargent are Wicksellian and not neo-Walrasian so Walras's Law as defined by Lange does not apply. Nevertheless, misuse of the neo-Walrasian terminology in this fashion probably accounts for the belief in a unique IS–LM structure as, for example, in the paper by McCaleb and Sellon (1980). Getting back to the Wicksellian interpretation of IS–LM analysis presented by Sargent, it must be acknowledged that Walras's Law does not apply to such a model. This is a point that many Keynesians have made over the years without apparently acknowledging the Wicksellian pedigree of their analysis. For example, imposing the wealth constraint implies that the money and bonds/equity market-clearing loci coincide and this is a common feature of many textbook versions of the IS–LM model (Dornbusch and Fischer, 1981:109–10).

But even if equities and bonds are not treated as perfect substitutes so that the yield on equities differs from that on bonds, the analysis proceeeds in a similar fashion. It differs only in that the market-clearing loci for assets (money and bonds/equities) no longer coincide and we require a separate analysis of each asset market along the lines sketched by Dornbusch (1976:105–10). Interestingly, this is the approach favoured by Brunner and Meltzer. As Dornbusch (1976:105) notes, 'A key feature of the B–M model is a distinction between debt and real capital; capital, *or equity*, and debt are imperfect substitutes and are therefore not aggregated into "bonds" in the manner that has proved so convenient in the Hicksian apparatus summarized in the LM schedule.' As we will see, Brunner and Meltzer make much of this issue to distinguish their work from that of the Keynesians *and* other monetarists. But as it turns out, the distinction is not theoretically significant. Although the return on bonds and the return on equities will diverge in the Brunner–Meltzer model in the short period, it is the discrepancy between the return on real capital and the yield on equities which operates as before to link the real and monetary sectors in the fashion of the Wicksellian distinction between natural and market rates of interest. The failure to draw a clear distinction between real capital and equity capital is, however, important because it confirms that it is *value* capital that is employed in these models. The role of these features in the Tobin and Brunner–Meltzer models can now be examined.

THE WICKSELL CONNECTION CONTINUED: TOBIN AND BRUNNER-MELTZER

In the discussion so far we have established that the defining characteristic of Wicksellian analysis is that capital is treated as *value* capital.

The marginal *value* product of capital then determines, along with *real* saving, the natural rate of interest. In Wicksell's analysis a discrepancy between the natural rate and the market rate in the short-period then induces forced saving (or dissaving), and a change in the price level.

The modern restatement of this analysis is in terms of portfolio balance theory. The portfolio decisions of households are analysed in terms of a wealth constraint containing money, bonds, and equities. If the latter two are considered to be good or perfect substitutes, their common rate of return is compared directly to the marginal product of capital in the same way that the market rate is compared to the natural rate by Wicksell. Whether equities and bonds are treated as perfect substitutes is therefore not the important issue.[4] The important link concerns the relationship between the marginal product of capital and the rate of return on equities, which may or may not *always* equal the rate on bonds – as it would if the two were perfect substitutes. Of course, if it is assumed that real capital and equities are perfect substitutes then their rates of return would never diverge and the link between the real and monetary forces would be broken and the Wicksellian connection lost. The central role of the Wicksell connection can now be illustrated by considering Tobin's general equilibrium analysis.

Tobin's money–capital model

The model(s) presented here are taken from Tobin (1969) but they embody the fundamental properties of the analysis that underlies all his work. The notation used by Tobin will be retained as it is sufficiently similar to that used in previous sections to allow for easy comparison. Unlike the previous models, however, Tobin concentrates exclusively on the analysis of the assets markets, leaving implicit the labour and commodity markets. A simple Tobin (1969) money–capital model contains the following relationships:

> *Wealth definition*
> $$W = qK + \frac{M}{p} \tag{5.8}$$

---

4. An alternative grouping of assets, considered by Tobin (1969:141) to be representative of Keynes's approach, involves money against all financial and physical assets: but see Chick (1973:94).

Balance equations

$$f_1\left(r_K, r_M, \frac{Y}{W}\right)W = qK \tag{5.9}$$

$$f_2\left(r_K, r_M, \frac{Y}{W}\right)W = \frac{M}{p} \tag{5.10}$$

Rate of return equations

$$r_K q = R \text{ or } q = \frac{R}{r_K} \tag{5.11}$$

$$r_M = r_M' - \rho_p^e \tag{5.12}$$

The model represents a single private sector (households) and two assets: money issued by the government to finance budget deficits and homogeneous *physical* capital (Tobin, 1969:326). Other variables are: p, the price of both currently produced capital and consumer goods; r_M and r_K, the real rates of return from holding money and capital; ρ_p^e, the expected rate of change in commodity prices; r_M', the nominal rate of interest on money (usually zero on cash or demand deposits); R, the marginal efficiency of capital relative to replacement cost; Y, income and W, wealth, both measured in goods. The capital stock, K, is not formally defined by Tobin. From the wealth definition, we deduce that $f_1 = 1 - f_2$, so one of the balance equations is redundant, which leaves four equations that are open to various interpretations depending on which four variables are taken as endogenous.

Tobin (1969) offers two interpretations, one of which represents a short-period and the other a long-period solution. For the short-period solution Tobin (1969:329) selects r_K, r_M, W and q as endogenous leaving $K, M, Y, p, R, \rho_p^e, r_M'$ as exogenous. However, before we examine this solution, it is necessary to consider some of the features of Tobin's analysis that obscure its links to the Wicksellian version of neoclassical theory. In this respect it is interesting to note that in two papers Tobin (1961:226, 1982:179) refers explicitly to the similarity between his analysis of the deviation between the rate of return on equities and the marginal *productivity* of capital, and Wicksell's distinction between the market and natural rates of interest.

The first point of importance is Tobin's definition of R as the *marginal efficiency* of capital relative to replacement cost. On other occasions, however, he defines R either as the *marginal productivity* of capital[5] or as the *marginal efficiency* of capital. It seems therefore that these two terms are used synonymously by Tobin. Now in terms of neoclassical theory, this is perhaps not unreasonable, because the function of the marginal productivity of capital determines the investment, or demand for capital, schedule. But in terms of Keynes's definition of the marginal efficiency of capital, the investment schedule is not derived directly from the marginal productivity of capital. In terms of Keynes's definition the marginal efficiency of capital is the rate of discount, *d*, which will equate the expected profit stream (if we assume a scrap value of zero and that profits accrue at the end of each year for a period of *n* years), and the price of new equipment, p_K. That is, the marginal efficiency of capital is found by solving the following for *d*:

$$p_K = \sum_{i=1}^{n} \frac{\pi_i}{(1 + d)^i}$$

In terms of this definition the marginal productivity of the type of capital in question will play a role in determining the profit stream π_i but there is no one-to-one relationship between it and the marginal *efficiency* of capital, *d* (Chick, 1973:92). By treating the two concepts as equivalent, Tobin embraces the neoclassical concept of capital.

This conclusion is confirmed by an examination of Tobin's continual slippage between the concepts of real physical capital and equity or value capital. As we have already remarked, within the Wicksellian brand of neoclassical theory, capital must be treated as a fund of *value* which at the same time must somehow embody itself in real physical capital. Tobin deals with this feature by identifying equities with real capital while at the same time allowing the equity valuation to deviate from the replacement cost of capital in the short period (or the marginal product of capital to deviate from the rate of return on equities). This enables him to use the term capital in an ambiguous sense in which it is seldom clear whether he is talking about real physical capital or equity (value) capital, as the following extract from Tobin (1963:384, emphasis added) makes clear (with comments by Chick (1973:101) in square brackets). Notice especially that Tobin refers to the marginal *productivity* of capital:

If investors [shareholders or businessmen?] are content with a low rate of

5. See, for example, Brainard and Tobin (1968:353,365) and the quote by Chick (1973:92) where Tobin again refers to *R* as the marginal *productivity* of capital. There is also the view of Lindahl and others that the marginal efficiency of capital is equivalent to Wicksell's concept of the natural rate. But, as we have already pointed out, that interpretation is not correct.

return on equity in real capital, relative to its [the capital's] *marginal productivity*, their bids for existing capital [equity shares or machines?] will cause its valuation [the valuation of capital equipment] to exceed its replacement cost; the difference will be an incentive to expand production of capital goods. But if investors require a relatively high rate of return on equity in real capital, the valuation of capital [goods] in place will be low relative to its replacement cost and will deter further production of investment goods. The course of economic activity, then, depends on the difference between two rates of return on ownership of capital [the return to shareholders and the return to firms, one might think]. One is the anticipated *marginal productivity of capital* [goods] determined by technology, factor supplies, and expectations about the economy. This cannot be controlled by the managers of money and public debt, except in the indirect sense that if they somehow successfully control the economy they control all economic magnitudes. The second rate of return on capital equity [equity now] is that rate at which the public would be willing to hold the existing stock of capital [?], valued at current prices. It is this rate of return, the *supply price of capital* [a rate, not the price of newly produced capital goods], which the monetary and debt authorities may hope to influence through changing the supplies and yields of assets and debts that compete with *real capital*, for a place in the portfolios and balance sheets of economic units.

Now apart from the ambiguity over real and equity capital Tobin is here clearly describing the relationship

$$q = \frac{R}{r_K}$$

In this case R is being referred to as the marginal *productivity* of capital (relative to replacement cost) and r_K, is, as usual, the rate of return on equity. The relationship between R and r_K described here by Tobin is also identical with Sargent's derivation of the so-called Keynesian investment function in expression (5.4′) above. Notice also that we are comparing the marginal productivity of capital with a rate of interest, r_K, which means that the marginal *value* productivity should be used (Howard, 1983:107). This can be seen from Tobin's alternative definition of q as $q = V/K$ where V = market value of equity and K the stock of capital at *replacement cost* (Brainard and Tobin,1968:353,355). This result is also equivalent to expression (5.4″) derived from Sargent's neoclassical (Keynesian) model.

The link between the monetary and real sectors in Tobin's analysis is therefore dependent on the relationship between R, the marginal productivity of capital (or the *natural* rate of return) and r_K, the return on equities (or the *market* rate of return). Brainard and Tobin (1968:357) describe the relationship as follows:

An increase in q, the market valuation, can occur as a result of an increase in the marginal efficiency of capital r [defined as the marginal productivity of capital on p.365], i.e. as a result of events exogenous to the financial sector. But an increase in q may also occur as a consequence of financial events that reduce r_K, the yield that investors require to hold equity capital. Indeed this is the sole linkage in the model through which financial events, including monetary policies, affect the real economy.

This relationship between the real and monetary rates of return is strictly within the Wicksellian tradition. These two rates may diverge in the short period, but in the long period they are brought into equality and we enter the realms of Tobin's (1955) dynamic aggregative (neoclassical) model. The relationship between these two aspects of the model can now be presented more formally in terms of the derivation of the short- and long-period solutions to Tobin's model.

The model presented here represents an adaptation or extension of Tobin's (1969) simple model to include an explicit analysis of the goods sector, along the lines suggested by Pettenati (1977). Despite Pettenati's claims, however, this does not make the model Keynesian rather than neoclassical. It differs from Wicksell's neoclassical model only in that income is not fixed at full employment. In Wicksell, all the adjustment fell on prices, i.e. inflation or deflation resulted, while the Keynesian interpretation allows for variable output at a fixed price level; recall the discussion in chapter 4. The equations of the model are as follows:

$$f_2\left(r_K, r_M, \frac{\Upsilon}{\dfrac{R}{r_K}K + \dfrac{M}{p}}\right)\left(\frac{R}{r_K}K + \frac{M}{p}\right) = \frac{M}{p} \tag{5.13}$$

$$\Upsilon = \left[a + I_n + I_n\left(\frac{R}{r_K} - 1\right)\right]\Bigg/(1 - b) \tag{5.14}$$

The first equation is a type of LM curve and is obtained by substitution from expressions (5.8)–(5.12) (Tobin, 1969:329). The second equation is a version of the IS curve similar to that suggested by Pettenati (1977) or as derived earlier from Sargent's model, expression (5.4′).[6] In terms of this interpretation and extension of the model, we have two equations in the variables r_K and Υ, with R, r_M,

6. Depreciation is ignored here. Expression (5.14) is derived from the following expressions:

$$C = a + b\Upsilon, \quad I = I_n + I_n(q - 1); \quad q = R/r_K, \quad \Upsilon = C + I.$$

In deriving (5.13) the price level p can be treated as exogenous, as it is by Tobin, or as the function $p = p(\bar{w}, y)$ as suggested by Pettenati (1977:366). The latter expression embodies the usual wage rigidity assumption of Keynesian economics.

K, M/p, a, b and I_n treated as exogenous. The variable I_n is the rate of investment or growth in the capital stock that would just keep the marginal productivity of capital at its natural rate R_n. Similarly Y_n is the level of income at which saving would just suffice to keep the capital stock consistent with the natural rate of growth of the economy (Tobin, 1969:331). Investment at this rate is compatible with $q = 1$ or $r_K = R_n$, the natural rate of interest.

The implications of this analysis and its relationship to the concepts of real saving and investment can be illustrated with reference to Figure 5.1. Expressions (5.13) and (5.14) are graphed as the LM and IS curves respectively and illustrate a short-period equilibrium solution in which $q < 1$; i.e. $r_K^e > R_n$. To see what is happening here note that both E and G lie on the IS curve which implies an equality between saving and investment. At G the forces of productivity and thrift (saving) determine the natural rate of interest, R_n, at the level of income Y_n. This implies that $q = 1$, i.e. $r_K = R_n$ so that $I = I_n$ which, from the definition $Y = C + I_n$ implies that $S = I_n$. That is, at Y_n, saving just suffices to increase the capital stock at the natural growth rate of the economy. Now at an income level lower than Y_n, say at Y_e, the natural rate of investment, I_n, would exceed the actual level of saving associated with Y_e. Therefore, the savings–investment equality requires a q less than one (Tobin, 1969:331). From $Y = C + I$ it follows that $S = I_n + I_n(q = 1)$. Hence at $Y_e < Y_n$, I_n will exceed S unless $q < 1$. In terms of the analysis of real saving and investment presented in Figure 5.2 we have the following situation. (See Sargent (1979:25) for a similar diagram.) At the level of income

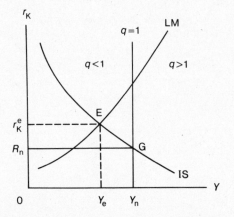

Fig. 5.1 Tobin's Wicksellian version of IS–LM

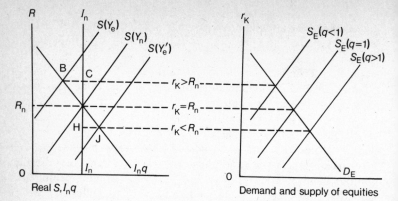

Fig. 5.2 Short- and long-period equilibrium of saving and investment in the Tobin model

Y_e the natural rate of investment I_n would exceed saving unless $q < 1$ as at point B. Similarly at a level of income greater than Y_n, say Y_e, the natural rate of investment would be insufficient to match saving unless $q > 1$. The relationship between R_n and r_K in Tobin's analysis therefore mimics precisely the relationship between the natural and market rates of interest in Wicksell's neoclassical model.[7] Consequently the wheel once again turns full circle to the neoclassical concept of capital and all that it entails. Tobin's analysis of short-period equilibrium simply represents a restatement of the Wicksellian neoclassical tradition. This conclusion is further confirmed by the specification of the long-period solution to the above model, which requires that $r_K = R_n$ so that E and G coincide (Figure 5.1), and Y_n implies full employment equilibrium in the labour market (Tobin, 1969:331). The market rate, r_K, is then equal to the natural rate, R_n, determined by the marginal productivity of capital, as in Wicksell. The only break with Wicksell is that output rather than prices is allowed to vary in the short period, and it is on this basis that the analysis qualifies for the title of Keynesian in the eyes of most observers. Despite this, the model remains strictly Wicksellian.

A Brunner–Meltzer model

In the discussion of Tobin's theoretical framework it was shown that

---

7. The only difference is that the notion of forced saving no longer arises because the level of income is changing and shifting the savings function. This latter property reflects the Keynesian feature introduced by Hicks.

the analysis continued to reflect the Wicksellian concept of capital and the notions of real saving and investment. In fact, Tobin's famous q-theory of investment is little more than a restatement of Wicksell's cumulative process in terms of output rather than prices. The objective in this section will be to show that Brunner–Meltzer employ exactly the same relationship between the rate of return on equity and the return on real capital. In this respect it is again important to point out that the distinction between bonds and equities as imperfect substitutes, of which Brunner–Meltzer make such a fuss (Dornbusch, 1976:105), is not the central issue. Rather the central issues concerns the relationship between the rates of return on equity and on real capital. In this respect it should also be noted that, like Tobin, Brunner–Meltzer do not make an adequate distinction between equity (value capital) and real capital. This failing is a symptom of the Wicksellian pedigree of the analysis which we will now proceed to demonstrate. This demonstration provides additional support for Benjamin Friedman's (1978) conclusion that the Tobin and Brunner–Meltzer models are essentially the same; they both embody the same (Wicksellian) theoretical structure.

The discussion and notation used here will be based on Dornbusch (1976) and Brunner–Meltzer (1976b:150–82) as this is somewhat simpler than the Brunner–Meltzer (1976a:67–103) notation but offers a faithful translation of their analysis, at least on the points of concern to us here. As Dornbusch (1976:105–9) points out, the Brunner–Meltzer model contains three assets in the wealth constraint: money, debt (bonds) and capital (equity). As noted earlier the distinction between real capital and equity is not clearly drawn. The analysis of these assets markets can be summarized in terms of the following equations (Brunner–Meltzer, 1976b:166):

$$B + vS + PK = W \quad \text{(wealth)} \tag{5.15}$$

$$B(i, P, p, e) = B \quad \text{(money)} \tag{5.16}$$

$$S(i, P, p, e) = vS \quad \text{(bonds)} \tag{5.17}$$

$$K(i, P, p, e) = PK \quad \text{(capital equity)} \tag{5.18}$$

The variables are defined as follows: B = monetary base; vS = value of public debt; PK = value of the capital stock; W = nominal wealth; i = yield on equity; S = the number of income streams yielding one dollar a year indefinitely; P = price of capital; p = price of output; e = real rental on capital.

There is a superficial resemblance between these equations and expressions (5.8)–(5.10) in the Tobin model. For example, both involve a wealth constraint and balance equations and Tobin (1969) also considers a model with three assets – money, bonds and equities

– although he treats bonds and equities as perfect substitutes. By contrast, Brunner–Meltzer treat bonds and equities as imperfect substitutes. Hence in the Brunner–Meltzer model there are three balance equations compared with two in the Tobin model. But this distinction is of no significance because the important analytical feature of both models is the link between the rate of return on equities and *real physical capital*. In Tobin's model this link is formalized in terms of the definition of q in expression (5.11). In the Brunner–Meltzer model the link is less explicit, but it is nonetheless there in the relationship between P, p and e. This is most readily apparent from Dornbusch's (1976:107) definition of the rate of return on equity as:

$$r = \frac{pe(w/p, K)}{P} = \left(\frac{p}{P}\right) e \qquad (5.19)$$

An analysis of this relationship then reveals that it plays the same role as expression (5.11) in Tobin's model, i.e. it plays the same role as Tobin's q.

To illustrate this claim note that Brunner–Meltzer impose the conditions $P = p$ and $i = e$ as long-period (steady state) conditions (Dornbusch, 1976:115; Brunner–Meltzer, 1976b:167n21). Brunner–Meltzer (1976a:72) derive this result by setting $i = (p/P)e + \pi$, ignoring inflation, π, and setting $p = P$ in long-period equilibrium to produce:

$$r = i = e \qquad (5.20)$$

which states simply that the long-period equilibrium requires equality of the rates of return on equities and bonds (debt) with the *real rental on capital*. But the *real rental on capital* is, in equilibrium, equal to the *marginal product of capital*; in the same way that the real wage is equal to the marginal product of labour in equilibrium. Thus, as in Tobin's analysis, the Brunner–Meltzer model defines long-period equilibrium in terms of the equality of the return on equities and the marginal productivity of capital in strictly neoclassical–Wicksellian fashion. Furthermore, outside of a long-period equilibrium solution r need not equal e because p and P need not coincide. Brunner–Meltzer (1976a:74) describe the relationship between short- and long-period situations as follows:

The asset price level [value of equities] is distinct from the price of new production [reproduction cost]. Costs of adjustment associated with the acquisition of real capital [machines], and costs of acquiring information about market opportunities, assure that p and P are generally not equal. In full long-period adjustment to a *steady state*, with all costs variable, all opportunities realized, and all anticipations equal to actual values, existing capital [equity] sells at reproduction cost, and the real return [marginal product of capital = real rental rate] to real capital [machines] equals the expected return e.[8]

If we did not know better, the above description could refer to the Brainard and Tobin explanation of the values of q in short- and long-period equilibrium. The Brunner–Meltzer model therefore embodies precisely the same link between the monetary and real sectors as does Tobin. Furthermore, this link represents a restatement of Wicksell's distinction between the market and natural rates of interest. It therefore suffers from all of the anomalies associated with the Wicksellian version of neoclassical analysis that were discussed in chapter 2.

A question of methodology

Before leaving the Tobin and Brunner–Meltzer theoretical frame-work it is instructive to examine the methodological implications of their use of the Wicksellian theme. In chapter 2 it was noted that the neoclassical 'parables' do at least apply in a one-commodity model and, interestingly, some neoclassical writers explicitly make this assumption when presenting their models. Sargent's (1979:6) discussion of these issues is a case in point. But if the analysis of the Wicksell connection is only valid for a one-commodity model, how are its conclusions to be applied to problems of policy in a multi-commodity world? There is clearly an important methodological issue at stake here.

The neoclassical response has been to treat the conclusions of the one-commodity model as useful 'parables' reflecting the fundamentals of interest rate theory. But if the one-commodity model is to generate useful 'parables' the assumptions used must only be simplifying or heuristic assumptions. This, of course, is precisely *not the case*. The assumptions used to generate the neoclassical 'parables' are clearly highly restrictive, i.e. the one-commodity model, and yet *necessary*. The method of successive approximation cannot therefore be applied, as any extension of the model – to include one more commodity for

---

8. Brunner–Meltzer (1976a:72) define e as the anticipated return to real capital. It may therefore not equal the marginal product of capital if anticipations are incorrect. This possibility obviously does not arise in long-period equilibrium as the quote by Brunner–Meltzer indicates. Introducing Rational Expectations would reduce some of the ambiguity about the interpretation of the model in short-period situations by imposing the condition that anticipations are correct on average, i.e. in a stochastic sense.

example – would cause the parables to collapse under the maze of contradictions exposed by the capital debate. Harris (1973:110) therefore concludes that 'no theory based on such foundations can lay claim to validity or generality or even to any significance as a "parable" or illustration of what exists in reality'.

Those Keynesians and monetarists currently exploiting the Wicksell connection are therefore also proceeding on shaky methodological ground. Consequently it comes as something of a surprise to find the new 'classical' economists proceeding in apparent oblivion of the limitations of neoclassical theory.

THE NEW 'CLASSICAL' MACROECONOMICS OR MONETARISM MARK II[9]

The new 'classical' macroeconomics swept into the literature with the claim that only unexpected policy actions would have a real impact on the economy. This conclusion was derived by applying the Rational Expectations hypothesis (REH) to the long-period solution of neoclassical models. Such a step appears to follow naturally from Muth's (1961) definition of expectations as rational if they were 'essentially the same as the predictions of the relevant economic theory', i.e. neoclassical theory. Alternatively, Muth suggested that expectations, in the form of the subjective probability distribution of outcomes, tend to be distributed, for the same information set, about the 'objective' probability distributions of outcomes. On the first definition any evaluation of the new 'classical' macroeconomics must identify the relevant economic theory which is to render expectations rational, e.g. which version of neoclassical general equilibrium theory is relevant? The second definition raises questions concerning the meaning of probability and although the relevance of the statistical foundations of the REH have been challenged by Davidson (1982/3) the issue will not be pursued here (it will be raised again in chapter 8). For the moment we concentrate on the role of neoclassical theory in the new 'classical' macroeconomics.

In this respect the 'relevant economic theory' turns out to be one or other version of *neoclassical* theory. As a number of observers have noted, e.g. Maddock and Carter (1982) and Rogers (1982), results generated by the new 'classical' macroeconomics are derived essentially from the 'relevant' version of neoclassical theory and do not

9. This section is based on Rogers (1982). The term 'monetarism mark II' is due to Tobin (1980).

follow from the REH *per se*. The latter may be applied to other models without producing the conclusions of the new 'classics' school. Once this issue has been clarified it is apparent that the new 'classical' macroeconomics is inevitably linked with the fate of neoclassical economics. It is, therefore, tempting to speculate that Muth's ideas could only have taken root at Chicago where the view that neoclassical theory provides a 'good approximation' to the real economy forms part of the current ideology; it appears to be taken as axiomatic. This theme is taken up again in chapter 6 when we discuss the Chicago view of economics and the implications of the new 'classical' macroeconomics for Chicago-style economics. Seen in this light it appears that the new 'classical' school may prove to be the undoing of this ideology by pushing it to a logically absurd conclusion.

As we have seen, the new 'classical' macroeconomics is inevitably involved with the theoretical and methodological fate of neoclassical economics. From this perspective an examination of some of the models used by the new 'classical' school proves particularly illuminating.

We begin with the macroeconomic models of which the Sargent and Wallace (1975,1976) models are perhaps the best known. These models are acknowledged to be of an *ad hoc* nature but they nevertheless serve to illustrate both essential features of the neoclassical synthesis and the limited role of the REH in the new 'classical' macroeconomics. As Shiller (1978) has illustrated, a simple version of the Sargent and Wallace framework can be produced by adding an IS–LM component to an aggregate supply function that embodies the natural rate hypothesis. A four-equation model of the following form results:

$$y_t = b_1 + b_2 r_t + b_3 G_t + b_4 Z_t + u_{1t} \tag{5.21}$$

$$M_t = P_t + c_1 y_t + c_2 r_t + u_{2t} \tag{5.22}$$

$$y_t = y_{nt} + \gamma(P_t - P_t^*) + u_{3t}, \qquad \gamma > 0 \tag{5.23}$$

$$P_t^* = E(P_t|I_t) \tag{5.24}$$

The variables are defined as follows: $P_t = $ log of price level; $y_t = $ log of aggregate output; $y_{nt} = $ log of aggregate output corresponding to the natural rate of unemployment; $r_t = $ nominal interest rate, $M_t = $ log of the money supply; $G_t = $ government expenditure, Z_t is an exogenous variable, u_{1t}, u_{2t} and u_{3t} are unforecastable error terms and b_1, b_2, b_3, b_4, c_1 and c_2 are fixed coefficients. The coefficient, γ may be related to the variance of P. The expected price level is given by P_t^* and is equated to the mathematical expectation of P_t conditional on the information available at time t, I_t. Included in I_t is the knowledge of the model (5.21)–(5.23). The model is written in log–linear form to avoid any complications with the calculation of mathematical expectations.

The first point to note about this model is that the aggregate supply function, expression (5.23), embodies the standard 'classical' analysis of the labour market as presented in any macroeconomics text that reflects the principles of the neoclassical synthesis. For example, Branson (1979) and Levacic and Rebmann (1982) present models that generate either a vertical supply curve ('classical' case) or a supply curve with a positive slope (Keynesian case!) depending on the assumptions made about the behaviour of money wages.

The Keynesian case emerges only on the introduction of the wage rigidity or money illusion assumptions. But the new 'classical' school is not prepared to accept the idea that these *ad hoc* assumptions are at all relevant. In a world of rational, pre-reconciled choices (by the auctioneer in the tâtonnement process?) there is no room for the unintended or involuntary, for malfunctioning and disorder. A neo-classical model, rigorously interpreted, implies the full employment of all resources and this is the view that lies behind the use of the natural rate hypothesis in equation (5.23). However, as we have seen, there is no coherent theoretical foundation for such a hypothesis within neoclassical theory – particularly in the case of the long-period equilibrium to which the concept of a natural rate supposedly applies. Despite a widespread belief to the contrary, the natural rate hypothesis has no coherent theoretical foundation within neoclassical theory. This is especially true of neo-Walrasian theory, despite Friedman's definition of the natural rate in a Walrasian setting, and this issue will be taken up in chapter 6. The discussion in chapters 2 and 4 has indicated that the natural rate of unemployment can be defined in terms of Wicksellian theory only in the context of a one-commodity world.

This brings us to the implications of the REH in the above model. The rational expectations assumption is expressed in equation (5.24). To see what it means, note that an aggregate demand function is obtained from equations (5.21) and (5.22) in the usual fashion. That is, we then have an aggregate demand function in P_t and y_t, with the exogenous variables being summarized by X_t; the error terms have simply been dropped.

$$y_t = -dP_t + eX_t \qquad (5.25)$$

Together with the aggregate supply curve the model can then be solved for P_t in terms of P_t^* and y_{nt} to give an expression of the form:

$$P_t = \frac{1}{\gamma + d}\left(\gamma P_t^* + eX_t - y_{nt} - u_{3t}\right) \qquad (5.26)$$

In terms of the REH the 'relevant economic theory' is the model used to generate P_t. It should be noted though that many applications of the REH do not involve the claim that individuals actually know the model and the probability distributions, but only that they act *as if* they had this knowledge. This view is open to the objections to be discussed in chapter 6. Hence the conditional expectation of P_t, in terms of expression (5.24) is given by:

$$P_t^* = E\left[\frac{1}{\gamma + d}(\gamma P_t^* + eX_t - y_{nt} - u_{3t})\right] \tag{5.27}$$

or

$$P_t^* = \frac{1}{\gamma + d}[\gamma P_t^* + eE(X_t) - y_{nt}] \tag{5.28}$$

Subtracting (5.28) from (5.26) and substituting the result into (5.23), produces, on rearrangement:

$$y_t - y_{nt} = \frac{\gamma}{\gamma + d}\{e[X_t - E(X_t)] - u_{3t}\} + u_{3t} \tag{5.29}$$

Expression (5.29) then embodies the conclusion that deviations of y_t from y_{nt} are dependent only on the unsystematic component of government policy (G_t and M_t are included in X_t). In effect the deviation of y_t from y_{nt} is purely random because $E[X_t - E(X_t)] = 0$ for any systematic policy rule. What we are left with is a random distribution of y_t about the natural level y_{nt}. In other words, all we have is a stochastic version of the standard 'classical' solution to a typical model of the neoclassical synthesis. In such a model the assumption of perfect foresight generates a vertical aggregate supply curve and the Sargent and Wallace analysis differs from this result only in the trivial sense that they use a stochastic version of the model. Models with this property exhibit certainty equivalence and it is difficult to see what purpose they can possibly serve (Maddock and Carter, 1982). For a visual presentation of this result see Burton (1982). These models exhibit the property of certainty equivalence in the sense that the analysis of the model under the assumption of perfect foresight results in the same solution as the stochastic version of the model under Rational Expectations (Begg, 1982:51–2). In particular, the policy conclusions are implicit in the 'classical' solution to the model and hence are independent of its stochastic Rational Expectations interpretation.

Now the debate between the Keynesians, monetarists and new 'classical' school is, if anything, over the slope of the long-period aggregate supply curve and this issue is not even addressed by using a model in which the aggregate supply curve is *assumed* to be vertical.

Furthermore the debate has added to the confusion over the distinction between long- and short-period equilibrium. Consider Shiller's (1978:11) comment that: 'The idea that deterministic monetary policy should have no effect on output in the long-period is a familiar argument of classical economics. Rational expectations models of this sort [Sargent and Wallace] make this true for the short-period as well.' The difficulty here, of course, is that the models of the neoclassical synthesis fail to make clear what notion of long-period equilibrium is being employed. Is it the Wicksellian notion defined in terms of a uniform rate of return or is it simply a redefinition of a neo-Walrasian market-clearing solution as long-period? These issues are seldom clarified so we can only speculate that models with a fixed capital stock – from which both 'classical' long-period and Keynesian results are derived – involve the Wicksellian approach. The discussion in chapters 4 and 5 would suggest that this is often a reasonable interpretation.

The above illustrations are typical of the kind of analysis encountered in the literature on the neoclassical synthesis. However, most neoclassical theorists regard such models as *ad hoc* and not worthy of serious attention. Hahn (1982b:36) is particularly harsh in this respect and dismisses these models with the remark that they consist of two or three equations plucked from an elementary micro-text and aggregated on the basis of faith and determination! Sargent and Wallace would seem to sympathize with this view as they recommend that the analysis should be conducted within the framework of a 'properly specified GE model'. But what is a properly specified general equilibrium model? In his conversation with Klamer (1984:70), Sargent is still far from clear and refers only to 'some notion of general equilibrium'. Perhaps Lucas is more specific?

In a well-known paper, Lucas (1975) presents a properly specified general equilibrium model in the guise of a 'fairly standard one-commodity neoclassical growth model'. He then proceeds to find the analogue of its solutions in a model with a continuum of separated markets or 'islands'. The idea behind this abstraction is that in the one-commodity model with a single market there is 'too much' information available to agents. This is perhaps putting it mildly in view of the fact that the future has collapsed into the present in such models (Harcourt, 1976:42). Nevertheless, the idea is to avoid the complete information feature of the original model. Even so trade takes place at market clearing prices. That is, the auctioneer is still employed, it is just that he is 'operating so rapidly that he is not noticed' (Lucas, 1980:711).

This model then serves as a basis for the equilibrium theory of the business cycle. Surprisingly, however, the analysis appears to rest on a new version of the money illusion assumption to generate the cycles. Random errors alone are clearly not sufficient to generate cycles; what is required is some moving average of these errors. To achieve this result it is assumed that agents mistake (temporarily?) a general increase in absolute prices for an increase in the relative price of the good they are selling. This leads them to increase their supply above the planned level. Since on average everyone is making the same mistake, aggregate output rises above what it would have been. In other words households see *wages* rise faster than expected but do not notice *prices* rising faster than expected. Firms notice the reverse! The properties of the 'surprise' supply function derive, therefore, from this asymmetrical gap in perception and are not implications of the REH. If anything this version of the 'illusion assumption' represents the latest attempt to reconcile the static GE model with the cyclical time-series data. An increase in aggregate demand which causes the general price level to rise leads therefore to an increase in output as agents mistake money price increases for real relative price increases. Firms expand their output and workers their supply of labour in the upswing phase of the cycle. The reverse procedure occurs on the downswing. What emerges is a business cycle theory based on the idea of mistakes rationally made! On closer inspection it seems that all this amounts to is another *ad hoc* attempt to generate some slope to the aggregate supply curve; an attempt that has a long tradition in the neoclassical synthesis.

In addition to these observations, the one-commodity model is open to the objections raised in this study. Essentially these amount to the charge that such a model is imaginary and hence incapable of generating empirical conclusions. How then does Lucas interpret these models? Fortunately he has made his views known and they amount to the following.

Along with most other economists Lucas views neoclassical models as highly artificial 'fictions' or abstractions that are patently 'unreal' (Lucas, 1980:711). Yet at the same time they must be capable of *imitating* how actual economies react. It is in this sense that more 'realism' is preferred to less. From these statements it is not entirely clear what Lucas (1980:697, emphasis added) has in mind but the following quote helps to clarify matters:

On this general view of the nature of economic theory then, a *'theory' is not a collection of assertions about the behaviour of the actual economy* but rather an explicit set of instructions for building a parallel or *analogue* system – a *mechanical imitation* economy. A 'good' model, from this point of view, will not be exactly more 'real' than a poor one, but will provide better imitations. Of course, what one means by a 'better imitation' will depend on the particular questions to which one wishes answers.

There are some similarities here with the Hahn rationale for the use of neo-Walrasian general equilibrium theory but more stress is placed on an analogue interpretation. In particular, Lucas appears, from his reliance on analogies, to give the model a theoretical interpretation. The Lucas view seems to be that 'patently artificial' models are best defended on the grounds that useful *analogies* can be drawn between the model and the real economy. There is an important distinction, however, between an analogue model and a model based on analogies (Achinstein, 1968:221–5). Unfortunately, Lucas is not clear on this point because he fails to spell out what these analogies are. Specifically, he does not answer the charge that a one-commodity model cannot lay claim to generality or even to any significance as a 'parable' (analogy?) of what happens in reality. Furthermore, if interpreted as a theoretical model, the one-commodity growth model can only be defended as part of a preliminary analysis. But as we have seen, the one-commodity model is not open to extension as required by the method of successive approximation and Lucas does not attempt such a defence. Consequently the one-commodity neoclassical growth model is best interpreted as an imaginary model that makes no real world references and is hence devoid of empirical content (Achinstein, 1968). As such it cannot offer a framework for an *explanation* of the real business cycle because to do so would require theoretical concepts that are given a literal or theoretical, rather than an analytical or *as if*, interpretation (Hausman, 1981). (Recall also the distinction between explanation and prediction drawn by Coddington, 1972,1975.) Furthermore, if the method of successive approximation is attempted, it will immediately encounter the theoretical and logical anomalies revealed by the capital debate when the model is extended beyond the one-commodity case. For these reasons the use of the REH in one-commodity neoclassical models, by Lucas and others, can only be defended on the grounds that they are imaginary models. They then provide no means whereby the conclusions reached can be transmitted to the real economy. What these models tell us about the real economy is simply anyone's guess.

From the perspective of methodology, Lucas's defence of neoclassical theory therefore appears most unsatisfactory and, as emerges from the discussion in chapter 6, this, to a large extent, is a reflection of the Chicago view of neoclassical economics. If we keep in mind that these economists see neoclassical theory as offering a 'good approximation' to the operation of the real economy then much of what they say is explained, even if it is hard to believe.

An examination of the REH hypothesis reveals that it is not directed at a solution of the anomalies that are now known to exist in neoclassical theory. In fact just the reverse is true. It is ironic that at the very moment that the leading exponents of neoclassical theory are pointing out its deficiencies, the new 'classical' school proceeds as if these deficiencies did not exist! As Fusfeld (1980) has remarked, the Rational Expectations revolution arrived too late to save neoclassical economics. The continued use of these models can then only be explained in terms of the Chicago view – an unsubstantiated form of free market ideology.

CONCLUDING REMARKS

In this chapter we have shown that the Keynesians, represented by Tobin, and the monetarists, represented by Brunner–Meltzer, both employ a restatement of Wicksellian monetary theory. The key feature of this analysis is the distinction between the natural rate of interest, determined by the marginal *productivity* of capital, and the market rate of interest. In Keynesian and monetarist interpretations the latter becomes the return on equities, but the principle involved is identical to that suggested by Wicksell.

In view of this conclusion it is obvious that Tobin and Brunner–Meltzer are using models that are open to the Cambridge critique. In particular it is not possible to prove the existence or stability of the long-period equilibrium solutions of these models, unless they are restricted to the one-commodity case. The models therefore have no coherent theoretical foundations within neoclassical economics, neither do they have a valid methodological rationale. Yet Tobin and Brunner–Meltzer clearly present their models in the context of discussions which examine monetary *policy*. As Clower (1975:10–12) pointed out with respect to neo-Walrasian theory, macroeconomists such as Patinkin and Lange proceeded to discuss policy issues in theoretical structures considered by their colleagues in pure theory to have no relevance for such questions; those monetary theorists following the Wicksell connection are open to the same criticism. Finally it was shown that the new 'classical' macroeconomics or the so-called Rational Expectations revolution does nothing to resolve the theoretical anomalies inherent in neoclassical monetary theory.

6

FRIEDMAN'S MONETARY FRAMEWORK: THE QUANTITY THEORY RESTATED?

INTRODUCTION

Any attempt to evaluate Friedman's monetary theory must first come to grips with a number of apparent anomalies in his position. To begin with, there is the obvious difficulty that Friedman has never explicitly presented a complete theoretical framework or model. This feature of Friedman's work is generally accepted (Shaw, 1983:423). His theoretical framework appears to have wandered through numerous phases beginning and ending with an attempt to impose the properties of the traditional quantity theory of money on to a system of unbacked fiat money and credit. The story begins in traditional quantity theory fashion with support for 100 per cent reserve banking (Friedman, 1953c), and ends on the same note with a call for an overhaul of the Federal Reserve system that will render control of the monetary base effective (Friedman, 1985). But in between these expressions of support for the traditional quantity theory Friedman engaged in several theoretical detours, notably: (i) a restatement of the quantity theory in the Cambridge tradition as a theory of the demand for money (Friedman, 1956, 1959); (ii) a reinterpretation of the IS–LM framework to include permanent income and Fisher's distinction between real and nominal interest rates (Friedman, 1974); (iii) the analysis of the natural rate of unemployment and the vertical long-period Phillips curve (Friedman, 1975); and (iv) the outline of a dynamic analysis designed to explain the overshooting of the final equilibrium position by nominal income and prices (Friedman, 1974; Friedman and Schwartz, 1982:ch. 2; Taylor, 1976). But what is offered in each case is only considered to be suggestive and not definitive. As Hahn (1980b:1) observes, Friedman urges theorists to paint with a broad Marshallian brush and not to worry too much about the finer (Walrasian?) details.[1]

However, coming from Friedman, this latter advice appears to involve a contradiction. For, despite describing himself as a Marshallian (Stein, 1976:311), Friedman makes continual reference to the quantity theory in a Walrasian setting and even defines the natural rate of unemployment in terms of the (suitably adjusted) Walrasian system of equations, e.g. Friedman (1974:31, 32, 44, 48, 55) and Friedman and Schwartz (1982:69) or Friedman (1968:8). Friedman also mentions Wicksell in connection with the concept of the natural rate of unemployment while simultaneously making use of Fisher and Keynes, which perhaps reflects his Chicago view of a unified economic theory. Strictly interpreted, however, his references to the quantity theory in a Walrasian setting would run into the difficulties discussed in chapter 3. Now, there are well-documented reasons why one cannot be a Marshallian and a Walrasian simultaneously. But in view of these references to the Walrasian system the temptation to interpret Friedman as a Walrasian when it comes to theory is quite strong and Frank Hahn (1980b, 1981) seems to have interpreted Friedman in this way.

Nevertheless, it can be argued that such an interpretation would not be correct. At least it is not consistent with Friedman's rejection of the Walrasian general equilibrium method (Friedman, 1953a, 1955). If anything it appears that Friedman employs the Marshallian partial equilibrium method. But Friedman's application of the Marshallian partial equilibrium method is clouded by two additional features. These are: (i) the Chicago vision of neoclassical economics; and (ii) the role played by the inductivist, conventionalist and instrumentalist elements in his methodology. Unless one takes all of these characteristics into account, Friedman's position remains an enigma.

The objective of this chapter is to examine all these dimensions of Friedman's approach to economic theory in an attempt to make some headway in understanding Friedman's brand of monetarism. The need to advance on such a broad front becomes apparent from even a superficial inspection of Friedman's position. To begin with, it appears that the limitations of neoclassical general equilibrium theories are not directly relevant to Friedman's analysis as he clearly rejects Walrasian general equilibrium theory (Friedman, 1953a, 1955). Instead he applies the Marshallian partial equilibrium method to partition reality into manageable 'bits' from which useful 'predictions' can be extracted (Hoover, 1984b). The Marshallian properties

1. It is interesting to note that Friedman consistently applies the traditional long-period method of economic theory in an attempt to distinguish between the persistent and transitory forces at work in the real economy (Eatwell, 1983c).

of his analytical style are, however, dominated by the inductivist/ empiricist element of his instrumentalist methodology. But as an inductivist logic does not exist, this effectively means that he is unable to provide the general or complete theoretical framework that his critics call for. A study of the 'models' of his 'theoretical framework' confirms this conclusion, as they consist of a set of *ad hoc* structures designed to explain (predict?) particular monetary phenomena.

As a result, it appears that much of Friedman's empirical work represents an attempt to develop a theory or 'model' by induction. The instrumentalist element in particular then shields him from some methodological criticism (Boland, 1979), while at the same time allowing him to treat the Walrasian system along conventionalist lines as a possibly useful 'filing system'. His naive instrumentalism, which treats theories as nothing more than instruments for generating predictions, serves the dual purpose of reinforcing the inductivist element, by restricting the concept of prediction to a narrow inter- pretation, while at the same time deflecting attention away from the theoretical underpinnings. This latter characteristic is reinforced by the Chicago vision of a unified neoclassical economics that underlies all economic theory. The Chicago view perhaps explains why, despite having described himself as a Marshallian, and Tobin as a Walrasian (!), Friedman considers that the issues that divide them are empirical and not theoretical. Yet, despite all the points that Friedman scores in debate he offers no solution to the dilemma of neoclassical monetary theory.

In addition to the theoretical vacuum, Friedman's reliance on instrumentalism also leaves him open to attack on methodological grounds. Despite the logical appeal of instrumentalism (Boland, 1979), and although the nature of Friedman's instrumentalism – whether Popperian or Deweyan – is still subject to debate (Hirsch and de Marchi, 1986), a number of points can be made which highlight the limitations of his methodology. These are, firstly, that it rules out the possibility of adopting a more progressive instrumentalism as suggested by Giedymin (1976). This route is closed to naive instru- mentalists like Friedman because they consider the truth content of neoclassical theory to be irrelevant. The second difficulty occurs because instrumentalism is only a useful methodology for those in- terested in 'predictions' of facts already known. For predictions, in the common sense interpretation of the term, instrumentalism is not a useful methodology. As Hoover (1984a:792) concludes: 'I have merely pointed out that instrumentalism, while logically flawless in dealing with any problem to which we already have the answer, is not a logically sound or efficacious methodology for any problem that matters.' It seems that this conclusion is valid whether we interpret Friedman's instrumentalism in the Popperian or the Deweyan sense. From this perspective the rather sterile meaning of Friedman's use of the term 'prediction' is revealed.

Assessing Friedman's approach to monetary theory along these lines reinforces the generally accepted conclusion that he has no complete theoretical framework other than perhaps the traditional quantity theory of money. Therefore, for those interested in the foundations of monetary theory Friedman's approach has little to offer.

THE CHICAGO VISION OF NEOCLASSICAL ECONOMICS

In a recent paper, Reder (1982) provided an invaluable service by outlining some of the key features of Chicago economics. In particular, these insights prove to be extremely helpful in understanding some aspects of Friedman's approach to monetary theory. As Reder (1982:11) explains, the key feature of the Chicago view rests on the hypothesis that decision-makers allocate resources so as to produce a Pareto-optimal solution. At the level of pure theory there is, in Reder's (1982:11) opinion, no difference between Chicago and non-Chicago views of neoclassical (neo-Walrasian or Marshallian?) theory: 'For problems [of] "pure theory" I do not consider that there are any generic differences between Chicago ... and non-Chicago ... theorists.' The Chicago view, or what Reder (1982:11) calls 'Tight Prior Equilibrium' (TP) theory, is based on the *belief* that neoclassical theory provides a useful 'first approximation' to the behaviour of the real economy. As Reder (1982:12) points out:

> in applied work, adherents of TP have a strong tendency to asume that, in the absence of sufficient evidence to the contrary, one may treat observed prices and quantities as good approximations to their long-period competitive values. Call this the 'good approximation assumption' ... Hard use of the good approximation assumption is the hallmark of Chicago applied research: but the assumption is not tested directly.

Use of the good approximation assumption reflects a belief in the stability of a free market economy (Wood, 1981). It seems, however, that Reder exaggerates the unity of the Chicago school. For as Hoover (1984b) has noted, there is a distinct difference between Friedman's use of the Marshallian partial equilibrium method and the use of the Walrasian general equilibrium method by Lucas, for example. Hence the use of the TP equilibrium assumption by Friedman in a partial equilibrium context must be carefully distinguished from the Lucas application in a general equilibrium context. For example, Friedman applies the TP equilibrium assumption in a partial equilibrium setting when developing the notion of permanent income while Lucas applies it in a general equilibrium setting when proposing his general equilibrium theory of the business cycle.

In addition to distinguishing the different applications of the TP assumption within Chicago economics, it is clear that non-Chicago economists are reluctant to make this assumption at all and in many cases reach precisely the opposite conclusion, i.e. that neoclassical theory is anything but a useful first approximation! Frank Hahn is a case in point. His work on neo-Walrasian theory has led him to the conclusion that models with Pareto-optimality properties can, at best, be used only to determine what cannot be said about the real economy. He thus adopts a 'counter-factual' methodology (Howard, 1983:86), which is the polar opposite of the Chicago view.

A simple example will clarify the features of this methodology. Frank Hahn (1980a:126, emphasis added) describes neo-Walrasian general equilibrium theory in the following terms:

General Equilibrium Theory is an *abstract* answer to an abstract and important question. Can a decentralised economy relying only on price signals be orderly? The answer of General Equilibrium Theory is clear and definitive: one can describe such an economy with these properties. *But this of course does not mean that any actual economy has been described.* An important and interesting theoretical question has been answered and that, in the first instance, is all that has been done.

In adopting this position, Hahn is interpreting the neo-Walrasian system as an imaginary model to which he then applies the counter-factual methodology as follows.[2]

In the quote, Hahn refers to the question of the orderly properties of a decentralised economy. This question he usually associates with a 200-year-old claim that a myriad of self-seeking agents, if left to themselves, will produce a coherent result. Neo-Walrasian theory, usually in the guise of the Arrow–Debreu model, then shows what the world *would have to look like* if this claim were true. As the Arrow–Debreu model contains many features which are *necessary* to generate the orderly result, and yet which are missing in the real economy, Hahn deduces that this 200-year-old claim is false. In other words this

2. As Achinstein (1968:222) points out, the proponents of imaginary models do not commit themselves to the truth or plausibility of the assumptions used. Instead their aim is to construct models which reveal what the system *could be like* if it satisfied the assumptions.

methodology maintains that one way of understanding the economic importance of money, for example, is to construct a model in which it is absent and then to compare its results either to another model or to the real economy in which money is present. This negative role of neo-Walrasian theory is considered to be sufficient justification for its continued use even though to date no neo-Walrasian model that includes money in an essential way has been constructed. In terms of Hahn's (1973a:14–15) methodology, Chicago economists therefore appear as 'ill-trained' theorists: 'This negative role of the Arrow–Debreu equilibrium I consider almost to be sufficient justification for it, since practical men and ill-trained theorists everywhere in the world do not understand what they are claiming to be the case when they claim a beneficient and coherent role for the invisible hand.' All this is not intended to suggest that Hahn's methodology is without defect but merely to make the comparison. For a discussion of the limitations of Hahn's methodology see Coddington (1975).

In view of the previous discussion of neoclassical monetary theory, it can only be concluded that the Lucas application of the Chicago 'good approximation assumption' to any existing capitalist economy rests on an act of faith if it is based on the Pareto-optimality properties of neo-Walrasian theory. As this seems to be the case in some instances we can only conclude that the generally acknowledged flaws in neoclassical theory have not yet penetrated as far as Chicago. However, Chicago economists who follow Friedman's use of the partial equilibrium approach are not open to this criticism. To assess Friedman's use of the Tight Prior equilibrium assumption we must therefore examine his methodology more closely.

FRIEDMAN'S METHODOLOGY

An important supplement to Friedman's application of the Marshallian partial equilibrium method is the methodology that accompanies it. Boland (1979:509–16) has pointed out three elements which are important: inductivism, conventionalism and instrumentalism. All three of these elements play important roles in Friedman's methodology and it is difficult to select one as the dominant feature. We therefore discuss each in turn.

Inductivists believe that theories can be true and that true theories are derived by applying inductive logic to observations. Thus, from true singular statements, i.e. observations, they believe it is possible to derive general statements (theories) by induction. To ensure that the singular statements employed will do the job, inductivists distinguish between normal and positive statements.[3] Only the latter are considered to be unambiguously true and can be used in the construction of theories. But as Boland (1979:507) explains, this distinction is not sufficient to support inductivism in the absence of an inductive logic: 'There is no type of argument that will validly proceed from assumptions that are singular to conclusions that are general statements.' The problem of induction simply remains unresolved. Nevertheless, Friedman's approach to monetary theory contains strong inductivist elements. This can be seen from his attempts to develop 'models' that explain/predict the observed behaviour of monetary phenomena. But when this behaviour changes, as for example was the case with the famous change in the secular decline in velocity, *ad hoc* extensions of the 'model' are introduced to account for the change. This leaves the distinct impression of Friedman as an inductivist.

But Friedman moves beyond simple inductivism to include elements of conventionalism and instrumentalism, both of which are methodologies that are unconcerned with the truth status of theories (Boland, 1979; Clark, 1979; Caldwell, 1980). In particular, the conventionalist view allows Friedman to stress the organisational function of theories and the criterion of simplicity in theory selection (Caldwell, 1980:367). Hence Friedman at times appears to treat the Walrasian system in conventionalist terms as a kind of 'filing system' (Friedman and Schwartz, 1982:37n35) or Friedman (1955).[4] Yet at other times he seems to treat the Walrasian system in Chicago TP fashion as a good 'first approximation'. His definition of the natural rate of unemployment would appear to be an illustration of the latter interpretation (Friedman, 1968:8). All this, it seems, Friedman is quite happy to combine with the Marshallian partial equilibrium method! Finally it is necessary to examine what is now considered to be the dominant feature of Friedman's methodology, namely instrumentalism.

3. Boland (1979:507n9) argues that this distinction is now best seen as an unexamined inductivist ritual within positive economics. Examples of Friedman's stress on *observation first* are: 'Lange largely dispenses with the *initial step* – a full and comprehensive set of observed and related *facts* to be generalized' (Friedman, 1953a:283, emphasis added); and, 'A far better way (to develop a theory) is to try to derive theoretical generalizations to fit as full and comprehensive a set of related *facts* about the real world as it is possible to get' (Friedman, 1953a:300, emphasis added).

4. Hahn, of course, takes these references at face value and points out that there is no basis for Friedman's quantity theory claims within neo-Walrasian economics. See, in particular, Hahn and Nield (1980) or Hahn (1982b). Friedman (1980) responds by accepting the limitations of neo-Walrasian theory and refers Hahn to the empirical evidence that supports the quantity theory. Friedman's response is quite understandable in terms of his methodology, although it strikes many observers as unacceptable.

The instrumentalist element in Friedman's methodology is apparent from his insistence that the purpose of science is prediction, and that the 'realism' of assumptions does not matter. These two statements can be interpreted as instrumentalist,[5] because, as we know, naive instrumentalists see theories as *nothing more* than instruments for generating predictions. Hence theories and the theoretical terms that they contain cannot be interpreted as true or false. But it should be noted that, in terms of the realist philosophy of science, 'realism' refers to the truth content of theories, and as Friedman accepts the instrumentalist label this is how his reference to realistic assumptions should be interpreted (Caldwell, 1980:368). In his famous essay on methodology Friedman was not clear on what he meant by 'realistic', but having accepted the instrumentalist label the above interpretation follows. By comparison, alternative interpretations appear trivial (Nagel, 1963). But once this interpretation is acknowledged, it appears from the arguments presented by Giedymin (1976) and Clark (1979:22) that Friedman is, at best, a naive instrumentalist.

This conclusion follows because naive instrumentalists are concerned *only* with the empirical content of *predictions* and not the assumptions. As Clark (1979:22) notes: 'Naive but not sophisticated instrumentalists assess the empirical applicability only of theorems. They ignore the direct testing of assumptions. Friedman shares this view.' Now Clark's notion of a naive instrumentalist is consistent with Caldwell's characterization of Friedman's position as 'methodological instrumentalism'. As Caldwell (1980) points out, instrumentalism and realism are often presented as opposing views in the philosophy of science. As such, instrumentalism is concerned also with the ontological status of entities referred to by theoretical terms; realists and sophisticated instrumentalists claim that theoretical terms should make real references while naive instrumentalists deny it (Caldwell, 1980; Boland, 1979). Thus, by ignoring the question of the ontological status of theoretical terms, Friedman embraces a naive instrumentalism.[6] It is for this reason that Caldwell (1980) describes Friedman as a 'methodological instrumentalist'. Both Clark (1979) and Caldwell

5. In any event we do not need to speculate about this as Friedman has accepted the instrumentalist label as 'entirely correct' (Caldwell, 1980:367). However, others have argued that there is no unique interpretation of Friedman's methodology (Helm, 1984b), or alternatively have associated Friedman's instrumentalism with the Deweyan rather than the Popperian brand (Wible, 1984; Hirsch and de Marchi, 1985, 1986).
6. This then leaves Friedman open to the Popper (1963) and Feyerabend (1964) critique of instrumentalism.

(1980) therefore come to the conclusion that Friedman has adopted too narrow a view of instrumentalism. In contrast to the impression created by Boland (1979), this means that his methodology is particularly weak. For example, Stewart (1979:131) comments on Friedman's approach as follows:

By choosing to ignore assumptions, we are giving up any attempt to fit our observations into the deductive framework of theory and by saying 'predictions are all that matter', we are denying that our reasoning can give any systematic help in controlling economic events – since, as we have seen, you may be able to predict an outcome without having any idea how to influence it.

The relevance of this observation in the current context is apparent once we recall that the imaginary models of neoclassical economics cannot generate the type of predictions in which Friedman is interested. Consequently Friedman is forced to rely on induction for the construction of 'models' because there is simply no link between neoclassical monetary models and the type of empirical work in which he is engaged. In addition, Friedman's naive instrumentalism means that he no longer considers the debate over the ontological status of neo-Walrasian or one-commodity Wicksellian models to be significant. Consequently Hahn's counterfactual methodology, which reflects concern (however limited) with the truth status of neo-Walrasian models, is dismissed by Friedman (1980) with the remark that he is well aware of the limitations of this type of theorizing. From his earlier reviews of Lange and Jaffee's translation of Walras this is no doubt true (Friedman, 1953a, 1955). Nevertheless it is hardly an adequate explanation for his own references to the quantity theory in a Walrasian setting! Such references reflect the conventionalist element in his methodology, reinforced no doubt by the 'good approximation' assumption of the Chicago view. Here we again see the role of the Chicago view in deflecting attention away from these crucial issues. If the neoclassical general equilibrium system (Wicksellian or Walrasian?) is *assumed* to offer a good approximation to the real economy, the ontological status of theoretical terms is not a question on the agenda; *it is solved by assumption*. But this again leaves the question of the theoretical foundations hanging in midair.

Finally, and in view of the bewildering maze of dimensions of Friedman's methodology, it is difficult to disagree with Stanley's (1985) characterization of it as the methodology of 'anything goes'.

FRIEDMAN'S THEORETICAL FRAMEWORK

The above features of Friedman's approach to economic theory can now be illustrated by considering some of his theoretical proposals in more detail. We begin with his restatement of the quantity theory and his use of the concept of permanent income to explain movements in velocity.

The quantity theory restated as a theory of the demand for money

Friedman (1956:3) opens his restatement of the quantity theory with the, by now familiar, observation that the quantity theory is a general approach rather than a well-defined theory; it is a theoretical approach which stresses that money is the dominant cause of fluctuations in nominal income. What was novel about Friedman's position at this time was his attempt to emphasize that the quantity theory is, in the first instance, a theory of the demand for money. An analysis of wealth-owning units' demand for assets, of which money is one, then leads to the conclusion that the demand for money has the general form:[7]

$$ M = d\left(P, r_b - \frac{1}{r_b}\frac{dr_b}{dt}, r_e + \frac{1}{P}\frac{dP}{dt} - \frac{1}{r_e}\frac{dr_e}{dt}, \frac{1}{P}\frac{dP}{dt}; w; \frac{Y}{r}; u\right) $$

(6.1)

Employing the simplifying assumptions that r is a weighted average of r_b and r_e and that the latter are stable over time, Friedman (1956:9–10)

7. Friedman (1956:9). The variables are defined as follows:

P = general price level;

$r_b - \dfrac{1}{r_b}\dfrac{dr_b}{dt}$ = the real return from holding \$1.00 of wealth in the form of bonds;

$r_e + \dfrac{1}{P}\dfrac{dP}{dt} - \dfrac{1}{r_e}\dfrac{dr_e}{dt}$ = the real return from holding \$1.00 in equities;

$\dfrac{1}{P}\dfrac{dP}{dt}$ = the nominal return per \$1.00 of physical goods; together with P it determines the real return;

w = ratio of human to non-human wealth;

$\dfrac{Y}{r}$ = estimate of total wealth;

u = summary of any other variables that affect tastes or preferences.

rewrites expression (6.1) in the form:

$$M = f\left(P, r_b, r_e, \frac{1}{P}\frac{dP}{dt}; w; Y; u\right) \tag{6.2}$$

which is homogeneous of degree one in P and Y. Hence (6.2) may be rewritten as:

$$\frac{M}{Y} = f\left(r_b, r_e, \frac{1}{P}\frac{dP}{dt}; w; \frac{P}{Y}; u\right) \tag{6.3}$$

or,

$$Y = V\left(r_b, r_e, \frac{1}{P}\frac{dP}{dt}; w; \frac{Y}{P}; u\right)M$$

In this way the demand for money, expression (6.1), is rewritten in the quantity theory form with V the income velocity.

A number of interesting points can now be made with reference to this interpretation of the quantity theory. To begin with, the demand for money function, expression (6.1), appears to be no more than an alternative formulation of Keynesian portfolio theory. Indeed the apparent similarity led Patinkin (1969:61) to conclude that: 'Milton Friedman provided us with a most elegant and sophisticated statement of modern Keynesian theory – misleadingly entitled "The Quantity Theory of Money – A Restatement".' There is, of course, some substance to this charge in the sense that all post-war monetary theorists have employed some version of the portfolio approach. Nevertheless, there are important differences between Friedman's use of this framework and the use to which it is put by Tobin or Brunner–Meltzer, for example. In particular, Friedman does not follow the Wicksellian route of comparing the market with the natural rate of interest to link the monetary and real sectors. Instead he employs an alternative concept of long-period equilibrium which reflects both the Chicago view and the inductivist element in his methodology. The concept we have in mind here is, of course, that of permanent income. The 'good approximation' assumption allows Friedman to treat actual income as a good approximation to permanent income if a reasonably large number of observations of actual income are used. In practice permanent income is defined as follows:

$$Y_{Pt} = (1 - \lambda)\sum_{i=1}^{n}\lambda^i Y_{t-i}, \text{ where } 0 < \lambda < 1$$

The use of permanent income then enables Friedman to explain secular and cyclical movements in velocity without recourse to the behaviour of interest rates. It should be noted, however, that the latter feature of Friedman's approach reflects a decision based on *empirical* and not theoretical considerations (Friedman, 1959:142n1). The relationship between money and income is, on these grounds, seen to be more direct than the influence via interest rates. The lack of investigation of the interest rate link by Friedman then leads to difficulties in explaining the money supply process or the transmission mechanism. Friedman's reliance on 'helicopter drops' is a reflection of this property of his approach to theory and obscures an issue of central importance: the endogeneity or exogeneity of the money supply. As we will see later, the concept of monetary equilibrium, of which orthodox portfolio theory is a particular characterization, enables us to specify the conditions under which the money supply is likely to be endogenous or exogenous. By ignoring the theoretical possibilities implicit in his specification of the demand for money in favour of some empirical generalizations, Friedman misses this point. The dominant role played by the inductivist element of Friedman's methodology in his restatement of the quantity theory can now be seen from his explanation of velocity changes.

Expression (6.3) is usually considered to be an improvement over the traditional specification of the quantity theory in which velocity was supposedly treated as a constant. Empirical studies showed, however, that velocity was certainly not constant. The naive quantity theory was therefore considered to be in some difficulty as a result. Now, however unjustified this interpretation of the quantity theory might be (Patinkin, 1972a), Friedman's restatement of the quantity theory is explicitly designed to take movements of velocity into account. Furthermore, these changes in velocity are explained in such a way that velocity, and hence the demand for money, is seen to be a stable *function* of a few variables. However, inspection of Friedman's 'explanation' clearly reveals its inductivist pedigree. The 'model' appears to work well in accounting for the secular decline in velocity prior to the early fifties, but fails entirely to explain the subsequent rise in velocity. It seems, therefore, that we do not have an adequate theoretical framework in Friedman's restatement of the quantity theory, but only an *ad hoc* means of explaining an observed statistical regularity. This conjecture is reinforced by a study of Friedman's argument.

Friedman (1959:122) defines the demand for money function (6.2) in the explicit form:

$$\log \frac{M}{NP_{\mathrm{p}}} = \gamma + \delta \log \left(\frac{Y_{\mathrm{p}}}{NP_{\mathrm{p}}} \right) \tag{6.4}$$

which expresses permanent real balances per capita as a function of permanent real income per capita. The variable δ is the elasticity of permanent real balances per head with respect to permanent income.[8] Estimates of (6.4) then yielded a value of $\delta = 1.8$. This result led Friedman to classify money as a luxury good, for, with every 1 per cent increase in Y_p/NP_p the demand for M/NP_p increases more than in proportion, i.e. by 1.8 per cent, which in turn implies a secular *decline* in the income velocity of money. This can be seen by taking the ratio of real permanent income per capita to real money balances per head (Rousseas, 1972:187):

$$\frac{(Y_p/NP_p)}{(M/NP_p)} = V_p = \frac{Y_p}{M} \tag{6.5}$$

where V_p = permanent income velocity. From (6.5) it is apparent that if M/NP_p rises more than in proportion to Y_p/NP_p permanent income velocity will fall. The cyclical movements in velocity can then be 'explained' by introducing the distinction between measured and permanent velocity. Measured velocity is defined as the ratio of nominal income per capita, Y/N, to nominal money balances per capita, M/N:

$$V_m = \frac{(Y/N)}{(M/N)} = \frac{Y}{M} = \left(\frac{Y}{Y_p}\right)\frac{Y_p}{M} = \left(\frac{Y}{Y_p}\right) V_p \tag{6.6}$$

Measured velocity, V_m, is therefore some multiple of permanent velocity where the multiple depends on the ratio of actual to permanent income. Over the business cycle, Y fluctuates more than Y_p. Hence in a downturn Y falls below Y_p while in an upswing Y rises above Y_p as a result of changes in transitory income. Measured velocity will therefore be expected to move in the same direction as nominal income, explaining the observed pro-cyclical movement in velocity. The introduction of permanent income into the demand for money function therefore serves the dual purpose of explaining the observed movements in velocity and doing so in terms of only a few variables. In this respect the empirical conclusion that interest rates do not play an important role is significant in restricting the number

8. The variables are defined as:

M = nominal money stock;

N = population;

Y_p = permanent aggregate nominal income;

P_p = permanent price level.

of variables in the function. Chick (1973:39) has noted, however, that other studies have found the interest rate to be significant even in equations that include permanent income. One reason for this discrepancy seems to be Friedman's inclusion of time deposits in his definition of money while other researchers use a narrower definition. The inverse relation between the interest rate and the demand for money may therefore be obscured in Friedman's data because the demand for time deposits varies positively with the interest rate. See also the comment in Rousseas (1972:190n17), who points out that in Friedman's (1959) paper the estimation technique biased the results against the rate of interest. And as Chick (1973:38) goes on to point out, the formulation of (6.2) contains so many variables that it could hardly fail to be stable. The use of permanent income avoids this charge by supporting the claim that velocity is a stable *function* in the sense that its behaviour can be predicted. In other words velocity is not a will-o'-the-wisp as seemed to be implied by some Keynesians.

A review of one example makes the point that Friedman's theoretical constructs are *ad hoc*. Over the initial period of Friedman's study the 'explanation' or 'prediction' of velocity apparently performed very well. Unfortunately, when the above 'explanation' was applied to the data from the early 1950s, it broke down. In fact Friedman's explanation is only consistent with the period 1870–1915 in the US (Rousseas, 1972:204). The period 1915–1929 showed no trend while 1929–1946 is the period disrupted by the Great Depression and World War II. From the early 1950s to the mid-1970s there was a distinct rise in velocity with an indication of a possible levelling off or fall since then (Friedman and Schwartz, 1982:312; Rousseas, 1972:200). This would seem to imply that Friedman's initial explanation of the secular movement in velocity in terms of permanent income represents only one of the infinite number of *ad hoc* specifications that could be constructed to fit the data *ex post facto*.[9] As Lipsey (1979:284, emphasis added) recently reminded us:

Of course, the proof of the pudding comes when the models are extrapolated to new data and here they fail in droves . . . (Therefore) we should not be very impressed with 'sunrise tests', testing the theory against the data *it was specifically constructed to explain* . . . We should not take a model seriously until it passes tests against new data . . . it was not *constructed* to fit.

9. Lipsey (1979:284) has also warned that as some *ad hoc* specification of almost any theory can be made to fit the data more or less well, we need to know which theory, if any, does consistently better. But such comparative testing is rare. In view of the difficulties for hypothesis testing revealed by the Duhem–Quine thesis this is, perhaps, not surprising.

Lipsey's advice is most appropriate when it comes to evaluating Friedman's restatement of the quantity theory. Friedman's explanation apparently does well for the initial data period but breaks down when time passes and new data become available. In this respect the episode serves to illustrate that Friedman uses the term prediction in a particularly narrow sense. As Hoover (1984a:790, emphasis added) describes it, Friedman (as an instrumentalist) is concerned with deriving 'neat summaries of *facts already known*'. That is to say, when Friedman refers to 'predictions', he means finding a model to mimic facts already known. But in that case Friedman's model has failed the real test of predictive accuracy. As Hirsch and de Marchi (1986:2) point out, numerous writers have criticised Friedman on this score for failing to live up to his supposedly falsificationist Popperian methodology (Blaug, 1980). By now, however, it should be clear that Friedman is not a Popperian. Embracing any form of instrumentalism is hardly compatible with Popper. If anything, it seems that Friedman rationalizes known evidence instead of framing a hypothesis and testing it against the evidence, i.e. he seeks to 'predict' facts already known! In the context of the present model the initial belief that it was able to predict the behaviour of velocity in terms of a stable velocity function is clearly unfounded. However well the model may 'predict' the behaviour of velocity over the data period for which it was constructed, it fails the only meaningful test – prediction of the future behaviour of velocity. By comparison to his initial restatement of the quantity theory, Friedman's attempts to rationalize the increasing trend in velocity appear even more *ad hoc* (Rousseas, 1972:204–21).[10]

An evaluation of Friedman's restatement of the quantity theory therefore leads to the conclusion that it represents an inductivist attempt at theory or 'model' construction. From what we know about inductivism such an attempt is bound to fail. A general theoretical framework cannot be constructed on that basis, and the change in the trend of velocity is an apt illustration of the dangers that lie in wait for those who seek to generalize from singular statements. Furthermore, Friedman's restatement of the quantity theory does not even

10. Interestingly, if the role of interest rate movements is taken into account then V_p and Y_p may move in the same upward direction (Rousseas, 1972:192). If the money supply is held constant the rise in the demand for real balances, as a result of the increase in Y_p will cause the interest rate to rise. This in turn has an inverse effect on the demand for real balances. If the negative interest rate effect dominates the positive Y_p effect the fall in the demand for real balances would imply a rise in V_p. But because Friedman has ruled out the interest rate effects on *empirical* grounds he does not employ this explanation.

appear to be consistent with the commonsense interpretation of the word 'prediction' because it fails the true test of prediction of future events.[11]

Friedman's version of IS–LM

In response to criticism of his presidential address to the American Economic Association (Friedman, 1968b), Friedman (1974) presented a theoretical framework based on the IS–LM structure that supposedly supported some of his claims. But again this model was only offered as suggestive and not definitive. This much is apparent from his response to the Brunner and Meltzer comments in Gordon (1974:135). Furthermore, in a later debate Friedman (1976b:315–16) appeared to consider the exercise only as an attempt to communicate with the Keynesians. Not surprisingly, in his more recent work with Anna Schwartz the restatement of the IS–LM model is dropped in favour of a more extensive description of his dynamic analysis. Now, despite the fact that this theoretical framework did not live up to Friedman's initial expectations, an examination of the model provides a useful comparison with the Wicksellian version of the IS–LM model discussed earlier. It also provides another illustration of Friedman's cavalier approach to economic theory.

Friedman's (1974:38–9) restatement of the IS–LM model consists of a monetary sector,[12]

$$M^{\text{D}} = Yl(r) \tag{6.7}$$

11. Friedman (1955) has a tendency to treat explanation and prediction as identical concepts. But as Stewart (1979:65–9, 128–32) and Coddington (1972:3–7) have pointed out, the two concepts are not equivalent. It is quite possible to predict successfully without being able to offer an explanation in any normal sense of the word. In addition it seems that if we are to make useful predictions *and* explanations, the ontological status of theoretical terms or assumptions must be approached along realist lines. Coddington (1972:6) makes this point as follows:

> When we present a causal narrative to accompany some observed regularity and thereby convert a prediction-rule into an explanation, we make claims as to what is literally the case; how in fact the regularity comes to be. An explanation in this sense – which seems to accord with the everyday sense of the word – therefore requires theoretical entities which are given a literal rather than an 'as if' interpretation.

12. The endogenous variables are M^{D}, M^{S}, Y, r, C/P, I/P, Y/P, ρ, ρ^*, and are defined as: M^{D} = nominal demand for money; M^{S} = nominal supply of money; Y = nominal income; r = nominal rate of interest; C/P = real consumption; I/P = real investment; Y/P = real income; ρ = real rate of interest; ρ^* = permanent level of the real rate of interest; $(1/Y \, dY/dt)^*$ = the permanent or anticipated rate of growth of nominal income; k_0 = the difference between the anticipated or permanent real rate of interest and the real growth rate, and is treated as a constant.

$$M^{\mathrm{S}} = h(r) \tag{6.8}$$

$$M^{\mathrm{D}} = M^{\mathrm{S}} \tag{6.9}$$

$$r = k_0 + \left(\frac{1}{\varUpsilon}\frac{d\varUpsilon}{dt}\right)^* \tag{6.10}$$

and a saving–investment sector,

$$\frac{C}{P} = f\left(\frac{\varUpsilon}{P}, \rho\right) \tag{6.11}$$

$$\frac{I}{P} = g(\rho) \tag{6.12}$$

$$\frac{\varUpsilon}{P} = \frac{C}{P} + \frac{I}{P} \tag{6.13}$$

$$\rho = \rho^* \tag{6.14}$$

$$\rho^* = \rho_0 \tag{6.15}$$

This is a system of nine equations in nine unknowns with some unusual features.

The first point of note is that Friedman again removes any role for the nominal rate of interest. Instead of following the Wicksellian distinction between the natural and market rates of interest, Friedman introduces Fisher's *definition* of real and nominal rates.[13] The nominal rate has no role to play; firstly because, from expression (6.10), it is a function of a constant, k_0, and permanent income; secondly, because Friedman (1974:38) then assumes that the money supply is exogenous so that (6.8) becomes

$$M^{\mathrm{S}} = \bar{M} \tag{6.8'}$$

Substituting from (6.7) and (6.9) then produces

$$\varUpsilon = \frac{\bar{M}}{l(r)} \tag{6.16}$$

or,

$$\varUpsilon = \bar{M}V(r)$$

13. The relationship between Fisher's real rate and Wicksell's natural rate was briefly discussed in chapter 2. It will be recalled that Pasinetti (1969) argued that Fisher attempted to relate the productivity of capital to his notion of the real rate. As we will see, Le Roy (1973) certainly equates Fisher's theoretical analysis of the real rate (as opposed to the *ex post* definition) to the marginal productivity of capital. In that case, Fisher's real rate is equivalent to Wicksell's natural rate and Fisher's analysis is open to the Cambridge critique. However, others, e.g. Dougherty (1980) and Tobin (1985), interpret Fisher as an early exponent of the neo-Walrasian tradition.

which from (6.10) means that we again get Friedman's (1974:41, expression (35)) result,

$$Y = \bar{M}V\left[k_0 + \left(\frac{1}{Y}\frac{dY}{dt}\right)^*\right]$$ (6.16′)

which is simply a restatement of velocity as a function of permanent income. Now expression (6.16′) can be used to determine the level of nominal income, Y, at any point in time, given $(1/Y\ dY/dt)^*$. But to determine the path of nominal income over time it is necessary to determine the anticipated (permanent) rate of change of nominal income, $(1/Y\ dY/dt)^*$. This Friedman proposes to do in his dynamic analysis which we will not consider here. It is more interesting to note that the saving–investment sector of Friedman's version of the IS–LM model has been completely bypassed! Friedman is well aware of this feature of his analysis and notes explicitly that he was unable to marry nominal and real values successfully in terms of his restated IS–LM model (Friedman, 1974:40). In essence then, Friedman had not provided a satisfactory restatement of the IS–LM model and he was well aware of it.

These two examples of Friedman's approach to economic theory serve to illustrate his empiricist application of the Marshallian partial equilibrium method to manageable bits of reality in an attempt to derive useful predictions. The collection of manageable bits of reality that results looks rather *ad hoc* by comparison to the general equilibrium approach of other monetary theorists. In particular, Friedman's approach stands in sharp contrast to other brands of monetarism discussed in chapter 5 and the difference has some interesting implications for monetarism mark II and Chicago economics in general.

FRIEDMAN, MONETARISM MARK II AND CHICAGO ECONOMICS

As Friedman is, in his own view, 'primarily an empirical economist, who uses a few deeply-held principles to sift through the facts in search of predictions' (Hoover, 1984b:66), it is revealing to compare Friedman's approach to that of the exponents of monetarism mark II, e.g. Lucas, Barro and Sargent.

In a recent paper on the two types of monetarism, Hoover (1984b) correctly identifies an important aspect of the distinction in Friedman's use of the Marshallian partial equilibrium method as opposed to the Walrasian general equilibrium method of the new 'classical' macroeconomists. With respect to economic theory it should be generally agreed with Hoover that Friedman sees no useful role for Walrasian general equilibrium theory in the generation of predictions. This much is at least apparent from his reviews of Lange and Jaffee's translation of Walras. However, this then raises some awkward questions for the relationship between monetarism mark II, Chicago economics and Friedman's quantity theory.

Friedman, as an instrumentalist/empiricist who employs the Marshallian method to partition reality into manageable bits, follows in the tradition of Wesley Mitchell. This tradition stands in sharp contrast to the younger generation of Chicago economists and exponents of monetarism mark II. To appreciate the significance of the difference it is necessary to recall that Wesley Mitchell felt that it was not his task 'to determine how the fact of cyclical oscillations in economic activity can be reconciled with the general theory of equilibrium or how the theory can be reconciled with the facts' (Hayek, 1931:39). This view of the limitations of Walrasian general equilibrium theory is shared by Friedman and is the polar opposite of the view adopted by exponents of monetarism mark II. The Friedman–Mitchell view is rejected by Lucas who argues that, given the existence of business cycles, 'the theorists' challenge is to reconcile them with general equilibrium theories' (Hoover, 1984b:67).

But, as we argued in chapter 5, the use of neoclassical general equilibrium theories by the exponents of monetarism mark II brings them into direct conflict with the dilemma of neoclassical monetary theory. This dilemma is not resolved by the Rational Expectations hypothesis and the Lucas attempt to produce a general equilibrium theory of the business cycle amounts to another failed attempt to reconcile the 'facts' with neoclassical general equilibrium theory. Moreover, the Lucas attempt to formalize some of Friedman's ideas in terms of neoclassical general equilibrium theory actually undermines the Chicago empiricist tradition by exposing it to the limitations of that theory. Monetarism mark II exposes Chicago economics to the Hahn critique of neo-Walrasian theory and/or the Cambridge critique of Wicksellian general equilibrium theory.

In this regard we must reject the argument by Hoover (1984b:67) that the new 'classical' macroeconomists cannot be considered to be Walrasians in the sense that they are not concerned with *purely* mathematical general equilibrium theory. The point is that the new 'classical' macroeconomists *cannot avoid* being classified as Walrasians in this sense. The mathematical and logical properties of the neo-Walrasian model cannot somehow be ignored in the process of reconciling the properties of the model with the existence of the business cycle. By embracing neoclassical monetary theory the exponents of monetarism mark II must inevitably reconcile the moneyless property of neo-Walrasian theory or the nonexistence of a long-period equilibrium solution in Wicksellian theory with the existence of the business cycle. This has not been done. Monetarism mark II cannot therefore provide a sound theoretical basis for Friedman's quantity theory view of the world. If anything, the exponents of monetarism mark II seem oblivious of the failings of neoclassical monetary theory. By exposing this dimension of the use of the Tight Prior equilibrium assumption, Chicago economics is undermined.

CONCLUDING REMARKS

The study of Friedman's theoretical framework presented here has attempted to convey some idea of the extreme complexity of his approach to economic analysis. Distinguishing between aspects of theory, method and methodology assists in unravelling that complexity.

At the level of *methodology* it is tempting to agree either with Helm (1984b), that there is no unique interpretation of Friedman's position, or with Stanley (1985), that Friedman's is the methodology of 'anything goes'. For although features of various methodologies can be identified in Friedman's writings, the precise interpretation of even the dominant instrumentalist element is open to debate. In particular, Hirsch and de Marchi (1985) have recently argued convincingly that Friedman's instrumentalism should be interpreted from a Deweyan rather than a Popperian perspective. On either interpretation, however, it seems that Friedman's methodology retains a strong inductivist/empiricist bias in the sense that he is concerned with deriving 'neat summaries of facts already known' (Hoover, 1984a:790). The importance of empirical studies to this endeavour should not, therefore, be underestimated. This aspect of Friedman's work provides the raw material – the 'facts already known' – to which theory is applied to derive convincing rationalizations. Seen from this perspective, the Hendry and Ericsson (1983) critique of Friedman's empirical research is far more damaging than any theoretical criticism directed by Keynesians and based on neoclassical general equilibrium theory. The Hendry–Ericsson critique attacks the 'raw material' on which Friedman's 'model' construction is based and is thus not limited to purely technical econometric issues.

At the level of *method* it seems clear enough that Friedman is an exponent of the Marshallian partial equilibrium approach. But this method he applies in the context of a *mélange* of elements from competing theories and methodologies. Despite having defined the natural rate of unemployment in Walrasian terms and incorporated ideas from Wicksell and Fisher, Friedman has no use for the Walrasian general equilibrium method and its concern with abstract completeness. On this score he stands apart from the younger generation of Chicago economists – the exponents of Rational Expectations or monetarism mark II. If anything the new 'classical' macroeconomists have weakened the Chicago tradition by bringing the neoclassical general equilibrium basis of the Tight Prior equilibrium assumption into the open. This is a step Friedman would never have taken and it points to a split in Chicago economics.

Thus, despite the complexity of Friedman's position, many aspects of his analysis are accounted for by the features of his method and methodology identified in the literature. But in addition, a further factor can be introduced to clarify the enigma that is Friedman's monetarism. This factor has been identified by Boland (1979) who observes that Friedman is only concerned with the sufficiency of a theory or set of assumptions. In more technical terms, Friedman employs *disjunctive-type* arguments which are very difficult to refute because each assumption or 'model' is treated as a sufficient condition for the conclusion which follows. We have seen evidence of this feature of Friedman's analysis in the reliance on a general approach in terms of which numerous apparently *ad hoc* models – none of which is presented as definitive – are presented as convincing rationalizations of the empirical evidence. If one or more of these models is refuted the argument is not lost as another plausible model can readily be found to replace it. The use of disjunctive-type arguments is characteristic of Friedman's analysis and no doubt partly accounts for the frustration experienced by his critics, particularly the Keynesians who employ neoclassical general equilibrium theory and *conjunctive-type* arguments. Conjunctive-type arguments are easier to refute as all that is necessary is the refutation of one of the assumptions (Boland, 1979:506).

Finally, at the level of *theory* it should now be apparent that to isolate the theoretical core of Friedman's monetary framework it is necessary to cut away many of the illustrative models he has used to generate plausible rationalizations. When this is done only the commitment to the quantity theory tradition remains. In terms of the taxonomy used in this study Friedman is therefore committed to the neutral money property of Real Analysis. But this raises the interesting question of the relationship between the new quantity theory – monetarism – and the classical quantity theory. Some observers suggest that monetarism is simply a new name for the classical quantity theory (Hayek, 1980). However, it seems that there are some important analytical issues that must be clarified before we can agree with that assessment.

Everyone would probably agree that the classical quantity theory applies in the case of a commodity money system. Commodity money is subject to analysis in terms of classical analytical principles in which costs of production determine natural prices and it is this analysis that forms the basis of the classical quantity theory. The challenge facing Friedman and other exponents of monetarism is to explain how the properties of the classical quantity theory can be imposed on a modern bank money economy., Suport for 100 per cent banking, monetary base control or a monetary growth rule would appear to be a monetarist attempt to get the bank money system to mimic the properties of the classical quantity theory. Despite all the rationaliz-ations of the empirical evidence offered by Friedman this is where the theoretical arrgument ultimately comes to rest. It concerns the answer to an apparently simple question. How can a modern bank money economy be made to behave *as if* it exhibited the desirable stability properties – from the point of view of the price level – of the classical quantity theory?

The monetarists' answer is that the money supply must somehow be fixed, i.e. rendered exogenous. Belief in the inherent stability of a capitalist economy then lends support to the idea that fixing the growth of the money supply will provide a stable financial environ-ment in which the real forces of the economy will ensure full employ-ment. If Friedman is to be interpreted as offering a restatement of the classical quantity theory then it must be along these lines that his analysis is assessed, namely how the classical quantity theory is to be made applicable to a bank money economy. Seen in this light it is apparent that not only has Friedman failed to resolve the dilemma of neoclassical monetary theory but he has instead led the monetarists face to face with one of the practical implications of that dilemma. For it is now generally accepted, no less by Friedman (1984) himself, that central bankers have not implemented monetarist policies. In par-ticular they have, by their actions, rejected the suggestion that the properties of the classical quantity theory can be imposed on a bank money system by implementing monetary base control and a monetary growth rule. Thus, monetarists have suffered the ultimate fate of all exponents of monetary theories in the tradition of Real Analysis; history has passed them by.

II

MONETARY ANALYSIS: FOUNDATIONS

7

RE-LAYING THE FOUNDATIONS OF MONETARY THEORY

INTRODUCTION

Looking back on the criticism of neoclassical monetary theory documented in previous chapters, we can perhaps be excused a feeling of frustration. Criticism, and negative criticism in particular, is all very well, but it provides little direct indication of how to proceed. The old adage that you can't beat something with nothing holds good. Where, then, do we go from here? The first step towards a more positive contribution can, it seems, be taken by placing the critique of neoclassical monetary theory in longer term historical perspective. To this end Schumpeter (1954:ch. 6) has provided a valuable insight which has been unduly neglected in the literature.[1] Within the history of monetary thought Schumpeter (1954:277–8) distinguishes between two major traditions which he labels Real Analysis and Monetary Analysis[2] and describes as follows:

Real Analysis proceeds from the principle that all the essential phenomena of

1. Kohn (1983, 1986) deserves the credit for drawing our attention to this crucial issue. It should be noted, however, that he fails to realize the full implications of the distinction. For example, he incorrectly classifies Wicksell's monetary theory in the tradition of Monetary Analysis and can find no theoretical innovations in Keynes so he interprets the contribution of the General Theory as the adoption of the equilibrium method instead of the sequence analysis favoured by 'classical' economists such as Dennis Robertson. As we will suggest below, this interpretation is fundamentally mistaken.
2. Schumpeter (1954:277) notes the ambiguity of the term 'real' but the sense in which it is used should become sufficiently clear as we proceed. The taxonomy suggested by Schumpeter and employed here should not be mistaken for Coddington's (1983:ch. 2) rather confusing distinction between what he calls the classical and Keynesian dichotomies and his attempt to assess the analytical implications of these dichotomies. The sterility of Coddington's attempt at taxonomy will become apparent when we again examine the distinction between loanable funds and liquidity preference theories in chapter 9.

economic life are capable of being described in terms of goods and services, of decisions about them, and of relations between them. Money enters the picture only in the modest role of a technical device that has been adopted in order to facilitate transactions . . . So long as it functions normally, it does not affect the economic process, which behaves in the same way as it would in a barter economy: this is essentially what the concept of Neutral Money implies.

On the other hand:

Monetary Analysis introduces the element of money on the very ground floor of our analytic structure and abandons the idea that all essential features of our economic life can be represented by a barter-economy model

From the perspective of this distinction it is apparent that the neoclassical monetary theory discussed in previous chapters falls within the tradition of Real Analysis. This conclusion is especially true of neo-Walrasian and Wicksellian monetary theory, but is also applicable to Friedman's monetary framework. Friedman (1974:27, emphasis added) states explicitly that: 'We have accepted the quantity theory presumption . . . that changes in the quantity of money *in the long run* have a negligible effect on real income so that non-monetary forces are "all that matter" for changes in real income over decades and *money "does not matter"*.' Such a point of view falls strictly within the tradition of Real Analysis, in which real and not monetary forces determine long-period equilibrium. Now this view leads to the rather paradoxical conclusion that, in the long run, if money 'does not matter' neither does inflation! Such a conclusion is obviously at odds with the widespread concern about, and evidence of, the negative effects of inflation on growth.[3] And, as Hahn (1982:105) has remarked, it is a truly astonishing feat 'to embrace a theory where inflation has negligible costs, and yet be the most vociferous advocates of curing inflation at any price'. This counterfactual conclusion is, of course, simply another symptom of the dilemma with which we opened this investigation and should not come as a surprise – it is a common characteristic of monetary theories in the tradition of Real Analysis.

The importance of the distinction between Real and Monetary Analysis is that it highlights the narrow base on which neoclassical monetary theory rests. It thereby offers the opportunity for recasting, within the context of Monetary rather than Real Analysis, those ideas in neoclassical monetary theory worth salvaging. The critique of neoclassical monetary theory discussed in part I clearly points in that

3. The argument that the variability in the rate of inflation is what causes all the problems is not an argument for reducing inflation but for holding it steady (Hahn, 1982b:102).

direction, as it is the breakdown of the Wicksellian real interest rate mechanism, and the realization that neo-Walrasian models are inescapably non-monetary, that has led to the collapse in the foundations of the subject. That is to say, it is the collapse in the monetary theories of Real Analysis which explains the collapse in the foundations of neoclassical monetary theory.

If the foundations of monetary theory are to be relaid, it is therefore within the tradition of Schumpeter's Monetary Analysis that we must proceed. Fortunately we do not have to look too far to find examples of Monetary Analysis. Schumpeter (1954:278–9) classifies Keynes's system as a leading example of Monetary Analysis which suggests that the monetary theories of both Keynes and Marx will repay closer investigation. For example, Keynes's (1933) description of a monetary economy is clearly compatible with the tradition of Monetary Analysis:

an economy in which money plays a part of its own and affects motives and decisions and is, in short, one of the operative factors in the situation, so that the course of events cannot be predicted, either in the long period or the short, without a knowledge of the behaviour of money between the first date and the last.

In a similar vein, Kenway (1983:156–9) notes that Marx was critical of Ricardo's neutral money analysis on grounds that are remarkably similar to the objections that are now made against the non-monetary analysis of neo-Walrasian theory:

In Ricardo's perception money acts as the means of exchange only, a convenience but no more than that. Money is only of transient importance; it plays no decisive role and its introduction makes no significant difference. For Marx, however, money is both the beginning and the end of the production cycle. In capitalist production money is indispensable to the cycle. The cycle is not completed until the sale phase is accomplished and neither can the cycle begin afresh until the previous cycle is complete and capital is back in its monetary form.

From these observations it would appear that the key issue in Monetary Analysis is the integration of monetary forces in the determination of long-period equilibrium positions. In other words, Monetary Analysis treats monetary forces as persistent rather than transitory. Monetary theories in the tradition of Real Analysis (both classical and neoclassical), treated monetary forces as only transitory, i.e. money could be non-neutral in the short period but was always neutral in the long period (Patinkin, 1972a). By way of contrast the essence of Monetary Analysis is the claim that monetary forces can be persistent. Money can be non-neutral even in the long period.

SOME PROPERTIES OF MONETARY ANALYSIS

Now it is true to say that all monetary theorists have attempted to integrate real and monetary forces in their analysis. For example, Patinkin's (1965) *Money, Interest and Prices* is subtitled *An Integration of Monetary and Value Theory*, while Wicksell clearly sought to integrate monetary and real forces in terms of the distinction between market and natural rates of interest. As we have noted, these attempts failed because they were conducted within the context of Real Analysis. In particular, Patinkin's attempt to integrate real and monetary forces via the real balance effect is not only unnecessary but compounds the already insoluble problems of stability analysis (Gale, 1982:ch.1; Grandmont, 1983). Nevertheless, Wicksell's distinction between market and natural rates of interest embodies an idea that can usefully be taken up in Monetary Analysis, as it reflects a relation common to a broad spectrum of monetary theories, some of which fall within the bounds of Monetary Analysis.

The idea that real and monetary sectors can be linked via the relationship between real and monetary rates of return has a long tradition in monetary theory. Turgot, for example, considered that captial was mobile between active (in production) and passive (in financial) uses. The rewards accruing to capital from these uses were kept in a kind of equilibrium by transfer of capital from one use to another in response to higher rewards. This did not mean that all rates of return were equalized, as profits earned on the active use of capital would be higher than interest earned in financial transactions to compensate for the greater uncertainty and trouble in employing capital actively. Consequently, competition, in the form of the mobility of liquid capital, operated, *ceteris paribus*, so as to impose some hierarchy on rates of return. Henry Thornton (1802) made a similar distinction between the rate of interest and the rate of mercantile profit and incorporated it as the linking mechanism between the real and monetary sectors. Wicksell independently formalized the idea in terms of his distinction between market and natural rates of interest. As we have seen, Keynesians and (some) monetarists employ the same link between real and monetary sectors. Not surprisingly, Keynes made use of the same mechanism both in the *Treatise* and in the *General Theory*. The important distinction in Keynes's case, however, is that in the *General Theory*, he explicitly repudiates the Real Analysis underlying his use of Wicksell's natural rate of interest in the *Treatise*, in favour of a monetary theory in the tradition of Monetary Analysis. Seen from this perspective, Keynes's monetary theory, and the analysis of the enigmatic chapter 17 of the *General Theory* in particular, differs significantly from the monetary orthodoxy of Real Analysis (classical or neoclassical). To prepare the ground for an assessment of Keynes's monetary theory it will prove useful to highlight some of the properties of Monetary Analysis.

Four aspects are of central importance: the nature of capitalist production, the distinction between interest and profit, the characteristics of bank money versus commodity money, and the principle of effective demand. These topics are all interdependent but it is helpful to distinguish between them for analytical purposes. The significance of the first point can be illustrated in terms of an assessment of the Keynes–Marx view of capitalist production.

Keynes and Marx on capitalist production

The significance of the difference in the vision of capitalist production held by monetary theorists in the tradition of Real Analysis, on the one hand, and the Monetary Analysis of Keynes and Marx on the other, can be illustrated in terms of the Marx–Keynes critiques of Ricardo. The similarity of the views of Keynes and Marx on this topic has recently been highlighted by Kenway (1983) and Dillard (1984). In this respect Marx was more explicit than Keynes, who replaced his initial discussion of the distinction between an entrepreneur economy and a co-operative economy in the early drafts of the *General Theory* with the postulates of the 'classical' economists and the attack on Say's Law (Torr, 1980; Dillard, 1984:423). Nevertheless, Keynes's discussion of the distinction between an entrepreneur economy and a co-operative economy is now available for direct comparison with Marx's views. Interestingly it also offers some insight into the reasons behind the rejection of Say's Law by both Marx and Keynes. In particular, this rejection appears to rest, in part, on the argument that 'classical' theory – in Keynes's sense – is seriously deficient as a model of capitalist production.

The essence of the 'classical' view of production is contained in the following quotation by Ricardo (1951–1973, I:290, emphasis added): 'No man produces, but with a *view to consume or sell*, and he never sells but with an intention to purchase some other commodity . . . By producing, then, he necessarily becomes *either the consumer of his own goods*, or the purchaser and consumer of the goods of some other person' (emphasis added, quoted by Kenway (1983:156)). Implicit in this interpretation of the process of production are the following assumptions. Either:

(i)   individuals produce for themselves; or,

(ii)   individuals need not sell their output – they may demand it
         for themselves; or,

(iii)   consumers and producers are identical.

Now it would be wrong to claim that no system of production could satisfy these conditions.[4] What Marx and Keynes argue is that these assumptions are totally inappropriate to capitalist production. Furthermore, as these assumptions underlie Say's Law, the latter is not relevant to capitalist production.

More specifically, Say's Law implies that productions are bought by productions; i.e. supply, the production of commodities, creates its own demand. As Hutt (1974:25) notes in refuting the entrepreneur's argument that money is scarce when sales are low: 'Sales are sluggish . . . not because money is scarce but because other products are.' Similarly, Hutt (1974:26, emphasis in original) makes it clear that Say's Law implies that producers may demand their own output: 'I can refrain from selling . . . any part of the output produced by my labour or produced through the services of the assets I own. But in that case I am myself demanding what I produce . . . Hence *all exercised "power to supply" is exercised "power to demand". There are no imaginable exceptions.*' The 'classical' vision of the production process is thus one in which Say's Law holds. But, as Keynes and Marx pointed out, the capitalist system of production does not meet the assumptions of the 'classical' analysis. In particular, they raised three objections:

(i) To claim that men produce for themselves is to ignore the division of labour which is the essence of capitalist production: 'In a situation where men produce for themselves, there is indeed no crisis, but neither is there capitalist production' (Marx, quoted by Kenway, 1983:156).

(ii) In capitalist production, producers must sell their output for money in the market: 'The capitalist's immediate objective is to turn his commodity, or rather his commodity capital, back into *money capital* and thereby to *realise* his profit . . . The immediate purpose of capitalist production is not "possession of other goods" but the appropriation of value, money, of abstract wealth' (Marx, quoted by Kenway, 1983:158, emphasis in original). In similar vein Keynes (1979:89) argues that: 'It [the firm] has no object in the world except to end up with more money than it started with. That is the essential

---

4. Simple barter production would suffice: 'In direct barter, the bulk of production is intended by the producer to satisfy his own needs or, where the division of labour is more developed, to satisfy the needs of his fellow producers, needs that are known to him' (Marx, quoted by Kenway, 1983:154).

characteristic of the entrepreneur economy.' Quoted by Torr (1980:431), also see Dillard (1984:424).

(iii) In capitalist production, decisions to produce are concentrated in the hands of the few: 'There is nothing more absurd as a means of denying crisis, than the assertion that the consumers (buyers) and producers (sellers) are identical in capitalist production' (Marx, quoted by Kenway, 1983:157).

Keynes's views on this matter are by now well known and clearly imply that in an entrepreneur economy it is the entrepreneurs who make the decisions on what to produce or the quantity of labour to employ and that outside of a co-operative economy there is no reason to expect firms to increase hiring at reduced real wages (Torr, 1980; Kregel, 1986).

To summarize, we may conclude that the first step in the Keynes–Marx objection to the Say's Law economy is that it is not a *capitalist* economy. Say's Law may be a property of a simple barter or co-operative economy but it does not hold for capitalist production.[5] A central implication of this view is that money is an essential element in the scheme of capitalist production. It is in this sense that the rejection of Say's Law opens up a meaningful role for money in the context of Monetary Analysis. It is important to be clear on this point. It is the existence of capitalist production that is a necessary condition for Monetary Analysis and not simply the existence of money *per se*. As we have seen, money can be added in a non-essential way to neoclassical models to produce the neutral money theories characteristic of Real Analysis. Acknowledging the properties of capitalist production avoids the neutral money route and allows for the integration of persistent real *and monetary* forces. This interdependence of the role of money and capitalist production is captured by Keynes's attempt to develop a '*Monetary* Theory of Production' – the original title of what was to become the *General Theory* (Dillard, 1984:423).

Interest and profit

Having established the point that it is in capitalist production that money has the potential to take on a non-neutral role, it is necessary

---

5. Keynes defines a barter or co-operative economy in the following terms: 'I define a barter economy as one in which the factors of production are rewarded by dividing up in agreed proportions the actual output of their co-operative efforts' (quoted by Torr, 1980:430). A modern example of a co-operative economy is the model of self-employed artisans used by Lucas (1977:16) and discussed by Torr (1984:200).

to re-examine the relationship between the rate of profit and the rate of interest in such a system. Marx's well known schematic representation of the cycle of production is particularly useful in this regard:

$$M \rightarrow M \rightarrow C \ldots P \ldots C' \rightarrow M' \rightarrow M'' \qquad (7.1)$$

Following Panico (1983), expression (7.1) can be discussed in terms of five stages:

Stage 1. Interest bearing liquid capital flows from the money capitalist to the industrial capitalist, $M \rightarrow M$;

Stage 2. The industrial capitalist buys factors of production, $M \rightarrow C$;

Stage 3. The industrial capitalist creates *potential* surplus value, $C \ldots P \ldots C'$ where $C' > C$;

Stage 4. Profits are *realised* by the sale of output for money, $C' \rightarrow M'$;

Stage 5. The industrial capitalist pays interest on the borrowed capital, $M' \rightarrow M''$ where $M < M'' < M'$.

Keynes presented no formal scheme equivalent to the above although he did, in the *Treatise*, distinguish between the financial and industrial circulations. In terms of Marx's scheme, the financial circulation refers to the dealings between money capitalists and industrial capitalists or between money capitalists themselves, stages 1 and 5, while stages 2 to 4 in Marx's scheme correspond to the industrial circulation of the *Treatise*. The industrial and financial circulations become the transactions and speculative demand in the *General Theory*.

Now the significance of labouring these distinctions is that they enable us to examine the relationship between the rate of profit and the rate of interest. The rate of profit emerges in the industrial circulation while the rate of interest emerges in the financial circulation. All monetary theorists have recognized this. But, as we have already noted, disagreement exists as to the precise relationship between the two rates.

The classical view of the relationship is that the rate of interest is determined by the rate of profit. This view was held by Adam Smith (Conard, 1963:12), and was most clearly stated by Ricardo: 'the rate of interest for money . . . is not regulated by the rate at which the Bank will lend . . . but by the rate of profits which can be made by the employment of capital.' (Ricardo, 1951–1973, I:363, quoted by Milgate, 1983:98).

The relevant neoclassical view is that of the Wicksellian distinction between market and natural rates of interest. (The neo-Walrasian interpretation of interest and profit is not relevant here for reasons that were spelt out in chapter 3.) The natural rate of interest, as determined by the forces of productivity and thrift, takes over the role of the rate of profit in classical theory in the sense that it acts as a centre of gravitation and determines the market rate of interest in long-period equilibrium.

Both Keynes and Marx reject this 'classical' view and argue instead that it is the rate of interest which, as the independent or exogenous variable, determines the normal rate of profit in long-period equilibrium (Milgate, 1983:98). But if the rate of interest is a monetary phenomenon determined independently of the process which generates profits in the real sector, what are the forces which determine its behaviour? In answering this question both Marx and Keynes reach the same conclusion, but not for the same reasons. Both reject the idea, common to Real Analysis, that the rate of profits or the natural rate of interest provides the centre of gravitation towards which the money rate of interest must adjust in the long period. Instead they argue that the money rate of interest is determined in empirical fashion by the institutional structure and the bargaining power of borrowers and lenders. On these points Marx is most explicit:

The average rate of interest prevailing in a certain country – as distinct from the continually fluctuating rates – cannot be determined by any law. In this sphere, there is no such thing as a natural rate of interest in the sense in which economists speak of a natural rate of profit or a natural rate of wage . . . there is no good reason why average conditions of competition, the balance between lender and borrower, should give the lender an interest of 3, 4, 5% etc., or else a certain percentage of the gross profits, say 20% or 50%, on his capital . . . The determination of (the average rate of interest) is accidental, purely empirical, and only pedantry or fantasy would seek to represent this accident as a necessity (Marx, quoted by Panico, 1983:173).

Panico (1983:172–5) then draws our attention to the similarity of these views on the rate of interest to those presented by Keynes in the *General Theory*. It is well known that Keynes explicitly rejected Wicksell's concept of the natural rate.[6] In its place he introduced the notion of the marginal efficiency of capital and employed the notion of a conventional rate of interest to provide the centre of gravitation for the system: 'It might be more accurate, perhaps, to say that the rate of interest is a highly conventional, rather than a highly psychological, phenomenon' (Keynes, 1936:203). The conventional rate of

---

6. 'I am now no longer of the opinion that the concept of a "natural" rate of interest, which previously seemed to me a most promising idea, has anything very useful or significant to contribute to our analysis' (Keynes, 1936:243). It should be noted that Marx is not referring to the natural rate in the sense used by Wicksell.

interest has, of course, no theoretical foundations and is given none by Keynes.

It is also apparent that Keynes (1936:204), in particular, envisages no mechanism whereby the conventional rate of interest, as an independent variable in a capitalist system, would automatically adjust to its full employment level: 'But it [the rate of interest] may fluctuate for decades about a level which is chronically too high for full employment; particularly if it is the prevailing opinion that the rate of interest is self-adjusting, so that the level established by convention is thought to be rooted in objective grounds much stronger than convention.' It is important to realize here that Keynes is suggesting that monetary phenomena can inhibit the tendency of the rate of interest to automatically adjust to the full employment level *in the long period*. As Eatwell (1983a:106) notes: 'So Keynes appears to be resting his case for a less-than-full employment equilibrium *not* on the proposition that a full employment rate of interest does not exist, but on the proposition that monetary phenomena will inhibit (or prohibit) the tendency of the rate of interest to attain the full employment rate.' Chick (1983:293) reaches a similar conclusion in assessing the role of money 'in establishing the possibility that unemployment is not merely a phenomenon of temporary dislocations', as do Harrod (1947:69) and Dillard (1984:423). These interpretations are only feasible from the perspective of Monetary Analysis, in which monetary forces may be persistent rather than merely transitory. However, as we will see below, Keynes does not appear to have stressed strongly enough the central role of the conventional rate of interest as an independent variable in liquidity preference theory.

In addition to reversing the roles of the natural and market rates of interest, Keynes formally abandons the natural rate of interest and introduces the marginal efficiency of capital to link the money rate of interest with the real sector. The concept of the marginal efficiency of capital as presented by Keynes provides a means of comparing the rates of return on the industrial and financial uses of liquid capital (Turgot's active and passive uses), without resort to the properties of Real Analysis which undermined Wicksell's concept of the natural rate of interest. As Pasinetti (1974:43) has explained:

there is absolutely no need to consider Keynes' marginal-efficiency-of-capital schedule as an expression of the marginal productivity theory of capital. This theory necessarily entails an inverse monotonic relation between capital intensity and the rate of interest. But that is not the case with Keynes' ranking of investment projects. In a slump situation the last project to be implemented might well be the least capital intensive of all, and therefore entail a decrease (not an increase) in the average amount of capital per employed labour.

Schumpeter (1954:1119n6) also notes the differences between Keynes's marginal efficiency of capital and Wicksell's natural rate.

The relationship between the natural rate of interest and the marginal efficiency of capital will be examined in detail in chapter 9. Here we need simply note that the natural rate remains as a component of the marginal efficiency of capital but neither the natural rate nor the marginal efficiency of capital determines the money rate of interest. In other words, the physical productivity of capital continues to play a role in the creation of potential profits but it does not determine the money rate of interest. Keynes (1973b:212) is most explicit on this point. To use Marshallian terminology, the physical productivity of capital only plays a role in determining the quasi-rents and excess profits. The expected profits are then discounted by the rate of interest and compared to the supply price of the unit of capital to determine whether it will generate profits over and above the interest charges. At the margin, the demand price of the unit of capital equals its supply price. (Recall the discussion in chapter 3.) In this fashion the relationship between profits and interest can be analysed in terms of Keynes's concept of the marginal efficiency of capital without running into the difficulties encountered by Wicksell.

Bank money versus commodity money

The previous discussion leads to the conclusion that monetary theories in the tradition of Real Analysis are based on a misspecification of both the nature of capitalist production and the rate of interest. Another dimension of this misspecification is the failure to follow through the distinction between commodity money and bank money.

By commodity money most economists mean one or other of the precious metals such as gold or silver, although shells or other similar scarce items have served as commodity money in some societies. Two key characteristics of commodity money are that it is a commodity subject to the 'laws' of production and that it is in relatively inelastic supply. For example, in a particular economy using gold as money, at any point in time the quantity of gold is effectively fixed. The growth in the supply of commodity money is small by comparison to the existing stock and subject either to developments on the balance of payments or gold mining output if the economy happens to possess some gold mines.

Bank money, by comparison, is a generic term which refers to unbacked fiat money and credit in all its forms. The fundamental characteristic of bank money is that it has negligible costs of production relative to its purchasing power. Because of this characteristic bank money is subject to analysis as a variety of natural monopoly. Supply is perfectly elastic but at a price set by the monetary authority, i.e. the central bank that acts as the monopoly supplier, or guarantor, of bank money.[7]

The major attraction of commodity money is that it appears to exhibit some desirable stability properties. In large measure this feature provides the rationale for support of the quantity theory. The objective is to re-establish what are perceived to be the admirable stability properties of the classical quantity theory. To illustrate the argument consider the following points.

In the case of commodity money an autonomous increase in the prices of some non-monetary commodities will (i) increase the costs of production and inhibit the supply of the money commodity; and (ii) make the monetary commodity relatively cheap and thus encourage its use for non-monetary purposes. Both of these effects act to reverse the initial autonomous increase in prices. The converse holds for an autonomous fall in the prices of non-monetary commodities (Friedman, 1953b:207). Commodity money therefore appears to have some attractive anti-inflationary properties: 'The existence of physical costs of production sets limits to the quantity of currency, and so runaway inflation is impossible so long as a commodity standard is adhered to' (Friedman, 1953b:209). However, the benefits do not come without cost (Friedman, 1953b:209–10). The major negative feature of commodity money is that considerable resources have to be devoted to its production. The potential saving in resources that can be achieved by employing a less costly medium of exchange ultimately leads to the adoption of unbacked fiat currency and credit: 'As already noted, the cost of a strict commodity standard is almost certain to lead to the adoption of devices designed to provide without cost at least some part of the annual addition to the circulating medium required to provide for secular growth' (Friedman, 1953b:243). Sir John Hicks (1967a:158–9) makes the same point: 'Metallic money is an expensive way of performing a simple function;

---

7. The distinction between bank and commodity money should not be confused with the distinction between inside and outside money introduced by Gurley and Shaw (1960). Makinen (1977:160) notes that the distinction between inside and outside money is best forgotten as the crucial distinction is that between money whose cost of production is less than its value (purchasing power), i.e. what we have called bank money in this study, and money whose cost of production equals its value, i.e. commodity money. However, we cannot agree with Makinen's suggestion that the Pigou effect is important in a bank money economy even though the latter does constitute positive net wealth as argued by Pesek and Saving (1967).

why waste resources in digging up gold when pieces of paper (or mere book entries) which can be provided, and transported, at a fraction of the cost will do as well? That is why the credit system grows; it provides a medium of exchange at much lower cost.' The forces of reduced cost and increased efficiency that lead to the evolution of bank money makes it virtually certain that schemes based on a return to convertibility, e.g. free banking (White, 1984), are not feasible. The evolution of bank money is irreversible and in any event it is highly unlikely that pure commodity money systems ever existed (Eichengreen, 1985:121–40).

The reasons for the evolution of bank money seem clear enough, but what are the dangers inherent in such a system? There are costs, as Hicks points out:

But on the other hand there is a penalty that the credit system is an unstable system . . . Thus in order for the credit system to work smoothly, it needs an institutional framework which will restrain it on the one hand, and shall support it on the other. To find a framework which can be relied on to give support when it is needed, and to impose restraint just when it is needed, is very difficult. I do not think that it has ever been perfectly solved. Even to this day we do not really know the answer.

Certainly, the potential instability of bank money has been well documented in the literature from Wicksell (1898a) to Minsky (1982). In terms of the classical quantity theory, the difficulty with bank money arises because it is practically costless to produce. Which means that under classical competitive conditions there is no effective limit to the supply of fiat money: 'There is *no stable competitive equilibrium* except when fiat currency declines so much in value that it becomes a commodity currency, the commodity being the paper and services used in producing the currency' (Friedman, 1953b:216, emphasis added). The monetarist solution for the control of the credit system is to impose a growth rule that will mimic the supply constraints of commodity money by placing quantitative restrictions on the issue of fiat currency. In this way it is hoped that the stability properties of commodity money can be combined with the low resource costs of bank money thereby obtaining the best features of both systems. This is surely the objective of both 100 per cent reserve banking and monetary base control.

It seems, therefore, that from a historical perspective, the distinguishing characteristic of bank money is that as it is not produced it is not subject to the 'laws' of production. Hence it is not amenable to analysis in terms of classical principles. This, ultimately, is the importance of the distinction between bank and commodity money for classical monetary theory. Similar conclusions apply to neoclassical monetary theory. Consequently, the crucial question facing monetary theorists, is whether the evolution of bank money makes any difference to their theories based on the properties of commodity money. Seen from the perspective of Monetary Analysis this question is fundamental. A strong case can be made for the argument that although monetary theorists within the tradition of Real Analysis, from Wicksell to Friedman, have acknowledged the existence, and some of the characteristics of credit, they have failed to follow the distinction to its analytical conclusion. Although Wicksell's pure credit model spells out the properties of bank money, it has since been tacitly assumed that bank money requires no special attention so long as it can be made to behave *as if* it were commodity money (Hicks, 1967a). But, as Schumpeter (1954:717) has argued, this has led to the development of a (commodity) money theory of credit instead of a *credit theory of money*. The distinction is not a play on words. It highlights a fundamental theoretical principle. In a bank money economy *the theoretical principles of neither classical nor neoclassical theory can be applied to explain the rate of interest*.

In this sense, monetary theories in the tradition of Real Analysis have no coherent theoretical explanation of the rate of interest. Marx, in terms of classical theory, rejects the notion of a natural rate of interest because money, i.e. fiat money or credit, is a 'commodity' *sui generis*, to which the laws of production do not apply (Panico, 1983:174). Hence credit cannot have a natural price in the classical sense of the term.[8] As far as neoclassical theory is concerned, we now know that the capital debate reveals that the natural rate of interest cannot be defined outside of a one-commodity model.

The properties of capitalist production and bank money are thus interdependent characteristics of monetary theories in the tradition of Monetary Analysis. This point has a long history but has recently been stressed by monetary theorists such as Kaldor (1970, 1982), Davidson (1978) and Moore (1979, 1984, 1986). Concerning the relationship between capitalist production and bank money Marc Lavoie (1984a:773–4) has summarized the position as follows:

The integration of money in the economic system must not be done when output is already specified, as in the exchange economy of general equilibrium models . . . but rather must be introduced as part of the production process . . . Those who organise production require access to existing resources, mainly human labour. This access is provided by credit money. Any flow of production requires a flow of new credit or the renewal of past flows

8. It should be noted, however, that Pasinetti (1981) uses a concept of the natural rate of interest based on a dynamic interpretation of Sraffa's standard commodity. How this concept is to overcome the objections raised by Marx to the use of the natural rate of interest in the classical model is not clear.

of credit. The banking system creates the necessary credit . . . Money is introduced into the economy through the productive activities of the firms, as these activities generate income. There can be no (bank) money without production.

What Lavoie is saying here is that the entrepreneur economy of capitalist production is a bank money economy in which the flow of credit cannot be analysed as if it were a given stock of commodity money. If anything, credit appears as a factor of production in a capitalist economy. Recognition of this point is fundamental in understanding the distinction between Real and Monetary Analysis.

In particular the role of money as *cause* or *effect* should be seen in terms of the distinction between commodity and bank money. Commodity money is clearly compatible with the classical quantity theory of money in which the quantity of money has a causal influence on the price level. Bank money, on the other hand, because it is generated in the process of production – or speculation – appears as part of a process and often as effect rather than cause. With the evolution of the banking system and the extensive use of credit, the question of causation has always posed particular difficulties for quantity theorists, wedded as they are to the properties of commodity money in the tradition of Real Analysis. But in the tradition of Monetary Analysis it is to the properties of bank money that we must turn. The nature of the money supply is of direct relevance here. The point is simply this: if the rate of interest is an independent variable, not determined by the forces of productivity and thrift but *exogenously* set by the monetary authorities, then the supply of credit becomes perfectly elastic in the short run at that rate of interest. This point was certainly recognized by Wicksell:

It is no longer possible to refer to the supply of money as an independent magnitude, differing from the demand for money. No matter what amount of money may be demanded from the banks, that is the amount which they are in a position to lend (so long as the security of the borrower is adequate). The banks have merely to enter a figure in the borrower's account to represent a credit granted or a deposit created. When a cheque is then drawn and subsequently presented to the banks, they credit the account of the owner of the cheque with a deposit of the appropriate amount (or reduce his debit by that amount). The 'supply of money' is thus furnished by the demand itself (quoted by Moore, 1986).[9]

9. This observation is of more than historical interest if central banks continue to implement monetary policy via control of short term interest rates. For example, Howells and Bain (1983) present an interpretation of the Bank of England's monetary control procedures which conforms almost exactly to Wicksell's description. In that case Monetary and not Real Analysis is the appropriate setting for an evaluation of monetary policy. Kaldor (1982) and Moore (1979) have been the principal exponents of this view.

Although Wicksell, like Keynes in the *Treatise*, sought only to extend the quantity theory tradition to an analysis of periods of transition in an economy with a well-developed banking system (Patinkin, 1976:48), all this was changed in the *General Theory*. There the quantity theory is given up. Modern Post Keynesian monetary theorists, such as Kaldor (1982) and Moore (1979, 1986), stress the point that in a world of bank money the quantity theory must be abandoned. As we will see, this conclusion is an inevitable consequence of the principle of effective demand. By contrast, modern monetary theorists in the tradition of Real Analysis treat the money supply as if it is, or can be made to *behave* as if it is, a fixed quantity of commodity money. This is true of both mainstream Keynesians, who employ the IS–LM model in which the quantity of money is fixed, and those monetarists who follow Friedman and argue for a fixed monetary growth rule. From the perspective of the distinction between commodity and bank money the monetarist's growth rule represents an attempt to ensure that a bank money system behaves as if it were a commodity money system. There are, of course, numerous implications for traditional money multiplier analysis and the monetarist position which follow from this point but these will be dealt with more fully below. At this stage it is sufficient to appreciate the interdependent relationship between capitalist production, the exogenous nature of the conventional rate of interest, and bank money. These three characteristics are in turn essential to an understanding of the principle of effective demand.

The principle of effective demand

The rejection of a Say's Law economy as the basis for the development of a monetary theory of production is a fundamental characteristic of Monetary Analysis. The rejection of Say's Law must, however, be made analytically watertight. To achieve this we need to introduce the principle of effective demand but we begin by considering Say's Law from another perspective so as to prepare the way for a clear statement of the principle of effective demand.

As Chick (1983:71) has pointed out, there are many versions of Say's Law but the basic idea is that production, by creating income, simultaneously creates the power to purchase (recall Hutt's defence of Say's Law). And, since the willingness to work is motivated by the desire to consume, there should be no impediment to the sale of *any* level of output and therefore no reason for unemployment. Output should expand up to the point of full employment of resources. In terms of the Weintraub (1958), Davidson and Smolensky (1964) or Chick (1983) analysis of aggregate demand and supply, the aggregate demand and supply curves would coincide as indicated by D = Z in Figure 7.1(a). This is the case described by Keynes (1936:29) and discussed by Patinkin (1976:89, 1982:128, 142). Alternatively, in the case of a marginal propensity to consume of less than one in a money-using economy, the 'classical' interest rate mechanism (loanable funds in conjunction with the quantity theory of money as explained in chapter 4) ensures an intersection of D and Z at full

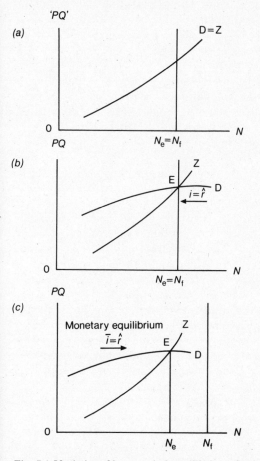

Fig. 7.1 Varieties of long-period equilibrium: Say's Law economies versus a monetary economy: (a) and (b) Say's Law economies (real exchange economies), (c) long-period unemployment equilibrium in a monetary economy

employment as in Figure 7.1(b). There is then no obstacle to the *profitable* expansion of output to the point of full employment, N_f in a Say's Law economy.

By contrast, the principle of effective demand refutes Say's Law by postulating that *there is a limit to the profitable expansion of output* (Chick, 1983:71). This observation is not quite sufficient to make the case, however, and the next step is to determine why there is a limit to the profitable expansion of output. The answer provided here relies on the reinterpretation of liquidity preference theory and the key role of the conventional rate of interest in the determination of what we will call monetary equilibrium. This term is taken from Myrdal (1939) and, although it differs in detail from his usage, it is in the same spirit as it is offered as a generalization of Wicksell and describes the condition for equilibrium of aggregate demand and supply (Shackle, 1967:97).

In shorthand terms, monetary equilibrium is defined by the equality between the conventional rate of interest and the marginal efficiency of capital. Given the conventional rate of interest, $\bar{i}$, the marginal efficiency of capital adjusts to the rate of interest and the rate of interest thereby determines the rate of investment. The rate of investment, an autonomous component of aggregate demand, then determines the point of effective demand, E, in Figure 7.1(c). At E monetary equilibrium exists in the sense that the rates of return on all forms of converting present into future wealth are equalized. That is, at the point of effective demand, we have long-period equilibrium in the classical sense of a uniform rate of return on all assets. Thus, in manufacturing industry, entrepreneurs are earning normal profits on their investment in productive capital and they have no incentive to expand production even if unemployment exists. This, in a nutshell, is the monetary theory of effective demand which integrates real and monetary forces in the determination of long-period equilibrium.[10]

Although Patinkin (1976:100) does not interpret the principle of effective demand as outlined here, he does suggest that, to the extent that Keynes's analysis can be represented graphically, it conforms to the aggregate demand and supply analysis of Figure 7.1 rather than to the Hicksian IS–LM model. As we have seen, the latter is essentially a Wicksellian structure and clearly lacks the principle of effective demand. By contrast, the principle of effective demand emerges as the key element in a monetary theory of production in the tradition of Monetary Analysis. An important characteristic of this concept of

10. The principle of effective demand as defined here differs from that employed by Patinkin (1976, 1982), Asimakopulos (1982, 1984), Milgate (1982:78) or Chick (1983). The significance of the difference will be discussed in chapter 9.

monetary equilibrium is the central role played by liquidity preference theory in defining monetary equilibrium, which in turn determines the rate of investment and the point of effective demand. Thus we see that the principle of effective demand and a non-neutral role for bank money are interdependent properties of capitalist production. And as, Chick (1985) and Lavoie (1984b:755) have recently reminded us, it is within this context that investment can determine savings. It is the ability to grant credit in advance of prior savings which leads to the reversal of the orthodox view of causality between saving and investment.

At this stage some preliminary comment on the exogenous nature of the rate of interest is necessary to avoid confusion. Two issues are relevant. The first arises from Sargent's (1979:92–5) demonstration that the traditional Keynesian model is inconsistent or overdetermined if the interest rate is treated as an exogenous variable. This result should not be confused with the analysis sketched above. The model used by Sargent is a co-operative model which embodies Say's Law as the labour market determines the full employment level of output. That is, Sargent's model does not include the principle of effective demand and as a result the full employment level of output determined by the labour market is inconsistent with the exogenous rate of interest.

The second issue arises from the tendency of most commentators to overlook the role of the conventional rate of interest as an exogenous variable in the liquidity preference theory.[11] In the absence of the natural rate of interest most observers find it difficult to make any sense of liquidity preference theory. Recent examples are the interpretations by Hutt (1979) and Coddington (1983) and these will be discussed in chapter 9. At this stage the significance of the difficulty can be illustrated by examining the disagreement between Garegnani (1983) and Kregel (1983) on the interpretation of the principle of effective demand. Both agree that monetary forces may determine real phenomena, such as the growth of output, but they disagree on the significance of Keynes's analysis of liquidity preference for the principle of effective demand. Garegnani (1983:78) recognizes the essential role of money in effective demand insofar as it allows for the

11. Not surprisingly it was an idea that puzzled the exponents of the loanable funds theory, as they were accustomed to employing the natural rate as the focus of the analysis; as we will see below this is still true today. Nevertheless, with the benefit of hindsight, we now know that the neoclassical foundations of the natural rate have been knocked out by the capital debate. Although not available to either Keynes or Marx, the result of that debate gives added support to their view that there is no theoretical explanation for the average or conventional level of the rate of interest.

break in the savings–investment link in the cycle of capitalist production, but feels that this 'has little to do with an explanation of the rate of interest by means of Keynes's liquidity preference'. Kregel, on the other hand, points to the importance of liquidity preference, and by implication the conventional rate of interest, for the principle of effective demand.

An examination of Garegnani's argument reveals that, at this point, he interprets liquidity preference theory too narrowly and as a result is led to overlook an important monetary aspect of the principle of effective demand. Essentially, Garegnani argues that Keynes had no long-period theory of the rate of interest and that liquidity preference theory is only a short-period analysis of transitory movements in the rate of interest. Consequently, he concludes that liquidity preference theory does not provide a basis for Keynes's claims on the determination of a long-period unemployment equilibrium and is thus easily absorbed into the neoclassical synthesis. In particular Garegnani (1983:78) argues that liquidity preference theory offers no explanation of why long-period flexibility of prices and wages will not produce full employment by causing the necessary adjustment in the rate of interest.

As we now know, however, these objections overlook the key role played by the conventional rate of interest in liquidity preference theory. Of course Garegnani is right to point out that Keynes has no *theory* of the long-period rate of interest. But that is precisely the point. Keynes like Marx, came to the conclusion that *it was not possible to provide a purely theoretical explanation of the long-period rate of interest* – i.e. the rate of interest is an exogenous-type variable. As Pasinetti (1974:47) notes: 'What this theory [of effective demand] requires, as far as the rate of interest is concerned, is not that the rate of interest is determined by liquidity preference, but that it is determined *exogenously* with respect to the income generation process. Whether, in particular, liquidity preference or anything else determines it, is entirely immaterial.' That there is no such thing as an endogenous equilibrium rate of interest was a point also stressed by Sraffa (Kregel, 1983:59, 66; Milgate, 1983:100).

Seen in this light it cannot be claimed that the neoclassical synthesis has incorporated liquidity preference theory. What the neoclassical synthesis incorporated was simply a generalization of loanable funds theory with liquidity preference theory standing in for the market rate of interest. This is obviously the case in most textbook presentations of the IS–LM model where 'liquidity preference theory' generates the LM curve and 'classical theory' (the forces of productivity and thrift) determines the IS curve, as explained in chapter 4.

There is no role for the principle of effective demand in such a model. Price and wage flexibility may (in a one-commodity model) restore full employment in the models of the neoclassical synthesis, but the question facing Keynes's statement of liquidity preference theory is whether a price and wage deflation will cause the exogenously determined *conventional* rate of interest to fall automatically to the full employment level. Both Keynes and Robinson (1947:86–92) gave negative answers to this question, and we will consider the issue in more detail below.

It seems, then, that Garegnani's arguments against liquidity preference theory are too narrowly based and if acted upon would lead to the neglect of an important influence of money on the point of effective demand. In particular, it should not be overlooked that the conventional rate of interest plays a key role in liquidity preference theory, akin to the natural rate in loanable funds theory, and that liquidity preference theory cannot therefore be interpreted as dealing only with the market or money rate of interest without reference to the conventional rate. The two theories are conceptually distinct as their key components, the conventional and natural rates of interest, are not comparable; they belong to separate conceptual frameworks.

CONCLUDING REMARKS

Schumpeter's distinction between Real and Monetary Analysis is important in explaining the paradoxical state of neoclassical monetary theory, in particular its inability to integrate monetary and value (real) theory. Neoclassical monetary theory falls within the confines of Real Analysis because it seeks to apply the assumptions of a neutral money Say's Law economy to the capitalist system. Monetary Analysis, on the other hand, is based on the premise that there are fundamental differences between capitalist production financed by bank money and the barter or co-operative production of a Say's Law economy. Recognizing this distinction is the first step in the development of Monetary Analysis. Once acknowledged, it opens up the route to the integration of real and monetary forces – both transitory *and persistent* – with the principle of effective demand. That is to say, monetary forces can then be integrated into the analysis of the long-period determination of output and employment – real variables. In particular, the relationship between real and monetary rates of return (the rate of profit, the marginal efficiency of capital, and the rate of interest) is correctly identified and can be re-examined without encountering the pitfalls of the neoclassical analysis. These points were stressed by Kregel (1983) and later chapters present a formal analysis of these issues.

Chapter 9 develops the Marshallian microeconomic foundations of monetary equilibrium. This exercise is intended to clarify the relationship between the rate of interest and the marginal efficiencies of other assets. In this sense, it offers an explanation of the relationship between the analysis of chapter 17 in the *General Theory* and the principle of effective demand. Chapter 10 then applies the concepts of monetary equilibrium and the principle of effective demand to three macroeconomic models: (i) the Fundamental Equations of the *Treatise on Money*; (ii) the aggregate demand and supply model of the Post Keynesians; and, (iii) the traditional IS–LM model. The latter provides an illustration of the principle of effective demand and the properties of Monetary Analysis in a context familiar to most macroeconomists. It also prepares the ground for the reconsideration of Shackle's notion of Keynesian kaleidics and contrasts this framework for Monetary Analysis with the 'classical' vision of Real Analysis. Before we engage in this endeavour, however, it is necessary to consider some further issues of method and methodology.

8

SOME FURTHER QUESTIONS OF METHOD AND METHODOLOGY

INTRODUCTION

The discussion of the previous chapter has established that the foundations of monetary theory must be sought within the framework of Schumpeter's Monetary Analysis. The work of Marx and Keynes – in the *General Theory* – falls within this tradition and it is with Keynes's monetary theory in particular that we will be concerned in later chapters. Before beginning with the analysis proper, however, it is necessary to examine some further issues of method and methodology. This need arises for two important reasons. Firstly, Keynes's monetary theory involves the application of Marshallian modes of thought, and the Marshallian partial equilibrium *method* is not properly understood by neoclassical general equilibrium theorists brought up on a neo-Walrasian or Wicksellian diet. Secondly, there are some issues of method and methodology outstanding from previous discussions that require clarification.

THE RICARDO–MARSHALL–KEYNES METHOD: PARTIAL EQUILIBRIUM

Although it should have been obvious all along, it is now generally acknowledged that Keynes must be evaluated from a Marshallian and not a neo-Walrasian or Wicksellian perspective.[1] Recent attempts to trace the Marshallian components and methods in the *General*

---

1. With the dominance of neo-Walrasian and Wicksellian modes of thought in the post-war period this obvious point was often overlooked and is still overlooked. For comments on this issue see Pasinetti (1974:ch. 2), Clower (1975), Davidson (1978) and Helm (1984a).

Theory have been made by Kregel (1981), Parinello (1983) and Asimakopulos (1982, 1984), for example. At first sight this may strike many readers as a little fanciful. After all, the *General Theory* supposedly initiated the development of macroeconomics while Marshallian economics is essentially microeconomics. This is the common perception. Such an assessment is, however, superficial. As Kregel (1981:1) reminds us, Joan Robinson was the first to suggest that Keynes's theory could be best understood as an extension of Marshallian tools to the analysis of output as a whole. Interestingly, Hoover (1984b:64) has recently pointed out that Friedman reached the same conclusion on the application of the Marshallian partial equilibrium method to macroeconomic issues.

The first point of which we must take note, then, is that partial equilibrium is not synonymous with microeconomics. In fact the partial equilibrium method was adapted by Keynes and applied to *macroeconomic* aggregates in both the *Treatise* and the *General Theory*. A moment's reflection should confirm that this is a legitimate interpretation, particularly if it is recalled that the general equilibrium method was applied by Walras to microeconomic analysis and only later adapted by neo-Walrasians to macroeconomics. Partial and general equilibrium approaches can therefore be compared at the level of *method* and not only in terms of whether they imply micro- or macroeconomic analysis. From the perspective of macroeconomic analysis, the term 'general' in neoclassical general equilibrium theory is particularly misleading because it has become associated with the idea that the analysis is concerned with the interdependence of the macro system, i.e. the 'whole system', while partial equilibrium is concerned with only part of the system under study. With the benefit of hindsight it now appears that this interpretation is particularly sterile. The partial equilibrium method when applied to macroeconomic issues is also general in the sense that it deals with the interdependence of the entire system.

But it deals with the entire system in a 'one problem at a time' fashion instead of attempting to solve for all endogenous variables simultaneously as in neo-Walrasian general equilibrium theory. Partial should therefore be interpreted to mean Marshall's one-at-a-time method (Kregel, 1976:218n). Furthermore, it appears that the *ceteris paribus* clause of the partial equilibrium method plays an important role in the notion of causality employed by Keynes, Marshall and, it seems, Ricardo. In this respect both Pasinetti (1974:43) and Schumpeter (1954:473) note the strong similarity in the *methods* of Keynes and Ricardo. In view of Marshall's claim to be extending and refining Ricardian economics, this link is perhaps not as surprising as it might seem at first sight. It should be stressed, however, that the use of the same *method* does not imply the use of the same *theory*. Keynes classed both Marshall (neoclassical) and Ricardo (classical) as 'classical' because their theories (for different reasons) had no role for the principle of effective demand: Ricardo because savings equalled investment by definition, and Marshall because the rate of interest equated real savings and investment. As for Keynes's own theoretical framework, Pasinetti (1974:43) argues that it is typically classical.

The fundamental issue at stake between partial and general equilibrium analysis is thus not the micro–macro distinction – the discussions of the microfoundations of macroeconomics, so popular in the recent literature, e.g. Harcourt (1977), provide ample illustrations of the confusion on this issue – but a question of method. Namely, how is the interdependence of the macroeconomic system best analysed – in terms of the neoclassical general equilibrium method or in terms of the Ricardo–Marshall–Keynes partial equilibrium method? In view of the failure of the neoclassical general equilibrium method, it is perhaps time that we took up Helm's (1984a) suggestion and reassessed the partial equilibrium alternative.

A key feature of the partial equilibrium method is its notion of causality. Pasinetti (1974:44–5) was one of the first to stress this point but the issue has recently been taken up by Hicks (1979), Helm (1984a, b) and Termini (1984). For example, it has been argued by both Pasinetti (1974:44) and Hicks (1979:80) that Keynes intended the long-term rate of interest, as an exogenous factor, to be treated as one of the causes of investment and Chick (1983:15) makes essentially the same point when she notes that in Keynes's method there is a distinct time-stream of events. The role of the conventional rate of interest as an exogenous factor is thus central to this notion of causality. As Hicks (1979:22) notes: 'From the point of view of the theory, an exogenous element (or the taking of some particular value by an exogenous element) cannot be an effect. It can only be a cause.' In a sense, it was this notion of causality which Hicks (1937) initially lost in his IS–LM interpretation of Keynes, when he insisted that the rate of interest should be determined endogenously in true neoclassical general equilibrium fashion, i.e. he overlooked the importance of the conventional rate of interest as an exogenous-type variable and by so doing abandoned Keynes's method.

Helm (1984a, b) has recently, and independently, reassessed the partial equilibrium method and reinforces Pasinetti's view that it is an essential complement to the notion of causality employed by Keynes. In particular, the *ceteris paribus* clause plays an important role in the method of counterfactuals. This method employs the use of hypothetical thought experiments to examine what would happen as a result of a change in one of the causal factors, assuming other causal factors remained constant.[2] That is to say, it is a method which attempts to provide an explanation in terms of cause and effect by isolating causes one at a time. The method has been discussed comprehensively by Termini (1981:61–4) in terms of the distinction between *logical* time and *calendar* or *historical* time. Thought experiments are conducted in logical and not calendar time.

A second key feature of the Ricardo–Marshall–Keynes method which requires attention is the role of the concept of long-period equilibrium. As the neo-Ricardians have recently reminded us, the excessive concentration on short-period equilibria, by Keynesians and others, represents a marked departure from the traditional method of economic theory. This method, as recently characterized by Milgate (1982:11, emphasis added), consists of:'specifying an abstract characterization of the *actual* economy so as to isolate a well-defined set of phenomena upon which to concentrate theoretical endeavour. This abstract characterization is meant to capture the *systematic, regular and persistent forces at work* in the system and thereby to permit the "theory" to exclude accidental, arbitrary and "temporary" phenomena.' In terms of traditional economic terminology, the systematic or persistent forces have always been analysed in terms of some notion of long-period equilibrium, while the temporary or transitory forces are relegated to short-period disturbances.

Now, despite the fact that some neo-Walrasians and so-called Keynesians have resorted to what looks like an analysis based solely on short-period equilibria, the point is not sufficient for a general critique of neo-Walrasian or Wicksellian general equilibrium theory, as both versions of neoclassical theory have some or other interpretation of a long-period equilibrium, however limited it may be. Examples of the traditional method of economic theory, in the sense that this entails the use of a long-period equilibrium concept, can, in fact, be found in all versions of neoclassical theory. (Recall the analysis in the appendix to chapter 3 for an illustration of the type of long-period equilibrium encountered in neo-Walrasian theory.) The traditional method of economic analysis is based on the view that theories are constructed by abstracting the persistent forces at work in the phenomena under investigation. If no such persistent forces exist then there will be no means of separating the systematic from the random, and consequently no way of constructing a theory. The existence of economics as a subject is therefore based on the view that

2. The use of counterfactuals in the partial equilibrium method should not be confused with Hahn's counterfactual methodology. Recall the discussion in chapter 3.

such persistent forces exist in capitalist economies and that they can be both detected and their analysis woven into some form of logically coherent theoretical structure.

In terms of such an endeavour, the notion of long-period equilibrium obviously proves particularly helpful because it specifies the conditions under which the persistent or dominant forces are in balance. It is not necessary that these forces be permanent but only that they change slowly over time. If no such state could be imagined (it need never actually have to be achieved) it is difficult to see in what way persistent and transitory forces could be distinguished. Most economists therefore proceed on the basis that the notion of long-period equilibrium is an indispensable theoretical construct. As Eatwell (1983c) notes, Friedman has always been faithful to this traditional method.

Nevertheless, many Keynesians took Keynes's concentration on the short run literally, and all but abandoned the concept of long-period equilibrium in the belief that in the long run we are all dead.[3] There are a number of obvious difficulties with such a position. Firstly, from the perspective of the history of economic thought, it makes no sense to claim as a *general* theory an analysis of output and employment in the short period; particularly in the case of a monetary theory. At least from the time of Hume it has been acknowledged that money may not be neutral in the short period (Patinkin, 1972b; Milgate, 1982:ch. 3; Eatwell, 1983a). By stressing the short-period aspects of Keynes's analysis and *ignoring* the long-period implications, the Keynesians therefore weakened their position. Under pressure from the monetarists they were grudgingly forced into considering some of the long-period implications of their analysis (Blinder and Solow, 1973; Tobin and Buiter, 1976; Tobin, 1980). But, as we have seen, this analysis turns out to be Wicksellian rather than Keynesian. To offer a positive response to neoclassical monetary theory it is therefore necessary to examine the influence of monetary forces in the determination of *long-period equilibrium* positions.

More importantly, Kregel (1983:51) makes it clear that it is not legitimate to treat short-period analysis as though it were a separate theory distinct from long-period theory. Both are different aspects of a single unitary theoretical framework – as in the familiar Marshallian three-period analysis, for example. Hence, although the notion of a long-period equilibrium may appear as a remote abstraction, it provides a systematic framework within which to discover and analyse the forces at work when the system is out of equilibrium, i.e.

3. This statement is made by Keynes (1923:80), as a quantity theorist, during a critique of simplistic interpretations of the quantity theory.

in the short period. As Robinson (1947:99) observes: 'But the motive for studying equilibrium positions is to discover forces which are at work when the system is out of equilibrium.' Note that this suggestion makes sense from a Marshallian but not a neo-Walrasian perspective. The latter has nothing to say about out-of-equilibrium positions.

Having established that some notion of long-period equilibrium is required, it remains to be decided what *concept* of equilibrium to employ. As Chick (1983:21) has pointed out, there appear to be two concepts of macro-equilibrium extant in economics. These are:

(i)   macro-equilibrium as a point of rest – forces leading to change are absent or countervailing;

(ii)   macro-equilibrium as a balance between supply and demand functions.

Now it is apparent that the first concept is broader than the second in the sense that it need not imply the second, i.e. (i) need not imply (ii) but (ii) implies (i). The second concept is, of course, that employed in neoclassical general equilibrium theory while the first has affinities with classical theory. For example, involuntary unemployment is not an idea that is compatible with the second concept of equilibrium but it may be consistent with the first.

The concept of monetary equilibrium used in this study is a macro-equilibrium in the first or classical sense of a state of rest. In static monetary equilibrium the rates of return on all assets are equalized but unemployment may result. In what follows, it is therefore important to bear in mind that a long-period macro-equilibrium can be treated as a position of rest which may not imply a macro-equilibrium of supply and demand functions – assuming that such functions could be constructed.

To summarize, we can say that key elements of the Ricardo–Marshall–Keynes method which need to be noted are the following. The partial equilibrium method is not limited to microeconomic analysis and should be compared to the general equilibrium *method* of neoclassical theory when applied to macroeconomic analysis. In particular, the partial equilibrium method represents an attempt to provide a causal explanation in terms of institutionally determined exogenous variables that cannot be given a theoretical explanation. Inherent in the method is the notion of a long-period equilibrium. Here, it seems, Marshall can be distinguished from Ricardo and Keynes in having adopted a narrower (neoclassical) concept of equilibrium based on the balance of demand and supply functions. Ricardo and Keynes, on the other hand, operate with the broader classical notion of competitive equilibrium as a state of rest.

METHODOLOGY UNDERLYING THE METHOD

In specifying what he perceives to be the long-period method, Milgate takes it for granted that classical theorists attempted to construct theories or models of *actual* economies. Such a view is, no doubt, understandable. But as we have seen, it cannot be taken for granted when evaluating the role of neo-Walrasian models. In fact, precisely the opposite view is taken by Frank Hahn in his brand of counterfactual methodology, in terms of which neo-Walrasian models are not supposed to refer to any actual economy. A fundamental issue of methodology is at stake here.

The issue at stake is, and has always been, the relationship between economic theories or models and the economies that they purport to analyse, i.e. the relationship between abstraction and realism. Now as everyone agrees that all theories abstract from reality, they must be unrealistic in a descriptive sense, so it is not with descriptive realism that we are concerned. Rather, it is the nature of abstraction that must be clarified. For this purpose the competing views of realists, conventionalists, instrumentalists and inductivists within the philosophy of science are of interest. Apart from the realists, all these positions have been discussed, so at this point we examine the realist view.

The central tenet of the realist position is that theories and theoretical terms should make real references. The use of analytic or theoretical terms that do not make such real references is rejected. That is, assumptions that do not refer to anything that actually exists are unacceptable. This point of view is neatly summarized by Katouzian (1980:80): 'If an abstraction has a counterpart in reality at all, then it is not a false description of reality; it is intended as a true description of reality in a set of well-defined circumstances which, like any other description, may turn out to be true or false.' The realist philosophy of science is therefore directly concerned with the ontological status of theoretical terms. Models or theories which embody this philosophy attempt to approximate the important features of the real economy. This, in essence, is what the debate over the 'realism' of assumptions is really about, although it has not always been conducted in these terms. Nevertheless, it proves particularly enlightening to compare the conventionalist methodology associated with neo-Walrasian model building and abstraction with Joan Robinson's concept of a historical model, as the latter appears to be consistent with the realist philosophy.

The distinction can be drawn by beginning with some common ground. Most theorists acknowledge that in the study of complex phenomena the method of successive approximation proves useful. This method is employed wherever the problem under investigation is so complex that its solution can only be approached in stages. In that way it is hoped that one manageable problem can be tackled at a time. Walras (1926:211), for example, stated that: 'Any order of phenomena, however complicated, may be studied scientifically provided the rule of proceeding from the simple to the complex is always observed.' Joan Robinson (1962:33) makes essentially the same point: 'A model which took account of all the variegation of reality would be of no more use than a map at the scale one to one. For a first sketch we may simplify the model...' When constructing theories or models of a capitalist economy, it therefore appears that most theories acknowledge the usefulness of the method of successive approximation.

To carry out the method, the theorist relies on heuristic or *simplifying* assumptions at the initial stages (Musgrave, 1981). In the initial stages the theorist may assume that a particular factor operates in such a way as not to affect the result. In later stages, or in applying the theory, he must take these factors into account and determine what difference they make to the previous results. The method of successive approximation thus enables the theorist to isolate the persistent forces and evaluate their impact separately before attempting to examine their interaction. In essence, it seems that this is another important function of the *ceteris paribus* clause, i.e. it enables the theorist, at the initial stages, to isolate the separate effects of the persistent forces. Everyone knows that when it comes to the real economy the *ceteri* are never *pares*, but nevertheless the economist's method should enable him to better identify the persistent forces at work in an apparently chaotic economic universe.

Joan Robinson (1962:25–6, emphasis in original) refers to models or theories constructed on this basis as *historical* models and describes their application in the following terms:

A model applicable to actual history has to be capable of getting out of equilibrium; indeed *it must normally not be in it*. To construct such a model, we specify the technical conditions obtaining in the economy, and the behaviour reactions of its inhabitants, and then, so to say, dump it down in a particular situation at a particular date in historic time and work out what will happen next. The initial position contains, as well as physical data, the state of expectations of the characters concerned (whether based on past experience or on traditional beliefs). The system may then work itself out so as to fulfil or so as to disappoint them ... In an historical model causal relations have to be specified.

In applying the lessons of the logical time analysis in this way we must face the complexity of *historical* time (Termini, 1981:73–81). The contrast with the conventionalist-type methodologies adopted by most neoclassical theorists could not be more stark. Hahn's use of a counterfactual methodology to justify the use of the Arrow–Debreu model is a prime example. For, although these theorists attempt to apply the method of successive approximation – by starting with simple exchange and then adding production and an intertemporal analysis, for example – the end result is not one that can be applied to concrete historical events, as Hahn acknowledges. Instead it appears that the same level of abstraction is always maintained.

In the neo-Walrasian case this entails always subjecting the extensions of the exchange model to the properties of a tâtonnement–recontract exchange equilibrium (Rogers, 1983). The assumptions that are made are thus never heuristic or simplifying assumptions, but are instead essential for retaining the properties of the exchange model, i.e. a particular version of a Say's Law economy. As Joan Robinson (1962:33) warned, in making simplifying assumptions 'we must be careful not to make a simplification in such a way that the model falls to pieces when it is removed.' Removing some of the neo-Walrasian 'simplifying' assumptions produces precisely this result. As the complexity of the analysis increases it is therefore not the case that the previous conclusions are revised as additional factors are taken into consideration. Rather, additional factors are always introduced in such a way that they do not disturb any existing conclusions – for example, production is treated as a variety of exchange. Interestingly, Friedman (1955:905) was one of the first to spot this weakness in the Walrasian methodology: 'In his final sentence, Jaffee speaks like a true Walrasian on methodology. One first constructs a pure theory, somehow on purely formal considerations without introducing any empirical content; one then turns to the "real" world, fills in the empty boxes, assigns numerical values to constants . . . This seems to me a basically false view.' But instead of following this insight to its logical conclusion and highlighting the importance of the truth status of assumptions, i.e. the 'realism' of assumptions, Friedman rather ironically ended up with precisely the opposite conclusion, the consequences of which were documented in chapter 6.

A fundamental issue in the methodology of the realists is the attention paid to the truth status of theoretical concepts. The realist philosophy is based on the *belief* that, although it may not be possible to prove that a theory is true or false, it is in fact true or false (Caldwell, 1980:372). It should also be noted that in the debate between realists and instrumentalists the 'realism' of assumptions refers to their truth status. Logical validity, although necessary, is not sufficient for theory construction. As Hoover (1984a) has reminded us, most logicians distinguish between logical validity and soundness, and classify a logically valid argument based on false assumptions as unsound. Aspects of neo-Walrasian models, for example, may thus be logically valid but they are unsound arguments about the capitalist system if based on false assumptions – as Hahn appears to concede they are.

AN ILLUSTRATION: THE ANALYSIS OF EXPECTATIONS

The treatment of expectations has recently received wide attention as a result of the application of the Rational Expectations hypothesis to neoclassical macroeconomic models. The implications of this development for economic theory were discussed in chapters 5 and 6 and require little further comment. It is important to note, however, that when discussing the basis on which expectations are founded, Keynes (1936:152) again turns to convention – the belief that the current state of affairs will continue unless we have specific reasons to expect a change. What is of relevance here, it seems, is the distinction between risk and uncertainty and the implications of this distinction for the analysis and treatment of expectations in economic models.

In addition to specifying the use of the relevant economic theory, the Rational Expectations hypothesis requires that individuals' (or the average of individuals') subjective probabilities should equal the objective probabilities, i.e. the observed frequencies of events. Now this latter requirement appears to be based on the view that economic events are replicable in the sense that they generate sufficient repetitions from which individuals can infer the objective frequencies. If the economic universe is not replicable in this sense then the statistical foundations of the Rational Expectations hypothesis may well be lost. There appear to be some grounds for believing that this is, in fact, the case.

This belief is based on the well-known distinction between risk and uncertainty. It has been traditional to argue that both Frank Knight and Keynes defined risk as a situation where replication occurs and the objective frequencies can be determined, and uncertainty as a situation where such frequencies cannot be established. This interpretation has, in the case of Knight, recently been challenged by Le Roy and Singell (1987) but there is little doubt that it is applicable to Keynes's case. For example, Keynes (1936:163) clearly appears to repudiate the relative frequency approach to the analysis of expectations when he remarks: 'We are merely reminding ourselves that human decisions affecting the future . . . cannot depend on strict mathematical expectations, since the basis for making such calculations does not exist.' Despite this apparently unequivocal rejection of the frequency approach to the analysis of expectations it is not uncommon to find Keynes interpreted, e.g. by Meltzer (1981), as an early exponent of the Rational Expectations hypothesis. But as Davidson (1982/3) and Bateman (1987) have recently reaffirmed, this interpretation is mistaken. Bateman, in particular, provides convincing evidence of why this is so. His discussion also enables us to see that the distinction between risk and uncertainty ultimately rests on alternative interpretations of the meaning of probability.

As Bateman (1987:99) explains, there are only two basic ideas about what probability is. The most familar is that the probability of an event is the long-term frequency of its occurrence. This concept of probability has been labelled *aleatory* probability because it is based on the proportion or percentage of times an event occurs, as in repeated trials of a fair game. It is this case that economists associate with situations characterized by risk. The other concept of probability relates to situations of uncertainty because it is based on the view that probability represents the degree of belief that an individual has in a particular outcome given his knowledge of the likelihood of its outcome rather than its relative frequency. This concept of probability is labelled *epistemic* probability (from *episteme*, the Greek word for knowledge).

These two basic concepts of the meaning of probability can both be interpreted from either a subjective or an objective perspective. An objective theory of probability is one in which probabilities of a given event are unique and the same for all individuals with the same information. Differences in assigned probabilities would then represent mistakes. This would not be the case with a subjective theory, as individuals may assign different probabilities to the same event even if they have the same information.

This taxonomy of views on the meaning of probability can now be employed to examine views on how expectations should be modelled. Taking the Rational Expectations hypothesis first, it is clear from Muth's definitions that this hypothesis is based on an objective theory of probability irrespective of whether the underlying view of probability is aleatory or epistemic. In fact Muth seems to employ both aleatory and epistemic views of probability. When specifying that individuals' subjective probabilities will coincide with the objective probabilities he seems to imply an aleatory view of probability but when he specifies expectations as the predictions of the relevant economic theory he seems to suggest an epistemic view. In the latter case he even leaves the door open to a subjective view if there is no agreement about what the relevant economic theory is. As we have noted in chapter 5, the new classical school eliminates the latter possibility by tacitly assuming that some unspecified but rigorous neoclassical general equilibrium model provides the relevant, and generally accepted, theory. This step effectively eliminates the subjective epistemic view of probability. But Bateman (1987) argues convincingly that this was the view of probability held by Keynes when he wrote the *General Theory* although it was not the view he held in the *Treatise on Probability*.

Bateman (1987:107) argues that in the latter work Keynes advocated an *objective epistemic* view of probability but at the time of the *General Theory* he had, under the influence of Ramsey, come to accept the *subjective epistemic* view. Bateman (1987:112) gives two reasons to explain Keynes's rejection of the application of the aleatory view of probability to economic phenomena. The first was that there was insufficient evidence to establish the existence of stable distributions of key variables: 'No one (including Tinbergen) had made enough observations under different circumstances to be able to legitimately make the assumption of stability that would be necessary to employ an aleatory conception of probability.' Although this objection holds out the hope that economics may, if the stability of these distributions can be established, emulate some branches of the natural sciences and employ an aleatory concept of probability, the second objection effectively undermines that hope. As Bateman notes, Keynes goes on to suggest that as economic agents employ subjective epistemic probabilities, their decision-making behaviour will not generate the stable distributions necessary to apply the aleatory concept of probability. Paul Davidson (1982/3) has made essentially the same point by stressing that we live in an economic environment in which stochastic processes are non-ergodic.

The difficulty with the subjective epistemic view of probability is, of course, that it opens the door to analytical nihilism. This, apparently, is the view held by Lucas (1977:15) when he suggests that economic theory is of little use in situations characterized by uncertainty rather than risk: 'In situations of risk, the hypothesis of rational behaviour on the part of agents will have usable content so that behaviour may be explainable in terms of economic theory. In such situations expectations are rational in Muth's sense. In cases of uncertainty economic reasoning will be of no value.' In similar vein, Bateman (1987:117n20) also registers a common perception when he notes that some supporters of a subjective epistemic view of probability, e.g. Shackle, encourage the view that it leads to analytical nihilism. However, as Bateman (1987:117) goes on to argue, there is no evidence that Keynes accepted this conclusion. Quite the contrary. Keynes (1973b:296–7) appears to have considered a subjective epistemic view of probability as quite compatible with the appropriate approach to model construction in economics:

> Economics is a science of thinking in terms of models joined to the art of choosing models which are relevant to the contemporary world. It is compelled to be this, because, unlike the typical natural science, the material to which it is applied is, in many respects, not homogeneous through time. The object of a model is to segregate the semi-permanent or relatively constant factors from those which are transitory or fluctuating so as to develop a logical way of thinking about the latter, and of understanding the time sequences to which they give rise in particular cases (quoted by Bateman, 1987:112).

Both Bateman (1987) and Torr (1984:198–9) make it clear that this view of the role of economic theory is compatible with a subjective epistemic approach to the analysis of expectations. But how can we deal with the analysis of expectations based on a subjective epistemic view of probability without falling into analytical nihilism? Some promising steps have been taken.

Following Lachmann's (1943:14) discussion, a useful starting point for the analysis of expectations that is consistent with the view of subjective epistemic probability is to draw a distinction between the need to treat expectations in *intelligible* fashion and the requirement that they should be *determinate*. This does not mean that expectations are treated in an *ad hoc* manner as is often claimed by exponents of Rational Expectations. Rather, it suggests that if expectations must be analysed in terms of the properties of subjective epistemic probability then it is pointless attempting to analyse them *as if* they are based on an objective aleatory view of probability. But giving up the idea that expectations must be objective and determinate does not mean that they are unintelligible. Nevertheless, if expectations cannot be treated along the lines suggested by Muth, how are they to be incorporated into economic analysis in an intelligible fashion? Everyone agrees that they should be incorporated, but can we make any progress in this endeavour? It seems that we can if we return to some of the ideas presented by Keynes (1936), Hicks (1939), Lachmann (1943) and Kregel (1976).

Following Lachmann's (1943) discussion, ideas that can be usefully taken up in this endeavour are such 'ideal types' as Keynes's long-term and short-term expectations or Hicks's sensitive and insensitive traders, the elasticity of expectations and their degree of convergence or divergence. An essential feature of this approach is that (at least in a static analysis) expectations are treated as part of the data that determine the equilibrium solution. In what follows, we attempt to sketch a treatment of expectations in economic analysis, based on a subjective epistemic view of probability and the role of model construction in economics, which is at least intelligible.

The first step in this endeavour is to assess the view that expectations can be analysed in terms of their degree of convergence or divergence. In a world of uncertainty it is reasonable to assume that a variety of opinion exists (Keynes, 1936:172). Keynes even suggests that the stability of the system is enhanced by the existence of divergent opinion. For example, transactions in financial assets, in particular, often provide evidence for differences in subjective opinion on the same information set. It is rare for there to be a market characterized by all bulls and no bears or vice versa. In general, the extent to which opinions differ is a matter of degree and will vary depending on the circumstances. Only if everyone held the same expectations would complete convergence occur. But then the market would have become thin to the point of non-existence in the sense that prices would adjust without the need for trading. Some Rational Expectations models suggest that this is the general case. For example, Tobin (1980:26–7) notes that: 'A disquieting feature of aggregative models which assume uniform expectations is that they don't explain why there are any transactions at all in existing assets.' This result was well known to Keynes (1936:198): 'If the change in the news affects the judgement and the requirements of everyone in the same way, the rate of interest will be adjusted forthwith to the new situation without any transactions being necessary.'

Complete convergence of expectations is thus a special case and in general a lesser degree of convergence will be encountered. Keynes goes on to suggest that we can gain some idea of the degree of convergence of expectations by observing the relationship between price movements and the volume of trading. The greater the price movement relative to the volume of trading, the more convergent the expectations: 'The movement in bond prices is, as the newspapers are accustomed to say, "out of all proportion to the activity of dealing" – which is as it should be, in view of individuals being much more similar than they are dissimilar in their reaction to the news' (Keynes, 1936:199). The Rational Expectations hypothesis, in its desire to make expectations objective, therefore runs into difficulties here because rationality is equated with objectivity. As objectivity requires unique probabilities and mathematical expectations, attempts to incorporate a diversity of opinion into models of Rational Expectations lead to the charge of irrationality (Torr, 1984:199). Seen from this perspective the Rational Expectations hypothesis looks like a special but not the general case.

Another aspect of the analysis of expectations which will prove useful to a more general treatment of expectations is the distinction, made by Hicks (1939:205), between elastic and inelastic expectations. He defines the concept as follows: 'I define the elasticity of a particular person's expectations of the price of a commodity *x* as the ratio of the proportional rise in the expected future prices of *x* to the proportional rise in the current price.' If prices are expected to rise more in the future than at present, then expectations are classified as elastic. Now as Lachmann (1943:19) notes, this classification in itself does not tell us why the elasticity should take on a particular value. However, if the classification is to be useful we need to be in a position to provide such an explanation. Lachmann (1943) therefore suggested that the elasticity of expectations is a function of the perceived behaviour of the persistent forces at work in the economy: 'A market will exhibit inelastic expectations only if it believes that price is ultimately governed by long-period forces, and if it has a fairly definite conception of what those forces are.' Here Lachmann appears to be echoing Keynes's view and suggesting that expectations are based on an analysis of the persistent forces at work in the economy which is the dominant view held by participants in the market.

There is, however, no one-to-one relationship between convergence and inelastic expectations based on an analysis of persistent forces. Convergent expectations may be highly *elastic*. Convergent expectations will be inelastic only if the persistent forces at work have not undergone, or are not expected to undergo, any major changes. Deviations in prices from their conventional or normal levels will then be interpreted as transitory disturbances which will soon be corrected, i.e. expectations are then *inelastic* and convergent. If, on the other hand, there has been a major structural change in the economy which has resulted in a realignment of the persistent forces, expectations may become *elastic* and convergent if there is consensus about the impact of these changes. During a period of transition, however, the degree of divergence in expectations is likely to increase, as participants are unsure whether the changes are transitory or persistent. (Recall that Keynes saw such divergence as a stabilizing factor.)

The above discussion indicates that it is possible to think systematically about expectations without having to restrict the analysis to conditions of risk alone. Furthermore, there is a method for introducing the subjective epistemic view of expectations into economic models in a systematic fashion. The method was employed by Keynes and has been extensively discussed by Kregel (1976). In addition, it is consistent with the features of method and methodology outlined above.

Kregel argues that there are three types of assumptions made about expectations in the *General Theory*. These are:

(i)　　　　long-term expectations are stable and short-term expectations are realized;

(ii)　　　long-term expectations are stable but short-term expectations may be disappointed;

(iii)　　long-term expectations are changing either (a) because they are affected by disappointed short-term expectations; or (b) because autonomous influences in long-term expectations are changing.

Kregel (1976:217) describes these models as (i) static, (ii) stationary, and (iii) shifting, which is a classification that illustrates the method of successive approximation as more factors, in this case expectations, are brought into play and allowed to interact. Kregel (1976:220) describes the process as follows: 'Thus, as Keynes reminds us, the examination of any actual problem can be eased by putting it first in the form of the stationary model and then passing to the shifting position, where "not one of the factors is not liable to change without much warning, and sometimes substantially. Hence the extreme complexity of the actual course of events" (Keynes, 1936:249).' The method proposed by Keynes therefore represents an attempt to tame the complexity of the real world, but without having to begin the analysis by assuming away uncertainty. As a first approximation, simplifying asumptions are made about expectations which are then locked in the *ceteris paribus* compound from where they may be released later. It is only in the static model that we have the special case of what looks like a Rational Expectations equilibrium in the sense that outcomes confirm expectations. The application of the Rational Expectations hypothesis to neoclassical models, by contrast, attempts to analyse situations with a restricted domain of application, e.g. risk not uncertainty, and then finds that it cannot get to grips with the complexity of reality because the method of successive approximation cannot be applied.

The Ricardo–Marshall–Keynes method is not subject to such a limitation. Keynes (1936:297, emphasis added) summarized the objectives of Marshall's partial or one-at-a-time method (Kregel, 1976:218n2, n3) as follows:

The object of our analysis is, not to provide a machine, or method of blind manipulation, which will furnish an infallible answer, *but to provide ourselves with an organised and orderly method of thinking out particular problems; and, after we have reached a provisional conclusion by isolating the complicating factors one by one, we then have to go back on ourselves and allow, as well as we can, for the probable interactions of the factors amongst themselves. This is the nature of economic thinking.* Any other way of applying our formal principles of thought (without which, however, we would be lost in the wood) will lead us into error.

The analysis which follows in chapters 9 and 10 applies this method to the analysis of monetary equilibrium. In other words, the long-period equilibrium solutions that are derived are determined only for a given conventional rate of interest, stable long-term expectations, i.e. the belief that the existing rate will continue, and realized short-term expectations. In short we are concerned initially only with Kregel's static equilibrium solution as a logical exercise in logical time. Termini (1981:61, emphasis in original) provides an apt description:

By logical time I mean a logical set of relations which links the variables in a *unique direction* implying a causal relationship between them. Because this causality is framed within a logical scheme, logical precedence does not entail any chronological precedence – i.e. the variables need not be dated.

The task of this type of analysis is to single out a *few fundamental relations* among a small defined group of basic variables in a causal ordering, which allows the *logical dynamics* of the system to be observed.

The exercise is, as Keynes suggested, intended to provide a logical analysis of the principle of effective demand so that we are in possession of an orderly method of thinking about the problem by isolating the complicating factors one at a time *before* allowing for their interaction. Having established the properties of monetary equilibrium in the context of the static equilibrium model we can then move on to the models of stationary and shifting equilibrium. Ultimately, in the model of shifting equilibrium, we encounter the final phase of the economics of Keynes and have to contend with the Keynesian kaleidics of Shackle (1974) or the economics-without-equilibrium of Kaldor (1985b). But we cannot appreciate the significance of this analysis without first developing the static equilibrium solution. As Termini (1981) notes, we are therefore not directly concerned with the adjustment process, the distinction between *ex post* and *ex ante* or the discrepancy between saving and investment.

CONCLUDING REMARKS

This chapter has attempted, somewhat briefly, to sketch the background to the method and methodology underlying the discussion of the examples of Monetary Analysis to be presented in the following chapters. In particular, it is important to recall that general equilibrium and partial equilibrium approaches can be interpreted as *methods* of macroeconomic analysis and should not be associated exclusively with macroeconomic and microeconomic analyses respectively. Macroeconomic equilibrium can be examined in terms of either the partial or the general equilibrium method. From the perspective of Monetary Analysis the partial equilibrium method appears to have some advantages because its associated notion of causality is compatible with the Keynes–Marx conclusion that certain key monetary and other variables (the wage level) are institutionally determined. Movements in these variables can then be treated as causes of movements in macroeconomic equilibrium. Associated with this approach is the view that economic theory is based on the detection and analysis of persistent forces. In terms of traditional terminology, this means that economic theory is concerned with the analysis of long-period equilibrium positions and the causes and implications of changes in those positions. With respect to the latter point it should not be forgotten that the economic universe is man-made, and the institutions that populate it have been designed by men to facilitate its orderly functioning and to reduce conflict. Such a universe is not as stable or as slowly evolving as the natural universe, and the method adopted by economic theorists should be capable of dealing with these features. The Ricardo–Marshall–Keynes method discussed above would appear to meet this requirement.

9

MARSHALLIAN MICROFOUNDATIONS OF MONETARY EQUILIBRIUM

INTRODUCTION

Although we can agree with Schumpeter that the *General Theory* lies within the tradition of Monetary Analysis it is not always clear that Keynes's argument is a coherent presentation of the properties of that analysis. Both Kaldor (1983) and Lavoie (1984b) have warned that Keynes should not always be followed too closely on some issues. In particular Kaldor (1983) identifies three limitations of the *General Theory* which are relevant here.[1] These are:

1. The failure to completely escape the quantity theory tradition and acknowledge that in a bank money system changes in the money supply are often the consequence and not the cause of the changes in prices and incomes;

2. Excessive reliance on the Marshallian microeconomic analysis of perfect competition;

3. The failure to deal with international trade and exchange rates, i.e. the closed economy assumption.

The first point has been thoroughly investigated by Moore (1986: ch. 13) who comes to the conclusion that although Keynes recognised the properties of bank money in the *Treatise*, the suppression of 'all technical monetary detail' in the *General Theory* led to his treatment of the money supply as fixed. In modern terminology this is usually interpreted to mean that Keynes treated the money supply as exogenous. But treating the money supply in this way is compatible with the quantity theory tradition and inconsistent with the treatment of the rate of interest as an exogenous variable. By contrast, within a bank money economy the money supply is generally endogenous and

---

1. A fourth shortcoming of the *General Theory* considered by Kaldor (1983: 12), the neglect of increasing returns, will not be considered here. See Kregel (1986).

driven by the demand for credit (Kaldor, 1982, 1985a).[2] As here we are not formally concerned with what Keynes really meant, but only with the development of a coherent monetary theory in the tradition of Monetary Analysis, we simply acknowledge this possible shortcoming in Keynes's exposition; for, despite its limitations, Keynes's approach still provides a useful platform for the development of Monetary Analysis.

Kaldor's objection to the Marshallian tools employed by Keynes is also valid in principle although it should not be forgotten that in seeking to take on the 'classics' on their own ground Keynes retained the Marshallian treatment of perfect competition (Chick, 1983: 25). Despite the validity of Kaldor's objection to Marshallian tools we nevertheless retain them for the sake of simplicity in what follows. In this sense the Marshallian tools are a means of making the point; however it could be made equally well using other microfoundations, e.g. by allowing for some degree of imperfect competition and assuming the state of competition to be given.

Finally, it is often taken for granted that the *General Theory* neglects both the importance of exports as an exogenous component of aggregate demand and the role of exchange rates. This view is open to qualification but we will not examine the issue here other than to note that, as Chick (1985: 15) points out, the main area of applicability of Keynes's analysis of speculative demand in these days of flexible exchange rates is undoubtedly the foreign exchange market. However, here we will focus attention on the analysis of monetary equilibrium in a closed economy.

Looking at the *General Theory* from the perspective of Monetary Analysis, chapter 17 on 'The Essential Properties of Interest and Money', immediately stands out as worthy of special attention. In fact, it seems that no matter what one's perspective, chapter 17 has always held a particular allure for monetary theorists. However, there appear to be two distinct reactions to its contents. On the one hand is the view that little would have been lost if it had not been written, e.g. see Hansen (1953: 159), Fender (1981: 82, 86) and, perhaps, Harcourt (1983). At the other extreme Nell (1983) goes so far as to see the chapter 17 analysis as a truly novel theory different from the rest of the *General Theory*. In Nell's view the chapter 17 analysis cannot be fully appreciated without taking into consideration the Sraffa rehabilitation of classical theory. Like Pasinetti (1974), Nell stresses the importance of the Ricardian (classical) roots of Keynes's analysis.

2. The terms endogenous and exogenous are given various interpretations in monetary debate and must be treated with caution. See the discussion in Makinen (1977: 426), Chick (1983: 234) and Cottrell (1986).

But this, it seems, is another objection to the Marshallian micro-foundations and it may be that the analysis outlined below could be conducted equally well in terms of a Sraffa model. We will not consider the issue directly, however, but will proceed instead to develop the notion of monetary equilibrium on the basis of Marshallian tools and the analysis of chapter 17 in the *General Theory*.

In particular, it is possible, using Marshallian tools and methods, along the lines suggested by Davidson (1978) and Kregel (1980, 1983), to recast the analysis of chapter 17 in terms of what we will call monetary equilibrium. With additional help from Kaldor (1960) and Conard (1963: ch. 8) in avoiding the ambiguities that surrounded earlier discussions (Chick, 1983: 295), it is shown that the concept of long-period monetary equilibrium integrates real and monetary forces in the determination of the point of effective demand. It is therefore possible to illustrate the basis for Keynes's claim to have integrated real and monetary forces in the analysis of rates of return, by replacing Wicksell's analysis of market and natural rates with the relationship between the conventional rate of interest and the marginal efficiency of capital. On this issue Keynes (1973b: 103) summarized his position as follows:

Put shortly, the orthodox theory maintains that the forces which determine the common value of the marginal efficiency of various assets are independent of money, which has, so to speak, no autonomous influence, and that prices move until the marginal efficiency of money, i.e. the rate of interest, falls into line with the common value of the marginal efficiency of other assets as determined by other forces. My theory, on the other hand, maintains that this is the special case and that over a wide range of possible cases almost the opposite is true, namely, that the marginal efficiency of money is determined by forces partly appropriate to itself, and that prices move until the marginal efficiency of other assets falls into line with the rate of interest.

Here Keynes is clearly making a claim compatible with the tradition of Monetary Analysis, as it is the rate of interest – a monetary phenomenon – which causes changes in the real sector. Furthermore these changes are not simply transitory, as Keynes is also explicitly reversing the direction of causation found in Wicksell's adjustment of the market rate to the natural rate of interest – the condition for long-period equilibrium.

Now it is well known that the discussion in chapter 17 is obscured by terminological confusion. It is therefore advisable to approach the analysis from a position where the issues are more clearly stated. In this respect Kregel (1980) has suggested that a study of the interest rate parity theorem provides a useful introduction to the concepts involved. We therefore follow this route.

THE INTEREST RATE PARITY THEOREM

As Kregel (1980) has argued, the origins of Keynes's theory of asset-holding can be traced to his earlier work on the interest rate parity theorem. According to this theorem the market is prepared to pay a premium for future delivery of a particular currency, on the foreign exchange market, when the return on deposits *in that currency*, i.e. the interest rate, is higher than that payable on other currencies. The forward discount or premium on a currency then provides a measure of the preference for holding funds in one centre rather than another. The forward discount or premium is in turn explained in terms of international interest rate differentials.

The theorem can be illustrated using Keynes's example of the relationship between interest rates in London and New York and the forward discount or premium on dollars per pound in London. In this respect it is important to note that Keynes uses the indirect method of quotation when describing the options open to a dollar holder in London. That is, he gives the dollar price per pound as the price of a dollar. In that case a dollar discount is represented by a future price of dollars *in excess* of spot (Kregel, 1980: 15). Keeping this possibly confusing terminology in mind, consider Keynes's (1923: 115–39) argument, which proceeds as follows. If dollars are quoted one month forward cheaper than spot dollars, i.e. one pound will buy more dollars forward than spot, then this reflects, in the case of competitive markets, the fact that short-term interest rates are higher in New York than in London by an amount equal to the discount on forward dollars in London. This relationship can be expressed in terms of a simple formula as follows:

$$i_{NY\$} = (P_f - P_s)/P_s + i_{L\pounds} \tag{9.1}$$

where,

$i_{NY\$}$ = the one month interest rate earned on dollars in New York;
$i_{L\pounds}$ = the one month interest rate earned on pounds in London;
P_f = the price, in London, of dollars per pound one month forward;
P_s = the price, in London, of dollars per pound, spot.

Consider the following numerical example (Keynes, 1923: 123). If spot dollars in London are worth \$4.40 to the pound and dollars one month forward \$4.405 to the pound, then in Keynes's terminology there is a forward discount of approximately 1.5 per cent per annum on dollars in London. This discount will exist if the short-term interest rate in New York is 1.5 per cent per annum *higher* than the equivalent rate in London. Under competitive conditions arbitrage operations between London and New York generally maintain this relationship. For example, if the interest rate differential between London and New York was less than 1.5 per cent per annum funds would flow to London to take advantage of the higher return on the foreign exchange market. The forward discount on dollars would then close to maintain the equilibrium relationship in (9.1). The forward discount on dollars in London therefore reflects a preference by market participants for keeping funds in New York rather than London.

Now, as Kregel (1980) points out, the intriguing aspect of this well-known analysis is that it can be directly related to Keynes's notion of liquidity preference and may be generalized to the analysis of 'own rates of interest' on all durable assets.

LIQUIDITY PREFERENCE AND OWN RATES OF OWN INTEREST

If, instead of discussing the foreign exchange market, we consider the borrowing and lending of money, the rate of interest as an indicator of liquidity preference is easily demonstrated. Interest, as everyone knows, is 'the percentage excess of a sum of money contracted for forward delivery ... over what we may call the "spot" or cash price of the sum thus contracted for forward delivery' (Keynes, 1936: 223). By analogy with the interest rate parity theorem, the market's preference for liquidity is given by the relationship $(Q_f - Q_s)/Q_s$ where Q_f now refers to the quantity of money that must be repaid per unit borrowed. For example, if $100 is borrowed at a rate of interest of 10 per cent per annum then $Q_f = \$110$ and $Q_s = \$100$. In terms of the convention on indirect quotation, forward liquidity is cheaper than spot as $1 spot can 'buy' $1.1 forward, i.e. there is a forward discount. (Recall that the indirect method of quotation used by Keynes implies a forward price in excess of spot in the case of a forward discount.) The money rate of interest therefore gives a measure of the market's preference for liquidity relative to illiquidity, in the same way that the forward discount on dollars, in London, indicates a preference for holding dollars in New York rather than pounds in London (Kregel, 1980).

There is, however, more to the interest rate parity theorem than the forward discount or premium on foreign exchange. The interest rate differentials between centres also played an important part. To generalize the framework to liquidity preference theory we must therefore extend the analysis to include the 'interest rates' on other durable *commodities* rather than in other *centres*.

To this end Keynes took up Sraffa's extension of the analysis of futures markets to the determination of 'commodity rates of interest' on all durable assets. Following Kaldor (1960) we will refer to these rates as own rates of own interest. Keynes (1936: ch. 17) referred to them as 'own rates of interest' but, as Kaldor (1960: ch. 2) shows, Keynes's terminology can be confusing. Own rates of own interest are defined as the return, *in terms of the commodity*, on a loan in that commodity; or, equivalently, as the amount of the commodity which can be bought for forward delivery in terms of a given amount of the same commodity for spot delivery. Consider, for example, the case of a grade of wheat for which both spot and futures markets exist. If the rate of interest is 5 per cent per annum, the one-year futures price of wheat $107 per tonne, and the spot price $100 per tonne, then 100 tonnes for spot delivery will only 'buy' approximately 98 tonnes for future delivery. The own rate of wheat interest is therefore -2 per cent. The owner of 100 tonnes sells spot for $100 and invests the proceeds at 5 per cent per annum. He then contracts to buy $105 worth of wheat in the futures market and obtains $105/107 = 98$ tonnes for a return of $(98 - 100)/100 = -2\%$. Note that we are following Kaldor's (1960) and not Lerner's (1952) terminology.

Similar calculations can be made for all durable assets even if no futures markets exist. The most well known, of course, is the 'marginal efficiency of capital' which is that rate of discount which equates the prospective yield from a unit of capital with its present *cost of production*, i.e. its supply price. In this respect it is necessary to distinguish between the marginal efficiency of holding, and the marginal efficiency of investing in, an asset. In the former case the asset is held for resale while in the latter case it is held in order to make a profit on the sale of its output. We will always refer to the latter case as the marginal efficiency of capital (MEC) in what follows. The point to note, however, is that own rates of own interest may be calculated on all assets irrespective of whether they possess forward or futures markets. The relationship between the marginal efficiencies of assets and their own rates of own interest will be discussed in full below.

By analogy with the interest rate parity theorem, own rates of own interest are likely to differ between commodities just as interest rates may differ between major trading centres. For purposes of comparison these rates must be converted into a common unit, usually money. The own rate of *money* interest can be calculated for each asset by allowing for the expected percentage appreciation or depreciation in the relative price of the asset in money terms. As was the case with expression (9.1), where the relationship between the two interest rates was maintained by the forward discount or premium, the equilibrium relationship between own rates of money interest is maintained by the expected percentage appreciation or depreciation in the relative price of the asset in money terms. In other words,

$$i_m = \pm a_w + \hat{r}_w \qquad (9.2)$$

where:

i_m = the known money rate of interest (the own rate of own interest on money);

a_w = the expected percentage appreciation or depreciation of the price of wheat in terms of money, determined either on spot and forward markets or by subjective judgement;

$\hat{r}_w$ = the own rate of wheat interest.

In terms of our previous example:

$$a_w = (107 - 100)/100 = 7\%$$

$$i_m = 5\%$$

$$\therefore \hat{r}_w = 5 - 7 = -2\% \text{ (from (9.2))}.$$

The relationship between own rates of interest and own rates of money interest is therefore maintained, in analogous fashion to the interest rate parity theorem, by the percentage appreciation or depreciation of the price of commodities in terms of money. Now the relationship described in expression (9.2) is entirely general and applies to all durable assets. Liquidity preference theory thus covers the whole spectrum of assets and not just money and bonds as some Keynesians have argued. Furthermore, it is apparent that the monetary asset plays an important role in integrating real and monetary rates of return. Expression (9.2) therefore applies explicitly to a monetary economy.

MONETARY EQUILIBRIUM DEFINED

In the previous section we defined own rates of own interest as the rate of return on an asset calculated in terms of that asset, i.e. the rate of return on wheat measured in terms of wheat. Alternatively the rate of return could have been calculated in money terms for all durable assets even if futures markets were non-existent and most of the elements in the calculation were subjective. As noted above, some of the methods of converting present into future assets are so significantly different from lending and borrowing or operating on the futures markets that they have been given different names: the marginal efficiency of holding (MEH) and the marginal efficiency of capital (MEC).

To clarify the properties of, and the relationship between, these concepts we begin by listing the three methods of converting present into future assets. Following Chick (1983: 297) these are:

(i)   borrowing and lending;

(ii)   buying or making a durable asset to hold
        (a) for later consumption, or
        (b) for resale;

(iii)   using a capital good to produce final goods for future sale.

The rate of interest is the term used to describe the rate of return from using the first method of conversion. The MEH and MEC are used to describe the second and third methods respectively. Having dispensed with this terminological issue it should be recalled that the rate of return from each of these methods may be calculated either in terms of the commodities involved or in terms of any other standard, including money. In the former case we have own rates of own interest: an 'own' MEH and an 'own' MEC. When calculated in money terms we have the MEC and MEH as traditionally defined. Now, although own rates of return are seldom calculated, they nevertheless form an important component of the MEH or MEC as traditionally measured.

As Conard (1963: 132–5) has shown, calculating the rate of interest, MEH or MEC, is most easily conducted using Fisher's expression for the marginal rate of return over cost. This is a legitimate step as Keynes (1936: 140–41) states explicitly that Fisher's rate of return over cost is identical with his definition of the marginal efficiency of capital. The rate of return over cost is defined as:

$$\text{(future value} - \text{present value)/present value} \qquad (9.3)$$

where the term 'value' is used in a broad sense to include quantities. Applying this definition of the own rate of return (or the own rate of own interest) on an asset gives:

$$\hat{r} = (Q_2 - Q_1)/Q_1 \qquad (9.4)$$

where $\hat{r}$ signifies an own rate of return and Q_2 and Q_1 refer to future and present quantities respectively. We may note in passing that, in the case of a real capital good, expression (9.4) captures the spirit of Wicksell's notion of the natural rate of interest as the rate obtained if capital were lent in kind rather than indirectly via the medium of money. (Recall the discussion in chapter 2.) Calculating the rate of return in money terms (or in terms of any asset) means that we must bring in the money price of the asset (or the price of the asset in terms of the standard asset). The money rate of return is then given by:

$$r = (P_2 Q_2 - P_1 Q_1)/P_1 Q_1 \qquad (9.5)$$

where P refers to the money price of the asset in a straightforward application of (9.3). By analogy with the interest rate parity theorem, there must exist an adjustment factor which, in equilibrium, will equate the money and own rates of return. To determine this factor, a, Conard (1963: 122) subtracts (9.4) from (9.5) as follows:

$$a = r - \hat{r}$$

$$a = (P_2 Q_2 - P_1 Q_1)/P_1 Q_1 - (Q_2 - Q_1)/Q_1$$

$$= \frac{P_2 Q_2 - P_1 Q_1 - P_1 (Q_2 - Q_1)}{P_1 Q_1}$$

$$a = (P_2 Q_2 - P_1 Q_2)/P_1 Q_1 = \frac{(P_2 - P_1)}{P_1}\left(\frac{Q_2}{Q_1}\right)$$

In equilibrium the money rate of interest equals the money rate of return on all durable assets, i.e.

$$(Q_2^m - Q_1^m)/Q_1^m = (P_2^i Q_2^i - P_1^i Q_1^i)/P_1^i Q_1^i$$

for all durable assets, i, and the latter expression may be broken up as in (9.6):

$$\left(\frac{P_2 Q_2 - P_1 Q_1}{P_1 Q_1}\right) = \left(\frac{P_2 - P_1}{P_1}\right)\left(\frac{Q_2}{Q_1}\right) + \left(\frac{Q_2 - Q_1}{Q_1}\right) \quad (9.6)$$

or,

$$r = a + \hat{r}$$

where r is the rate of interest in money terms, a the adjustment factor and $\hat{r}$ the own rate of own interest, i.e. the proxy for Wicksell's natural rate of interest. The rate of return on any asset, measured in terms of money, therefore consists of these two components, a and $\hat{r}$, despite the fact that they may not be calculated explicitly. Again, the relationship to the Wicksellian theme is apparent as, in the case of a real capital good, the marginal efficiency of capital contains what looks like the natural rate of interest, $\hat{r}$, as a component on the right-hand side of expression (9.6). As we will see below, this suggests that Wicksell's analysis of the relationship between natural and market rates of interest is a special case of the relationship between the marginal efficiency of capital and the rate of interest.

To illustrate the relationship between the components in (9.6), consider the *short-period* equilibrium relationship between the money rate of interest, the marginal efficiency of holding food (wheat) and the marginal efficiency of capital in the production of clothing. The example illustrated in Table 9.1 describes a situation where food is

Table 9.1. *Money and own rates of return: short-period equilibrium*

Time	Quantity Relations			Implied money prices		Rates of Return				
	Money	Food	Clothing	Food	Clothing	Money rate	Own MEH food	Own MEC clothing	MEH food in money terms	MEC clothing in money terms
This year	100	100	100	$1.00	$1.00	$\dfrac{104 - 100}{100}$	$\dfrac{80 - 100}{100}$	$\dfrac{130 - 100}{100}$	$\dfrac{80(1.30) - 100(1.00)}{100(1.00)}$	$\dfrac{130(0.80) - 100(1.00)}{100(1.00)}$
Next year	104	80	130	$1.30	$0.80	$= 4\%$	$= -20\%$	$= 30\%$	$= 4\%$	$= 4\%$

$$a_c = \frac{(0.8 - 1.00)}{1.00} \times \frac{130}{100} = -26\%$$

$$a_f = \frac{(1.30 - 1.00)}{1.00} \times \frac{80}{100} = 24\%$$

expected to be scarce in the future (next year) relative to the present (this year). The example is taken from Conard (1963: 123–5, 144–5) and the numbers are chosen to illustrate a *short-period* equilibrium position. Carrying costs are assumed to be 20 per cent, so of 100 units of food held for a year, only 80 will remain. Nevertheless the higher price expected next year makes it profitable to store food. In the case of clothing production, the cost of acquiring the capital to produce the clothing is 100 units, *measured in clothing*, and the expected output 130 units.

From this information, which we are treating as certain although in any real situation some of the elements would be subjective, the implied prices of clothing and food are derived from the assumption of short-period equilibrium, which requires that the MEH and MEC equal the rate of interest of 4 per cent. The relationship between the own MEH and MEC on food and clothing and their respective marginal efficiencies in money terms is given by the adjustment factor, a. For example, in the case of clothing, the MEC in clothing production measured in money (column 11 in Table 9.1) equals the own marginal efficiency measured in terms of clothing (column 9 in Table 9.1) plus the adjustment factor, $a_c = -26\%$ (shown below Table 9.1 and derived from the information contained in columns 4 and 6). The same relationship holds between the own MEH food, the adjustment factor and the MEH food measured in terms of money. In equilibrium the marginal efficiency of storing food (MEH) is equated with the marginal efficiency of producing clothing (MEC) when both are calculated in the same units, e.g. money.

Having reached this point, we are now in possession of an analysis of the relationship between real and money rates of return which all monetary theorists have seen as fundamental to the integration of real and monetary forces and which we define as monetary equilibrium. The framework can now be used to re-examine Wicksell's analysis of the relationship between the natural and market rates of interest.

Monetary equilibrium: Wicksell reconsidered

From the theory of asset-holding discussed in the previous section we know that short-period monetary equilibrium requires the following condition:

$$i_m = r_j = a_j + f_j; \quad \forall j, j = 1, 2, \ldots, n \quad (9.7)$$

where i_m is 'the' rate of interest and the r_j's are the marginal efficiencies from alternative methods of transforming present into future assets. For the sake of simplicity we are abstracting here from the question of the term structure of interest rates and employing a single rate as 'the' rate of interest. In any event, Kaldor (1960: 64–8) shows that the analysis is easily extended to incorporate a treatment of the term structure of interest rates. Also, it is not necessary that (9.7) be satisfied as an equality. A hierarchy of rates of return as between active and passive uses of capital is more realistic but for the sake of simplicity (9.7) is retained as an equality. Consequently, in the next section, it will prove useful at times to consider only one of the $\hat{r}_j$'s as a proxy for the 'natural' rate of interest. With this simplified framework we can concentrate on the relation between the market and 'natural' rates of interest.

The first step in the argument which follows is the re-examination of Wicksell's analysis of the relationship between market and 'natural' rates of interest using a Marshallian comparative static analysis of the process of adjustment to monetary equilibrium. We distinguish between market period, short-period and long-period equilibrium but do not extend the analysis to Marshall's fourth period – the study of secular changes. It seems that such a step would take us into the realms of growth theory à la Harrod (1939). And although Kregel (1983: 57) does not see that Keynes's analysis has anything to do with Marshallian periods, it is difficult to separate out the strands in Keynes's argument if these periods are not employed.

This exercise then leads to the conclusion that changes in the market rate of interest, i_m, can cause changes in the 'natural' rate, $\hat{r}_j$. The argument is then extended in the following section by examining Keynes's analysis of the relation between the rate of interest, the market for capital goods and the MEC.

Following Kaldor (1960), a Marshallian analysis of the process of adjustment to monetary equilibrium can usefully be illustrated by beginning with the long-period equilibrium, or stationary state. In such an equilibrium, market prices equal short-period supply prices which in turn equal the normal or long-period supply prices. Hence the adjustment factors, the a_j, in all the marginal efficiencies are zero as spot and forward prices are identical. In long-period equilibrium, monetary equilibrium therefore reduces to

$$i_m = \hat{r}_j; \quad \forall j, j = 1, 2, \ldots, n \qquad (9.8)$$

where the $\hat{r}_j$ are the 'own' marginal efficiencies and all adjustment factors are zero.

The adjustment factors play an important role, however, in providing the price signals during the process of adjustment towards long-period equilibrium once it is disturbed. Assume, for example, that the stationary state is disturbed by an increase in the rate of interest from i_m to i_m^0. In terms of Marshallian comparative static analysis, equilibrium is maintained in the market period by a fall in the spot prices of all durable assets. As the rate of interest rises, lending money offers a better return than alternative methods of transforming present into future assets, so the demand for these assets falls in the market period and equilibrium is maintained by the emergence of a positive adjustment factor in the MEC or MEH of those assets. That is, market period equilibrium produces:

$$i_m^0 = [(P_{fj} - P_{sj})/P_{sj}](Q_{fj}/Q_{sj}) + \hat{r}_j; \quad \forall j, j = 1, 2, \ldots, n$$

(9.9)

with,

$$a_j = [(P_{fj} - P_{sj})/P_{sj}](Q_{fj}/Q_{sj}) > 0 \text{ as } P_{sj} < P_{fj}$$

A rise in the rate of interest causes an initial fall in spot prices, P_{sj}, but the process does not end there. As Kaldor (1960: 70) points out, the fall of spot prices below their long-period supply prices (normal prices) means that these assets will not be produced: 'assets whose own rate of own interest $[\hat{r}_j]$ falls below their own rate of money interest $[r_j]$ can no longer be newly produced'. In more conventional terminology this simply means that assets whose market demand prices (spot prices) fall below their normal supply prices can only be produced at a loss. The long-period supply price or normal price represents costs of production (including normal profit), so when the market price falls below this level losses will be made.

All this is no doubt familiar from Marshall's three-period analysis as a neoclassical formalization of the classical law of supply and demand. In terms of this law, resources are directed to increase the supply of those commodities whose prices exceed their normal costs and withdrawn from the production of those commodities where market prices are below normal costs. Keynes (1936: 228) describes the situation thus: 'Now those assets of which the normal supply-price is less than the demand-price will be newly produced; and these will be those assets of which the [own] marginal efficiency would be greater . . . than the rate of interest . . . As the stock of assets . . . is increased, their [own] marginal efficiency tends to fall. Thus a point will come at which it no longer pays to produce them, *unless the rate of interest falls pari passu*.'

In the short period, the process of adjustment continues via a reduction in output, which tends to reverse the downward movement in spot prices by reducing supply. Short-period prices are therefore higher than market period prices and the 'own' marginal efficiencies increase as a result of a reduction in output (assuming diminishing returns) or stock holdings (by reducing carrying costs). Long-period equilibrium is then achieved in a continuation of this process via a reduction in the capital stock. This maintains monetary equilibrium at the higher rate of interest and 'own' marginal efficiencies, i.e. 'natural rates', as a reduction in the capital stock causes $\hat{r}_j$ to rise. Thus:

$$i_m^0 = \hat{r}_j^0; \quad \forall j, j = 1, 2, \ldots, n \tag{9.10}$$

with

$$\hat{r}_j^0 > \hat{r}_j \text{ in response to } i_m^0 > i_m$$

This latter conclusion emerges from a straightforward application of Marshallian principles at the macro level instead of the industry level. In other words, a Marshallian comparative static analysis of the relationship between the rate of interest and the marginal efficiency of a non-monetary asset leads to the conclusion that the marginal efficiency of the non-monetary asset may adjust to the rate of interest. In Wicksellian terms the natural rate of interest, $\hat{r}$, adjusts to the market rate, i. In this sense the analysis exhibits the property of hysteresis, i.e. the natural rate of interest adjusts to the market or actual rate of interest. We have here, it seems, the basis for Keynes's claim to have reversed the direction of causation between the marginal efficiencies of assets and the rate of interest. It is also apparent that, when interpreted from a Marshallian perspective, Keynes's analysis of the relationship between the rate of interest and the marginal efficiency of capital is a generalization of Wicksell. In Keynes's analysis it is true that the proxy for the natural rate of interest, $\hat{r}$, is always equal to the money rate in long-period equilibrium. But this equality can occur at various levels of output and employment and the direction of causation, in the main, runs from the conventional rate of interest to the natural rate. (The reverse influence from $\hat{r}$ to i is, of course, not excluded.)

Monetary equilibrium: Keynes on the MEC and the market for capital goods

The principles of the analysis outlined above can now be reinforced by examining the role of the capital goods market in the relationship between the rate of interest and the MEC. As we noted in chapter 4, in an economy in which capital goods are produced, the rate of interest does not equate the demand for capital (investment) with the supply of capital (saving). Instead, as Keynes (1936: 186n) argued, 'the equality between the stock of capital goods offered and the stock demanded will be brought about by the *prices* of capital goods, not by the rate of interest'. The relationship between the rate of interest and the MEC in a capitalist economy therefore involves an analysis of the capital goods market. Following Davidson (1978: ch. 4) this relationship can be examined in terms of Marshallian principles. The first step, however, is to relate the MEC to the Marshallian concepts of demand and supply prices.

The demand price of a capital good is obtained by discounting its prospective yield by the rate of interest. Keynes (1930: 1202, quoted by Davidson, 1978: 730) explained the relationship as follows: 'the demand price of capital goods . . . depends on *two* things – on the estimated net prospective yield from the fixed capital (estimated by the opinion of the market after such allowances as they choose to make for the uncertainty of anticipations, etc.) measured in money, and the rate of interest at which this yield is capitalized'. Keynes (1936: 137) also defined the demand price in similar fashion in the *General Theory*: 'If Q_r is the prospective yield from an asset at time r, and d_r is the present value of £1 deferred r years *at the current rate of interest* then $\Sigma Q_r d_r$ is the demand price'. The supply price of a capital good, on the other hand, is either the short- or long-period supply price as determined in orthodox Marshallian fashion from the firms' cost functions in the capital goods industries. Investment is then pushed to the point where the demand price of capital is equal to the supply price. In short-period equilibrium the demand price of capital is equal to the short-period supply price and the MEC is equal to the rate of interest. Another way of saying the same thing is that the MEC is a rate of discount which equates the demand price of a capital good with the supply price. In terms of our previous definition, the MEC is the rate of discount, d, which equates P_K, the supply price, with the present value of the expected profit stream, π_i (if we assume a scrap value of zero and that profits accrue at the end of each year for a period of n years) in the expression,

$$P_K = \sum_{i=1}^{n} \frac{\pi_i}{(1 + d)^i}$$

A possible complicating factor with these calculations is the existence of multiple solutions (Davidson, 1978: 57–8).

The rate of interest therefore interacts with the MEC via changes in the demand and supply prices of capital goods. What happens to output and employment then depends on the relationship between market or short-period demand prices and the long-period supply prices of capital goods. To examine this relationship we require an analysis of the demand and supply functions of the capital goods market.

To derive these functions we assume, for the sake of simplicity, a representative firm. Such an assumption enables us to avoid the technical problems posed by the aggregation of heterogeneous physical units of capital. Such an aggregation problem is, however, quite distinct from the logical problem of the valuation of capital in Wicksellian theory. The aggregation problem faced here is common to all macroeconomic analysis but does not involve any logical difficulties that need concern us (Davidson, 1978: 71n3). Given the rate of interest and the expected yield, the relationship between the demand price of capital and the quantity of capital demanded by a firm can be plotted as a conventional downward sloping demand curve. The problems of slope which affect the Wicksellian investment function do not arise in this case as we are dealing with the prices of capital goods, and not the rate of interest, as the dependent variable (Pasinetti, 1974: 43). A similar curve is considered to exist at the macro level. Davidson (1978: 72) writes this demand function as:

$$D_k = f_1(P_k, i, \phi, E) \qquad (9.11)$$
$$f'_{1P_k} < 0; f'_{1i} < 0; f'_{1\phi} > 0; f'_{1E} > 0$$

where P_k is the price of capital, i 'the' rate of discount, ϕ the state of expectations about the future stream of profits to be earned by each unit of capital (recall the discussion in chapter 8), and E represents the number of entrepreneurs who can obtain the necessary finance. Now although there are four independent variables, P_k, i, ϕ, and E, the latter three are in the nature of shift parameters which are themselves interdependent. If the rate of interest were to increase, for example, the demand function would shift to the left as the demand price for any quantity of capital was reduced. But at the same time expectations, ϕ, may be revised as a result of the change in price. Finally, we need to add the depreciation demand for capital to the above function. This can be done by assuming that the capital stock, S_k, wears out at a constant rate such that the flow demand for capital $d_k = nS_k$, where n is the rate of depreciation and $0 < n < 1$. The total demand for capital is thus $D_k + d_k$.

On the supply side we have, in addition to the existing stock of capital, S_k, a short-period flow supply curve derived from Marshallian principles. This supply curve may be written as:

$$s_k = f_2(P_k) \qquad (9.12)$$

The total supply of capital is then $S_k + s_k$ and the demand and supply schedules may now be combined in a single diagram that relates the rate of interest, via the prices of capital goods, to the MEC. Figure 9.1 then illustrates the case of the stationary state examined earlier. For

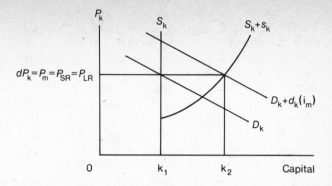

Fig. 9.1 Capital goods market: long-run equilibrium (stationary state)

a more detailed version of this diagram see Davidson (1978: 83, Figure 4.5(b)). For our purposes the simpler diagram is adequate. Inspection of Figure 9.1 reveals the characteristics of the stationary state with the market price, P_m, equal to both the short-period supply price, P_{SR}, and the long-period supply price, P_{LR}. Also, the demand price, dP_k is equal to the normal or long-period supply price as capital accumulation has ceased and only replacement investment of $k_1 k_2$ occurs to maintain the capital stock, S_k. Long-period equilibrium exists as $i_m = \hat{r}_j; \forall j, j = 1, 2, \ldots, n$.

To illustrate Keynes's argument about the relationship between the rate of interest and the prices of capital goods we now disturb the stationary state by increasing the rate of interest (Figure 9.2). The impact of an increase of the rate of interest on the capital goods market is, *ceteris paribus*, to shift the demand function for capital to the left. As a result, the (notional)[3] spot price falls below the short-period supply price, P_{SR}, and both of these prices also lie below the long-period supply price, P_{LR}. The investment that is occurring, $k_1 k_3$, is not sufficient to maintain the capital stock which would require replacement at the rate $k_2 k_3$ which is greater than $k_1 k_3$.

Consequently, if the rate of interest i_m is maintained, the capital stock will run down until a new stationary state is achieved as $k_1 S_k$ shifts to the left. This is a simplified solution which ignores the possibility of a wage and price decline and a fall in the long-period supply price P_{LR}. From a Marshallian perspective, monetary equilibrium is therefore maintained initially (in the market period) by a fall

3. We refer to the notional spot price, not in Clower's (1965) sense of the term, but to indicate that there is no well-developed spot market for units of secondhand capital. Retaining the spot price is, however, useful for indicating how secondhand capital is valued relative to newly-produced capital. See Davidson (1978: ch. 4).

in the spot price, then by a change in output and supply price in the short period, and finally by a change in the capital stock in the long period. Moreover, although the rate of interest always equals the MEC in a Marshallian comparative static analysis, the rate of interest has an impact on the real economy as a result of the divergence of the prices of capital, and other, goods from their normal levels. With the demand price of capital goods, dP_k, below the long-period supply prices, the capital goods industry would make losses if it attempted to maintain the initial capital stock. In terms of expression (9.9) P_{fj} is the long-period supply price and P_{sj} the demand price. Finally, as a matter of interest, we can note that this analysis provides a basis for Tobin's q-theory of investment that does not rest on Wicksellian foundations. For example, if $P_{sj} > P_{fj}$ then demand prices exceed supply prices and Tobin's $q > 1$ so there is no reason why Tobin's analysis should not be extended to the concept of monetary equilibrium.

Applying Marshallian tools to an analysis of the relationship between the rate of interest and the MEC thus reveals the route by which the conventional rate of interest causes adjustments in the real sector. If the marginal efficiencies of assets can adjust to the rate of interest, as Keynes claims is possible in a wide range of circumstances, then the behaviour of the rate of interest has important implications for the theory of output and employment. Keynes (1936: 222, emphasis in original) summarizes the position as follows: 'It seems, then, that the *rate of interest on money* plays a peculiar part in setting a

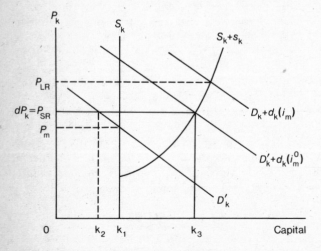

Fig. 9.2 Capital goods market: a contango

limit to the level of employment, since it sets a standard to which the marginal efficiency of a capital-asset must attain if it is to be newly produced.' If the rate of interest can set the level to which the marginal efficiencies of other assets must adjust, then it is the money rate of interest which determines monetary equilibrium and defines the point of effective demand. (Recall the discussion in chapter 7.)

MONETARY EQUILIBRIUM AND THE POINT OF EFFECTIVE DEMAND

The notion of monetary equilibrium developed in the previous sections can now be integrated with the principle of effective demand. As noted in chapter 7, the principle of effective demand is offered as a refutation of Say's Law because it postulates a limit to the profitable expansion of output which may occur before full employment is achieved. The relationship between the rate of interest and the MEC outlined in the previous section explains how this can happen.

In the context of Monetary Analysis the rate of interest is a variable that cannot be explained by the principles of either classical or neoclassical theory. In this sense the money rate of interest appears as an exogenous-type variable, $\bar{i}_m$, which, as Keynes and Marx both suggested, is based on the interaction of such factors as monetary policy, conventions employed in financial markets and the confidence in those conventions. There is no reason to expect that these factors will combine so as to determine a long term rate of interest which will generate a demand price for capital goods and a resultant rate of investment that will ensure full employment. The rate of investment that emerges once monetary equilibrium has been established may well determine a point of effective demand that is not sufficient to fully employ the labour force. Furthermore, when monetary equilibrium establishes the point of effective demand, rates of return are equalized for all forms of converting present into future wealth. There is therefore no incentive for entrepreneurs to expand production of capital goods. That is, if the demand price of capital goods is such that producers only earn normal profits then there is no incentive to increase production. Thus, the condition of monetary equilibrium, viz:

$$i_m^- = \hat{r}_j; \; \forall j, j = 1, 2, \ldots, n$$

is a long-period equilibrium in the classical sense of a uniform rate of return on all assets. Say's Law is broken because supply does not create its own demand if increased output cannot be sold at a profit.

If it is also the case that flexibility in the rest of the system cannot induce monetary equilibrium to occur at the level of full employment then the monetary theory of effective demand provides an explanation for the existence of a long-period *equilibrium* with unemployment. That is, the analysis of the principle of effective demand presented here provides the analytical basis for Keynes's (1936: 204) claim that the interest rate may fluctuate for decades about a level that is too high for full employment.

In this respect the analysis also supports Keynes's claim to have demonstrated the existence of an unemployment equilibrium. However, the general consensus is that Keynes failed to make the case in support of this claim. For example, Patinkin (1965: ch. 13, 1976: 113, 1982: ch. 5) has consistently argued that Keynes offered an analysis of unemployment *disequilibrium* rather than unemployment equilibrium and this interpretation is widely accepted. Nevertheless it differs fundamentally from the analysis presented here. Two points of difference are worth examining in more detail.

The first point of difference is that the concept of monetary equilibrium employed here is the traditional long-period equilibrium of Marshall and the classics. By comparison, the conventional wisdom among Keynesians is that the *General Theory* is concerned only with the short period. But as we have noted, this interpretation makes very little sense when viewed from the perspective of the history of thought. Surely no monetary theorist brought up in the Marshallian tradition would claim an analysis of short-period equilibrium as a general theory? Moreover, analytically, it is not possible to partition the analysis of the short period from the analysis of long-period equilibrium. Nevertheless, Patinkin (1982: 153) reflects the general consensus when he interprets the *General Theory* as the analysis of unemployment disequilibrium. The reason for Patinkin's conclusion can be traced to his interpretation of the principle of effective demand.

Patinkin (1982: 153) interprets what he calls the theory of effective demand to mean that the economy is brought into equilibrium via changes in output. Although this is partly true it does not specify the conditions which define the state of equilibrium. In other words, Patinkin's interpretation of the principle of effective demand allows, in effect, the operation of Say's Law as there is no possibility of a limit to the profitable expansion of output until the physical constraint of full employment of resources is encountered. Thus although Patinkin (1982: 143) identifies the role of profits along the lines sketched in this study, his analysis does not contain the definition of the point of effective demand. Hence he interprets Say's Law too narrowly as referring only to the case where the D and Z curves coincide, e.g. as in Figure 7.1a (Patinkin, 1982: 144). But Say's Law holds also for the case where the D and Z curves do not coincide, which means that if the point of effective demand is not defined as suggested here in terms of monetary equilibrium, there is then no limit to the profitable expansion of output. On this interpretation Keynes's analysis therefore inevitably becomes the economics of *unemployment disequilibrium*.

The second point of difference is accounted for by the fact that Patinkin (1976, 1982) employs the traditional neoclassical analysis of the demand for labour. This means that he is inevitably concerned with the process of adjustment of output to full employment equilibrium because the marginal, profit-maximising conditions are satisfied along the so-called demand for labour function. There is then no limit to the profitable expansion of employment and unemployment can result only if there are impediments to the adjustment of the real wage. Unemployment is then inevitably a disequilibrium phenomenon. In terms of the terminology used in this study, Patinkin's interpretation would, at best, be treated as part of the analysis of shifting equilibria. In this regard Patinkin's analysis also differs from Keynes's own claims that wage and price flexibility need not restore full employment equilibrium; this question will be taken up below. Patinkin's (1976: 105–7) optimistic conclusion appears, ultimately, to be based on the view that his interpretation of the theory of effective demand is consistent with Walrasian general equilibrium theory! This relationship is most obvious in Patinkin (1965) but is explicitly supported by the claim that 'the analysis of the *General Theory* is in effect a Walrasian, general equilibrium one' (Patinkin, 1976: 100). Based on the assessment of neo-Walrasian theory presented in part I of this study this interpretation would appear to be fundamentally misconceived.

LIQUIDITY PREFERENCE VERSUS LOANABLE FUNDS: EPILOGUE

The debate between liquidity preference and loanable funds theories of the rate of interest has been examined from various perspectives in previous discussion. However, in view of the restatement of the principle of effective demand presented above, a final word is required. It seems that these comments are necessary because there is still widespread misunderstanding of liquidity preference theory. Recent evidence in support of this view is provided by the dispute between

Garegnani and Kregel identified in chapter 7 but appears in stark relief in the work of Hutt (1979) and Coddington (1983).

The major difficulty that Hutt and Coddington have with the liquidity preference theory is that they overlook (or cannot accept) that the natural rate of interest (the personification of the forces of productivity and thrift) has lost its role as the centre of gravitation in liquidity preference theory.[4] For example, in his discussion of the nature of the Keynesian thesis, Hutt (1979: 112–17) continually chides Keynes and his disciples for talking about the market rate of interest instead of the relationship between market and natural rates (in the Wicksellian sense (Hutt, 1979: 112n16)). The point can be illustrated by considering Hutt's reaction to Harrod's description of Keynes's statement of liquidity preference theory. This description is particularly useful because it confirms the interpretation presented in this study. Harrod (1947: 69, emphasis added) summarizes Keynes's views as follows:

The theory of interest is, I think, the central point in his scheme. He departs from the old orthodoxy in holding that the failure of the system to move to a position of full activity is not primarily due to friction, rigidity, immobility or to phenomena essentially connected with the trade cycle. If a *certain level of interest is established, which is inconsistent with full activity, no flexibility or mobility in the other parts of the system will get the system to move to full activity.* But this wrong rate of interest, as we may call it, is not itself a rigidity or inflexibility. It is natural, durable, and, in a certain sense, in a free system, inevitable.

Hutt's (1979: 116) reaction to this passage is to complain that both Harrod and Keynes are thinking about the absolute level of the market rate of interest rather than its relation to the natural rate! From this reaction, and many others scattered throughout the discussion, it is clear that Hutt fails to understand the role of the conventional rate of interest as an exogenous-type variable in liquidity preference theory. Consequently he cannot make any sense of the principle of effective demand and the critique of Say's Law. Hutt remains trapped by the 'classical' vision.

A similar conclusion applies to Coddington's attempts to get to grips with liquidity preference theory. Like Hutt, Coddington is bemused by the absence of the natural rate of interest as a centre of gravitation. After noting that the central thesis of Wicksell's analysis is the deviation between market and real rates of interest, Coddington (1983: 81) goes on to complain that:

Keynes introduces, and indeed focuses on, such monetary disturbances in the

---

4. By contrast, Tsiang (1956) seeks to reconcile liquidity preference and loanable funds theories of the rate of interest but makes no mention of the role of the natural rate in loanable funds theory.

determination of interest rates. What he does not tell us is what it is that is being disturbed: what the monetary disturbance is a disturbance of.

Keynes's theory of the speculative demand for money must therefore be seen as an essay in the economics of pure chaos. The speculators speculate but what are they really speculating on?

With this rather plaintive plea by Coddington we have, of course, come full circle to Dennis Robertson's objections to liquidity preference theory discussed in chapter 2.

Coddington goes on to distinguish between the underlying forces of productivity and thrift that determine the level of interest rates, and speculative movements around that level, which, by analogy with boiling soup, represent bubbles on the surface. But, Coddington concludes, one cannot have bubbles without a surface to keep them up there so by implication the market rates (bubbles) need a natural rate (the surface of the soup). Unfortunately for Coddington the analogy is not relevant in this case. Liquidity preference theory is, as Harrod describes it, at the centre of Keynes's Monetary Analysis in which the principle of effective demand breaks Say's Law. In liquidity preference theory the conventional money rate of interest has taken over the role of the surface of the soup and the proxy for Wicksell's natural rate adjusts to this. The idea that Coddington and Hutt have difficulty grasping, or accepting, is that the conventional rate of interest must be treated as an exogenous-type variable because the money rate of interest cannot be explained in terms of either classical or neoclassical principles.

Interpreted in this way the loanable funds theory emerges as a special case of liquidity preference theory in the sense that it represents the case where equality between money and natural rates of interest occurs at full employment. The money rate of interest at which this occurs Keynes (1936: 243) called the neutral or optimum rate. But there is no reason to believe that this rate would occur automatically as a result of the operation of the forces of productivity and thrift. The equality of money and natural rates of interest could occur at various levels of output and employment – their equality at the optimum rate is a special case from the set of possible long-period equilibria.

MONETARY EQUILIBRIUM: KEYNES VERSUS FISHER ON REAL RATES OF INTEREST AND INFLATIONARY EXPECTATIONS

The relevance of the notion of monetary equilibrium proposed here can be further reinforced by considering the opposing views of Keynes and Fisher on the relationship between inflation, nominal and real rates of interest. Concerning this relationship Fisher (1930: 414–15) argued that: 'If men had perfect foresight, they would adjust the money interest rate so as exactly to counterbalance or offset the effect of changes in the price level, thus causing the real interest rate to remain unchanged at the normal rate.' A reading of any macro-economics text will reveal that Fisher's analysis forms part of conventional wisdom on interest rate theory. It is certainly the point of view adopted by monetarists. In symbols we can write the relationship as: $r = i - \dot{p}^e$, where $\dot{p}^e$ is the expected rate of inflation. In a sense the continued use of the Fisher hypothesis is surprising given the widespread acknowledgement that Fisher's analysis is not confirmed by the empirical evidence (Summers, 1983; Carmichael and Stebbing, 1983: 619). In fact Fisher himself was aware that his analysis did not agree with the evidence. He attributed the lack of confirmation to the existence of money illusion (Fisher, 1930: 415): 'The erratic behaviour of real interest rates is evidently a trick played on the money market by the "money illusion" when contracts are made in unstable money.'

Keynes (1936), Harrod (1970) and Davidson (1981) reject both Fisher's analysis and his attempt to reconcile it with the facts. Their objection is based on the view that adjustment of monetary equilibrium to inflationary expectations occurs via the marginal efficiencies of assets and not via the rate of interest. When discussing Fisher's analysis Keynes (1936: 142) notes:

The mistake lies in supposing that it is the rate of interest on which prospective changes in the value of money will directly react, instead of the marginal efficiency of a given stock of capital. The prices of *existing* assets will always adjust themselves to changes in expectation concerning the prospective value of money. The significance of such changes in expectation lies in their effect on the readiness to produce new assets through their reaction on the marginal efficiency of capital.

The argument here is the same as that outlined in the previous section – in general the MEH and MEC adjust to the rate of interest rather than vice versa. Referring to the condition for monetary equilibrium: $i = a_j + \dot{r}_j$, Keynes, Harrod and Davidson argue that inflationary expectations operate on the a_j and not on the money rate, i. If perfect foresight or Rational Expectations is assumed then the spot prices of assets will immediately adjust and capital gains will be made only by the initial holders of these assets. As Keynes (1936: 142) noted:

if it [inflation] is foreseen, the prices of existing goods will be forthwith so adjusted that the advantages of holding money and of holding goods are again equalised, and it will be too late for holders of money to gain or to suffer a change in the rate of interest which will offset the prospective change during the period of the loan in the value of money lent.

To understand the theoretical basis for the failure of the Fisher hypothesis it is necessary to first distinguish between the *definition* of the real rate of interest and the *theory* of the real rate. The definition is simply: $r' = i - \dot{p}$, where $\dot{p}$ is the actual rate of inflation. This is, of course, an *ex post* relation that always holds. However, Fisher is not concerned with this definition but rather with the theory of the real rate of interest. As Le Roy (1973: 13) explains, Fisher is concerned with the view that the real rate:

is . . . ultimately related to the marginal productivity of physical capital, which in turn is determined by individuals' saving behaviour and the state of technology. Since the productivity of capital is not affected by inflationary expectations, at least not in any obvious way, the real interest rate on fixed money assets will also be unaffected, implying that changes in the rate of inflation will result in equal changes in nominal interest rates.

This interpretation of Fisher's concept of the real rate of interest is consistent with Pasinetti's (1969) discussion which outlines Fisher's attempts to relate his notion of the real rate to Wicksell's concept of the natural rate. If that interpretation is correct, and there seems to be no reason to doubt that it is, then Fisher's concept of the real rate, as determined by the forces of time preference operating on the marginal productivity of capital (Carmichael and Stebbing, 1983: 620), amounts to a simple restatement of Wicksell's natural rate of interest. Fisher's analysis is then subject to all the limitations outlined in chapter 2. Hence there would appear to be no *a priori* grounds for believing that expected inflation will impact on the nominal rate of interest as postulated by Fisher. Instead, expected inflation will impact on the marginal efficiencies of other assets as explained by Keynes and Harrod. This view has recently been tested by Carmichael and Stebbing (1983: 629) and they conclude that: 'Contrary to some widely held beliefs, it would therefore seem that, as far as financial markets are concerned, the impact of inflation has fallen dominantly on real rates of return with little influence on nominal interest rates in either the short or the long run.'

The impact of inflation on the marginal efficiencies of assets in monetary equilibrium can be further illuminated by considering the characteristics of different types of assets. To examine the relationship between the money rate of interest and the marginal efficiency of holding an asset or the marginal efficiency of capital, Keynes (1936: ch. 17) proceeds by identifying three elements which determine the net benefit from converting present into future assets. Each asset has a yield, q, which may be its ability to produce saleable output or its capacity to satisfy needs directly. In addition each asset has carrying costs, c, and a liquidity premium l, which reflects the ease with which it can be exchanged for something else. These properties then determine the own rate of own interest of an asset, i.e. its natural rate. Thus,

$$\hat{r}_j \equiv q_j - c_j + l_j; \quad \forall j, j = 1, 2, \ldots, n \qquad (9.13)$$

and in similar fashion own rates of money interest are obtained by adding the adjustment factor, a,

$$r_j \equiv a_j + q_j - c_j + l_j; \quad \forall j, j = 1, 2, \ldots, n \qquad (9.14)$$

Approaching the analysis of own rates of own interest from this perspective is particularly useful because it is immediately obvious that each of the above properties is not of equal significance for all types of assets. For example, in the case of a real capital asset used to produce output for sale, the yield, q, is of paramount importance. (It is here that the physical productivity of capital is important.) In the case of holding an asset for later resale then the carrying costs, c, and the liquidity premium, l, are important.

That different assets have different characteristics is important when it comes to explaining the impact of inflationary expectations on the marginal efficiencies of assets. As Davidson (1981) has argued, when a higher rate of inflation is widely expected, lenders, i.e. those with surplus funds, do not adjust the rate of interest to incorporate an inflationary premium. In general they simply do not have the power to set interest rates. Instead they increase their demand for those assets whose resale prices (net of carrying costs) are expected, at least, to keep pace with the rate of inflation. That is, savers seek those assets which act as a hedge against inflation. Adjustment to monetary equilibrium in the face of expectations of a higher inflation rate therefore occurs to the marginal efficiencies of durable assets and not to the rate of interest (Le Roy, 1973: 14–15).

Assets which act as a hedge against inflation have a number of distinct characteristics. Firstly, they are usually non-reproducible commodities in relatively fixed supply; secondly, a well developed spot market must exist to provide the necessary liquidity premium; and, finally, carrying and transactions costs must be relatively low. Assets which have these characteristics are ideal for the development of a market in which capital gains can be made. In particular the inelasticity of supply means that a rising spot price cannot induce a significant increase in supply and thereby moderate the price rise in the longer term. Also, the normal prices of non-reproducibles, $P_{\hat{y}}$, are not tied to costs of production but rest on subjective factors which are more prone to shift when the 'news' spreads. Expectations are then more likely to be elastic – in the Hicksian sense – than is the case with reproducibles whose normal prices are tied to their costs of production. Consequently, when the spot prices of these types of asset begin to rise and attract attention, expectations of capital gains become self-fulfilling and rates of return can be substantial. The process is, of course, not unending and becomes more fragile the longer it continues. Nevertheless, during the inflation of the 1970s a wide range of such non-reproducible assets provided rates of return well in excess of the inflation rate for almost a decade. As Evans (1981: 37) has pointed out: 'consumers put what little saving they did, not into the traditional financial market instruments – savings accounts, bonds and stocks – but into assets that were in fixed supply. In addition to real estate, these covered a wide range of additional assets: gold, silver, oriental rugs and ceramics, *objets d'art*, and so forth.' During the 1970s the rates of return on these assets far exceeded the inflation rate – as measured by the consumer price index – but the situation abruptly reversed itself in the early 1980s as inflation began to moderate (Evans, 1981: 38).

Moreover, it seems that, as a result of this inflation, investment funds were diverted from productive to non-productive uses. Durable assets used in production do not possess the characteristics of inflation-hedged assets, because they have high carrying costs and there is usually no well-developed spot market in plant and equipment (Davidson, 1978). Consequently, investment is diverted to non-productive uses. If anything this suggests that, under inflationary conditions, the point of effective demand is likely to move away from that which would generate full employment. That is, as wealth is diverted from productive to non-productive uses, this has the same effect on employment as a rise in the conventional long rate of interest. Thus, under inflationary conditions, unemployment can be expected to rise; inflation is not neutral as it leads to a distortion in the accumulation of wealth from productive to non-productive assets.

The experience with stagflation is, therefore, understandable in terms of Keynes's analysis of the relationship between inflationary expectations and the rate of interest. By comparison, those who seek to salvage Fisher's position have to explain how inflation, or expectations of inflation, causes a decline in the real rate of interest. Such explanations have, in fact, been given, most notably by Mundell (1963), while more recently Neil Wallace reportedly remarked that: 'Fisher was wrong. *Real* interest rates are high because monetary policy is tight' (quoted by Zucker, 1982: 65).

Although we can only speculate about the rationale behind Wallace's statement, Mundell's argument is clear enough. He employs a model based on Metzler's (1951) analysis in terms of which the real rate of interest ensures equilibrium between real saving and investment and generates a locus analogous to the IS curve. The money or nominal rate of interest ensures equilibrium in the money market and generates an LM-type curve as illustrated in Figure 9.3. The curves are plotted for a given level of output with real balances on the abscissa and real and nominal interest rates on the ordinate (recall the discussion in chapter 4). If the ordinate is interpreted as the real rate of interest then Mundell shifts the LM curve down by the anticipated rate of inflation, leaving the IS curve unaltered. The real rate of interest then falls from r_0 to r_1 while the money rate rises from i_0 to i_1. Thus, inflation causes a decline in the real rate of interest and – Mundell claims – this analysis is more consistent with Fisher's own empirical observations. However, it is not, as Mundell also claims, consistent with Keynes's theoretical criticism of Fisher. Mundell's analysis (1963: 281), it is clear, is based on the properties of the loanable funds theory in which the real or natural rate of interest is defined in terms of real saving and real investment. His explanation is therefore open to the objections raised in chapters 2, 4 and 5. By contrast, Keynes's analysis and the concept of monetary equilibrium employed in this study, fall within the tradition of Monetary Analysis. In terms of this analysis the impact of expected inflation is on the marginal efficiencies of durable assets and not on the nominal rate of interest.

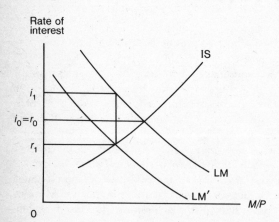

Fig. 9.3 Mundell's IS–LM analysis of real and nominal interest rates

In this section we have employed the concept of monetary equilibrium to highlight the analytical basis for Keynes's objection to Fisher's analysis of inflationary expectations and real rates of interest. The impact of expected inflation is then seen to fall on the spot prices of those assets which can act as hedges against inflation and not on the nominal rate of interest. Therefore, although a demand-pull inflation may stimulate output, the danger is that a misallocation of resources will result as investment is diverted from productive to non-productive uses. In this sense inflation is not neutral as output, employment and growth decline in the long term.

MONETARY EQUILIBRIUM AND THE NEO-RICARDIANS

At this point it is useful to return to the question of Garegnani's objection to Keynes's analysis of the relationship between the rate of interest and the marginal efficiency of capital. The issue has also been discussed by Eatwell and Milgate. The crux of their objection seems to be that Keynes's analysis of the rate of interest and the MEC is simply a restatement of the neoclassical analysis of the relation between the rate of interest and investment. For example, Eatwell (1983a: 121, emphasis added) states:

The lack of any logical foundation for the construction of an elastic demand schedule for investment as a function of the rate of interest is simultaneously a critique of the neoclassical theory of output *and of Keynes's concept of the marginal efficiency of capital – which was itself derived from the neoclassical schedule.*

This view is attributed to Garegnani by Eatwell and Milgate (1983: 89) and amounts to the conclusion that Keynes's analysis of the marginal efficiency of capital is equivalent to the neoclassical analysis of the natural rate of interest.

However, from the perspective of the Marshallian analysis of the concept of monetary equilibrium developed in this chapter, this conclusion is seen to be false. The relationship between the normal or conventional rate of interest and the marginal efficiency of capital is not equivalent to the neoclassical analysis of the natural and market rates of interest. (Recall also the discussion by Pasinetti (1974) who points out that the schedule of the marginal efficiency of capital should not be confused with that of the marginal productivity of capital.) Another way of saying the same thing is that the liquidity preference theory is not equivalent to the loanable funds theory. Because of his erroneous association of Keynes's treatment of the MEC with neoclassical theory, Garegnani is led to the wrong conclusion as to the properties of liquidity preference theory. The analysis of the relation between the rate of interest and the MEC outlined in this chapter is not open to the Cambridge critique. That is the first point.

The second point concerns the coherence of liquidity preference theory. As noted in chapter 7, Garegnani is unhappy about liquidity preference theory, as a long-period analysis of the rate of interest, because it appears to rest on views about the 'normal' rate of interest – 'views which the theory does not explain'. But as we noted, Keynes, like Sraffa and Marx, is simply acknowledging that economic theory provides no sound theoretical explanation of the rate of interest. The position becomes a little clearer when it is recalled, firstly, that from the perspective of classical theory, credit money does not have a natural price: 'According to Marx, interest is the price to be paid for the interest-bearing capital [credit], which is a commodity *sui generis* since it never enters the process of production' (Panico, 1983: 174). The natural rate of interest cannot, therefore, be defined in terms of classical principles. Secondly, we know as a result of the capital debate that the same conclusion holds for neoclassical theory. So where does that leave us? Surely it leaves us with a notion something like the conventional rate of interest as an independent variable?

Now, at one point, it seems that Garegnani (1978) actually comes to this conclusion. While bemoaning the existence of a lacuna in Keynes's long-period theory of the rate of interest, he notes that it can be filled by a radical rejection of traditional neoclassical theory. What this radical rejection would involve is summarized in the accompanying footnote which reads:

There are *hints* in this latter direction in the *General Theory*. Keynes, in fact asserts the 'conventional' character of the rate of interest, and hence the capacity of the monetary authorities to control the average level of the interest rate on long-term loans, if they act with sufficient 'persistence and consistency of purpose' (cf. Keynes, 1936: 204). *This idea which, if consistently applied, would lead to a theory of value and distribution radically different from the marginalist theory . . . does not seem to have been taken up in the subsequent literature* (Garegnani 1978: 73n, emphasis added).

Milgate (1982: 98–101) makes a similar point when he notes that there is, in principle, no incompatibility between Keynes and classical theory if the rate of interest is treated as an exogenous variable that determines the normal rate of profit. One of the major objectives of this study has been to present a comprehensive statement of these ideas in terms of the goals set by Kregel (1983).

A final point which distinguishes the approach adopted here from that of the neo-Ricardians concerns the definition of the principle of effective demand. Milgate (1982: 78) defines the principle of effective demand as the formal proposition that saving and investment are brought into equality by variations in the level of income (output). By comparison, the definition used here applies the concept of monetary equilibrium to define the point of effective demand as that level of output beyond which it is not profitable to expand production. This is a definition in the classical sense of equilibrium as a point of rest, and, as we will see from the discussion of the Fundamental Equations in chapter 10, saving equals investment in long-period monetary equilibrium. There is no question of a divergence between the two.

 The distinction between the two definitions can be seen more clearly if we recall the discussion in chapter 8 of the three types of assumptions about expectations which Kregel distinguishes in the *General Theory*. The model discussed in this chapter corresponds to the static model identified by Kregel. Long-period equilibrium is derived for a given state of long-term expectations and short-term expectations are realized. In this model there is thus no question of a discrepancy between saving and investment and there is no point in distinguishing between *ex post* and *ex ante*. Rather the objective is to establish, as a theoretical or logical matter, that the point of effective demand can determine a long-period equilibrium at almost any level of employment.

 The Milgate definition is, by contrast, concerned specifically with the discrepancy between *ex ante* saving and investment and the process of income adjustment which brings them to equality. In terms of Kregel's classification, this is a process which can only be dealt with in the model of stationary or shifting equilibrium. But, as a theoretical principle, Milgate's definition does not define the point of effective demand. Thus, in terms of Keynes's objectives, the Milgate definition does not appear to address the central issue: 'The main point is to distinguish the forces determining the position of equilibrium from the technique of trial and error by means of which the entrepreneur discovers where the position is' (Keynes, quoted by Davidson and Kregel, 1980: 139). Milgate's definition (like that of Patinkin, 1976, 1982) does not isolate the forces determining the position of equilibrium but concentrates instead on the process of trial and error in the stationary/shifting model without defining the point of effective demand. In this sense it is difficult to see in what way Milgate's definition is an advance over the equilibrium concept employed in the analysis of the simple Keynesian cross.

CONCLUDING REMARKS

An investigation of Keynes's Monetary Analysis reveals that it can be readily interpreted as the application and adaptation of Marshallian tools and modes of thought to the analysis of monetary equilibrium. In particular, the partial equilibrium or one-at-a-time method is much in evidence in the sense that it is applied to isolate the monetary aspects of the principle of effective demand. Here Keynes has reversed the direction of causation, postulated by 'classical' theory, between real and monetary rates of interest and has abandoned the notion of a natural rate of interest. Although it may be argued that Keynes did not fully appreciate the significance of the role of the conventional rate of interest it is a straightforward matter to show, applying Marshallian tools of analysis, that the money rate of interest may determine long-period monetary equilibrium with unemployment. In a capitalist system the long rate of interest is set by convention – the balance of power between *rentiers* and capitalists as mediated by the monetary authorities. It is certainly not subject to the behaviour of pure market forces. These forces operate on the short-period fluctuations of market rates of interest around the normal rate. There is therefore no natural, unique centre of gravitation in a capitalist system that exists independently of the normal rate of interest. Instead, monetary equilibrium may determine a point of effective demand over a range of output which includes full employment as only one of this set of possible solutions. In terms of neo-Walrasian terminology, monetary equilibrium is not unique.

10

MACROECONOMIC ANALYSIS AND MONETARY EQUILIBRIUM

INTRODUCTION

The previous chapter outlined the Marshallian microfoundations of the concept of monetary equilibrium. We now move on to consider the implications of that concept for macroeconomic analysis. There are three areas of application that will repay attention. These are: (i) the Fundamental Equations of the *Treatise on Money*; (ii) the Weintraub–Davidson analysis of aggregate demand and supply; and (iii) the IS–LM model of the mainstream Keynesians. The concept of monetary equilibrium can be employed to reinterpret all these structures from the perspective of Monetary rather than Real Analysis.

The application of the concept of monetary equilibrium to the Fundamental Equations avoids the contradictions encountered by Keynes, and explains the significance of the principle of effective demand for the development of the *General Theory*. A useful spin-off from this reassessment is that the quantity theory is seen to be a special case or interpretation of monetary equilibrium. It is easily shown that the quantity equation holds at all monetary equilibria. The quantity *theory* then appears as the restriction of monetary equilibrium to full employment in the case where the money stock is exogenous.

A similar application of the concept of monetary equilibrium to the macroeconomic models of both Post Keynesians and more mainstream Keynesians can then be made to provide a unified theoretical structure for the Keynesian position. The Post Keynesian macroeconomic analyses of Kaldor (1981) and Davidson (1978) for example, can then be reinterpreted in the more familiar garb of the IS–LM structure employed by Tobin – but one that exhibits the properties of Monetary rather than Real Analysis. All that this requires is the introduction of the concept of monetary equilibrium to

233

apply the principle of effective demand in the IS–LM structure. From this perspective, Post Keynesian monetary theory is seen to be a generalization of Wicksell. In this respect, the version of the IS–LM model employed to illustrate the argument is taken from Meltzer's (1981) attempt to interpret Keynes. On reflection this should not come as a surprise. For although we have seen that Meltzer is a monetarist he shares a common Wicksellian general equilibrium structure with Tobin. Also it is clear that, in intent, Meltzer's interpretation of Keynes is compatible with the properties of Monetary Analysis discussed in this study; but as his interpretation lacks the concept of monetary equilibrium he is unable to define the principle of effective demand and reach the conclusions offered here.

Finally, on a theoretical level, the concept of monetary equilibrium also allows us to incorporate the work of the so-called fundamentalist Keynesians such as George Shackle. Exponents of Real Analysis, be they Keynesians, monetarists or neo-Ricardians, have treated Shackle's work as an exercise in the economics of pure chaos or, perhaps more kindly, as an elegant nihilism of no practical relevance. However, this is a fundamental mistake. Shackle's work is important not only for its treatment of expectations but also for the message it carries about the method of economic analysis. Shackle's work in fact identifies the conditions under which the traditional analysis of long-period equilibrium can proceed. In other words it identifies the conditions that circumscribe the use of the equilibrium method, namely, that the key exogenous variables in the system must be stable. This message has unfortunately gone undetected by the exponents of Real Analysis because the properties of their models obscure its theoretical and policy relevance.

However, the capitalist system does not operate in accordance with the properties of Real Analysis. In a modern capitalist system certain key variables, such as the long rate of interest, provide the centre of gravitation around which the system will fluctuate. As there are no forces that will ensure that this centre of gravitation is the optimum it is the role of policy to ensure that a closer approximation to the optimum outcome is at least possible. Shackle's work spells out the dangers that await those who implement policy in the belief that the self-adjusting world of Real Analysis is the appropriate model. In fact, if policy were to be implemented solely on the basis of a belief in the properties of Real Analysis the economics of chaos would indeed result. The point will be illustrated in chapter 11 by a reassessment of Post Keynesian, Keynesian and monetarist proposals for stabilizing a capitalist economy.

THE FUNDAMENTAL EQUATIONS: A REASSESSMENT

The obvious point at which to begin a macroeconomic application of the concept of monetary equilibrium is with the Fundamental Equations of the *Treatise on Money* as even a superficial inspection reveals that the Fundamental Equations involve the application of Marshallian analytical tools to macroeconomic variables. Consequently, applying the Marshallian microfoundations developed in chapter 9 allows for a reassessment of the limitations of the Fundamental Equations. This exercise then provides the basis for the development of a more comprehensive macroeconomic framework which embodies the properties of Monetary Analysis outlined in earlier chapters. It enables us to apply the concept of monetary equilibrium to the models of both the Keynesians and the Post Keynesians. In addition it provides for a revealing comparison with the quantity theory tradition of Real Analysis.

In this regard it is shown that, at best, the quantity *theory* emerges as a special case of monetary equilibrium which relies on two crucial assumptions: the uniqueness of long-period equilibrium and the exogeneity of the money stock. By comparison, when the Fundamental Equations are interpreted from the perspective of Monetary Analysis, the existence of multiple equilibria is seen to be the norm. The quantity *equation* holds at all monetary equilibria but is quite incapable of explaining how these equilibria are attained. It is in this sense that Keynes's attempt to treat the quantity equation in dynamic causal fashion, in terms of the Fundamental Equations, ultimately leads, in the *General Theory*, to the abandonment of the quantity theory.

It should be stressed, however, that this discussion is not intended to suggest that Keynes had made the crucial break between Real and Monetary Analysis in the *Treatise*. Rather, it appears that, in the *Treatise*, Keynes was still thinking along the lines of Real Analysis by applying the Fundamental Equations to analyse periods of transition between, or disturbances of, long-period equilibrium (Moggridge, 1973; Milgate, 1983). In terms of this view the quantity theory remained valid in the long period but needed to be augmented by an analysis of short-period disturbances. That is to say, Keynes was at this point only concerned with the integration of real and monetary forces in the short period. Certainly it is clear that in the *Treatise* Keynes had no notion of the principle of effective demand. In this respect Keynes's analysis is similar in intent to that of Fisher's analysis of the periods of transition (Makinen, 1977:72), or with Wicksell's interpretation of the role of the cumulative process as augmenting but not replacing the quantity theory, which remained valid for long-period analysis.

The same conclusion does not appear to apply to Joan Robinson (1933a:52), however, who, when discussing reaction to the *Treatise*, noted that: 'the Theory of Money has recently undergone a violent revolution. It has ceased to be the Theory of Money, and become the *Analysis* of output.' Here Robinson appears to indicate that she is aware of the revolutionary implications of Keynes's *Treatise* analysis once it is pushed to its logical conclusion, i.e. when real and monetary forces are integrated in the analysis of long-period positions. When such an integration is achieved the theory of money and the theory of output are seen to be interdependent strands of the same analysis.

Once this point is accepted, the ground is prepared for the macroeconomic analysis of monetary equilibrium within the tradition of Monetary Analysis. The Fundamental Equations alone are not sufficient in this regard as they are formally equivalent to the quantity equation. What is required is a more formal framework which incorporates the properties of Monetary Analysis outlined in chapter 7: capitalist production, exogenous interest rate, endogenous money supply and the principle of effective demand. Kaldor (1981) has, in fact, provided such a framework; and although he makes no mention of Monetary Analysis, his model can be interpreted as exhibiting all the properties of that analysis. The model therefore provides a macroeconomic framework within the tradition of Monetary Analysis that can form the common basis for Keynesian and Post Keynesian monetary theory. Furthermore the model provides for a direct comparison with the 'classical' and Keynesian models of the neoclassical synthesis. The first step in the understanding of this framework is a reassessment of the Fundamental Equations.

The Fundamental Equations of the *Treatise* were developed by Keynes in response to a widely felt dissatisfaction with aspects of the quantity theory. The issues at stake were described by Keynes (1930: 133, emphasis added) in the following terms:

The Fundamental Problem of Monetary Theory is not merely to establish identities or statical equations relating (e.g.) the turnover of monetary instruments to the turnover of things traded for money. The real task of such a Theory is to treat the problem dynamically, analysing the different elements involved, in such a manner as to exhibit the *causal* process by which the price-level is determined, and the method of transition from one position of equilibrium to another. The forms of the Quantity Theory, however, on which we have all been brought up ... are but ill adapted for this purpose.

The Fundamental Equations of the *Treatise* are designed to achieve this purpose by applying Marshallian modes of thought to macroeconomic, rather than microeconomic, variables. But the attempt to treat the problem dynamically did not mean that Keynes intended to give up the quantity theory for long-period analysis. Nevertheless, interpreted in the light of the analysis of previous chapters, Keynes's arguments lead to the conclusion that the quantity theory is seriously misleading as an analysis of long-period equilibrium.

Many writers have commented on the utility of the Fundamental Equations for the analysis of inflation, but few have noted their more general applicability to the analysis of the interaction of real and monetary forces. A notable exception in this regard is Shackle (1974: 25), who notes that the Fundamental Equations provide the basis for 'a complete macro-dynamic theory, a formal frame able to provide a place for all the questions about the movements of the great aggregative variables'.

Unfortunately, in the *Treatise*, Keynes did not push the analysis implicit in his Fundamental Equations to its logical conclusion. The major reason for this appears to be that he retained Wicksell's notion of the natural rate of interest (if somewhat reinterpreted) and the associated view that the economy operates at full employment. In other words, the principle of effective demand is missing in the *Treatise*. As Joan Robinson (1933b:84) was quick to observe, this led to a paradoxical state of affairs in which the reader of the *Treatise* was expected to 'visualize an acute slump with full employment, and a trade boom without an increase in output'. This paradoxical state of affairs is remedied, however, once it is realized that Keynes's analysis implies that changes in monetary factors could cause a change in the long-period equilibrium position itself. The limitations to Keynes's analysis are, moreover, easily overcome by replacing the natural rate of interest, i.e. loanable funds theory of the rate of interest, with the analysis of the money rate of interest and the MEC, i.e. liquidity preference theory, presented in chapter 9. The Fundamental Equations then provide a macroeconomic illustration of the interaction of real and monetary forces in terms of the analysis of monetary equilibrium outlined in the previous chapter.

At the same time, this reinterpretation of the Fundamental Equations provides an opportunity for demonstrating that the quantity theory can at best only be interpreted as a special case of monetary equilibrium. The quantity equation will hold at all long-period monetary equilibria, but as it is an entirely static construct it cannot be used to explain how these equilibria are achieved. The quantity theory is then hardly a theory but simply that statement of the quantity equation which holds when the condition for long-period equilibrium, $\bar{i} = \hat{r}$, occurs at full employment. Traditional applications of the quantity theory avoid this issue by assuming that real forces always establish monetary equilibrium at full employment.

The analytical structure of the *Treatise* rested on the two Fundamental Equations which determined the price level of consumption goods and the price level of output as a whole, i.e.

$$P = \frac{E}{O} + \frac{I' - S}{R} \tag{10.1}$$

$$\Pi = \frac{E}{O} + \frac{I - S}{O} \tag{10.2}$$

Following Shackle (1967:167), these equations are best explained by adapting the *Treatise* notation somewhat. Decomposing total consumer spending, U, into income earned from the production of consumption goods, E', plus income earned from the production of investment goods, I', less what is saved, S, we can write:

$$U = E' + I' - S$$

If R represents the physical number of units of output of consumption goods then the price level of consumption goods is:

$$P = U/R = (E' + I' - S)/R \text{ or, } P = E'/R + (I' - S)/R$$

As Keynes's (1930:135) physical unit of production is the same for consumption and investment goods, the unit production cost of consumption goods, E'/R is the same as E/O, the unit production cost of goods in general, where O is total output. This produces the first Fundamental Equation, i.e. the price level for consumption goods can then be written as in (10.1).

The second Fundamental Equation relates the overall price level, Π, to the price level of consumption goods, P, and the price level of new investment goods, P':

$$\Pi = (PR + P'C)/O$$

The latter price level, P', is influenced by the money rate of interest and, as we will see, it is via this mechanism that the natural rate of interest and the equality of saving and investment enter the analysis. This link will be examined in some detail below. If C is the output of investment goods and E is total money income so that $E = E' + I'$ then we can write $PR = E - S$, and the value of new investment goods as $P'C = I$ (as opposed to their cost of production I'). Making these substitutions produces

$$\Pi = (E - S + I)/O = E/O + (I - S)/O$$

which is the second Fundamental Equation.

At this point it seems advisable to repeat Keynes's (1930: 138) reminder that these equations are identities which tell us nothing in themselves – like the quantity equation, of which they are simply an alternative version. When approached from the perspective of monetary equilibrium, however, both the quantity theory and the Fundamental Equations are placed in a different light.

To relate the Fundamental Equations to the previous discussion it is necessary to change them into a form which distinguishes between efficiency earnings and profits. This Keynes does by defining windfall (or excess) profits in the production and sale of consumption goods as Q_1, and the corresponding profit on investment goods as Q_2. Total profit equals the sum of profits in each sector, i.e. $Q = Q_1 + Q_2$. Profit in the production of consumption goods, Q_1 equals sales revenue less costs, i.e. $Q_1 = PR - E'$, hence $Q_1 = E' + I' - S - E' = I' - S$, and since $Q_2 = I - I'$ and $Q = Q_1 + Q_2$ it follows that $Q = I' - S + I - I'$ which reduces to $Q = I - S$.

These adjustments enable us to examine the impact of a change in the rate of interest on the profits in the consumption and investment goods sectors. These profits (or losses) arise as a result of changes in the prices of capital and consumption goods relative to their normal or long-period supply prices. The latter levels are determined by the rate of efficiency earnings, i.e. the ratio of total money income to output. Thus the rate of efficiency earnings is $W_1 = E/O$ and is related to the rate of earnings per unit of human effort, W, via the coefficient of efficiency, e, so that $W = eW_1$. The fundamental principle reflected by these substitutions is that long-period supply prices are determined by efficiency earnings (costs of production including normal profit) and that short-period deviations in the market prices cause windfall (excess) profits or losses. The analysis is thus in the Marshallian long-period tradition. This can be most clearly seen by the transformed equations which now appear as:

$$P = W_1 + \frac{Q_1}{R} \tag{10.3}$$

$$\Pi = W_1 + \frac{Q}{O} \tag{10.4}$$

and state, for example, that the price of consumption goods, P, is equal to the rate of efficiency earnings plus (minus) the excess profits (losses) obtained in their production. The same conclusion holds for the price of output as a whole.

In the long period, windfall profits are zero and the Fundamental

Equations reduce to

$$P = W_1 = \Pi \tag{10.5}$$

and prices correspond to the money-rate of efficiency earnings (Keynes, 1930:152). We are now in a position to put the Fundamental Equations to work.

Macro-equilibrium: multiple monetary equilibria

As with all identities, the Fundamental Equations tell us very little unless augmented with some theory of how their component parts are related. In particular, the *causal* direction of change in Keynes's discussion emerges from the Fundamental Equations as a consequence of applying Wicksell's distinction between the market and natural rates of interest. In long-period equilibrium the two rates coincide and the second terms in the Fundamental Equations are zero, i.e. if $\overline{\imath} = \hat{\imath}$ then $P = W_1 = \Pi$ as $Q_1 = Q_2 = 0$. This clearly indicates that, in the *Treatise*, Keynes is employing the Wicksellian analysis of saving and investment as determinants of the rate of interest, i.e. he is employing the loanable funds theory. As we will see this led him into difficulty with the analysis of unemployment.

A divergence between the two rates of interest then causes the emergence of excess profits or losses, initially in the investment-goods sector and later in the consumption-goods sector. As Keynes (1930: 154, 203–6) notes:

the higher the rate of interest, the lower, other things being equal, will be the value of capital goods. Therefore, if the rate of interest rises, P' will tend to fall, which will lower the rate of profit on the production of capital-goods, which will be a deterrent to new investment. Thus a high rate of interest will tend to diminish ... the volume of output of capital-goods. The rate of saving on the other hand is stimulated by a high rate of interest ... It follows that an increase in the rate of interest tends – other things being equal – to make the rate of investment ... decline relatively to the rate of saving, i.e. to move the second term of both Fundamental Equations in the negative direction, so that the price-levels tend to fall.

Following Wicksell, it will be convenient to call the rate of interest which would cause the second term of our Fundamental Equation to be zero, the *natural-rate* of interest, and the rate which actually prevails the *market-rate* of interest. Thus the natural-rate of interest is the rate at which saving and the value of investment are exactly balanced, so the price level of output as a whole ... exactly corresponds to the money-rate of efficiency-earnings of the Factors of Production.

...

the initial consequence of a higher bank rate will be a fall in the price of capital goods, and therefore in P′, the price-level of new investment goods ... But if the change in the market-rate does *not* exactly correspond to a change in the natural rate ... the decline in the rate of investment will cause a fall in P ... therefore, we have a fall in both P and P', consequent losses to *all* classes of entrepreneurs, and a resulting diminution in the volume of employment ... This state of unemployment may be expected to ensue, and to continue, until the rise in bank rate is reversed, or by a chance, something happens to alter the natural-rate of interest so as to bring it back to equality with the new market-rate.

In these passages the Wicksellian or 'classical' theory of the rate of interest clearly provides the basis for Keynes's Marshallian application of the Fundamental Equations to examine the influence of price changes on output and employment in the investment and consumption goods sectors. However, when Wicksell's natural rate of interest is abandoned and the analysis pushed to its logical conclusion along the lines sketched in chapter 9, changes in output and employment emerge in both the short *and* the long period. The condition of monetary equilibrium, $\bar{i} = \hat{\imath}$ then defines a point of effective demand which may imply a long-period unemployment equilibrium that cannot be corrected by flexibility in the rest of the system. But in the *Treatise* Keynes had not yet arrived at the principle of effective demand. Nevertheless, Hicks (1967b:199) senses the implications:

As we have seen, the equilibrium of the *Treatise* is a condition in which the earnings of *entrepreneurs* are normal, in the sense that 'they have no motive to increase or to decrease their scale of operations'. The economy can be in equilibrium, in this limited sense, even though the scale of operations is far below capacity: for nothing is said about capacity, or about employment, in this definition. There can be equilibrium, in this sense, at the bottom of a slump ...

Hicks's statement clearly reflects the tension in Keynes's own views on the implications of the changes he was discussing for equilibrium – was it long- or short-period equilibrium? Hicks appears to treat it as a short-period equilibrium at the bottom of a slump. That is to say, the unemployment equilibrium referred to by Hicks appears to be a short-period equilibrium – part of cyclical unemployment – even though the equilibrium is one of normal profits – the Marshallian notion of long-period equilibrium!

Joan Robinson, on the other hand, was adamant that Keynes had failed to realize the full implications of his analysis. In her view there were a number of illustrations of this conclusion:

A second example of Mr. Keynes's failure to realize the nature of the revolution he was carrying on is to be found in the emphasis which he lays upon the relationship of the quantity of investment to the quantity of saving. He points out that if savings exceed investment, consumption goods can only be sold at a loss. Their output will consequently decline until the real income of the population is reduced to such a low level that savings are perforce reduced to equality with investment. But he completely overlooks the significance of this discovery, and throws it out in the most casual way without pausing to remark that he has proved *that output may be in equilibrium at any number of different levels* and that while there is a natural tendency towards equilibrium between savings and investment (in the very long-period) there is no natural tendency towards full employment of the factors of production. The mechanism of thought involved in the equations of saving and investment compels its exponent to talk only of short-period disequilibrium positions. And it was only with disequilibrium positions that Mr. Keynes was consciously concerned when he wrote the *Treatise* – he failed to notice that he had incidently evolved *a new theory of the long-period analysis of output* (Robinson, 1947:55–6, emphasis added).

With the benefit of hindsight – and early discussions of the *General Theory* – Robinson is therefore able to reinterpret the analysis of the Fundamental Equations as providing the basis for a new theory of the *long-period* analysis of output. Furthermore, it is quite clear that she realized that multiple monetary equilibria were the norm and not the exception. Kregel (1983:64) reaches the same conclusion as to the intent of the *General Theory*: 'Keynes was first interested to show that there is no "natural tendency" for the system to maintain full employment at its "natural" position. This he achieved by showing that within Wicksell's terminology, there could be any number of equilibria.'

In this respect, it should always be remembered that the use of unique equilibrium solutions by general equilibrium theorists is based on an assumption for which there is simply no empirical or theoretical basis. Uniqueness and global stability are recognized as extreme possibilities by most neoclassical general equilibrium theorists, but the fact is nevertheless often ignored when it comes to the question of macro-equilibrium with unemployment. However, the analysis of monetary equilibrium presented in the previous chapter clearly reveals that multiple equilibria are the norm. If changes in monetary factors, in the guise of the conventional rate of interest, can cause changes in the capital stock then monetary equilibrium is not unique.

The neoclassical notions of existence and stability must therefore be replaced by a broader concept. Such a concept was presented by Wicksell (1901:101) and is best conveyed in terms of an analogy to the behaviour of:

a cylinder, which rests on a horizontal plane in so-called neutral equilibrium. The plane is somewhat rough and a certain force is required to set the price-cylinder in motion and to keep it in motion. But so long as the force – the rising or lowering of the rate of interest – remains in operation, the cylinder continues to move in the same direction ... Once the cylinder has come to rest, there is no tendency for it to be restored to its original position.

This concept of equilibrium is most apt once it is applied to the notion of monetary equilibrium which defines the point of effective demand. If monetary equilibrium is, in general, obtained by the adjustment of $\hat{\imath}$ to $\bar{\imath}$ then Wicksell's analogy describes the property of hysteresis. Long-period equilibrium is then not unique and may occur with unemployment.

This, it seems, was one of the central conclusions reached by Keynes (1979:55, some emphasis added) after his transition from the *Treatise* to the *General Theory*:

On my view, there is no unique *long-period* position of equilibrium equally valid regardless of the character of the policy of the monetary authority. On the contrary there are a number of such positions corresponding to different policies. Moreover there is no reason to suppose that positions of *long-period* equilibrium have an inherent tendency or likelihood to be positions of optimum output. A *long-period* position of optimum output is a *special case* corresponding to a special kind of policy on the part of the monetary authority.

From this perspective, monetary policy takes on an added significance because money matters, not only for the determination of nominal income, but for the determination of the long-period equilibrium itself. *Monetary* forces therefore have a strong impact not only on the inflationary process but also on unemployment, output and growth.

The Fundamental Equations and the quantity theory

Reinterpreting the Fundamental Equations of the *Treatise*, in terms of the properties of Monetary Analysis, reveals that the neoclassical notions of uniqueness and stability of long-period equilibrium are highly restrictive. Monetary Analysis suggests the existence of multiple equilibria and the movement between equilibria rather than the global stability of a unique long-period equilibrium. What this implies is that the quantity theory assumes a special case of monetary equilibria which applies, at best, only if the money stock is exogenous. This conclusion follows in a trivial fashion from Keynes's (1930: 149) reconciliation of the Fundamental Equations with Fisher's equation of exchange. In long-period equilibrium only normal profits are earned and $Q_1 = Q_2 = 0$. If M_1 is the total of income deposits and

V_1 their velocity of circulation then $E = M_1 V_1$ (as $V_1 = E/M_1$ by definition). In any long-period equilibrium the Fundamental Equations then become:

$$\Pi = P = M_1 V_1/O \text{ or, } PO = M_1 V_1$$

whenever $\bar{i} = \hat{i}$. This statement of the quantity equation is similar to Fisher's version except that O represents output rather than transactions and $M_1 V_1$ refers to income deposits and their velocity rather than cash deposits and their velocity. The quantity *equation* therefore holds at *all monetary equilibria* and yet is quite incapable of giving any clue as to how these equilibria are established. The quantity *theory* thus emerges as a special case of monetary equilibrium based on two key assumptions: the uniqueness of long-period equilibrium at full employment and the exogeneity of the money stock.

On the first point it is clear that if changes in prices *and output* can occur in the long period, the quantity theory loses much of its analytical appeal. The traditional response to the difficulty has been to invoke the authority of neoclassical theory for the assumption of long-period full employment.[1] Once this step is taken the need to examine the long-period interaction of real and monetary forces is assumed away and the adjustment falls entirely on the price level. However, as we have seen, there is no theoretical basis for such a belief.

The second assumption is crucial to the quantity theory and today is the centre of attention in the debate between monetarists and Post Keynesians. At the time of Locke and Hume, exponents of the old quantity theory, the assumption of an exogenous money stock may have been appropriate, although it is doubtful that a pure commodity money system has ever existed. Money in the form of credit has always augmented commodity money to a greater or lesser extent. Nevertheless, assuming the case of pure commodity money for the sake of comparison, it is then usually argued that in the case of a commodity money, such as gold or silver, the amount is exogenously fixed and may be augmented only by mining, trade or plunder. There is, under these conditions, an independent supply function based on the costs of production of the money commodity.

In the world of bank money, however, the situation is quite different. As Wicksell and Myrdal both recognized, here the supply of money is not independent of the demand. In this case an independent money supply function does not exist and the quantity *theory* fails as

---

1. Patinkin (1972a:20), has, however, argued that some quantity theorists recognized the non-neutrality of money in the long period on the grounds that monetary changes could affect the real stock of physical capital and hence the real (natural) rate of interest.

the quantity equation $MV = PT$ can be read from right to left rather than vice versa (Robinson, 1970). These issues will be taken up in greater detail in the following chapter but for the moment it is sufficient to note that the treatment of the conventional rate of interest as an exogenous variable implies that the money supply is largely endogenous. When pushed to its logical conclusion, Keynes's desire to treat monetary theory in a dynamic causal fashion leads, therefore, to the abandonment of the quantity *theory* as a tool of analysis.

A POST KEYNESIAN MACROECONOMIC ANALYSIS OF
MONETARY EQUILIBRIUM: STATIC EQUILIBRIUM

Having illustrated that the quantity theory is, at best, a special case of monetary equilibrium, the need for a more general analytical framework is readily apparent. Such a framework, which can be adapted to meet all the criteria of Monetary Analysis, has been sketched by Kaldor (1981) and, with the necessary adjustments, consists of the following five relationships.

$$PQ = MV \tag{10.6}$$

$$P = (1 + \pi)\, w\, \frac{N}{Q} \text{ or,} \tag{10.7}$$

$$P = (1 + \lambda)\, \frac{dN}{dQ}\, w \tag{10.7a}$$

$$MV \equiv D \equiv Y = \frac{1}{1 - c}\, I(\bar{i} = \hat{r}) \tag{10.8}$$

$$M = \frac{Y}{V(i)} \text{ or,} \tag{10.9}$$

$$M = \frac{Y}{V(i,\, \bar{i})} \tag{10.9a}$$

$$i = \bar{i} \tag{10.10}$$

The first expression (10.6) is the traditional quantity equation which relates the price level to the monetary variables. The equation may, however, be read in either direction permitting the distinction between cost-push and demand-pull inflation.[2] This is readily

---

2. Initially monetarists ridiculed this distinction. But on reflection we can see that their position was based on the implicit assumption that the money stock was fixed, i.e. exogenous. Under those conditions a rise in the price of oil, say, means that more of the fixed money stock is used to buy oil leaving less to buy other goods. Hence only relative prices, and not the absolute price level, should change. This is the result that could occur in a world of commodity money. In a world of credit money things are quite different and cost-push inflations are a reality.

apparent from expression (10.7), which Kaldor (1981: 8) calls the Pigou amendment to the quantity theory, and which relates the price level to the exogenous level of money wages, w. The variables N/Q and π refer respectively to the average direct labour cost per unit of output and the percentage margin on direct costs added for overhead costs and profit.[3] Although expression (10.7a) bears a close resemblance to the neoclassical 'demand for labour function' it cannot be so interpreted in this model for reasons that will be provided below. Furthermore, as Kaldor (1981: 9) suggests, treating Q as a dependent variable in expression (10.7) means abandoning full employment (one of the main pillars of the quantity theory) and allows for the existence of long-lasting or permanent unemployment.

The reason for this change lies in expression (10.8) which introduces the principle of effective demand or the principle of income generation in a capitalist economy (Kaldor, 1981: 10n1). The essence of this principle is that monetary equilibrium, $\bar{i} = \hat{r}$, establishes a limit to the profitable expansion of output. In long-period equilibrium the long rate of interest establishes the rate of investment, an autonomous component of aggregate demand, and the point of effective demand. The point of effective demand determines employment and once monetary equilibrium is established, flexibility in the rest of the system, e.g. money wages and prices, cannot induce an adjustment to full employment. In the simple framework presented above investment, I, is the sole source of autonomous expenditure. Other important sources such as government expenditure and exports are ignored at this point. The expression $1/(1 - c)$ is the familiar multiplier.

Expression (10.9) is the so-called liquidity preference relation. From what we have said earlier about the interpretation of liquidity preference theory it should not come as a surprise to find that the first four expressions present a somewhat incomplete picture. As Kaldor (1981) has explained at length, Keynes, and his early Keynesian interpreters, appeared to treat the framework as complete at this point.[4] But, in that case, the model consists of four equations to determine the four unknowns, P (the price level), Q (real output), V (the velocity of circulation) and i (the money rate of interest). The

3. The profit margin on turnover is taken to be one which, at normal utilization of capacity, generates the desired or normal rate of return for a particular industry (Kaldor, 1981:8–9). Kaldor also refers to (10.7) as the short-period cost function but it is difficult to relate this designation with the notion of normal profit incorporated in π (see Kaldor, footnote 11) or the existence of permanent unemployment.

4. Robertson, like Hutt and Coddington, among others, overlooked the role of the conventional rate and as a result interpreted liquidity preference theory as dealing only with the market rate of interest (Danes, 1979).

exogenous variables are presumed to be: M (the quantity of money); w (the level of money wages); I (the level of investment) and c (the propensity to consume), while the 'behavioural' relations are the production function $Q(N)$ and the liquidity preference function $V(i)$. Since $Y \equiv PQ$, Y is not a separate variable. However, the framework at this point is, as explained above, lacking the essential component of the liquidity preference theory (the conventional rate of interest) and hence the principle of effective demand is missing.

As a result of this oversight the model is, up this point, readily reincorporated into neoclassical loanable funds theory with the liquidity trap and wage rigidity as special cases which may, or may not, be of some practical significance. All of this changes with the addition of expression (10.10) and the replacement of (10.9) by (10.9a). The model sketched in expressions (10.6) to (10.10) cannot then be interpreted in terms of the properties of Real Analysis that characterize the models of the neoclassical synthesis. There are several significant features which should make that clear.

Firstly, the model is causal–recursive and cannot be solved as a set of simultaneous equations as is the now standard practice with macroeconomic models. Secondly, the long term rate of interest, $\bar{i}$, is treated as an exogenous variable, which together with the marginal efficiency of capital, defines the point of effective demand and determines employment, i.e. Say's Law does not hold. Thirdly, there is no role for the neoclassical analysis of the labour market even if there is an inverse relationship between real wages and employment. Finally, although the quantity equation holds at the point of effective demand, the quantity theory is abandoned and money is non-neutral in the long period.

That the model should be interpreted as a causal system needs little further elaboration in view of the discussion of the characteristics of these models in chapter 7. The second point is perhaps more interesting as it has often been suggested that Keynes imposed the condition $i = \bar{i}$, but that this leads to problems of inconsistency or overdetermination. Examples of this interpretation can be found in Modigliani (1944) and Sargent (1979: 92–5) and the issue has recently been discussed by Kohn (1981b) who makes some revealing observations. He begins by suggesting, correctly, that if an unemployment equilibrium is possible then the rate of interest is indeterminate, so that a so-called bootstrap theory of interest becomes a necessity (Kohn, 1981b: 861). As we have seen, this is in fact the case when the liquidity preference theory is interpreted as outlined in chapter 9. However, he then goes on to conclude that the problem of overdetermination that troubled Modigliani can be resolved once it is realized that the model is in a disequilibrium state (Kohn, 1981b:878)! This latter conclusion illustrates how easy it is to miss the point when the principle of effective demand is not understood. For without the principle of effective demand it is not possible to determine a long-period equilibrium other than at the point of full employment in a Say's Law economy. Hence, without the principle of effective demand, the conclusion is inevitably reached that Monetary Analysis is concerned with disequilibrium (Kohn, 1981b; 1986), or that it involves inconsistency (Sargent, 1979: 92–5), or that an unemployment equilibrium requires the assumption of rigid wages. This latter interpretation brings us to the third issue, the interpretation of the labour market in this model.

Although Roy Weintraub (1979: 45–6) does not appear to grasp the nature of the principle of effective demand as outlined in this study, he does correctly perceive that the labour market cannot be interpreted along neoclassical lines in this Post Keynesian system. He correctly concludes that: 'For the Keynesian system clearly the labor market must go in the sense that the demand curve for labor is *not* given by any aggregate marginal productivity relationship.' Instead, in Keynes's system, 'employment is already determined, ... since the intersection of aggregate supply and demand occurs in income–employment space. Consequently, the "labor market" is redundant.' This point has been made consistently over the years by Paul Davidson and we will return to it again below.

For the moment it is sufficient to note that expression (10.7a) should not be interpreted as a neoclassical demand for labour function. To do so, and to explain employment in terms of the level of real wages, is to confuse consequences with causes. Asimakopulos (1982:30n25) reminds us that in the 1933 draft of the *General Theory* Keynes made this point when he argued that 'we may well discover empirically a correlation between employment and real wages. But this will occur, not because the one causes the other, but because they are both consequences of the same cause.' Keynes then goes on to explain that the common cause is a shift in the point of effective demand. Employment is determined by the point of effective demand and not by a co-operative interaction between demanders and suppliers of labour at a market-clearing real wage. Hence the marginal disutility of labour also does not play a direct role in the determination of employment. In this sense we are dealing with an entrepreneur and not a co-operative economy because entrepreneurs determine the level of employment and have no incentive to increase output and employment beyond the point of effective demand.

The final point concerns the nature of the money supply and the non-neutral role of money in this model. First, a brief background on Keynesian monetary theory is necessary. The initial Keynesian interpretation of liquidity preference theory as comprising only expression (10.9) led to the view that the velocity of circulation could conveniently be stretched or shrunk to accommodate changes in the level of incomes or expenditures. In that sense, it appeared as if the Keynesian model implied that money did not matter – it was an unimportant quantity. In this way it seems that many Keynesians were led to a view contrary to the spirit of Monetary Analysis. The new quantity theorists (the monetarists) took advantage of this Keynesian weakness and made much of the close correlation between movements in Y and M. However, as Kaldor and others have often pointed out, correlation does not reveal anything about causality and Friedman's empirical findings, on which he places so much weight, are equally consistent with the hypothesis that changes in the supply of money simply accommodate changes in the demand for money, i.e. they are consistent with the fact that there is no independent supply function for money. If anything the monetarist 'evidence' for the 'stability' of the velocity of circulation, or the demand for money, is no more than a reflection of the fact that the supply of money has been adjusted to the demand by the banking system and the central bank. In that sense the monetarist 'evidence' may equally well be interpreted to mean that the money supply is endogenous (Kaldor, 1981:19).

In this regard, treating the long-term rate of interest as an exogenous variable is consistent with the view that the money supply is endogenous. As we have noted, Wicksell argued that in an economy with a well-developed banking system the supply of money was determined by the demand. Further, as Rousseas (1986:67) points out, Myrdal (1939) held the same view and stressed that there was no one-way causal connection from the money supply to the price level. Modern Post Keynesian monetary theorists such as Kaldor, Davidson and Moore have, of course, been stressing this point for some time. The interpretation of Kaldor's model presented here is consistent with this view, as the quantity theory has no role to play. Although it is true that the quantity equation, expression (10.6), always holds at the monetary equilibrium established by the point of effective demand, the neutrality of money and the quantity theory have been given up.

These points can be readily illustrated by relating the analysis to the aggregate demand and supply model proposed by Weintraub (1958) and Davidson and Smolensky (1964). These functions have been the subject of considerable analysis some of which has generated controversy (Patinkin, 1982:ch. 5). Nevertheless, and although

Patinkin does not employ the principle of effective demand as defined in this study (so inevitably he interprets Keynes as the economics of unemployment *disequilibrium*), the interpretation of the curves offered here is consistent with the spirit expressed by Patinkin (1982:143, 153). In this regard expression (10.7) can be interpreted as an aggregate supply function, Z, which relates expected proceeds, PQ, to employment, N, given the wage rate, profit mark-up, state of technology and labour productivity. A reasonable interpretation of this aggregate supply function suggests that, at least, normal profits must be earned if any particular level of employment is to be maintained. Expression (10.8) is comparable to the aggregate demand function, D, given the rate of interest, the marginal propensity to consume, stable long-period expectations and realised short-period expectations. The two functions can then be plotted as illustrated in Figure 10.1. Given the long rate of interest, long-period monetary equilibrium, $\bar{i} = \hat{r}$ then establishes the point of effective demand at E. Competition ensures that output would expand up to this point as excess profits would be removed by competition in the long period. For the representative firm, E is the point of maximum profit in the sense that there is no incentive for the firm to move away from it (Patinkin, 1982:143). In equilibrium the quantity equation, expression (10.6) does hold but it plays no role in the determination of equilibrium.

It is clear from this summary of the model that the conventional rate of interest, as an independent variable, plays a central role in

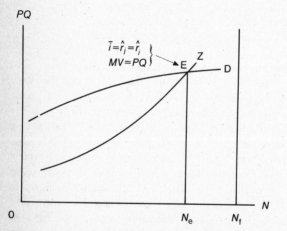

Fig. 10.1 Monetary equilibrium in the Post Keynesian aggregate demand and supply model

determining the point of effective demand. We therefore begin a more detailed illustration of the properties of the model with a discussion of the conventional rate of interest.

The conventional rate of interest: interest rate regimes

At one point Chick (1983:10) remarks that Keynes 'comes to the astonishing conclusion that the chief cause of unemployment is not so much that the real wage is too high, but that the rate of interest is too high'. This conclusion, she goes on to say, is at first sight most implausible. After all, 'what relationship could there possibly be between unemployment, the most human of problems, and the rate of interest, the driest of economic variables?' The answer has been provided by the analysis of monetary equilibrium in previous sections. This analysis hinges on the notion of the conventional rate of interest which we must now consider in more detail.

The importance of the fact that the rate of interest is an exogenous or independent variable cannot be overemphasized. It receives strong theoretical support from the analysis conducted in chapters 2 to 9 and is also widely acknowledged by central bankers who conduct monetary policy via manipulation of interest rates. Although they have more control over short rates, this control has a direct effect on the entire interest rate structure. This issue will be considered briefly in the next chapter. At this stage we need to examine some of the properties of the conventional rate of interest specified in expression (10.10).

It is necessary to consider two issues: the relationship between short and long rates of interest and the distinction between persistent and transitory changes in rates. In respect of the former, it is interesting to note the different transmission mechanisms highlighted by Hawtrey and Keynes. As Davis (1980:718) has pointed out, Hawtrey stressed the influence of Bank rate on short rates and the inventory decisions of firms, while Keynes stressed the term structure aspect, the relationship between short and long rates and the influence of long rates on investment. The behaviour of i in expression (10.10) thus summarizes the term structure and the influence on I, in expression (10.8), which operates via both of these mechanisms. The efficacy of monetary policy in stimulating investment is thus dependent on the efficiency of these two mechanisms. The more crucial of the two would seem to be the relation between Bank rate and long rates via the term structure. This relation is somewhat elastic and manipulations of Bank rate to change long rates may not always be effective.

Secondly, a distinction must be drawn between transitory and persistent changes in rates. This distinction allows for temporary or short-term fluctuations of the market rate around the conventional rate. In the model of monetary equilibrium presented above, a similar distinction can be drawn between the conventional rate of interest, $\bar{i}$, and the market rate, i, which will deviate from the conventional rate from time to time as a result of short-term disturbances in the financial markets. This distinction should be familiar as it still forms the basis of some explanations of liquidity preference theory in which the inelastic expectations of 'norm believers' stabilize interest rate movements about the normal or conventional rate.

The important point here is that movements in the long rate which are not intended or perceived to be transitory are the crucial factor. It is the long rate of interest which is treated, by Keynes and others, as one of the causal elements in the determination of long-period monetary or macro-equilibrium. It should also be recalled that Keynes offers no theory of the long rate of interest but argues instead, like Marx, that this rate depends on convention, which is itself determined by institutional and other empirical factors – including monetary policy.[5] Psychological factors play a role in the sense that market participants must have confidence in a particular normal or conventional rate. Only if such confidence exists will expectations be inelastic and market deviations self-correcting. If confidence fails, expectations become elastic and the market exhibits signs of instability. Because the rate of interest cannot be determined by objective or real factors the monetary authorities carry the burden of maintaining confidence and thereby keeping the potentially unstable subjective factors in check. As we will see this is one of the implications of Shackle's analysis.

A useful illustration of an analysis based on the concept of a conventional rate of interest is in fact found in the Radcliffe Report (1959: 176–7). The Report distinguishes between various interest rate regimes, which it classifies in terms of a mechanical analogy as 'low', 'middle' and 'top gear'. Changes of gear amount to changes in the entire structure of interest rates including the long rate. It is these changes of gear which have important implications for capital formation and growth:

Those concerned with the planning of capital developments, especially if these are of the more long-lasting and less hazardous kinds, work on the basis

5. After completion of this manuscript a paper by Panico (1987) appeared which documents the evolution of Keynes's thought on the theory of the rate of interest between the *Treatise* and the *General Theory*. The points of Keynesian exegesis made by Panico are fully compatible with the analytical structure adopted in this study.

of some conventional rate of interest, often 5 per cent. This is the 'middle gear' rate of interest; if rates go 'top gear' ... (and) if planners become persuaded that the new level of interest rates has come to stay, their habits will gradually change, and the range of worthwhile capital development will be adapted to the new level of interest rates (Radcliffe Report, 1959: 176).

Although we are not directly concerned with issues of policy at this point, it follows that changes of gear, or the ability of the monetary authorities to initiate such changes, have important implications. The implied strategy is summarized by the Radcliffe Report (1959: 177–8) as follows:

Our conclusion on the rate of interest policy is therefore that, while there can be no reliance on the weapon as a major short-term stabiliser of demand, the authorities should think of rates of interest – and particularly long rates – as relevant to the domestic economic situation ... If the authorities were to take the view that a fall in total demand was a sign of a more lasting collapse in the demand for capital development, definite measures to bring down the whole structure of interest rates – amounting to a change in gear – would be appropriate.

Now the interesting aspect of these recommendations by the Radcliffe Committee is that, from a theoretical perspective, there is no mention of the natural rate of interest. Instead, the structure of interest rates is seen to be a matter of convention subject to the objectives of monetary policy. The views expressed by the Radcliffe Committee are thus consistent with the Keynes–Marx view of interest rates, which is one of the characteristics of Monetary rather than Real Analysis. In terms of the latter analysis the monetary authorities must allow pure market forces automatically to adjust the market rate of interest to the natural rate, which is itself determined by the 'real' forces of productivity and thrift. Anything but a *laissez-faire* interest rate policy would then produce inflationary or deflationary pressure. From the perspective of Monetary Analysis, however, there is no such thing as the natural rate of interest and its associated pure market forces. Markets are man-made, as are the institutions and rules under which they operate. The structure of interest rates which results in a particular economy is then not something that can be given a purely theoretical explanation in terms of classical or neoclassical theory – rather the interest rate reflects psychological, institutional and other historical factors which cannot be specified *a priori*.

When examining the impact of changes emanating in the real sector on interest rates, we must, from the perspective of Monetary Analysis, determine whether there will be any impact on the conventional interest rate structure. Will these changes lead to a change in the conventional rate of interest or not? Transitory adjustments which leave the conventional rate, or expectations about it, unchanged will not have any implications for long-period macro-equilibrium.

As a corollary of the above position we may remind the reader that debates over the liquidity preference and loanable funds theories have often ended inconclusively because they have overlooked the crucial role played by the conventional rate of interest in the liquidity preference theory. In liquidity preference theory the conventional rate of interest plays a role akin to the natural rate in Wicksell's monetary theory because the direction of causation has been reversed and the conventional money rate acts as the centre of gravitation. Ignoring the role of the conventional rate is to miss an essential element of the theory.

Existence of static monetary equilibrium with unemployment

In terms of the notion of monetary equilibrium outlined in chapter 9 it was shown that multiple equilibria are to be expected and that the money rate of interest can set the level to which the marginal efficiencies of real assets adjust. At this point we need to highlight the implications of monetary equilibrium for the relationship between the conventional rate of interest, $\bar{\imath}$, in expression (10.10) and the principle of effective demand incorporated in expression (10.8). The point that needs to be made is that the rate of investment established in monetary equilibrium is not necessarily sufficient to ensure full employment. In other words, long-period monetary equilibrium may well generate a point of effective demand which implies unemployment. To recall Hicks's (1967b: 199) description of the equilibrium concept of the *Treatise*, the system is in equilibrium even though the scale of operations is far below potential capacity because entrepreneurs are earning normal profits and therefore *have no incentive to change their scale of operations*. This, it seems, is the concept of unemployment equilibrium that Keynes (1973b:122–3, emphasis added) had in mind:

In a system in which the level of money income is capable of fluctuating, the orthodox theory is one equation short of what is required to give a solution. Undoubtedly, the reason why the orthodox system has failed to discover this discrepancy is because it has always tacitly assumed that income *is* given, namely, at the level corresponding to the employment of all the available resources. *In other words, it is tacitly assuming that the monetary policy is such as to maintain the rate of interest at that level which is compatible with full employment.*

The missing 'equation' to which Keynes is referring here is the principle of effective demand and it is apparent that Keynes sees the rate of interest as playing a central role in determining the level of aggregate demand. It is in this sense that the mysterious analysis of chapter 17 – the general theory of asset-holding – or what we have called monetary equilibrium, is related to the principle of effective demand.

The next point to note with respect to the possibility of an unemployment equilibrium in Keynes's framework is the treatment of the labour market. Firstly, we have noted that although expression (10.7) includes the real wage and – in (10.7a) – the marginal product of labour, it cannot be treated as a demand for labour function in traditional neoclassical fashion. This latter point was initially raised by Sidney Weintraub and has been stressed by Davidson (1967, 1983) who argues that the traditional neoclassical treatment of the demand for labour function as the derivative of the production function with respect to the labour input, is, at best, only a market equilibrium curve. The argument is repeated in Weintraub (1979:45) and is reinforced by the Cambridge critique of the neoclassical production function (Garegnani, 1983). As all undergraduate students are told – but soon forget when they move on to neoclassical general equilibrium theory – the demand for labour is a derived demand; derived from the demand for output. The aggregate demand function, or what Keynes called the point of effective demand, and not the derivative of a neoclassical production function and the marginal disutility of labour, then determines the level of employment.

The argument can be illustrated by employing the notion of monetary equilibrium to determine the point of effective demand in terms of the Davidson–Weintraub analysis of aggregate demand and supply functions discussed above. Following Davidson (1983), the aggregate supply schedule, which plots money proceeds as a function of employment, is represented by Z in Figure 10.2(a). The aggregate demand function in money terms is indicated by D and can be derived given the propensity to consume and the rate of investment, as in expression (10.8). Long-run monetary equilibrium, indicated by $\bar{i} = \hat{r}_i = \hat{r}_j$ in Figure 10.1, establishes the rate of investment, and the resultant point of effective demand at E then determines a long-period equilibrium with unemployment.

This analysis appears to be in accordance with Keynes's claim that:

the volume of employment is not determined by the marginal disutility of labour measured in terms of real wages, except in so far as the supply of labour available at a given real wage sets a *maximum* level of employment. The propensity to consume and the rate of new investment determine between them the volume of employment (Keynes, 1936: 30, quoted by Davidson, 1983: 54).

Thus the labour market is not treated as an auction market in terms of which entrepreneurs and workers can co-operate to establish a market-clearing real wage. In an entrepreneur, as opposed to a co-operative economy, entrepreneurs determine employment via the demand for goods and services, i.e. entrepreneurs are not directly interested in employment. Once monetary equilibrium establishes a point of effective demand with unemployment, there is no rational basis for expecting entrepreneurs to engage in negotiations with

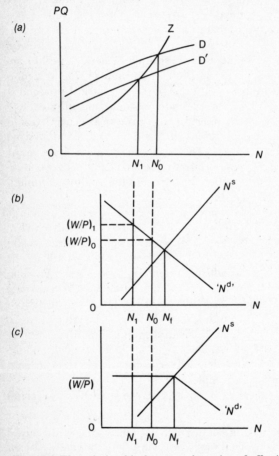

Fig. 10.2 The relationship between the point of effective demand and real wages

workers about real wages if they have achieved equilibrium and are earning normal profits. As Hicks (1967b) noted, entrepreneurs have no such incentive; so, if monetary policy has set interest rates in too high a gear to achieve full employment, the economy settles into a long-period unemployment equilibrium.

The implication of this analysis is that the real wage is essentially independent of the level of employment. As Davidson (1983) argues, the relationship between the real wage and employment may be constant or declining as illustrated in Figures 10.2(b) and (c). There is no necessary inverse relationship between the real wage and employment. The money wage rate is, like the interest rate, an exogenous-type variable. Furthermore, flexible money and/or real wages cannot then restore full employment, N_f in Figure 10.2, unless they lead to a shift in the point of effective demand. An autonomous increase in investment by the authorities would, of course, shift the point of effective demand and reduce involuntary unemployment. We need now to consider whether the unemployment equilibrium associated with the point of effective demand at E can be shifted by flexible wages and/or prices.

Stability of static monetary equilibrium with unemployment

The issue which we must now consider is the question of the persistence or stability of long-period monetary equilibrium with unemployment. In this respect we have already noted that, in the context of the static model, it is the movement between equilibria, and not the return to a unique full employment equilibrium, that the question of stability must address. For example, if Keynes is claiming that the long rate of interest may persist for decades at a level which holds the economy on a growth path with unemployment, then adjustment factors which would automatically restore full employment must be non-existent or inoperative. Thus, as Joan Robinson (1947: 86) put it, 'We must now meet the argument that it is unnatural to suppose that the rate of interest can be permanently maintained at a level at which unemployment occurs.' The orthodox Keynesian response to this question is well known and relies on the existence of a liquidity trap to prevent the rate of interest from falling to a level consistent with full employment. This explanation is still quite popular despite the fact that Keynes (1936:207) remarked that he knew of no case where absolute liquidity preference had been of practical importance.

Associated with this analysis is the assumption of wage rigidity used by both 'classical' and Keynesian theorists. Surprisingly, it appears that in answering her own question Joan Robinson presents either the liquidity trap explanation – the (long?) rate of interest reaches a point below which it cannot fall before full employment is reached (Robinson, 1947:870 – or the perverse relationship between the rate of interest and capital per man that is encountered in multi-commodity neoclassical models (Robinson, 1947: 91n1 and n2). Falling prices and wages which cause the rate of interest to fall cannot therefore be relied on to restore full employment. Now the latter argument may be a valid critique of the Real Analysis of neoclassical monetary theory, but it throws little light on the issue with respect to monetary equilibrium. To evaluate this case we need to examine the impact of changes in money wages on monetary equilibrium, i.e. on the MEC and the rate of interest. Keynes (1936:265) concludes that, in the case of a closed economy, the impact of wage cuts on the propensity to consume cannot be relied upon to restore full employment.

As far as the MEC is concerned, it is instructive to note that Keynes (1936: 265) argues that the most favourable result would occur if wages were to be cut across the board (economy-wide) to a level from which the only expected changes would be upward. Here it seems that Keynes is implicitly assuming that the price level remains unchanged and only moves upwards if and when money wages are increased. Under these circumstances a cut in money wages would be favourable to the MEC because it would lower long-period or normal supply prices relative to demand prices and support the expectation of increased aggregate demand in the future. Output and employment would then increase. The most unfavourable contingency occurs with money wages sagging slowly downwards, presumably bringing prices with them, and doing nothing to improve the prospect of profits. Keynes then rejects the favourable alternative as impractical under a system of free wage bargaining in a capitalist system – although he does not rule out the possibility that it might work in a centrally planned authoritarian system. Nevertheless, that leaves little hope that falling wages and prices can act as automatic stabilizers by influencing the MEC in a capitalist economy.

The only route that remains then, is the influence of falling wages and prices on the rate of interest. Here Keynes argues that, with a virtually fixed money supply, falling money wages could, in principle, increase the quantity of money and lower the rate of interest. (If the quantity of money is a function of the wage and price level then this route is closed (Keynes, 1936:266).) But if that were the case, then it would make more sense to use monetary policy directly as it has decided advantages (Keynes, 1936:267–8). However, Keynes (1936: 164) was sceptical about the likely success of attacking monetary equilibrium only from the side of the interest rate, using monetary policy alone. In terms of the above model, the level of aggregate demand is a function of investment, in expression (10.8), which is influenced not only by the long rate of interest but also by the animal spirits of entrepreneurs – their expectations of profits; and if the latter have collapsed, falling interest rates may not stimulate investment sufficiently to achieve full employment. Hence additional steps to influence the MEC directly would be required, otherwise the variability of the market estimation of the MEC would be too great to be offset by any practical changes in the rate of interest. Thus, although changes of gear – to use the Radcliffe terminology – may be necessary to restore or maintain full employment equilibrium, Keynes was of the opinion that, used alone, monetary *policy* would not be sufficient. Hence, as wage reductions were analytically the same as an increase in the money supply, 'It follows that wage reductions, as a method of securing full employment, are also subject to the same limitations as the method of increasing the quantity of money' (Keynes, 1936: 266).

The above conclusion can, moreover, be strengthened by introducing the conventional rate of interest and the endogeneity of bank money. Certainly a falling wage level during a recession may increase the real quantity of money. But unless that leads to an *automatic* fall in the conventional rate of interest via a change in Bank rate and/or an increase in the demand for credit, output and employment will not increase. Furthermore, to the extent that the money supply is credit driven, it is always difficult to operate an expansionary monetary policy during a recession unless other means (fiscal policy) can be found to stimulate the demand for credit.

In addition, Keynes noted that if reliance were placed on wage reductions in a capitalist system, the reductions would be achieved in a haphazard fashion. If they succeeded in reducing the rate of interest it would still do little good. The slowly sagging wage level might induce a sagging rate of interest, but it would also be accompanied by a sagging MEC, as the demand price for capital goods followed the supply price down. The restoration of equilibrium is then problematic as the falling rate of interest is accompanied by a squeeze on profits (Keynes, 1936:269). Under these conditions aggregate demand collapses and the point of effective demand may move further to the left in Figure 10.2(a).

Keynes's (1936:269) analysis of the impact of price and wage flexibility on monetary equilibrium thus leads to the conclusion that a capitalist economy cannot be made self-adjusting along *laissez-faire* lines: 'to suppose that a flexible wage policy is a right and proper adjunct of a system which on the whole is one of *laissez-faire*, is the opposite of the truth. It is only in a highly authoritarian society, where sudden, substantial, all-round changes could be decreed that a flexible wage policy could function with success.' Although they do not employ the principle of effective demand and hence cannot see that Keynes does establish an unemployment equilibrium, mainstream Keynesians like Tobin (1975) do argue that wage and price flexibility is too weak to eliminate persistent unemployment. Their argument can therefore be strengthened by introducing the concept of monetary equilibrium to define the point of effective demand.

A KEYNESIAN MACROECONOMIC ANALYSIS OF MONETARY EQUILIBRIUM: THE IS–LM MODEL REHABILITATED

The analysis that we have sketched so far can now be recast in the more familiar IS–LM structure. The most convenient vehicle for doing this is Meltzer's (1981) attempt to interpret the *General Theory* in terms of an IS–LM model. Now although Meltzer is a monetarist who has employed the Wicksellian version of the IS–LM model (recall the discussion in chapter 5), his interpretation of Keynes is of particular interest because it appears in intent to be remarkably similar to the analysis presented in this study. However, although the general interpretation is similar to that suggested here, when we examine the analytical details of Meltzer's arguments more closely it is apparent that his model retains most of the essential features of a Say's Law economy and cannot, therefore, generate a long-period unemployment equilibrium as a state of rest. Instead Meltzer continually refers only to the *average level* of output and employment as less than the full employment level, although it is clear that he intends – and attributes a similar intention to Keynes – the average level of unemployment to be more than a transitory phenomenon. For example, he notes that Keynes describes a system that seems capable of remaining in a chronic condition of subnormal activity for a considerable period of time without a tendency to either total collapse or recovery (Meltzer, 1981:40).

The limitations inherent in Meltzer's analysis are, however, easily overcome to yield a working version of the IS–LM model that reflects the properties of Monetary rather than Real Analysis. From the perspective of Monetary Analysis, and the concept of monetary equilibrium in particular, the analytical features of Meltzer's model which account for its failure to establish the existence of a long-period unemployment *equilibrium* are:

(i)   the inadequate specification of the principle of effective demand; and,

(ii)   the neoclassical analysis of the labour market.

These two features are crucial as they allow Say's Law in by the back door. In Meltzer's system the point of effective demand is not defined and there is therefore no limit to the profitable expansion of output. This explains his description of the state of long-term unemployment as the *average level* of unemployment. Nevertheless these two features are readily corrected.

Meltzer (1981:52–4) summarizes his interpretation of Keynes in terms of the following system of equations:

$$\frac{S}{W} = \frac{I}{W} \qquad (10.11)$$

$$\frac{S}{W} = S\left(\frac{Y}{W}, \hat{r}\right) \qquad (10.12)$$

$$\frac{I}{W} = I(\hat{r}, E) \qquad (10.13)$$

$$\frac{M}{W} = L\left(i, \bar{i}, \frac{Y}{W}\right) \qquad (10.14)$$

$$\frac{Y}{W} = F(K, \mathcal{N}) \qquad (10.15)$$

$$\mathcal{N}^d = f(W/P) \qquad (10.16)$$

$$\mathcal{N}^s = g(W) \text{ or } g(W, P) \qquad (10.17)$$

$$\mathcal{N} = \mathcal{N}^d \leqslant \mathcal{N}^s \qquad (10.18)$$

Apart from the specification of interest rates, where the notation has been adapted to make it compatible with that used in this study, no other changes have been made. In most equations nominal values are deflated by the money wage, W. The first three equations, (10.11)–(10.13), derive what Meltzer (1981:52) considers to be a conventional IS curve. Similarly, expression (10.14) is, with the exception of the variable $\bar{i}$ (which corresponds to the variable r^e in Meltzer's paper), a conventional LM curve. We will have more to say about the latter variable in a moment.

Before considering that issue it is important to point out that the conventional IS–LM model sketched by Meltzer is in fact the Wicksellian version. Thus, the IS curve generates a locus of quasi-natural rates, $\hat{r}$, while the LM curve generates the market rates, i, although Meltzer follows the usual practice and does not distinguish between the two. In this sense it would be tempting to interpret the first four expressions as a statement of the loanable funds theory of the rate of interest in which the forces of productivity, I, and thrift, S, determine the natural rates of interest while the demand and supply of money determines the market rates. However, this would be premature. The relationship between market and natural rates can be generalized along the lines sketched in chapter 9 and Meltzer (1981:52, 56) appears to take some steps in that direction when he introduces the expected long rate of interest, $\bar{i}$, which is determined by psychological and institutional factors. In intent and interpretation this rate of interest is equivalent to what we have called the conventional rate of interest; that is, it is an exogenous variable not explained by the theory.

At this point Meltzer appears to be in danger of combining the key elements of both the loanable funds and the liquidity preference theories of the rate of interest! However, this is only a problem for Meltzer's own interpretation. Analytically it poses no difficulty because the liquidity preference theory is a generalization of the loanable funds theory (recall the discussion in chapter 9). Meltzer's ambivalence on this issue does, nevertheless, indicate that he provides no clear statement of the principle of effective demand. The main reason for this is that Meltzer (1981:53n30) only introduces $\bar{i}$ at the insistence of Paul Davidson. The variable $\bar{i}$ therefore appears as more of an afterthought than as an integral part of the analysis and we will come back to its role again below.

The remaining expressions, (10.15) to (10.18) specify an orthodox supply side and Meltzer (1981:53) argues that Keynes accepted the 'classical' theory of the demand for labour. As we have noted, however, the weight of evidence is against this interpretation, e.g. Davidson (1967, 1983), Roy Weintraub (1979) and Asimakopulos (1982), and its continued use is another indication that Meltzer does not provide an adequate specification of the principle of effective demand.[6] By including the 'classical' theory of the demand for labour, Meltzer eliminates any impediment, e.g. the point of effective demand, to the profitable expansion of output, as falling real wages

6. Another aspect of Meltzer's (1981:57) discussion which illustrates the lack of any role for the principle of effective demand is the description of the equation for the money wage as 'the missing equation' which permits a solution at less than full employment. Although Meltzer notes that Keynes's solution does not rely on the assumption of rigid wages the reference to the 'missing equation' appears to contradict this assertion. Davidson (1983: 54) notes that Meltzer appears to contradict himself by arguing both that Keynes did not rely on the rigid wage assumption but then using it himself to demonstrate the existence of unemployment equilibrium. He concludes: 'Meltzer's equational restatement should – almost half a century after Keynes – be able to encompass fixed as well as variable wages and prices.' In response to criticism of this nature Meltzer (1984:538, some emphasis added) responds with the following explanation: 'On my interpretation, the system is an *underemployment equilibrium* with $W = W_0$. Everyone expects output to fluctuate around Y_0/W_0. Hence everyone expects money wages to fluctuate around W_0'. On reflection it is difficult to avoid the conclusion that Meltzer is resorting to semantics and introducing the wage rigidity explanation for unemployment by the back door.

always lead to the profitable expansion of output. However, this aspect of Meltzer's interpretation is also readily replaced by introducing the Davidson–Weintraub analysis of the labour market to underpin the aggregate supply curve.

The eight expressions are reduced by Meltzer to three equations containing eight variables, (10.19)–(10.21). Meltzer argues that Keynes treated M, W, K, $\bar{i}$ and E (expected income) as exogenous variables and solved for Y/W, P and $\hat{r}$.

$$\text{IS:} \quad \frac{Y}{W} = A\left(\hat{r}, \frac{Y}{W}, E\right) \tag{10.19}$$

$$\text{LM:} \quad \frac{Y}{W} = B\left(i, \bar{i}, \frac{M}{W}\right) \tag{10.20}$$

$$\text{SS:} \quad \frac{Y}{W} = F[K, \mathcal{N}(W, P)] \tag{10.21}$$

Meltzer (1981:54) now compares this specification to the D and Z model sketched earlier. He equates expression (10.21), the aggregate supply function, with the Z function and expressions (10.19) and (10.20) with the D function. This comparison should allow a clear assessment of where the differences lie. To see where these are we need to establish how unemployment arises in Meltzer's system; but because Meltzer does not talk about an unemployment equilibrium, only about the average level of employment, his explanation is not always as clear as it might be. Nevertheless the argument seems to run as follows.

It begins with what appears to be no more than an assertion that the average level of output is below the full employment level. Expectations are supposed to be rational and expected output equals the average level of output (Meltzer, 1981:55). This point can be illustrated with reference to Meltzer's two-panel diagram which is reproduced here as Figure 10.3. If $E_0 = Y_0/W_0$ aggregate demand is given by IS_0. All this suggests that pessimistic expectations are to blame for the gap between Y_0/W_0 and Y^*/W^* and the resultant unemployment. In fact Meltzer (1981:55) goes on to note that optimistic expectations allow the economy to reach Y^*/W^* but the high rate of capital accumulation that results reduces the marginal efficiency of capital, reducing the demand for investment, and output falls back to Y_0/W_0. However, it is not entirely clear from Meltzer's description why this should happen unless for some reason entrepreneurs find it unprofitable to produce output Y^*/W^*.

The gap in Meltzer's story can be filled by applying the concept of monetary equilibrium and the Marshallian microfoundations developed in chapter 9, and previously applied to the Fundamental

Equations and the Post Keynesian model. The analysis then proceeds
as follows. An improvement in 'animal spirits' causes the demand
price of capital goods to rise above their long-period supply prices.
The resultant investment reduces the natural rate and unless the
exogenous long rate, $\bar{\imath}$, happens to fall *pari passu*, expectations prove
to have been too optimistic and we have what turns out to be a cycle
of expansion and contraction characterized by malinvestment. In
terms of the Marshallian analysis, a bout of optimistic 'animal spirits'
raises the demand price of capital goods relative to their long-period
supply prices and initially produces only disequilibrium as neither $\bar{\imath}_0$
nor $\hat{r}_0$ has changed. But as the investment is put in place, $\hat{r}$ falls (as a
result of diminishing returns) and expectations are prone to sharp
downward revision as the expansion continues. A downward revision
of expectations necessary to reduce the demand price below the

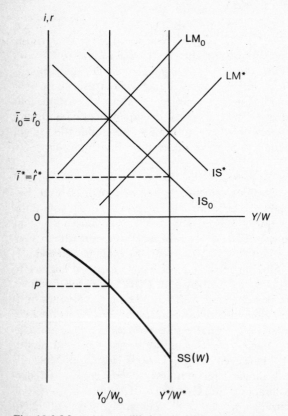

Fig. 10.3 Monetary equilibrium in Meltzer's IS–LM model

supply price may well be required to allow for a contraction of the capital stock and to restore $\hat{r}$ to equality with $\bar{i}_0$.

As Meltzer suggests, this interpretation appears to be consistent with Keynes's discussion of the trade cycle. For example, when applying his analysis to an interpretation of the trade cycle, Keynes (1936:315–22, emphasis added) makes the following observations:

> The latter stages of the boom are characterised by optimistic expectations as to the future yield of capital-goods sufficiently strong to offset their growing abundance and their rising costs of production, and, probably, a rise in the rate of interest also ... The disillusion comes because doubts suddenly arise concerning the reliability of the prospective yield ... The situation, which I am indicating as typical, is ... one ... where investment is being made *in conditions which are unstable* and cannot endure, because it is promoted by *expectations which are destined to be disappointed* ... The boom which is destined to end in a slump is caused, therefore, by the combination of a rate of interest $[\bar{i}_0]$, which is a correct state of expectation would be too high for full employment, with a misguided state of expectation which, so long as it lasts, prevents this rate of interest from being in fact a deterrent. A boom is a situation in which over-optimism triumphs over a rate of interest which, in a cooler light, would be seen to be excessive.

There is little doubt from this description that Keynes envisaged no mechanism whereby optimistic expectations could produce a long-period full employment equilibrium if 'the' rate of interest, i.e. the conventional or normal long rate, was itself too high to ensure full employment.

Similarly, Meltzer (1981:56) goes on to make many of the points sketched earlier when he argues that falling money (and real) wages in Keynes's model would not necessarily restore full employment:

> Keynes's involuntary unemployment is the difference between Y^*/W^* and Y_0/W_0. Workers cannot permanently reduce this level of unemployment by reducing (money) and real wages. A reduction in money wages (or an increase in M) shifts LM to the right, say to LM* in Figure 10.3. At LM*, output is near to Y^*/W^* but, Keynes explains, if the marginal efficiency of capital is unchanged while the rate of interest has fallen below the rate determined by psychological and institutional considerations, $\bar{i}_0$, 'entrepreneurs will necessarily make losses ... Hence the capital stock and the level of employment will have to shrink ...' (Keynes, 1936:217–18). The economy returns to Y_0/W_0.

In this statement Meltzer gets as close to describing the principle of effective demand as it is possible to get without actually defining it! Although in intent it appears that he is describing the point of effective demand as defined in this study, it is again not clear from his description why entrepreneurs are making losses. The reason for this lack of clarity can, of course, be traced to the fact that Meltzer does not employ Marshallian analytical techniques or the concept of monetary equilibrium and, consequently, he is unable to define the point of effective demand. Another dimension to the source of confusion in Meltzer's analysis seems to be that the loanable funds and liquidity preference theories are not clearly distinguished (as we noted above, the key element of liquidity preference theory, the exogenously determined long rate, $\bar{\imath}$, appears to be something of an afterthought added at the prompting of Paul Davidson). However, when the full implications of the liquidity preference theory and the principle of effective demand are recognized, Meltzer's analysis can again be clarified along Marshallian lines.

The money rate of interest, $\bar{\imath}$, is an exogenous variable determined by psychological and institutional factors. There is therefore no reason why it should be such as to generate just that rate of investment which would produce the full employment level of output, Y^*/W^*. If it does not then the IS_0 and LM_0 curves intersect at the level of output Y_0/W_0. In our terminology, long-period monetary equilibrium now exists as $\bar{\imath}_0 = \hat{r}_0$, and Say's Law is broken because there is a limit to the profitable expansion of output. If falling money wages do lead to a fall in the market rate of interest without a change in $\bar{\imath}_0$, then any attempt to increase investment will depress the natural rate below $\hat{r}_0$ and, as Meltzer notes, losses will be made. In Marshallian comparative static terms a fall in the quasi-natural rate, $\hat{r}$, below the conventional rate, $\bar{\imath}_0$, will mean that the demand prices of capital goods fall below their long-period supply prices. That is, we have the *short-period* equilibrium result:

$$\bar{\imath}_0 = (LPS_k - DP_k)/DP_k + \hat{r}_1 \qquad (10.22)$$

where $\hat{r}_1 < \hat{r}_0$ and $DP_k < LPS_k$, the latter two variables referring, respectively, to the demand prices and long-period supply prices of capital goods. With demand prices below supply prices investment will fall and the capital stock will shrink. This, it seems, is the process that Keynes, and Meltzer, have in mind but which Meltzer is unable to describe accurately because his analysis lacks a clear specification of the principle of effective demand. Nevertheless, in his diagram, Figure 10.3, $\bar{\imath}_0$ then determines the position of the LM_0 curve. Movements along the curve represent transitory or short-term disturbances of the money rate around the normal or conventional rate while changes in the normal rate, what the Radcliffe Committee called changes of gear, would shift the LM curve. (A derivation of the LM curve consistent with this analysis is presented by Howells and Bain (1983). Given the locus of quasi-natural rates along the IS_0 curve, monetary equilibrium is established at the level of output

Y_0/W_0 and long-term unemployment results. Similarly, movements in the market rate of interest around the conventional rate due to an increase in M/W may then induce a temporary expansion of output and employment towards Y^*/W^* but the intersection of IS_0 and LM^* is only the short-period equilibrium described by (10.22)! In the long period, investment will decline and output will fall to the level dictated by the point of effective demand.[7] It seems, therefore, that we now have an IS–LM illustration of Keynes's claim that, if the normal rate of interest is too high, then the economy may fluctuate for decades around a level of output that is too low for full employment. We may also note in passing that, given the IS_0 curve, the neutral or optimum rate of interest referred to by Keynes (1936:183) is $\bar{\imath}^* = \hat{r}^*$.

The discussion so far has been conducted within the confines of the static equilibrium model with the rate of interest and expectations held constant as it were. This, of course, is hardly the basis for a comprehensive analysis of stability and the preceding discussion is therefore best interpreted as only a partial analysis of the problem. It is concerned only with the analysis of wage flexibility and the objective is to show that, without taking other complicating factors into account, wage flexibility cannot be relied on to restore full employment. To provide a more comprehensive analysis of stability these complicating factors have to be taken into account. We then have to face the implications of Keynesian kaleidics (to use Shackle's phrase).

MONETARY EQUILIBRIUM AND KEYNESIAN KALEIDICS

As Davidson and Kregel (1980:143) observe, in Keynes's analysis the threat of chronic instability is always present. This is a theme that has been examined by both Minsky (1975, 1982) and Vicarelli (1984) and, on reflection, it is apparent that the source of the threat can be traced to the role of bank money in a capitalist system. Many monetary theorists have noted the potential instability of money systems based on credit – Wicksell's (1898a) pure credit model is a well known example – and the issue inevitably arises in the case of monetary equilibrium.

Monetary equilibrium rests on the existence of a conventional rate

---

7. Meltzer (1981:56) argues that Keynes does not envisage a multitude of potential solutions but only one alternative equilibrium position. In view of Keynes's (1979:35) statement that there are a number of long-period equilibrium positions it is difficult to see how Meltzer arrives at this conclusion. He seems to think that Keynes considered the only alternative equilibrium solution to be one in which the marginal efficiency of capital was zero. But this is only a special case from a range of possible monetary equilibria.

of interest on which long-period expectations are based. The conventional rate of interest thus provides the centre of gravitation of the system. However, unlike the case of either classical or neoclassical theory, objective factors such as costs of production or the forces of productivity and thrift do not determine the rate of interest in a bank money economy. The centre of gravitation of the system is then not determined by real or objective factors and the potential for instability is plain enough. Once this is accepted, we come face to face with the Keynesian kaleidics of George Shackle (1967:247, emphasis added):

> The interest rate in a money economy. This was the enigma that led Keynes to the nihilism of his final position ... The interest rate depends on expectations of its own future. It is expectational, subjective, psychic, indeterminate. And so is the rest of the economic system. The stability, once doubted, is destroyed, and cascading disorder must intervene before the landslide grounds in a new fortuitous position. *Such is the last phase of Keynesian economics. But Keynes showed governments how to prolong the suspension of doubt.*

Here Shackle takes great delight in spelling out the danger that lurks behind the reassuring facade of the static equilibrium model. To most economists, including both neoclassicists and neo-Ricardians, this blatant flirtation with indeterminacy and chaos is too much to stomach and Shackle's work is generally disregarded as of no practical significance. This is a fundamental mistake. To see why, let us consider a recent critique of Shackle's work.

Using Shackle as the high priest of what he calls Keynesian fundamentalism – a term attributed to Coddington (1976) who raised similar objections – Magnani (1983:249, emphasis added) argues that:

> Shackle's critique of neoclassical theory *amounts to an attack on the long-period method*. In fact, by rejecting the very possibility of formulating *general* statements about the working of the economy, *he must also abandon the possibility of building a theory based on the isolation of persistent forces* which define the centres of gravity [sic] of the system.

From what we now know of the concept of monetary equilibrium it is apparent that Magnani's argument is not sound. Although Shackle stresses the indeterminacy that can result in the case of shifting equilibrium, this does not mean that it is not possible to build a theory based on the isolation of persistent forces. The analysis of monetary equilibrium in the static equilibrium model presented above is just such a case. The potential indeterminacy which Shackle stresses arises because it is not possible to define the centres of gravitation of the system in objective terms. To isolate persistent forces it is then necessary to identify and fix the independent variables in the system. What is more, as these independent variables cannot be determined on an objective basis it follows that the long-period method can only be applied on the basis of the convention that they remain fixed. Thus far from abandoning the long-period method, *Shackle's analysis actually isolates the conditions under which it can be applied to a capitalist economy*. The logic of Shackle's position is not that it is inevitable that no general statements can be made about the working of the economy, but that the possibility of deriving such statements is dependent on the existence of fixed independent variables together with confidence in their stability.

Far from lacking practical significance, this conclusion is surely of fundamental importance to policy makers. If the independent variables of the system, in particular the interest rate, are not determined by objective real forces, as is claimed by monetary theories in the tradition of Real Analysis, then the responsibility for their stability must rest with the monetary authorities. Seen from this perspective the message of the so-called fundamentalist Keynesians is not that the world is inevitably chaotic but that the stability that we do enjoy has a rather fragile basis. If anything it directs attention to the fact that steps must be taken to ensure the stability of the independent variables in the system. As Shackle put it, Keynes showed governments how to prolong the suspension of doubt. This conclusion has particular significance for independent variables such as the rate of interest, the wage rate and, in an open economy, the exchange rate. If these variables are not stabilized but are left to the whim of the market in the mistaken belief that market rates are determined by objective forces, then the economy is cut free from its moorings, as it were, and Shackle's nihilistic conclusion follows. In this sense it seems that recent monetary policy has, under the influence of monetarism, actually created the shifting equilibrium world of Shackle's Keynesian kaleidics.

CONCLUDING REMARKS

This chapter has presented some macroeconomic applications of the concept of monetary equilibrium outlined in chapter 9. Beginning with the Fundamental Equations of the *Treatise* it has demonstrated that the quantity *theory* is, at best, a special case of monetary equilibrium. This special case rests on two assumptions: the existence of a unique long-period equilibrium at full employment and the exogeneity of the money stock. Both of these assumptions are not true of a modern capitalist economy and are consequently abandoned in the development of a framework for Monetary Analysis.

In this respect the Fundamental Equations are not sufficient to provide a comprehensive macroeconomic framework for Monetary Analysis as they are formally equivalent to Fisher's quantity equation. Kaldor's (1981) model, on the other hand, does provide the basis for the macroeconomic analysis of monetary equilibrium. The model, sketched in terms of expressions (10.6)–(10.10), when interpreted from the perspective of monetary equilibrium, exhibits all the properties of Monetary Analysis outlined in chapter 7 and provides the basis for contemporary Post Keynesian monetary theory. It also offers a genuine comparison with both the 'classical' and Keynesian models of the neoclassical synthesis. Both of these categories of models fall within the tradition of Real Analysis.

The key contribution of the monetary analysis offered here is the integration of the concept of monetary equilibrium with the principle of effective demand. Given that the rate of interest is a variable that cannot be explained in terms of classical or neoclassical principles, the concept of monetary equilibrium establishes the rate of investment and thus the point of effective demand beyond which it is not profitable to expand output. There is no mechanism in a capitalist economy that relates the rate of interest, via the rate of investment, to the full employment level of output in the long period. Given a particular monetary policy and rate of interest, the rate of investment may well be insufficient to generate a point of effective demand that ensures full employment. Furthermore, at the point of effective demand, entrepreneurs have no incentive to expand production; monetary equilibrium exists and the rates of return on all methods of converting present into future wealth are equalized. The concept of monetary equilibrium explains why the principle of effective demand breaks Say's Law.

The model therefore also explains the existence of a long-period equilibrium with unemployment even if wages and prices are flexible. In particular a flexible wage policy cannot be relied upon to restore full employment unless declining wages and prices impact favourably on the rate of interest and/or the marginal efficiency of capital. But, as Keynes and others have argued, a favourable outcome is unlikely. Rather, it is far more likely that a falling wage and price level would succeed only in depressing aggregate demand even further and shifting the point of effective demand away from the full employment level. Keynes (1936:266) therefore suggested that a rigid money wage *policy* would be preferable. In a capitalist bank money economy there is simply no mechanism that ensures that the long rate of interest adjusts automatically to the level necessary to ensure full employment. By comparison, 'classical' and pseudo-Keynesian models in the tradition of Real Analysis all exhibit the properties of Say's Law, neutral money and a co-operative auction-market analysis of employment. In these models a dichotomy exists between real and monetary sectors and long-period equilibrium is determined by real factors.

The concept of monetary equilibrium can also be applied to a reassessment of the IS–LM model. The reinterpretation of the IS–LM model presented here clearly has a number of implications worth spelling out. Apart from the obvious conclusion that it satisfies all the properties of Monetary Analysis sketched in previous chapters it also provides a reconciliation of the Post Keynesian D–Z model and the IS–LM model of the neoclassical Keynesians. (Perhaps this explains why Keynes raised no fundamental objections to Hicks's IS–LM structure.) The latter have always been at a disadvantage in debate with exponents of the 'classical' stream of the neoclassical synthesis over their inability to demonstrate the existence of an unemployment equilibrium, except on *ad hoc* terms. But once the common properties which underlie both models are recognized the way is open for an alliance of all Keynesians against the 'classical' vision in all its guises.

In addition, the options facing macroeconomic policy, both monetary and fiscal policy in both closed and open economies – the analysis is readily extended to deal with an open economy – can then be posed in a meaningful fashion. For example, the debate between Keynesians and monetarists can be summarized as a debate over whether the economy is best stabilized by stabilizing investment or stabilizing the money stock. Fiscalists and some Keynesians advocated compensatory fiscal policy. But as Meltzer (1981: 41) notes, there is no evidence of this view in Keynes. Rather, Keynes advocated the stabilization of investment. The implications of this position have been examined by Kregel (1985). In terms of the IS–LM model sketched above it implies the stabilisation of the IS curve at a level closer to full employment (as at IS* in Figure 10.3). The policy implication is clearly based on the conclusion that, if the normal rate of interest is too high, investment will be too low and the economy will settle at a level of output too low for full employment. Such an outcome is conceivable in a world to which the properties of Monetary Analysis are applicable.

SUMMARY

11

REAL ANALYSIS AND MONETARY ANALYSIS: THE CENTRAL ARGUMENTS

INTRODUCTION

This study opened by posing the dilemma currently facing neoclassical monetary theorists. Ultimately this dilemma was seen to arise from the contradictions which result from attempts to develop monetary theory within the tradition of what Schumpeter called Real Analysis. In Real Analysis, real forces determine long-period equilibrium and money is neutral, i.e. a veil. One objective of this study has been both to highlight the sterility of this view and to remind the reader that it is based on a historically dated concept of the economy; an agricultural, commodity money economy of self-employed farmers and artisans in which Say's Law holds. In a capitalist economy with a well-developed financial sector, the assumptions of the Say's Law economy are no longer valid. To avoid the dilemma of neoclassical monetary theory it is therefore necessary to abandon the framework of Real Analysis and begin with the foundations of monetary theory in the tradition of Monetary Analysis. The behaviour of a capitalist economy is compatible with the properties of Monetary but not Real Analysis. The foundations of monetary theory are thus to be found within the tradition of Monetary Analysis – this is a fundamental conclusion. Accordingly, this chapter summarizes the arguments which support it and briefly draws out some policy implications.

REAL ANALYSIS: CRITIQUE

To appreciate the significance of the dilemma facing neoclassical monetary theory, it is necessary to distinguish between its two main streams of analysis – the Wicksellian and the neo-Walrasian. The

275

taxonomy is important because each theory has its own properties which are subject to distinct critiques. The foundations of neoclassical monetary theory must, in the first instance, be evaluated in terms of the Wicksellian or neo-Walrasian variant.

Wicksellian and neo-Walrasian foundations of neoclassical monetary theory

The defining characteristic of Wicksellian general equilibrium theory of relevance here is the treatment of the *given* capital endowment as a *value* magnitude. As a result of the capital debate, models with this property are now known to be incapable, in general, of generating a long-period equilibrium solution unless restricted to the case of a single commodity. In multi-commodity models the value of the capital endowment will be a function of the prices of the various capital goods and, as the latter are endogenous variables, the value of the capital endowment cannot be fixed, i.e. the value of the capital endowment cannot be treated as an exogenous variable. This, of course, is simply an alternative statement of Joan Robinson's charge of circular reasoning. If the value of the capital endowment is a function of the endogenous variables it is supposed to determine, the argument is circular, and the logical basis for the determination of a long-period equilibrium solution collapses. In terms of neoclassical jargon, the *existence* of an equilibrium solution cannot then be established and the theoretical structure is, or at least should be, of no further interest to a neoclassical economist. Other implications of the capital debate lead to similar conclusions when we consider the question of stability.

The significance of these conclusions for Wicksellian monetary theory is that they effectively undermine the concept of the natural rate of interest. There is then no theoretical foundation for Wicksell's distinction between natural and market rates of interest. The Wicksellian foundations of the loanable funds theory, in which the natural rate of interest plays a key role, and the notion of a real rate of interest are thus swept away. Rather ironically, the market rate of interest is left hanging by its own bootstraps (to use Hicks's phrase). With reference to the dilemma in neoclassical monetary theory the Wicksellian foundations are now seen to have collapsed.

The treatment of capital in neo-Walrasian theory, on the other hand, avoids the difficulties encountered by Wicksellian theory, because capital is specified as a fixed *quantity*, i.e. as an array of machines which forms part of the initial endowments. The neo-Walrasian treatment of capital is thus not open to the Cambridge critique. Nevertheless, neo-Walrasian theory is also unable to provide foundations for neoclassical monetary theory. There are many difficulties, but the most fundamental from the point of view of monetary theory is the issue raised by Hahn, viz. finding a role for money in a theoretical structure in which money is not required! The quotation by Hahn which opened chapter 1 refers to the Arrow–Debreu model as the, supposedly, most sophisticated model in the neo-Walrasian tradition. Such a model has no role for money because it assumes the existence of all conceivable contingent futures markets. All trades from creation to eternity can then be 'negotiated' via the single tâtonnement process which occurs on the day of creation. It seems intuitively obvious that in such a world no one would need or want money, and a model with these properties is, at best, an exercise in logic only.

To escape the sterile implications of this logic, neo-Walrasian monetary theorists turned to the so-called temporary equilibrium models, in which a complete array of contingent features markets does not exist. Nevertheless it is still not possible to find a role for money in such models. A full Walrasian tâtonnement is still retained, with all choices pre-reconciled (even at fix-price equilibria). Hence, the attempt to introduce some uncertainty, and thereby provide a rationale for the role of money as a means of avoiding uncertainty, runs into the same difficulties as the Arrow–Debreu model. Pre-reconciled choices are not compatible with uncertainty. Money, in the form of some durable medium of exchange and store of value, may always be added to these neo-Walrasian models, but it is strictly inessential in the sense that there 'is nothing we can say about the equilibrium of an economy with money which we cannot also say about the equilibrium of a non-monetary economy' (Hahn, 1973b:231).

Attempts to introduce money into neo-Walrasian models via the finance constraint also fail to address the central issue – the inessential nature of money in these models – and have not solved the problem. Similarly the addition of the quantity equation to the neo-Walrasian system of equations imposes the condition that money must be used to carry out the exchanges. In other words, the quantity equation in a neo-Walrasian model imposes the constraint that trade can only occur with the aid of a monetary medium, and it cannot therefore be interpreted as a demand for money function in the Cambridge tradition. The neo-Walrasian statement of the quantity equation is therefore not compatible with the Cambridge interpretation of the quantity theory. In a neo-Walrasian model the demand for money is the mirror image of the supply of commodities. The use of a quantity equation in a neo-Walrasian model is in fact a simple example of what

Clower has called the finance constraint. This, it is found, is the analytical basis of the Valavanis objection to Patinkin's critique of the so-called 'classical dichotomy'. From this perspective Patinkin's critique is seen to be in error. In particular, there is no meaningful sense in which a neo-Walrasian model which includes the quantity equation – the model used by Patinkin to investigate the 'classical dichotomy' – can be dichotomized as suggested by Patinkin. Hence there is no basis for Patinkin's claim that the real balance effect is necessary to integrate monetary and value theory. Apart from the technical limitations of Patinkin's argument, it is now apparent that he was employing a model in which money is inessential. His attempted integration of monetary and value theory was then bound to fail.

The existence of a monetary equilibrium within neo-Walrasian theory has therefore not been established. In particular, Hahn's (1965) objections to Patinkin's analysis have not been answered, and the existence proofs that have been developed are valid only for non-monetary models. The question of stability is in a similar unsatisfactory state, even in non-monetary models, so the question of stability of monetary equilibrium also has not yet been faced (Fisher, 1976; Hahn and Nield, 1980).

In view of these observations it is concluded that the foundations of neoclassical monetary theory have yet to be laid. The conclusion reached by Hahn (1973b) is still valid today. A fundamental corollary of this conclusion reached in this study is, of course, that these foundations cannot be laid within the tradition of Real Analysis and that the search must proceed on the basis of Monetary and not Real Analysis. Nevertheless it is necessary to examine the implications of this conclusion for the monetary theories of Keynesians and monetarists.

The neoclassical synthesis: Keynesians, monetarists and Friedman

The limitations of neoclassical monetary theory sketched above obviously place monetarists or Keynesians who propose to build on neoclassical foundations in some difficulty. An examination of the literature in fact reveals that both Wicksellian and neo-Walrasian foundations are currently in use. This trend began with what is often referred to as the neoclassical synthesis, and it is important to realize that there are both Wicksellian and neo-Walrasian versions of its most popular creation, the IS–LM model. In particular, the synthesis which arose as a result of the 'Keynes versus classics' debate embodies implicitly the Wicksellian distinction between the market and natural rates of interest. On the other hand, the version of the IS–LM model presented by Patinkin is strictly neo-Walrasian in structure, and it was the properties of this approach that, at one time, featured prominently in the liquidity preference versus loanable funds debate (recall the discussion in the appendix to chapter 4). Nevertheless, it is the Wicksellian version of IS–LM that dominates the textbooks and now forms the basis for Tobin's Keynesian model as well as the monetarist model of Brunner and Meltzer. This similarity in theoretical structure recently drew comment from Samuelson (1983:25) who noted:

In 1976 when Professor Benjamin Friedman of Harvard wrote down for the monetarists Karl Brunner and Allen Meltzer what their model of monetarism was, it turned out not to be qualitatively distinguishable from James Tobin's Keynesian model.

Benjamin Friedman's finding that the two models are qualitatively indistinguishable can, of course, be explained on the grounds of their shared Wicksellian foundations.

The Wicksell connection emerges most clearly in Tobin's famous q-theory of investment and the Brunner–Meltzer attempt to formalize the monetarist transmission mechanism. An examination of both these theoretical structures shows that they embody the Wicksellian distinction between the natural rate of interest, derived from the marginal productivity of capital, and the market rate of interest. Discrepancies between these two rates provide the link between the real and monetary sectors in strictly Wicksellian fashion. Tobin, as a Keynesian, places more emphasis on output changes, while Brunner and Meltzer, as monetarists, are more concerned with inflation. Both, however, employ the same Wicksellian foundations. The Keynesian interpretation follows by fixing the price level and allowing adjustment to fall on output, while the monetarist interpretation is closer to Wicksell's cumulative adjustment of the price level with output fixed at full employment. However, if monetarists and Keynesians are building on Wicksellian foundations, then their models are open to the objections raised in the capital debate, i.e. they cannot be employed outside of a one-commodity world. The foundations of Wicksellian monetary theory have been undermined, yet the Keynesians and monetarists seem unaware that they are building on sand. For example, there is then no theoretical basis for the belief in the Pigou effect, which is in general unable to restore equilibrium in a multi-commodity Wicksellian model – even in principle.

The neoclassical foundations of Milton Friedman's brand of monetarism are similarly undermined, yet the direct impact on his position is less dramatic than for Tobin or Brunner–Meltzer. The reason for the lack of a direct link between the Wicksellian or neo-

Walrasian foundations and Friedman's monetarism can be traced to a number of factors. To begin with, it now seems clear that Friedman employs the Marshallian *partial equilibrium* method to partition reality in search of predictions of facts already known. In this sense Friedman emerges as an inductivist/empiricist. In particular, his instrumentalist methodology – whether interpreted from a Deweyan or Popperian perspective – although it may be logically consistent, is not a useful methodology for any problems to which we do not have the answer (Hoover, 1984a).

At the level of theory it is also apparent that Friedman has no particular use for neoclassical *general equilibrium* theory. His references to this work amount to no more than misleading *obiter dicta* of no significance to his own position. Ultimately Friedman's theoretical position rests on the view that the classical quantity theory of money can be applied to a modern capitalist system so long as credit money can be made to behave as if it were commodity money. Friedman seeks to achieve this result by fixing the quantity of money. There is, however, no basis for believing that a capitalist economy can be made self-adjusting along those lines and Friedman provides no theoretical analysis to support this belief. Like other neoclassical monetary theorists in the tradition of Real Analysis, Friedman is proceeding without any theoretical foundations.

In view of this assessment, it must be concluded that the foundations of modern monetary theory are highly unsatisfactory. As all economists hold the view that an adequate discussion of policy issues can only be conducted on the basis of a coherent theoretical framework, the implications of this conclusion are self-evident. Certainly much of the debate between the Keynesians and monetarists, at the academic level at least, has been conducted with models which preclude consideration of the relevant alternatives. In the case of the theoretical debate, this has led to unwarranted swings in fashion from Keynesian to monetarist positions on the basis of superficial applications of neoclassical monetary theory. The implications for empirical research, like those for policy, are also negative. It is simply not possible to relate the results of empirical studies to the moneyless neo-Walrasian world of exchange or the one-commodity Wicksellian world. Empirical research is thus proceeding without any sound theoretical foundations in neoclassical monetary theory. This observation applies with particular force to Friedman, who appears to have resorted to induction as a means of avoiding the theoretical quicksand of neoclassical monetary theory.

MONETARY ANALYSIS: FOUNDATIONS

The critique of Real Analysis presented above thus leaves the neo-classical monetary theorist facing a dilemma: either he must be theoretically rigorous, but deal only with models in which money is inessential; or he must sacrifice the rigour of the neoclassical foundations in an attempt to deal with monetary phenomena. Most economists with a passion for policy issues have opted for the latter route without realizing that this is what they have done, i.e. they proceed in the belief that their models have sound neoclassical foundations. By contrast, Hahn is an example of a 'pure' theorist who has opted for the former route in the belief that ultimately monetary phenomena will succumb to the rigour of his analysis. A far better way to proceed, of course, is to develop a theoretical structure which avoids the dilemma by integrating money into the analysis from the start. The tradition in monetary theory which proceeds on this premise was labelled by Schumpeter (1954) as Monetary Analysis.

A useful source of ideas in this tradition is to be found in the years of 'high theory' in the 1930s. Numerous developments occurred in monetary theory at this time which were swamped in the post-war years by the neoclassical synthesis or the Keynesian revolution. Yet, in the pre-war years, the tradition of Monetary Analysis was in ascendancy. Within the tradition of Monetary Analysis the notion of the neutrality of money is, of course, given up. As Schumpeter (1954:278) put it, 'it has to be recognised that essential features of the capitalist process depend upon the "veil" and that the "face behind it" is incomplete without it'. Leading monetary theorists of the 1930s were much concerned with this view. For example, Hayek (1931:110, emphasis added) argued that:

no analysis of actual economic phenomena is complete if the role played by money is neglected. *This means that we have definitely to give up the opinion* which is still widely prevalent, that, in the words of John Stuart Mill, '. . . there cannot, in short be intrinsically a more insignificant thing, in the economy of society, than money' which 'like many other kinds of machinery only exerts a distinction and independent influence of its own when it gets out of order'.

Similar observations were made by Myrdal (1939:16), from whom we have borrowed the term monetary equilibrium, and who suggested that the analysis of natural rates of interest in a monetary economy would be different from that of a barter economy, and by Keynes (1933, emphasis in original) who drew the distinction as follows:

An economy, which uses money but uses it merely as a neutral link between transactions in real things and real assets and does not allow it to enter into motives or decisions, might be called – for want of a better name – a *real-exchange economy*. The theory which I desiderate would deal, in contradistinction to this, with an economy in which money plays a part of its own and affects motives and decisions and is, in short, one of the operative factors in the situation, so the course of events cannot be predicted, either in the long period or in the short, without a knowledge of the behaviour of money between the first state and the last. And it is this which we ought to mean when we speak of a *monetary economy*.

After reading this it seems that Hahn (1973b) rediscovered the fact that neo-Walrasian analysis is an example of a real-exchange economy – forty years on! With the benefit of hindsight it now appears that, of Keynes, Myrdal and Hayek, Keynes made the most significant progress in the development of Monetary Analysis. The remainder of this study therefore concentrated on a re-evaluation of Keynes's monetary theory, especially that in the *General Theory*, as the basis for the development of monetary theory in the tradition of Monetary Analysis. A distinction between Keynes and the Keynesians has, of course, been drawn by Leijonhufvud (1968), but the distinction under review here has generally been neglected in the mainstream literature. In fact, one of the major reasons for the failure of Keynesian monetary theory has been its reliance on Real rather than Monetary Analysis. To develop a rigorous analytical framework for Monetary Analysis a re-evaluation of Keynes's monetary theory proves to be a useful point at which to begin. To this end a few basic principles were established.

A Say's Law economy and a capitalist economy

The distinction between a Say's Law or a co-operative commodity money economy and a capitalist bank money economy proves to be fundamental to understanding Monetary Analysis. Needless to say the distinction is lost in Real Analysis. The first odd feature of a Say's Law economy is the view that individuals produce for themselves; hence they may demand their own output if they cannot sell it, and consumers and producers are identical. This view of the production process is implicit in the belief that in terms of Say's Law productions buy productions. But, as both Marx and Keynes argued, this interpretation of production is not compatible with capitalist production. In particular it ignores the division of labour and the need to realize money profits, which are essential features of capitalism.

However, the essential problem with Say's Law when applied to a capitalist economy is that it implies that there is no limit to the profitable expansion of production. Output will therefore expand up to the point at which the labour force is fully employed. Now it is well known that Keynes claimed to refute Say's Law by proposing that the principle of effective demand established a limit to the profitable expansion of output and that equilibrium could therefore be established at almost any level of employment. To establish this claim, the refutation of Say's Law must be made analytically watertight. In this regard, the concept of monetary equilibrium was adapted from chapter 17 of the *General Theory* using Marshallian principles, and then applied to demonstrate the existence of a point of effective demand which establishes a long-period equilibrium with unemployment. That is, the concept of monetary equilibrium was employed, in a static context, to integrate real and monetary factors in a Monetary Analysis of the principle of effective demand.

Monetary equilibrium and the principle of effective demand

Attempts to develop the notion of monetary equilibrium have a long history in both classical and neoclassical theory, but perhaps the most well-known illustration is Wicksell's specification in terms of the natural and market rates of interest. Wicksell, however, employed the idea of monetary equilibrium, in the context of a neoclassical monetary theory in the tradition of Real Analysis. On the other hand, although Keynes retained the concept of monetary equilibrium, it can be argued that he applied it in a manner compatible with the tradition of Monetary Analysis. In this regard he rejected the Wicksellian concept of the natural rate and replaced it with what he called the conventional or normal rate of interest. To appreciate the analytical significance of this point it is necessary to consider the implications of the distinction between bank and commodity money from the perspective of classical theory and the capital debate in the case of neoclassical theory. From the perspective of classical theory, the rate of interest associated with bank money cannot be analysed in terms of a natural rate because credit is a 'commodity' *sui generis* and therefore not subject to the laws of production. There is, therefore, no classical theory of the natural rate of interest on a par with the analysis of the natural prices of other commodities. It is in this sense that the distinction between credit and commodity money is important to classical theory.

From the perspective of neoclassical theory the argument is somewhat different and rests on the realization that the capital debate has undermined any hope of defining the natural rate of interest in terms of neoclassical principles. With the neo-Walrasians confined to perfect barter, and hence moneyless models, this leads inevitably to the conclusion that there is no possibility of developing a theory of the rate of interest using neoclassical general equilibrium principles! Once this fact is acknowledged the way is open to the integration of real and monetary forces in the determination of long-period equilibrium.

In this respect the solution offered in this book is a vindication of the conclusions reached by Nell (1983:87) (although Nell's own solution is too opaque to follow): 'If Keynes has grounds for his revised Quantity Theory and his rejection of the neutrality of money in equilibrium (as well as in the movement towards equilibrium), they can only come from the approach based largely on the neglected chapter 17', or Kregel (1983:61): 'If the equality $r_i = r_m$ [monetary equilibrium] occurs before all available real resources are fully utilised the system has reached a stable, less-than-full employment equilibrium.' To this end chapter 9 applied traditional Marshallian micro-economic analytical tools to restate the analysis of chapter 17 in the *General Theory* in terms of a concept of monetary equilibrium in which, given the conventional rate of interest, equilibrium is established between all forms of converting present into future wealth. This is, after all, the classical notion of equilibrium as a state of rest. In this case, however, it is the rate of interest which determines the level to which the marginal efficiencies of other assets adjust. In this respect it could be argued that Keynes is still very much in the classical tradition. However, the concept of monetary equilibrium suggested here provides the analytical basis for the principle of effective demand which breaks Say's Law.

Monetary equilibrium, at which the rates of return across all assets are equalized – given risk differentials – then establishes a point of effective demand beyond which it is *not profitable* to expand output. The conventional rate of interest which may be (but is not automatically) influenced by monetary policy in terms of Bank rate and its link to the long rate via the term structure, is an independent or exogenous-type variable. There is therefore no adjustment mechanism that can automatically set the rate of interest at a level which will establish a demand price for capital goods that in turn generates just that rate of investment necessary to ensure full employment, even in the long period. In shorthand terms, long-period monetary equilibrium which establishes equality between the rate of interest and the MEC can generate a rate of investment which is compatible with almost any level of employment. In terms of a static analysis – given long-run expectations and realised short-period expectations – entrepreneurs are then in long-period equilibrium earning normal profits and have no incentive to expand production. The point of effective demand determined by monetary equilibrium therefore establishes a limit to the profitable expansion of production and breaks Say's Law. Wage flexibility will then only increase employment if it can shift the point of effective demand by operating on the marginal propensity to consume, the rate of interest and/or the MEC. At best the outcome is indeterminate. The most likely outcome of wage flexibility, however, is to shift the point of effective demand *away* from the full employment level.

Monetary equilibrium and Keynesian monetary theory

The concept of monetary equilibrium outlined in chapters 9 and 10 is, it seems, formally compatible with most of Post Keynesian monetary theory as reflected in the work by Kaldor, Davidson, Kregel, Chick, Minsky and Moore, among others. If anything, a reading of Davidson and Kregel (1980), who set out 'Keynes's paradigm: a theoretical framework for monetary analysis', leads to the conclusion that the introduction of the concept of monetary equilibrium, as the determinant of the point of effective demand, considerably strengthens the Post Keynesian analysis. For example, many Post Keynesian statements of aggregate demand and supply analysis appear to suggest that it is *expected proceeds* that determine the point of effective demand, e.g. Asimakopulos (1984). But in that case the analysis is open to the charge that only if expectations are depressed will unemployment equilibrium result. This is not what Keynes claimed. The concept of monetary equilibrium avoids this potential problem. Instead, it provides a rigorous analysis of long-period equilibrium with unemployment based on Marshallian principles and the classical notion of equilibrium as a state of rest. In addition the analysis presented here can be interpreted as the static component of a historical model, in Joan Robinson's sense, as the analysis is readily extended to incorporate the stationary and shifting models identified by Kregel (1976). Expectations can thus be incorporated into the analysis in an intelligible way *after* the principle of effective demand has been established (Davidson and Kregel, 1980:139).

The analysis also rehabilitates the liquidity preference theory by acknowledging that the notion of the conventional rate of interest cannot be given a theoretical explanation in terms of classical or neoclassical principles. The conventional rate thus plays a key role in liquidity preference theory analogous to the role played by the natural rate in the loanable funds theory. Although this interpretation of liquidity preference theory is not widely acknowledged – Chick is a notable exception – it is compatible with the work of Kaldor and Moore on the endogenous nature of the money supply in a credit money economy. In fact, the concept of monetary equilibrium proposed here links the Kaldor–Moore analysis with the principle of effective demand (as in Kaldor's model discussed in chapter 10) and thereby undermines other key features of monetarism or pseudo-Keynesianism such as the notion of a natural rate of unemployment and the neutrality of money.

The analysis presented here also appears to make some contribution to Keynesian exegesis although that was not the major objective. No claim is made that the interpretation offered here is what Keynes really meant. Nevertheless, the analysis presented in chapters 9 and 10 does meet the claims that Keynes made for his analysis in the *General Theory* and it does so without resorting to the usual arguments based on a discrepancy between *ex ante* saving and investment. The concept of monetary equilibrium is employed in the context of Kregel's (1976) static model to demonstrate, as a theoretical or logical principle, that the point of effective demand can determine a long-period equilibrium at almost any level of employment. This demonstration is not based on the discrepancy between *ex ante* saving and investment to break Say's Law; in fact such a discrepancy cannot arise in the static model. This property of the analysis seems to be consistent with Keynes's response to interpretations of the *General Theory*.

For other economists, I find, lay the whole emphasis, and find the whole explanation in the *differences* between effective demand and income, and they are so convinced that this is the right course that they do not notice that in my treatment it is not so . . . *The main point is to distinguish the forces determining the position of equilibrium from the technique of trial and error by means of which the entrepreneur discovers where the position is* . . . (but even if we) suppose the identity of *ex post* and *ex ante*, my theory remains (Keynes, 1973b:181–3; quoted by Davidson and Kregel, 1980:139, emphasis added).

Keynes thus explicitly repudiates the distinction between *ex ante* saving and investment as important in determining the position of equilibrium. The neo-Ricardians and some Post Keynesians appear to have overlooked this point. In addition, when summarizing the *General Theory*, Keynes (1936:245) explicitly states that the rate of interest is treated as one of the *independent* variables along with the marginal propensity to consume and the schedule of marginal efficiency of capital. Some early expositions of Keynes's system actually incorporated the exogenous nature of the rate of interest but only as an exercise to demonstrate that Keynes's model was supposedly logically inconsistent or indeterminate (Weintraub, 1977:54). The next step was to 'endogenize' the interest rate along Hicksian lines in the derivation of the IS–LM model; but, in the process, monetary theory took a wrong turn and lost contact with the monetary theory of production and the principle of effective demand.

To put monetary theory back on track and rehabilitate the IS–LM structure it is therefore necessary to return to the properties of Monetary Analysis. When this is done the IS–LM model can be rehabilitated along the lines sketched in chapter 10. This involves reintroducing the long rate of interest as an exogenous variable and generalizing Wicksell's treatment of monetary equilibrium to define the point of effective demand. The IS–LM model can then be interpreted in a fashion that is compatible with the aggregate demand and supply model of the Post Keynesians as it generates multiple long-period equilibria some of which imply unemployment.

Finally, it is also apparent that the concept of monetary equilibrium suggested here is compatible with the potential instability and indeterminacy stressed by fundamentalist Keynesians such as George Shackle. Once we move beyond the confines of the static equilibrium model into the realm of shifting equilibrium we come face to face with the question of economics without equilibrium (Davidson and Kregel, 1980:147). This, ultimately, is what wage, interest, and exchange rate stability is all about in a bank money economy. In a modern capitalist economy these variables are the independent variables on which the stability of the system rests. If these variables are not stabilized (this does not mean fixed) by policy then, contrary to neoclassical theory, they are not subject to market forces that will propel them to their natural levels. Once they start moving the centre of gravitation of the system moves with them, i.e. the system exhibits the property of hysteresis and we are dealing with the model of shifting equilibrium. This is the indeterminate world of Shackle. To suggest, on the basis of neoclassical theory, that these variables should be allowed to fluctuate so as to produce an optimum allocation of resources, capital accumulation and employment, is the opposite of the truth.

SOME POLICY IMPLICATIONS

Although we are not explicitly concerned with policy issues in this book the principles of Monetary Analysis developed here do have some policy implications that are worth nothing. At the most fundamental level, it is apparent that the concept of monetary equilibrium rests on the notion of a conventional rate of interest which is not given a theoretical explanation. The same can be said of the money and real wage rates which cannot be determined in 'objective' fashion as postulated by the neoclassical analysis of the labour market. Another key macroeconomic variable which has the same property is the exchange rate. For once it is realized that the interest rate does not have a natural equilibrium value it must be conceded that the exchange rate also, has no natural rate; like the interest rate it is a variable that rests on conventions. These observations have important implications for the implementation of monetary policy particularly when that policy is influenced by monetarist ideas.

The implications of Monetary Analysis for the implementation of macroeconomic policy can be illustrated in terms of the rehabilitated version of the IS–LM model presented in chapter 10. This model provides an opportunity for isolating the fundamental policy differences that separate Keynes from the modern 'classics' – both Keynesian and monetarist. The distinction can be briefly illustrated with reference to Figure 10.3. In terms of the traditional IS–LM framework, i.e. the Wicksellian version, monetarists seek to stabilize the economy by fixing the money stock, i.e. stabilizing the LM curve, and allowing price and wage flexibility to maintain full employment in the long period. Keynesians adopt essentially the same theoretical framework but argue that the adjustment process is slow and consequently government intervention is necessary to speed up the process of adjustment to long-period full employment. For this purpose Keynesians favour fiscal measures such as built-in stabilizers augmented by active (fine tuning?) budget adjustment of revenue and/or expenditure. As both Meltzer (1981:56) and Kregel (1985:33) point out, Keynes's macroeconomic policy proposals are quite different from either of these.

Keynes's proposals are understandable in terms of the theoretical framework outlined in chapters 9 and 10 when we introduce the further observation that private investment is the most volatile component of aggregate demand. Given the volatile nature of expectations about prospective yields, private investment is subject to potentially large and sudden fluctuations at any normal rate of interest. For monetary policy to offset these fluctuations would require equally large fluctuations in the normal rate of interest. Keynes considered that the variability of the marginal efficiency of capital would be too great to be offset by movements in the normal rate of interest, even if it were possible to engineer quickly. Moreover, as we will note below, there may well be negative side effects if the normal rate of interest is subjected to wild fluctuations. Hence Keynes was not optimistic about active use of monetary policy to stabilize the economy. Instead he suggested the 'socialization of investment'. What this amounted to was a programme of government investment which accounted for between two-thirds and three-quarters of total investment (Kregel, 1985:33, 40). Without going into the micro-economic issues necessary to maintain efficiency it is clear that the intention is to provide a long-term stabilizing influence on aggregate demand.

In terms of Figure 10.3 this means that the IS curve is stabilized so that the economy may fluctuate about a lower level of unemployment than would otherwise be the case. Thus the essence of Keynes's policy proposals rests on the stabilization of investment and does not rely on the active countercyclical fiscal or monetary policy as advocated by Keynesians. As Kregel (1985:32–3) reminds us, Keynes regarded the emergence of budget deficits as a symptom of failure to achieve the stabilization of investment. Budget deficits were not seen by Keynes as a remedy for unemployment except in the case of extreme emergency. This latter solution is the legacy of the fiscalists or exponents of functional finance, e.g. Lerner, which now passes for Keynesian policy in the IS–LM models of the textbooks. This policy may, however, be destabilizing in the long term as it takes no steps to stabilize the economy but offers only a response to shocks. If the economy is subjected to a series of stagflationary shocks that increase the average level of inflation and unemployment, then transfer and interest payments may well come to generate large budget deficits. The long-term implications of such a deficit and the inability of demand management to deal with supply shocks then leads inevitably to the view that Keynesian policies are no longer relevant. However, as Kregel (1985) remarks, the policies advocated by Keynes have not been tried.

By comparison to Keynesian activism, monetarism does at least have the virtue that it aims to provide a stable basis around which the economy may fluctuate. However, monetarism failed because it represented an attempt at stabilization that is incompatible with the properties of a capitalist system. In theoretical terms, monetarism simply assumes that fixing the money stock will establish monetary equilibrium at full employment. As we now know, however, fixing the money stock may generate monetary equilibrium at any of a number of levels of employment in the long period. Restraining the growth in the money supply may well produce more than a temporary increase in unemployment. More technically, monetarism represents an attempt to force a modern bank money, capitalist economy to behave as if it were a commodity money economy.

Seen from this perspective, monetarism, as the new quantity theory, differs from the classical quantity theory because it seeks to impose the properties of the classical quantity theory on bank money. The originators of the classical quantity theory applied it, with justification it seems, to commodity money. Many monetarists are not so careful and fail to realize the implications of the properties of bank money. Reimposing the properties of the quantity theory appeals to monetarists because the economy is then supposedly in a position to adjust to its natural equilibrium with interest rates and other financial variables, e.g. the exchange rate, at their natural and therefore stable levels. This, of course, is the attraction of the doctrine of neutral money. However, it is not possible to reimpose the properties of a commodity money world on the bank money systems of modern capitalist economies. Credit is now – and always has been – an interdependent part of capitalist production, i.e. it is in effect a factor of production, and any attempt to fix the quantity of money whether via 100 per cent reserve banking or via monetary base control will not only fail but may well destabilize the economy. The attempt will fail because restrictions on reserves will only encourage the provision of money substitutes, i.e. credit as a factor of production, by institutions lying outside the formal banking system. It may destabilize the economy because the monetarist belief in the natural rate of unemployment or the natural rate of interest has no theoretical basis in a bank money, capitalist economy.

If the conventions on which interest rates and exchange rates are based are broken, say by an explicit change of philosophy on the part of the monetary authorities in an attempt to implement monetarist policy and fix the money supply so as to allow interest and exchange rates to be 'market-determined', then the stabilizing influence of *inelastic* expectations in the financial markets may well be lost. Short-term interest rates or exchange rates then become volatile, because there is *no natural rate that can be objectively determined* – in the case of the exchange rate, purchasing power parity is not an objective measure to which the actual exchange rate must adjust. If central banks attempt to allow interest rates and exchange rates to be solely determined by market forces in the face of a shock to the system, there is no indication for market participants about the stable levels of these variables, i.e. where will the views of bulls and bears come into balance? Under these conditions expectations are prone to become elastic and rate movements exaggerated rather than dampened. It is in this sense that liquidity preference theory is applicable to the analysis of floating exchange rates in the period since the collapse of the Bretton Woods agreement. Without a commitment to a particular exchange rate, participants in the foreign exchange market often have no indication whether short-term movements in the rate will be reversed or not. That is, they have no clear idea of the normal or conventional rate and consequently expectations tend to be elastic rather than inelastic.

Interestingly, Friedman (1953d:158) only argues for freely floating exchange rates if a domestic monetary regime based on 100 per cent reserve banking is in place. He believed that if domestic money stocks were fixed, then exchange rates and interest rates could be entirely market-determined because they would fluctuate in stable fashion around their natural levels. To the extent that an economy is susceptible to wage/price spirals this is due to an unstable monetary system and/or policy that should be stabilized by imposing control on the money stock. However, as we know, although central banks have implemented monetary targets this is quite different from imposing a fixed rate of growth on the money stock. Central banks have found it impossible to impose the properties of commodity money on the bank money systems of capitalist economies. Hence the necessary conditions for exchange rate stability set by Friedman for freely floating exchange rates have never been met. Foreign exchange rates then have no natural equilibrium levels. Under these conditions foreign exchange markets attract speculators who can exploit the elasticity of expectations to make gains.

The volatility of interest and exchange rates under these conditions serves no useful purpose in promoting capital accumulation and growth – if anything it discourages it. In terms of Kregel's (1976) classification, the monetarist experiment, by seeking to impose the properties of the quantity theory on a capitalist economy, has in fact *created* an extreme example of the model of shifting equilibrium, i.e. attempts to implement monetarist policies have created the indeterminacy of Shackle's world. The economy then has no natural equilibrium to which it will adjust. Instead it is subjected to a period of 'tail-chasing' without any prospect of a satisfactory result. In a sense it is ironic that, in opting for free markets and price flexibility, the monetarists are actually creating the conditions stressed by the so-called Keynesian fundamentalists who highlight the importance of expectations and the impossibility of objective analysis. Certainly, by sweeping away existing conventions, attempts to implement monetarist-type policies have *increased* uncertainty and *created* indeterminacy.

Fortunately, although central bankers have flirted with monetarism and revelled in its rhetoric, they have pulled back from the brink when it came to an attempt to impose the properties of the quantity theory in a modern capitalist system (Friedman, 1984; Poole, 1982). Nevertheless, many economists still have a preference for flexible interest rates and exchange rates in the belief that these promote an optimal allocation of resources, capital accumulation and employment. The analysis of monetary equilibrium presented here suggests that this conclusion is the opposite of the truth. Key financial variables such as interest and exchange rates cannot be allowed to float freely or be perfectly flexible for, in a capitalist economy using bank money, there is no mechanism whereby these variables can automatically provide the configuration that would ensure the result envisaged by the monetarists. Instead, and disregarding the negative effect that increased interest rate volatility will have on investment in productive capital, the interest rate structure which does emerge may well establish a point of effective demand that generates unemployment. A modern capitalist economy cannot be made self-adjusting by allowing for flexible interest, exchange and wage rates. The concept of monetary equilibrium and the analysis of the principle of effective demand presented here explain why this is so. This, as I understand it, is the message of Keynes and Post Keynesian monetary theory.

REFERENCES

Achinstein, P. 1968. *Concepts of Science*, Baltimore: Johns Hopkins Press.

Ackley, G. 1961. *Macroeconomic Theory*, New York: Macmillan.

Ackley, G. 1978. *Macroeconomics: Theory and Policy*, New York: Macmillan.

Allingham, M. 1983. *Value*, London: Macmillan.

Archibald, G.C. and Lipsey, R.G. 1958. Monetary and Value Theory: A Critique of Lange and Patinkin, *Review of Economic Studies*, 26, 1–22.

Arrow, K.J. and Hahn, F.H. 1971. *General Competitive Analysis*, San Francisco: Holden-Day Inc.

Asimakopulos, A. 1982. Keynes' Theory of Effective Demand Revisited, *Australian Economic Papers*, 21, 18–36.

Asimakopulos, A. 1984. The General Theory and its Marshallian Micro-foundations, *Metroeconomica*, 36, 161–175.

Bailey, R. 1976. On the Analytical Foundations of Wicksell's Cumulative Process, *The Manchester School*, 44, 52–71.

Barro, R.J. and Grossman, H.I. 1976. *Money, Employment and Inflation*, New York: Cambridge University Press.

Bateman, W.B. 1987. Keynes's Changing Conception of Probability, *Economics and Philosophy*, 3, 97–120.

Bauer, P.T. 1939. Interest and Quasi-Rent, *Economic Journal*, 49, 154–157.

Begg, D.K.H. 1982. *The Rational Expectations Revolution in Macroeconomics*, Oxford: Philip Allan.

Benavie, A. 1977. Keynesian Versus Perfect Market Macromodels, *Atlantic Economic Journal*, 5, 1–10.

Bilas, R.A. 1967. *Microeconomic Theory: A Graphical Analysis*, New York: McGraw-Hill.

Blaug, M. 1980. *The Methodology of Economics*, Cambridge: Cambridge University Press.

Blinder, A.S. and Solow, R.M. 1973. Does Fiscal Policy Matter?, *Journal of Public Economics*, 2, 319–337.

Boland, L.A. 1979. A Critique of Friedman's Critics, *Journal of Economic Literature*, 17, 503–522.

Brainard, W.C. and Tobin, J. 1968. Pitfalls in Financial Model Building, reprinted in *Essays in Economics*, 1971, ed. J. Tobin, vol. i, 352–377.

293

Branson, W.H. 1979. *Macroeconomic Theory and Policy*, 2nd edn, New York: Harper and Row.

Brunner, K. and Meltzer, A. 1976a. An Aggregative Theory for a Closed Economy, in *Monetarism*, ed. J.L. Stein, 67–103, Amsterdam: North-Holland.

Brunner, K. and Meltzer, A. 1976b. Reply to Comments by Dornbusch, Rasche and Mayer, in *Monetarism*, ed. J.L. Stein, 150–182, Amsterdam: North-Holland.

Burton, J. 1982. Varieties of Monetarism and their Policy Implications, *Three Banks Review*, no. 134, 14–31.

Caldwell, B.J. 1980. A Critique of Friedman's Methodological Instrumental-ism, *Southern Economic Journal*, 47, 366–374.

Caravale, G.A. and Tosato, D.A. 1980. *Ricardo and the Theory of Value, Distribution and Growth*, London: Routledge and Kegan Paul.

Carmichael, J. and Stebbing, P.W. 1983. Fisher's Paradox and the Theory of Interest, *American Economic Review*, 73, 619–630.

Chick, V. 1973. *The Theory of Monetary Policy*, 1st edn, Oxford: Blackwell.

Chick, V. 1978. The Nature of the Keynesian Revolution: A Reassessment, *Australian Economic Papers*, 17, 1–20.

Chick, V. 1983. *Macroeconomics After Keynes*, London: Philip Allan.

Chick, V. 1985. Monetary Increases and their Consequences: Backwaters and Floods, University College London: discussion paper, 85–06.

Clark, R.L. 1979. Methodology as a Barrier to the Solution of the Keynesian/Monetarist Controversy, *Indian Economic Journal*, 27, 16–36.

Clower, R.W. 1963. Classical Monetary Theory Revisited, *Economica*, 30, 165–170.

Clower, R.W. 1965. The Keynesian Counter-Revolution: A Theoretical Appraisal, in *The Theory of Interest Rates*, eds. F.H. Hahn and F.P.R. Brechling, 103–125, London: Macmillan.

Clower, R.W. 1967. A Reconsideration of the Microfoundations of Monetary Theory, *Western Economic Journal*, 6, 1–9. Reprinted in Clower, R.W. (ed.), 1969a.

Clower, R.W. 1969a. (ed.) *Monetary Theory: Selected Readings*, Harmondsworth: Penguin.

Clower, R.W. 1969b. Introduction to *Monetary Theory: Selected Readings*, ed. R.W. Clower, 7–21, Harmondsworth: Penguin.

Clower, R.W. 1975. Reflections on the Keynesian Perplex, *Zeitschrift für Nationalökonomie*, 35, 1–24.

Cochrane, J.L. 1970. *Macroeconomics Before Keynes*, Glenview, Illinois: Scott, Foresman and Company.

Coddington, A. 1972. Positive Economics, *Canadian Journal of Economics*, 5, 1–15.

Coddington, A. 1975. The Rationale of General Equilibrium Theory, *Economic Inquiry*, 13, 539–558.

Coddington, A. 1976. Keynesian Economics: The Search for First Principles, *Journal of Economic Literature*, 14, 1258–1273.

Coddington, A. 1983. *Keynesian Economics: The Search for First Principles*,

London: George Allen and Unwin.

Conard, J.W. 1963. *An Introduction to the Theory of Interest*, Los Angeles: University of California Press.

Cottrell, A. 1986. The Endogeneity of Money and Money–Income Causality, *Scottish Journal of Political Economy*, 33, 2–27.

Cowen, T. 1983. Temporary Equilibrium and the Microfoundations of Macroeconomic Theory, unpublished manuscript, Harvard University.

Danes, M.K. 1979. Dennis Robertson and the Construction of Aggregative Theory, unpublished Ph.D. dissertation, Queen Mary College, University of London.

Davidson, P. 1967. A Keynesian View of Patinkin's Theory of Employment, *Economic Journal*, 77, 559–578.

Davidson, P. 1977. Money and General Equilibrium, *Economie Appliquée*, 31, 541–563.

Davidson, P. 1978. *Money and the Real World*, 2nd edn, London: Macmillan.

Davidson, P. 1981. A Critical Analysis of the Monetarist–Rational Expectations–Supply Side Incentive Economics Approach to Accumulation During a Period of Inflationary Expectations, *Kredit und Kapital*, no. 4, 496–503.

Davidson, P. 1982. Rational Expectations: A Fallacious Foundation for Studying Crucial Decision Making Processes, *Journal of Post Keynesian Economics*, 5, 182–198.

Davidson, P. 1983. The Dubious Labour Market Analysis in Meltzer's Restatement of Keynes' Theory, *Journal of Economic Literature*, 21, 52–56.

Davidson, P. and Kregel, J.A. 1980. Keynes's Paradigm: A Theoretical Framework for Monetary Analysis, in *Growth, Profits and Property*, ed. E.J. Nell, 137–150, Cambridge: Cambridge University Press.

Davidson, P. and Smolensky, E. 1964. *Aggregate Demand and Supply Analysis*, New York: Harper and Row.

Davis, E.G. 1980. The Correspondence Between R.G. Hawtrey and J.M. Keynes on the Treatise: The Genesis of Output Adjustment Models, *Canadian Journal of Economics*, 13, 716–724.

Desai, M. 1981. *Testing Monetarism*, London: Frances Pinter.

Dillard, D. 1948. *The Economics of John Maynard Keynes: The Theory of a Monetary Economy*, New York: Prentice Hall.

Dillard, D. 1984. Keynes and Marx: A Centennial Appraisal, *Journal of Post Keynesian Economics*, 6, 421–432.

Dornbusch, R. 1976. Comment on Brunner and Meltzer, in *Monetarism*, ed. J.L. Stein, 104–126, Amsterdam: North-Holland.

Dornbusch, R. and Fischer, S. 1981. *Macroeconomics*, 2nd edn, New York: McGraw-Hill.

Dougherty, C. 1980. *Interest and Profit*, London: Methuen.

Eatwell, J. 1983a. Theories of Value, Output and Employment, in *Keynes's Economics and the Theory of Value and Distribution*, eds. J. Eatwell and M. Milgate, 93–128, London: Duckworth.

Eatwell, J. 1983b. The Long-Period Theory of Employment, *Cambridge Journal of Economics*, 7, 269–286.

Eatwell, J. 1983c. The Analytical Foundations of Monetarism, in *Keynes's Economics and the Theory of Value and Distribution*, eds. J. Eatwell and M. Milgate, 203–213, London: Duckworth.

Eatwell, J. and Milgate, M. 1983. (eds.) *Keynes's Economics and the Theory of Value and Distribution*, London: Duckworth.

Eichberger, J. 1986. Review of 'Money and Markets: Essays by Robert W. Clower', *Economic Record*, 62, 346–348.

Eichengreen, B. 1985. *The Gold Standard in Theory and Practice*, New York: Methuen.

Evans, M.K. 1981. *The Truth About Supply Side Economics*, New York: Basic Books.

Fender, J. 1981. *Understanding Keynes*, London: Wheatsheaf Books.

Feyerabend, P. 1964. Realism and Instrumentalism: Comments on the Logic of Factual Support, in *The Critical Approach to Science and Philosophy*, ed. M. Bunge, 280–308, London: The Free Press of Glencoe.

Fisher, F.M. 1971. Aggregate Production Functions and the Explanation of Wages: A Simulation Experiment, *The Review of Economics and Statistics*, 53, 305–325.

Fisher, F.M. 1976. The Stability of General Equilibrium: Results and Problems, in *Essays in Economic Analysis*, eds. M. Artis and R. Nobay, 3–29, Cambridge: Cambridge University Press.

Fisher, I. 1911. *The Purchasing Power of Money*, New York: Macmillan.

Fisher, I. 1930. *The Theory of Interest*, New York: Macmillan.

Friedman, B. 1978. The Theoretical Non-Debate about Monetarism, in *The Structure of Monetarism*, ed. T. Mayer, 94–112, New York: Norton and Company.

Friedman, M. 1953a. Lange on Price Flexibility and Employment: A Methodological Criticism, in *Essays in Positive Economics*, 277–300, Chicago: Chicago University Press.

Friedman, M. 1953b. Commodity-Reserve Currency, in *Essays in Positive Economics*, 204–250, Chicago: Chicago University Press.

Friedman, M. 1953c. A Monetary and Fiscal Framework for Economic Stability, in *Essays in Positive Economics*, 133–156, Chicago: Chicago University Press.

Friedman, M. 1953d. The Case for Flexible Exchange Rates, in *Essays in Positive Economics*, 157–203, Chicago: Chicago University Press.

Friedman, M. 1955. Leon Walras and his Economic System: A Review Article, *American Economic Review*, 45, 900–909.

Friedman, M. 1956. The Quantity Theory of Money – A Re-statement, in *Studies in the Quantity Theory of Money*, ed. M. Friedman, 3–21, Chicago: Chicago University Press.

Friedman, M. 1959. The Demand for Money: Some Theoretical and Empirical Results, reprinted in *The Optimum Quantity of Money*, 1969, 111–139.

Friedman, M. 1966. Interest Rates and the Demand for Money, reprinted in *The Optimum Quantity of Money*, 1969, 142–155.

Friedman, M. 1968. The Role of Monetary Policy, *American Economic Review*, 57, 1–17.

Friedman, M. 1969. *The Optimum Quantity of Money*, London: Macmillan.

Friedman, M. 1974. A Theoretical Framework for Monetary Analysis, in *Milton Friedman's Monetary Framework*, ed. R.J. Gordon, 1–62, Chicago: Chicago University Press.

Friedman, M. 1975. Unemployment versus Inflation? An Evaluation of the Phillips Curve, *Occasional Paper* no. 44, Institute of Economic Affairs, London.

Friedman, M. 1976. Comments on Tobin and Buiter, in *Monetarism*, ed. J.L. Stein, 310–317, Amsterdam: North-Holland.

Friedman, M. 1980. Monetarism: A Reply to the Critics, *The Times* London, 3 March.

Friedman, M. 1984. Lessons from the 1979–82 Monetary Policy Experiment, *American Economic Review*, Papers and Proceedings, 74, 397–400.

Friedman, M. 1985. The Case for Overhauling the Federal Reserve, *Challenge*, July–August, 4–12.

Friedman, M. and Schwartz, A.J. 1982. *Monetary Trends in the United States and the United Kingdom*, Chicago: Chicago University Press.

Fusfeld, D.R. 1980. 'Is Optimising Rational?', paper presented to the Annual Meeting of the American Economic Association, Denver, Colorado.

Gale, D. 1982. *Money: In Equilibrium*, Cambridge: Cambridge University Press.

Gale, D. 1983. *Money: In Disequilibrium*, Cambridge: Cambridge University Press.

Garegnani, P. 1970. Heterogeneous Capital, the Production Function and the Theory of Distribution, *Review of Economic Studies*, 37, 407–437.

Garegnani, P. 1978. Notes on Consumption, Investment and Effective Demand, Parts I and II, *Cambridge Journal of Economics*, 2, 335–353; 3, 63–82.

Garegnani, P. 1983. Two Routes to Effective Demand, in *Distribution, Effective Demand and International Economic Relations*, ed. J.A. Kregel, 69–80, London: Macmillan.

Giedymin, J. 1976. Instrumentalism and its Critique: A Reappraisal, *Boston Studies in the Philosophy of Science*, 39, 179–207.

Gilbert, J.C. 1982. *Keynes's Impact on Monetary Economics*, London: Butterworth.

Gordon, R.J. 1974. (ed.) *Milton Friedman's Monetary Framework: A Debate with his Critics*, Chicago: Chicago University Press.

Grandmont, J.M. 1974. On the Short-Run Equilibrium in a Monetary Economy, in *Allocation under Uncertainty: Equilibrium and Optimality*, ed. J.H. Dreze, 213–228, London: Macmillan.

Grandmont, J.M. 1977. Temporary General Equilibrium Theory, *Econometrica*, 45, 535–571.

Grandmont, J.M. 1983. *Money and Value: A Reconsideration of Classical and Neoclassical Monetary Theories*, Cambridge: Cambridge University Press.

Grandmont, J.M. and Younes, Y. 1972. On the Role of Money and the Existence of a Monetary Equilibrium, *Review of Economic Studies*, 39, 355–372.

Gupta, S.B. 1969. The Invalidity of the Dichotomy in the Pure Inside-Money Model, *Journal of Political Economy*, 77, 118–121.

Gurley, J.G. and Shaw, E.S. 1960. *Money in a Theory of Finance*, Washington, D.C.: Brookings Institution.

Hahn, F.H. 1965. On Some Problems of Proving the Existence of an Equilibrium in a Monetary Economy, in *The Theory of Interest Rates*, ed. F.H. Hahn and F.P.R. Brechling, 126–135, London: Macmillan.

Hahn, F.H. 1972. *The Share of Wages in the National Income*, London: Weidenfeld and Nicolson.

Hahn, F.H. 1973a. *On the Notion of Equilibrium in Economics*, Cambridge: Cambridge University Press.

Hahn, F.H. 1973b. On the Foundations of Monetary Theory, in *Essays in Modern Economics*, ed. M. Parkin, 230–242, London: Longman.

Hahn, F.H. 1977. Keynesian Economics and General Equilibrium Theory: Reflections on Some Current Debates, in *The Microfoundations of Macroeconomics*, ed. G.C. Harcourt, 25–40, London: Macmillan.

Hahn, F.H. 1980a. General Equilibrium Theory, *The Public Interest*, 58 (Special Issue), 123–138.

Hahn, F.H. 1980b. Monetarism and Economic Theory, *Economica*, 47, 1–17.

Hahn, F.H. 1981. Review of Beenstock: A Neoclassical Analysis of Macroeconomic Policy, *Economic Journal*, 91, 1036–1039.

Hahn, F.H. 1982a. The Neo-Ricardians, *Cambridge Journal of Economics*, 6, 353–374.

Hahn, F.H. 1982b. *Money and Inflation*, Oxford: Blackwell.

Hahn, F.H. and Negishi, T. 1962. A Theorem on Non-Tâtonnement Stability, *Econometrica*, 30, 463–469.

Hahn, F.H. and Nield, R. 1980. Why Mrs Thatcher Should Beware, *The Times* London, 25 February.

Hansen, A.H. 1953. *A Guide to Keynes*, New York: McGraw-Hill.

Harcourt, G.C. 1972. *Some Controversies in the Theory of Capital*, Cambridge: Cambridge University Press.

Harcourt, G.C. 1976. The Cambridge Controversies: Old Ways and New Horizons – or Dead End?, *Oxford Economic Papers*, 28, 25–65.

Harcourt, G.C. 1977. (ed.) *The Microfoundations of Macroeconomics*, London: Macmillan.

Harcourt, G.C. 1981. Marshall, Sraffa and Keynes: Incompatible Bedfellows?, *Eastern Economic Journal*, 7, 39–50.

Harcourt, G.C. 1983. Keynes's College Bursar View of Investment, in *Distribution, Effective Demand and International Economic Relations*, ed. J.A. Kregel, 81–84, London: Macmillan.

Harrington, R. 1971. The Monetarist Controversy, *The Manchester School*, 39, 269–292.

Harris, D.J. 1973. Capital, Distribution and the Aggregate Production Function, *American Economic Review*, 63, 100–112.

Harris, D.J. 1980. A Post-Mortem on the Neoclassical 'Parable', in *Growth, Profits and Property*, ed. E.J. Nell, 43–63, New York: Cambridge University Press.

Harrod, R.F. 1939. An Essay on Dynamic Theory, *Economic Journal*, 49, 14–33.

Harrod, R.F. 1947. Keynes, the Economist, in *The New Economics: Keynes' Influence on Theory and Policy*, ed. S.E. Harris, 65–72, New York: Alfred A. Knopf.

Harrod, R.F. 1970. Discussion paper, in *Monetary Theory and Policy in the 1970's*, eds. G. Clayton, J.C. Gilbert and R. Sedgwick, 58–63, London: Oxford University Press.

Hausman, D.M. 1981. Are General Equilibrium Theories Explanatory?, in *Philosophy in Economics*, ed. C.J. Pitt, 17–32, Dordrecht: Reidel.

Hayek, F.A. 1931. *Prices and Production*, London: George Routledge and Sons.

Hayek, F.A. 1932. A Note on the Development of the Doctrine of 'Forced Saving', *Quarterly Journal of Economics*, 47, 123–133.

Hayek, F.A. 1980. Letter to *The Times* London, 5 March.

Helm, D.R. 1984a. Marshallians and Walrasians: Hicks, LSE and Cambridge in the 1930s, paper presented at the History of Economic Thought Conference, University of Surrey, 5–7 September.

Helm, D.R. 1984b. Predictions and Causes: A Comparison of Friedman and Hicks on Method, in *Economic Theory and Hicksian Themes*, eds. D.A. Collard, D.R. Helm, M.G. Scott and A.K. Sen, *Oxford Economic Papers*, Supplement, 36, 118–134.

Hendry, D.F. and Ericsson, N.R. 1983. Assertion without Empirical Basis: An Econometric Appraisal of Friedman and Schwartz' 'Monetary trends in . . . the United Kingdom', paper presented at the Twenty-second Meeting of the Panel of Academic Consultants to the Bank of England, October.

Hickman, W.B. 1950. The Determinacy of Absolute Prices in Classical Economic Theory, *Econometrica*, 18, 9–20.

Hicks, J.R. 1937. Mr Keynes and the Classics: A Suggested Interpretation, *Econometrica*, 5, 147–159.

Hicks, J.R. 1939. *Value and Capital*, Oxford: Oxford University Press.

Hicks, J.R. 1950. *A Contribution to the Theory of the Trade Cycle*, Oxford: Oxford University Press.

Hicks, J.R. 1957. A Rehabilitation of 'Classical' Economics?, *Economic Journal*, 67, 279–289.

Hicks, J.R. 1967a. Monetary Theory and History: an Attempt at Perspective, in *Critical Essays in Monetary Theory*, 155–173, Oxford: Clarendon Press.

Hicks, J.R. 1967b. A Note on the Treatise, in *Critical Essays in Monetary Theory*, 189–202, Oxford: Clarendon Press.

Hicks, J.R. 1976. Some Questions of Time in Economics, in *Evolution, Welfare, and Time in Economics*, ed. A.M. Tang *et al.*, 135–151, Lexington, Mass.: Heath Lexington Books.

Hicks, J.R. 1979. *Causality in Economics*, Oxford: Blackwell.

Hirsch, A. and de Marchi, N. 1985. The Methodology of Positive Economics as *Via Media*, unpublished mimeograph.

Hirsch, A. and de Marchi, N. 1986. Making a Case when Theory is Unfalsefiable: Friedman's Monetary History, *Economics and Philosophy*, 2, 1–21.

Honohan, P. 1981. A New Look at Wicksell's Inflationary Process, *The Manchester School*, 49, 319–333.

Hoover, K.D. 1984a. The False Promise of Instrumentalism: A Comment on Frazer and Boland, *American Economic Review*, 74, 789–792.

Hoover, K.D. 1984b. Two Types of Monetarism, *Journal of Economic Literature*, 22, 58–76.

Howard, M.C. 1979. *Modern Theories of Income Distribution*, London: Macmillan.

Howard, M. 1983. *Profits in Economic Theory*, London: Macmillan.

Howells, P.G.A. and Bain, K. 1983. The Derivation of the LM Schedule – a Pedagogical Note, *British Review of Economic Issues*, 5, 57–65.

Howitt, P.W. 1973. Walras and Monetary Theory, *Western Economic Journal*, 11, 487–499.

Howitt, P.W. 1974. Stability and the Quantity Theory, *Journal of Political Economy*, 82, 133–151.

Hutchison, T.W. 1964. '*Positive*' *Economics and Policy Objectives*, London: Allen and Unwin.

Hutt, W.H. 1974. *A Rehabilitation of Say's Law*, Athens: Ohio University Press.

Hutt, W.H. 1979. *The Keynesian Episode: A Reassessment*, Indianapolis: Liberty Press.

Jaffé, W. 1942. Leon Walras's Theory of Capital Accumulation, in *Studies in Mathematical Economics and Econometrics*, eds. O. Lange, F. McIntyre and T.O. Yntema, 37–48, Chicago: Chicago University Press.

Johnson, H.G. 1965. A Quantity Theorist's History of the United States, *Economic Journal*, 75, 388–396.

Johnson, H.G. 1967. Money in a Neo-Classical One-Sector Growth Model, in *Essays in Monetary Economics*, 2nd edn, 141–178, London: George Allen and Unwin.

Johnson, H.G. 1971. *Macroeconomics and Monetary Theory*, London: Grey-Mills.

Kaldor, N. 1960. Keynes' Theory of Own-Rates of Interest, in *Essays on Economic Stability and Growth*, 59–74, London: Duckworth.

Kaldor, N. 1970. The New Monetarism, *Lloyds Bank Review*, no. 97 (July), 1–18.

Kaldor, N. 1981. *Origins of the New Monetarism*, Cardiff: University College of Cardiff Press.

Kaldor, N. 1982. *The Scourge of Monetarism*, Oxford: Oxford University Press.

Kaldor, N. 1983. *Limitations of the General Theory*, Keynes Lecture in Economics, The British Academy, Oxford: Oxford University Press.

Kaldor, N. 1985a. How Monetarism Failed, *Challenge*, May–June, 4–13.

Kaldor, N. 1985b. *Economics Without Equilibrium*, New York: M.E. Sharpe Inc.

Kaldor, N. and Trevithick, J. 1981. A Keynesian Perspective on Money, *Lloyds Bank Review*, no. 139 (January), 1–19.

Katouzian, H. 1980. *Ideology and Method in Economics*, London: Macmillan.

Kenway, P. 1983. Marx, Keynes and the Possibility of Crisis, in *Keynes's Economics and the Theory of Value and Distribution*, eds. J. Eatwell and M. Milgate, 149–166, London: Duckworth.

Keynes, J.M. 1923. *A Tract on Monetary Reform*, London: Macmillan.

Keynes, J.M. 1930. *A Treatise on Money*, vol. I, London: Macmillan.

Keynes, J.M. 1933. The Monetary Theory of Production, reprinted in *Collected Writings*, ed. D. Moggridge, vol. XXIX (1979), 408–411, London: Macmillan.

Keynes, J.M. 1936. *The General Theory of Employment, Interest and Money*, London: Macmillan.

Keynes, J.M. 1973a. *Collected Writings*, ed. D. Moggridge, vol. XIII, The General Theory and After: Part I, Preparation, London: Macmillan.

Keynes, J.M. 1973b. *Collected Writings*, ed. D. Moggridge, vol. XIV, The General Theory and After: Part II, Defence and Development, London: Macmillan.

Keynes, J.M. 1979. *Collected Writings*, ed. D. Moggridge, vol. XXIX, The General Theory and After: A Supplement, London: Macmillan.

Klamer, A. 1984. *The New Classical Macroeconomics*, Brighton: Harvester Press.

Kohn, M. 1979. On the Foundations of Monetary Theory and the Monetary Foundations of Macroeconomics, unpublished manuscript, Dartmouth College.

Kohn, M. 1981a. In Defence of the Finance Constraint, *Economic Inquiry*, 19, 177–195.

Kohn, M. 1981b. A Loanable Funds Theory of Unemployment and Monetary Disequilibrium, *American Economic Review*, 71, 859–879.

Kohn, M. 1983. Monetary Analysis, the Equilibrium Method, and Keynes' General Theory, unpublished mimeo., Dartmouth College. (Now published as Kohn 1986.)

Kohn, M. 1986. Monetary Analysis, the Equilibrium Method, and Keynes' General Theory, *Journal of Political Economy*, 94, 1191–1224.

Kregel, J.A. 1971. *Rate of Profit, Distribution and Growth*, London: Macmillan.

Kregel, J.A. 1976. Economic Methodology in the Face of Uncertainty: The Modelling Methods of Keynes and the Post-Keynesians, *Economic Journal*, 86, 209–225.

Kregel, J.A. 1980. Expectations and Rationality within a Capitalist Framework, paper presented to the Annual Meeting of the American Economic Association, Denver, Colorado.

Kregel, J.A. 1981. Marshall's 'Supply Point' as the Precursor of Keynes's 'Point of Effective Demand', unpublished mimeograph.

Kregel, J.A. 1983. Effective Demand: Origins and Development of the Notion, in *Distribution, Effective Demand and International Economic Relations*, ed. J.A. Kregel, 50–68, London: Macmillan.

Kregel, J.A. 1984. A Critical Appraisal of the Process of Integration of the Post Keynesian and Surplus Approach 1980–1984, paper presented at the Conference on Streams of Economic Thought, Trieste, 1–3 September.

Kregel, J.A. 1985. Budget Deficits, Stabilisation Policy and Liquidity Preference, Keynes's Post-War Policy Proposals, in *Keynes's Relevance Today*, ed. F. Vicarelli, 28–50, London: Macmillan.

Kregel, J.A. 1986. The Effective Demand Approach to Employment and Inflation Analysis, paper presented to the Annual Meeting of the

American Economic Association, New Orleans, Louisiana.

Lachmann, L.M. 1943. The Role of Expectations in Economics as a Social Science, *Economica*, 10, 12–23.

Lachmann, L.M. 1982. The Salvage of Ideas: Problems of the Revival of Austrian Economic Thought, *Gneiting*, 19 May, 1–17.

Laidler, D. 1972. On Wicksell's Theory of Price Level Dynamics, *The Manchester School*, 40, 125–144.

Lange, O. 1942. Say's Law: A Restatement and Criticism, in *Studies in Mathematical Economics and Econometrics*, eds. O. Lange, F. McIntyre and T.O. Yntema, 49–68, Chicago: Chicago University Press.

Lange, O. 1944. *Price Flexibility and Employment*, Bloomington, Ind.: Principia Press.

Lavoie, M. 1984a. The Endogenous Flow of Credit and the Post Keynesian Theory of Money, *Journal of Economic Issues*, 18, 771–797.

Lavoie, M. 1984b. Credit and Money: The Dynamic Circuit, Overdraft Economics, and Post Keynesian Economics, in *Money and Macroeconomic Policy*, ed. M. Jarsulic, 63–84, Boston: Kluwer Nijhoff.

Leijonhufvud, A. 1968. *On Keynesian Economics and the Economics of Keynes*, London: Oxford University Press.

Leijonhufvud, A. 1981. The Wicksell Connection: Variations on a Theme, in *Information and Coordination: Essays in Macroeconomic Theory*, 131–202, Oxford: Oxford University Press.

Lerner, A.P. 1952. Essential Properties of Interest and Money, *Quarterly Journal of Economics*, 66, 172–193.

Le Roy, S. 1973. Interest Rates and the Inflation Premium, *Federal Reserve Bank of Kansas Review*, May, 11–18.

Le Roy, S. and Singell, L.D. 1987. Knight on Risk and Uncertainty, *Journal of Political Economy*, 95, 394–406.

Levacic, R. and Rebmann, A. 1982. *Macroeconomics*, London: Macmillan.

Lindahl, E. 1939. *Studies in the Theory of Money and Capital*, New York: Rinehart and Co.

Lipsey, R.G. 1979. World Inflation, *Economic Record*, 55, 283–296.

Lucas, R.E. 1975. An Equilibrium Model of the Business Cycle, *Journal of Political Economy*, 83, 1113–1144.

Lucas, R.E. 1977. Understanding Business Cycles, *Carnegie–Rochester Conference Series on Public Policy*, 5, 7–29.

Lucas, R.E. 1980. Methods and Problems in Business Cycle Theory, *Journal of Money, Credit and Banking*, 12, part 2, 696–715.

McCaleb, T.S. and Sellon, G.H. 1980. On the Consistent Specification of Asset Markets in Macroeconomic Models, *Journal of Monetary Economics*, 6, 401–417.

McCallum, B.T. 1983a. The Role of Overlapping-Generations Models in Monetary Economics, in *Money, Monetary Policy, and Financial Institutions*, *Carnegie–Rochester Conference Series on Public Policy*, eds. K. Brunner and A.H. Meltzer, 18, 9–44.

McCallum, B.T. 1983b. Comments on 'A Model of Commodity Money' by Thomas J. Sargent and Neil Wallace, *Journal of Monetary Economics*, 12, 189–196.

McCallum, B.T. 1985. Bank Deregulation, Accounting Systems of Exchange, and the Unit of Account: A Critical Review, in *Carnegie–Rochester Conference Series on Public Policy*, 23, 13–46.

Maddock, R. and Carter, M. 1982. A Child's Guide to Rational Expectations, *Journal of Economic Literature*, 20, 39–51.

Magnani, M. 1983. 'Keynesian Fundamentalism': A Critique, in *Keynes's Economics and the Theory of Value and Distribution*, ed. J. Eatwell and M. Milgate, 247–259, London: Duckworth.

Makinen, G.E. 1977. *Money, The Price Level, and Interest Rates*, Englewood Cliffs: Prentice-Hall.

Malinvaud, E. 1977. *The Theory of Unemployment Reconsidered*, Oxford: Blackwell.

Mason, W.E. 1980. Some Negative Thoughts on Friedman's Positive Economics, *Journal of Post-Keynesian Economics*, 3, 235–255.

Mayer, T. 1982. Monetary Trends in the United States and the United Kingdom: A Review Article, *Journal of Economic Literature*, 20, 1528–1539.

Meltzer, A.H. 1981. Keynes's General Theory: A Different Perspective, *Journal of Economic Literature*, 19, 34–64.

Meltzer, A.H. 1984. Keynes's Labour Market: A Reply, *Journal of Post-Keynesian Economics*, 6, 532–539.

Metzler, L. 1951. Wealth, Saving and the Rate of Interest, *Journal of Political Economy*, 59, 93–116.

Milgate, M. 1982. *Capital and Employment*, London: Academic Press.

Milgate, M. 1983. The 'New' Keynes Papers, in *Keynes's Economics and the Theory of Value and Distribution*, ed. J. Eatwell and M. Milgate, 187–199, London: Duckworth.

Minsky, H.P. 1975. *John Maynard Keynes*, New York: Macmillan.

Minsky, H.P. 1982. *Can 'It' Happen Again? Essays on Instability and Finance*, New York: M.E. Sharpe.

Modigliani, F. 1944. Liquidity Preference and the Theory of Interest and Money, *Econometrica*, 12, 45–88.

Moggridge, D.E. 1973. From the Treatise to the General Theory: An Exercise in Chronology, *History of Political Economy*, 5, 72–88.

Moore, B.J. 1979. The Endogenous Money Stock, *Journal of Post-Keynesian Economics*, 2, 49–70.

Moore, B.J. 1984. Contemporaneous Reserve Accounting: Can Reserves be Quantity Constrained?, *Journal of Post-Keynesian Economics*, 7, 103–113.

Moore, B.J. 1986. Horizontalists and Verticalists: The Macroeconomics of Endogenous Money, unpublished manuscript, Wesleyan University, Middletown, Connecticut.

Morishima, M. 1977. *Walras's Economics: A Pure Theory of Capital and Money*, Cambridge: Cambridge University Press.

Moss, S. 1980. The End of Orthodox Capital Theory, in *Growth, Profits and Property*, ed. E.J. Nell, 64–79, New York: Cambridge University Press.

Mundell, R.A. 1963. Inflation and Real Interest, *Journal of Political Economy*, 71, 280–283.

Musgrave, A. 1981. Unreal Assumptions in Economic Theory: The F-twist

Untwisted, *Kyklos*, 34, 377–387.

Muth, J.F. 1961. Rational Expectations and the Theory of Price Movements, *Economica*, 29, 315–335.

Myrdal, G. 1939. *Monetary Equilibrium*, London: William Hodge.

Nagel, E. 1963. Assumptions in Economic Theory, *American Economic Review*, Papers and Proceedings, 53, 211–219.

Nell, E.J. 1983. Keynes after Sraffa: The Essential Properties of Keynes's Theory of Interest and Money, in *Distribution, Effective Demand and International Economic Relations*, ed. J.A. Kregel, 85–103, London: Macmillan.

Ostroy, J.M. 1973. The Informational Efficiency of Monetary Exchange, *American Economic Review*, 63, 597–610.

Ostroy, J.M. and Starr, R.M. 1974. Money and the Decentralization of Exchange, *Econometrica*, 42, 1093–1113.

Panico, C. 1983. Marx's Analysis of the Relationship between the Rate of Interest and the Rate of Profits, in *Keynes's Economics and the Theory of Value and Distribution*, eds. J. Eatwell and M. Milgate, 167–186, London: Duckworth.

Panico, C. 1987. The Evolution of Keynes's Thought on the Rate of Interest, *Contributions to Political Economy*, 6, 53–61.

Parinello, S. 1983. The Marshallian Core of the General Theory, paper presented at the Colloque International 'Keynes Aujourd'hui: Théories et Politiques' held at Université Paris I Pantheon–Sorbonne.

Pasinetti, L.L. 1969. Switches of Technique and the 'Rate of Return' in Capital Theory, *Economic Journal*, 79, 508–531.

Pasinetti, L.L. 1974. *Growth and Income Distribution: Essays in Economic Theory*, Cambridge: Cambridge University Press.

Pasinetti, L.L. 1981. *Structural Change and Economic Growth*, Cambridge: Cambridge University Press.

Patinkin, D. 1952. Wicksell's Cumulative Process, *Economic Journal*, 62, 835–847.

Patinkin, D. 1958. Liquidity Preference and Loanable Funds: Stock and Flow Analysis, *Economica*, 25, 300–318.

Patinkin, D. 1965. *Money, Interest and Prices*, 2nd edn, New York: Harper and Row.

Patinkin, D. 1969. The Chicago Tradition, The Quantity Theory and Friedman, *Journal of Money, Credit and Banking*, 1, 56–70.

Patinkin, D. 1972a. On the Short-Run Non-Neutrality of Money in the Quantity Theory, *Banca Nazionale del Lavoro*, 25, 3–22.

Patinkin, D. 1972b. Samuelson on the Neoclassical Dichotomy: A Comment, *Canadian Journal of Economics*, 5, 279–283.

Patinkin, D. 1976. *Keynes' Monetary Thought: A Study of its Development*, Durham, NS: Duke University Press.

Patinkin, D. 1982. *Anticipations of the General Theory?* Oxford: Blackwell.

Patinkin, D. 1983. New Perspective or Old Pitfall? Some Comments on Allan Meltzer's Interpretation of the General Theory, *Journal of Economic Literature*, 21, 47–51.

Pesek, B. and Saving, T. 1967. *Money, Wealth and Economic Theory*, New York: Macmillan.

Petri, F. 1978. The Difference between Long-Period and Short-Period General Equilibrium and the Capital Controversy, *Australian Economic Papers*, 17, 246–260.

Pettenati, P. 1977. Alternative Theories of a Money-Capital Economy: Keynes, Tobin and the Neoclassics, *Oxford Economic Papers*, 29, 351–369.

Pierce, D.G. and Shaw, D.M. 1974. *Monetary Economics*, London: Butterworth.

Pierce, D.G. and Tysome, P.J. 1985. *Monetary Economics: Theories, Evidence and Policy*, 2nd edn, London: Butterworth.

Poole, W. 1982. Federal Reserve Operating Procedures: A Survey and Evaluation of the Historical Record Since October 1979, *Journal of Money, Credit and Banking*, 14, 575–596.

Popper, K. 1963. Three Views Concerning Human Knowledge, in *Conjectures and Refutations*, 97–119, London: Routledge and Kegan Paul.

Quirk, J. and Saposnik, R. 1968. *Introduction to General Equilibrium Theory and Welfare Economics*, New York: McGraw-Hill.

Radcliffe Report 1959. Report of the Committee on the Working of the Monetary System, Cmnd 827, London: HMSO.

Reder, M.W. 1982. Chicago Economics: Permanence and Change, *Journal of Economic Literature*, 20, 1–38.

Rhodes, J.R. 1984. Walras's Law and Clower's Inequality, *Australian Economic Papers*, 23, 112–122.

Ricardo, D. 1951–1973. *The Works and Correspondence of David Ricardo*, ed. P. Sraffa with the collaboration of M. Dobb, Cambridge: Cambridge University Press.

Robertson, D. 1934. Industrial Fluctuations and the Natural Rate of Interest, *Economic Journal*, 44, 650–656.

Robertson, D. 1966. *Essays in Money and Interest*, London: Fontana.

Robinson, J. 1933a. The Theory of Money and the Analysis of Output, in *Collected Economic Papers*, J. Robinson, vol. I, 52–58, Oxford: Blackwell.

Robinson, J. 1933b. A Parable on Saving and Investment, *Economica*, 13, 75–84.

Robinson, J. 1947. The Long-Period Theory of Employment, in *Essays in the Theory of Employment*, J. Robinson, 75–100, Oxford: Blackwell.

Robinson, J. 1962. *Essays in the Theory of Economic Growth*, London: Macmillan.

Robinson, J. 1970. Quantity Theories Old and New: A Comment, *Journal of Money, Credit and Banking*, 2, 504–512.

Rogers, C. 1982. Rational Expectations and Neoclassical Economics: The Methodology of the New Classical Macroeconomics, *South African Journal of Economics*, 50, 318–339.

Rogers, C. 1983. Neo-Walrasian Macroeconomics, Microfoundations and Pseudo-Production Models, *Australian Economic Papers*, 22, 201–220.

Rogers, C. 1985. A Critique of Clower's Dual Decision Hypothesis, *South African Journal of Economics*, 53, 111–123.

Rosenstein-Rodan, P.N. 1936. The Co-ordination of the General Theories of Money and Price, *Economica*, 3, 257–280.

Rousseas, S.W. 1972. *Monetary Theory*, New York: Alfred A. Knopf.

Rousseas, S.W. 1986. *Post Keynesian Monetary Theory*, New York: M.E. Sharpe.

Samuelson, P.A. 1962. Parable and Realism in Capital Theory: The Surrogate Production Function, *Review of Economic Studies*, 39, 193–206.

Samuelson, P.A. 1983. Sympathy from the Other Cambridge, *The Economist*, 25 June.

Sargent, T.J. 1979. *Macroeconomic Theory*, New York: Academic Press.

Sargent, T.J. and Wallace, N. 1975. Rational Expectations, the Optimal Monetary Instrument and the Optimal Money Supply Rule, *Journal of Political Economy*, 83, 241–255.

Sargent, T.J. and Wallace, N. 1976. Rational Expectations and the Theory of Economic Policy, *Journal of Monetary Economics*, 2, 169–184.

Sargent, T.J. and Wallace, N. 1983. A Model of Commodity Money, *Journal of Monetary Economics*, 12, 163–187.

Schumpeter, J.A. 1954. *History of Economic Analysis*, New York: Oxford University Press.

Shackle, G.L.S. 1967. *The Years of High Theory: Invention and Tradition in Economic Thought 1926–1939*, Cambridge: Cambridge University Press.

Shackle, G.L.S. 1974. *Keynesian Kaleidics*, Edinburgh: Edinburgh University Press.

Shaikh, A. 1980. Laws of Production and Laws of Algebra: Humbug II, in *Growth, Profits and Property*, ed. E.J. Nell, 80–95, Cambridge: Cambridge University Press.

Shaw, G.K. 1983. Review of Friedman and Schwartz, *Economic Journal*, 93, 422–424.

Shiller, R.J. 1978. Rational Expectations and the Dynamic Structure of Macroeconomic Models: A Critical Review, *Journal of Monetary Economics*, 4, 1–44.

Shubik, M. 1985. Review of 'Money: In Equilibrium', *Journal of Money, Credit and Banking*, 17, 126–128.

Sowell, T. 1974. *Classical Economics Reconsidered*, Princeton: Princeton University Press.

Stanley, T.D. 1985. Positive Economics and its Instrumental Defence, *Economica*, 52, 305–319.

Stein, J.L. 1976. *Monetarism*, Amsterdam: North-Holland.

Stewart, I.M.T. 1979. *Reasoning and Method in Economics*, London: McGraw-Hill.

Summers, L.H. 1983. The Non-adjustment of Nominal Interest Rates: A Study of the Fisher Effect, in *Macroeconomics, Prices and Quantities*, ed. J. Tobin, 201–241, Oxford: Blackwell.

Taylor, D. 1976. Friedman's Dynamic Models: Empirical Results, *Journal of Monetary Economics*, 2, 531–538.

Termini, V. 1981. Logical, Mechanical and Historical Time in Economics, *Economic Notes* by Monte dei Paschi di Siena, no. 3.

Termini, V. 1984. A Note on Hicks's 'Contemporaneous Causality', *Cambridge Journal of Economics*, 8, 87–92.

Thornton, H. 1802. *An Enquiry into the Nature and Effects of the Paper Credit of Great Britain*, London: Allen and Unwin (1939).

Tobin, J. 1955. A Dynamic Aggregative Model, reprinted in *Essays in Economics*, 1971, vol. I, 115–132.

Tobin, J. 1961. Money, Capital, and other Stores of Values, reprinted in *Essays in Economics*, 1971, vol. I, 217–228.

Tobin, J. 1963. An Essay in the Principles of Debt Management, reprinted in *Essays in Economics*, 1971, vol. I, 378–455.

Tobin, J. 1965. Money and Economic Growth, reprinted in *Essays in Economics*, 1971, vol. I, 133–145.

Tobin, J. 1969. A General Equilibrium Approach to Monetary Theory, reprinted in *Essays in Economics*, 1971, vol. I, 322–338.

Tobin, J. 1971. *Essays in Economics*, vol. I, Amsterdam: North-Holland.

Tobin, J. 1975. Keynesian Models of Recession and Depression, *American Economic Review*, Papers and Proceedings, 65, 195–202.

Tobin, J. 1980. *Asset Accumulation and Economic Activity*, Oxford: Blackwell.

Tobin, J. 1982. Money and Finance in the Macroeconomic Process, *Journal of Money, Credit and Banking*, 14, 171–204.

Tobin, J. 1983. Keynes' Policies in Theory and Practice, *Challenge*, 26, 5–11.

Tobin, J. 1985. Neoclassical Theory in America: J.B. Clark and Fisher, *American Economic Review*, Papers and Proceedings, 75, 28–38.

Tobin, J. and Buiter, W. 1976. Long-Run Effects of Fiscal and Monetary Policy on Aggregate Demand, in *Monetarism*, ed. J.L. Stein, 273–309, Amsterdam: North-Holland.

Torr, C.S.W. 1980. The Distinction between an Entrepreneur Economy and a Co-operative Economy: A Review Note, *South African Journal of Economics*, 48, 429–434.

Torr, C.S.W. 1981. Microfoundations for Keynes's Point of Effective Demand, *South African Journal of Economics*, 49, 334–348.

Torr, C.S.W. 1984. Expectations and the New Classical Economics, *Australian Economic Papers*, 23, 197–205.

Tosato, D. 1969. Sur la Théorie Walrasienne de la Capitalisation, *Economie Appliquée*, 22, 533–595.

Tsiang, S.C. 1956. Liquidity Preference and Loanable Funds Theories, Multiplier and Velocity Analysis: A Synthesis, *American Economic Review*, 46, 539–564.

Tsiang, S.C. 1966. Walras' Law, Say's Law and Liquidity Preference in General Equilibrium Analysis, *International Economic Review*, 7, 329–345.

Valavanis, S. 1955. A Denial of Patinkin's Contradiction, *Kyklos*, 8, 351–368.

Vicarelli, F. 1984. *Keynes: The Instability of Capitalism*, Philadelphia: University of Philadelphia Press.

Vicarelli, F. 1985. (ed.) *Keynes's Relevance Today*, London: Macmillan.

Walker, D.A. 1984. (ed.) *Money and Markets: Essays by Robert Clower*, Cambridge: Cambridge University Press.

Walras, L. 1926. *Elements of Pure Economics*, translated and edited by W. Jaffé, London: Allen and Unwin (1954).

Walsh, V. and Gram, H. 1980. *Classical and Neoclassical Theories of General Equilibrium*, New York: Oxford University Press.

Weintraub, E.R. 1979. *Microfoundations: The Compatibility of Microeconomics and Macroeconomics*, Cambridge: Cambridge University Press.

Weintraub, S. 1958. *An Approach to the Theory of Income Distribution*, Philadelphia: Clifton.

Weintraub, S. 1977. Hicksian Keynesianism: Dominance and Decline, in *Modern Economic Thought*, ed. S. Weintraub, 45–66, Oxford: Blackwell.

White, L.H. 1984. *Free Banking in Britain*, Cambridge: Cambridge University Press.

Wible, J.R. 1984. The Instrumentalism of Dewey and Friedman, *Journal of Economic Issues*, 18, 1049–1070.

Wicksell, K. 1893. *Value, Capital and Rent*, New York: A.M. Kelley (1954).

Wicksell, K. 1898a. *Interest and Prices*, translated by R.F. Kahn, London: Macmillan (1936).

Wicksell, K. 1898b. The Influence of the Rate of Interest on Commodity Prices, in *Knut Wicksell: Selected Papers on Economic Theory*, ed. E. Lindahl, 67–89, London: Allen and Unwin (1958).

Wicksell, K. 1901. *Lectures in Political Economy*, vols. i and ii, translated by E. Claasen and L. Robbins, London: Routledge (1935).

Woods, J.H. 1981. The Economics of Professor Friedman, in *Essays in Contemporary Fields of Economics*, eds. G. Horwich and J.P. Quirk, 191–241, West Lafayette, Indiana: Purdue University Press.

Yeager, L. 1968. Essential Properties of a Medium of Exchange, *Kyklos*, 21, 45–68.

Zucker, S. 1982. Why Interest Rates Don't Follow Inflation Down, *International Business Week*, 21 June, 65.

INDEX